Hands-On Reactive Programming in Spring 5

Build cloud-ready, reactive systems with Spring 5 and Project Reactor

Oleh Dokuka
Igor Lozynskyi

BIRMINGHAM - MUMBAI

Hands-On Reactive Programming in Spring 5

Copyright © 2018 Packt Publishing

Commissioning Editor: Aaron Lazar
Acquisition Editor: Alok Dhuri
Content Development Editor: Tiksha Sarang
Technical Editor: Abhishek Sharma
Copy Editor: Safis Editing
Project Coordinator: Prajakta Naik
Proofreader: Safis Editing
Indexer: Rekha Nair
Graphics: Jisha Chirayil
Production Coordinator: Arvindkumar Gupta

First published: October 2018

Production reference: 2041018

Published by Packt Publishing Ltd.
Livery Place
35 Livery Street
Birmingham
B3 2PB, UK.

ISBN 978-1-78728-495-1

www.packtpub.com

In the memory of my father, Ivan

– Igor Lozynskyi

`mapt.io`

Mapt is an online digital library that gives you full access to over 5,000 books and videos, as well as industry leading tools to help you plan your personal development and advance your career. For more information, please visit our website.

Why subscribe?

- Spend less time learning and more time coding with practical eBooks and videos from over 4,000 industry professionals

- Improve your learning with Skill Plans built especially for you

- Get a free eBook or video every month

- Mapt is fully searchable

- Copy and paste, print, and bookmark content

Packt.com

Did you know that Packt offers eBook versions of every book published, with PDF and ePub files available? You can upgrade to the eBook version at `www.Packt.com` and as a print book customer, you are entitled to a discount on the eBook copy. Get in touch with us at `customercare@packtpub.com` for more details.

At `www.Packt.com`, you can also read a collection of free technical articles, sign up for a range of free newsletters, and receive exclusive discounts and offers on Packt books and eBooks.

Foreword

Reactive programming is finally getting the attention it deserves with the help of famous Java names such as Spring Boot and Spring Framework. Which qualifier would you use to describe Spring solutions? The usual answer I hear and read from various users—pragmatic. The reactive support offered is no exception, and the team has chosen to keep supporting both reactive and non-reactive stacks. With choice comes responsibility, it is, therefore, critical to understand when to design your application "the reactive way" and what best practices you can apply to your next production-ready systems.

Spring positions itself as a provider of the best tooling available to write all kinds of microservices. With its reactive stack, Spring helps developers to create incredibly efficient, available, and resilient endpoints. As a byproduct, reactive Spring microservices tolerate network latency and cope with failure in a much less impacting way. Think about it—it's the right solution if you are writing an Edge API, a mobile backend, or a heavily mutualized microservice! The secret? Reactive microservices isolate slow transactions and reward the fastest.

Once you have qualified your needs, Project Reactor will be a reactive foundation of choice that will naturally pair with your reactive Spring project. In its latest 3.x iterations, it implements most of the Reactive extensions described first by Microsoft in 2011. Along with a standard vocabulary, Reactor introduces first-class support for Reactive Streams flow control at every functional stage and unique features such as Context passing.

In a synthetic but not simplistic set of example-driven chapters, Oleh and Igor describe a fantastic journey into reactive programming and reactive systems. After a quick context setting, reminding the history and challenges of Project Reactor, we quickly dive into ready-to-use examples running on Spring Boot 2. The book never does miss an occasion to seriously cover testing, giving a clear idea on how to produce quality reactive code.

Oleh and Igor perfectly introduce their readers to those reactive design patterns for the scalability needs of today and tomorrow. The authors cover more than reactive programming with plenty of guidance on Spring Boot or Spring Framework. In a forward-looking chapter, authors stimulate the readers' curiosity with some details about reactive communications using RSocket—a promising technology poised to deliver reactive benefits to the transport layer.

I hope you will take as much pleasure from reading this book as I did and keep learning new ways of writing applications.

Stéphane Maldini

Lead developer, Project Reactor

Contributors

About the authors

Oleh Dokuka is an experienced software engineer, Pivotal Champion, and one of the top contributors to Project Reactor and Spring Framework. He knows the internals of both frameworks very well and advocates reactive programming with Project Reactor on a daily basis. Along with that, the author applies Spring Framework and Project Reactor in software development, so he knows how to build reactive systems using these technologies.

Igor Lozynskyi is a senior Java developer who primarily focuses on developing reliable, scalable, and blazingly fast systems. He has over seven years of experience with the Java platform. He is passionate about interesting and dynamic projects both in life and in software development.

About the reviewers

Mikalai Alimenkou is a senior delivery manager, Java tech lead, and experienced coach. An expert in Java development, scalable architecture, agile engineering practices, QA processes, and project management, he has more than 14 years of development experience, specializes in complex, distributed, scalable systems, and global company transformations. He's an active participant and speaker at many international conferences and is the founder and an independent consultant at XP Injection—a training and consulting provider. He's an organizer and founder of Selenium Camp, JEEConf, and XP Days Ukraine international conferences, as well as the Active Anonymous Developers Club (UADEVCLUB).

Nazarii Cherkas works as a solutions architect at Hazelcast—a company that develops open source projects such as Hazelcast IMDG and Hazelcast Jet. Nazarii has many years of experience of working in different positions, from Java engineer to team lead. He has been involved in various projects for different industries, from telecoms and healthcare to critical systems serving the infrastructure of one of world's biggest airlines. He holds a master's degree in computer science of the Yuriy Fedkovych Chernivtsi National University.

Tomasz Nurkiewicz is a Java champion. He had spent half of his life programming. On a daily basis, he works in the e-commerce sector. He's involved in open source, is DZone's most valuable blogger, and used to be very active on Stack Overflow. He's an author, trainer, conference speaker, technical reviewer, and runner. He claims that code that's not tested automatically is not a feature but just a rumor. He also wrote a book on RxJava.

Packt is searching for authors like you

If you're interested in becoming an author for Packt, please visit authors.packtpub.com and apply today. We have worked with thousands of developers and tech professionals, just like you, to help them share their insight with the global tech community. You can make a general application, apply for a specific hot topic that we are recruiting an author for, or submit your own idea.

Table of Contents

Preface

Reactive systems are responsive at all times, which is what most businesses demand. The development of such systems is a complex task and requires a deep understanding of the domain. Fortunately, developers of the Spring Framework have created a new, reactive version of the project.

With *Reactive Programming in Spring 5,* you'll explore the fascinating process of developing a Reactive system using Spring Framework 5.

This book begins with the foundation of Spring Reactive programming. You will gain an understanding of the possibilities of the framework and learn about the fundamentals of reactivity. Further on, you will study the techniques of reactive programming, learn how to apply them to databases, and use them for cross-server communication. All of these tasks will be applied to a real project example, which will enable you to practice the skills learned.

Get on board with the reactive revolution in Spring 5!

Who this book is for

This book is for Java developers who use Spring to develop their applications and want to be able to build robust and reactive applications that can scale in the cloud. Basic knowledge of distributed systems and asynchronous programming is assumed.

What this book covers

Chapter 1, *Why Reactive Spring?*, covers the business cases in which reactivity fits very well. You will see why a reactive solution is better than a proactive one. Also, you will get an overview of a few code examples that show different ways of cross-server communication, as well as an understanding of today's business needs and their requirements of the modern Spring Framework.

Chapter 2, *Reactive Programming in Spring - Basic Concepts*, expands on the potential of reactive programming and its central concepts by means of code examples. The chapter then shows the power of reactive, asynchronous, non-blocking programming in the Spring Framework with code examples, and applies this technique in business cases. You'll garner an overview of the publisher-subscriber model in examples of code, understand the power of reactive Flow events, and learn about the application of these techniques in real-world scenarios.

Chapter 3, *Reactive Streams - the New Streams' Standard*, concentrates on the problems that are introduced by Reactive Extensions. Code examples are used to explore the different approaches and expand upon the nature of the problems. The chapter also delves into problem-solving and the introduction of the Reactive Streams specification, which introduces new components to the well-known publisher-subscriber model.

Chapter 4, *Project Reactor - the Foundation for Reactive Apps*, looks at the realization of the reactive library; that is, fully implementing the Reactive Streams specification. Firstly, this chapter emphasizes the advantages of implementing Reactor, and then it takes a survey of the reasons that motivated Spring developers to develop their own new solution. Also, this chapter embraces the fundamentals of this impressive library—here you'll get an understanding of Mono and Flux, as well as the applications for reactive types.

Chapter 5, *Going Reactive with Spring Boot 2*, introduces the Spring 5 reactive modules required for reactive application development. Here you'll learn how to get started with modules, and how Spring Boot 2 helps developers configure applications fast.

Chapter 6, *WebFlux Async Non-Blocking Communication*, covers the primary module, Spring WebFlux, which is the essential tool for the organization of asynchronous, non-blocking communication with both the user and external services. This chapter gives an overview of the advantages of this module and the comparison with Spring MVC.

Chapter 7, *Reactive Database Access*, goes into the Spring 5-based reactive programming model for data access. This chapter's emphasis is upon reactive reinforcement in Spring Data modules and explores the features that come out of the box with Spring 5, Reactive Streams, and Project Reactor. In this chapter, you will encounter code that shows a reactive approach for communication with different databases, such as SQL and NoSQL databases.

Chapter 8, *Scaling Up with Cloud Streams*, will introduce you to the reactive features of Spring Cloud Streams. Before starting to learn about the new brilliant capabilities of the module, you'll be given an overview of business case gaps and the problems that you can be faced with when scaling on different servers. This chapter reveals to you the power of the Spring Cloud solution, covering its implementation via code examples of the relevant Spring Boot 2 configuration.

Chapter 9, *Testing the Reactive Application*, covers the basics required for reactive pipeline testing. This chapter introduces the Spring 5 Test and Project Reactor Test modules for writing tests. Here you will see how to manipulate the frequency of events, move timelines, enhance thread pools, mock results, and assert passed messages.

Chapter 10, *And, Finally, Release It!*, is a step-by-step guide to current solution deployment and monitoring. Here you will see how to monitoring reactive microservices, for which Spring 5 modules are required. Also, the chapter covers the tools that will be useful for monitoring the aggregation and display of results.

To get the most out of this book

The development of reactive systems is a complex task, requiring a deep understanding of the domain. A knowledge of distributed systems and asynchronous programming is required.

Download the example code files

You can download the example code files for this book from your account at www.packt.com. If you purchased this book elsewhere, you can visit www.packt.com/support and register to have the files emailed directly to you.

You can download the code files by following these steps:

1. Log in or register at www.packt.com.
2. Select the **SUPPORT** tab.
3. Click on **Code Downloads & Errata**.
4. Enter the name of the book in the **Search** box and follow the onscreen instructions.

Once the file is downloaded, please make sure that you unzip or extract the folder using the latest version of:

- WinRAR/7-Zip for Windows
- Zipeg/iZip/UnRarX for Mac
- 7-Zip/PeaZip for Linux

The code bundle for the book is also hosted on GitHub at `https://github.com/PacktPublishing/Hands-On-Reactive-Programming-in-Spring-5`. In case there's an update to the code, it will be updated on the existing GitHub repository.

We also have other code bundles from our rich catalog of books and videos available at `https://github.com/PacktPublishing/`. Check them out!

Download the color images

We also provide a PDF file that has color images of the screenshots/diagrams used in this book. You can download it here: `https://www.packtpub.com/sites/default/files/downloads/9781787284951_ColorImages.pdf`.

Conventions used

There are a number of text conventions used throughout this book.

`CodeInText`: Indicates code words in text, database table names, folder names, filenames, file extensions, pathnames, dummy URLs, user input, and Twitter handles. Here is an example: "The first call invokes `onSubscribe()`, which stores `Subscription` locally and then notifies `Publisher` about their readiness to receive newsletters via the `request()` method."

A block of code is set as follows:

```
@Override
public long maxElementsFromPublisher() {
    return 1;
}
```

Any command-line input or output is written as follows:

```
./gradlew clean build
```

Bold: Indicates a new term, an important word, or words that you see onscreen.

 Warnings or important notes appear like this.

 Tips and tricks appear like this.

Get in touch

Feedback from our readers is always welcome.

General feedback: If you have questions about any aspect of this book, mention the book title in the subject of your message and email us at customercare@packtpub.com.

Errata: Although we have taken every care to ensure the accuracy of our content, mistakes do happen. If you have found a mistake in this book, we would be grateful if you would report this to us. Please visit www.packt.com/submit-errata, selecting your book, clicking on the Errata Submission Form link, and entering the details.

Piracy: If you come across any illegal copies of our works in any form on the Internet, we would be grateful if you would provide us with the location address or website name. Please contact us at copyright@packt.com with a link to the material.

If you are interested in becoming an author: If there is a topic that you have expertise in and you are interested in either writing or contributing to a book, please visit authors.packtpub.com.

Reviews

Please leave a review. Once you have read and used this book, why not leave a review on the site that you purchased it from? Potential readers can then see and use your unbiased opinion to make purchase decisions, we at Packt can understand what you think about our products, and our authors can see your feedback on their book. Thank you!

For more information about Packt, please visit packt.com.

Why Reactive Spring? 1

In this chapter, we are going to explain the concept of **reactivity**, looking at why reactive approaches are better than traditional approaches. To do this, we will look at examples in which traditional approaches failed. In addition to this, we will explore the fundamental principles of building a robust system, which is mostly referred to as **reactive systems**. We will also take an overview of the conceptual reasons for building message-driven communication between distributed servers, covering business cases in which reactivity fits well. Then, we will expand the meaning of **reactive programming** to build a fine-grained reactive system. We will also discuss why the Spring Framework team decided to include a reactive approach as the core part of **Spring Framework 5**. Based on the content of this chapter, we will understand the importance of reactivity and why it is a good idea to move our projects to the reactive world.

In this chapter, we will cover the following topics:

- Why we need reactivity
- The fundamental principles of the reactive system
- Business cases in which a reactive system design matches perfectly
- Programming techniques that are more suitable for a reactive system
- Reasons for moving Spring Framework to reactivity

Why reactive?

Nowadays, **reactive** is a buzzword—so exciting but so confusing. However, should we still care about reactivity even if it takes an honorable place in conferences around the world? If we google the word reactive, we will see that the most popular association is programming, in which it defines the meaning of a programming model. However, that is not the only meaning for reactivity. Behind that word, there are hidden fundamental design principles aimed at building a robust system. To understand the value of reactivity as an essential design principle, let's imagine that we are developing a small business.

Suppose our small business is a web store with a few cutting-edge products at an attractive price. As is the case with the majority of projects in this sector, we will hire software engineers to solve any problems that we encounter. We opted for the traditional approaches to development, and, during a few development interactions, we created our store.

Usually, our service is visited by about one thousand users per hour. To serve the usual demand, we bought a modern computer and ran the Tomcat web server as well as configuring Tomcat's thread pool with 500 allocated threads. The average response time for the majority of user requests is about 250 milliseconds. By doing a naive calculation of the capacity for that configuration, we can be sure that the system can handle about 2,000 user requests per second. According to statistics, the number of users previously mentioned produced around 1,000 requests per second on average. Consequently, the current system's capacity will be enough for the average load.

To summarize, we configured our application with the margin regarding capacity. Moreover, our web store had been working stably until the last Friday in November, which is Black Friday.

Black Friday is a valuable day for both customers and retailers. For the customer, it is a chance to buy goods at discounted prices. And for retailers, it is a way to earn money and popularize products. However, this day is characterized by an unusual influx of clients, and that may be a significant cause of failure in production.

And, of course, we failed! At some point in time, the load exceeded all expectations. There were no vacant threads in the thread pool to process user requests. In turn, the backup server was not able to handle such an unpredictable invasion, and, in the end, this caused a rise in the response time and periodic service outage. At this point, we started losing some user requests, and, finally, our clients became dissatisfied and preferred dealing with competitors.

In the end, a lot of potential customers and money were lost, and the store's rating decreased. This was all a result of the fact that we couldn't stay responsive under the increased workload.

But, don't worry, this is nothing new. At one point in time, giants such as Amazon and Walmart also faced this problem and have since found a solution. Nevertheless, we will follow the same roads as our predecessors, gaining an understanding of the central principles of designing robust systems and then providing a general definition for them.

To learn more about giants failures see:

- Amazon.com hit with outages (`https://www.cnet.com/news/amazon-com-hit-with-outages/`)
- Amazon.com Goes Down, Loses $66,240 Per Minute (`https://www.forbes.com/sites/kellyclay/2013/08/19/amazon-com-goes-down-loses-66240-per-minute/#3fd8db37495c`)
- Walmart's Black Friday Disaster: Website Crippled, Violence In Stores (`https://techcrunch.com/2011/11/25/walmart-black-friday/`)

Now, the central question that should remain in our minds is—How should we be responsive? As we might now understand from the example given previously, an application should react to changes. This should include changes in demand (load) and changes in the availability of external services. In other words, it should be reactive to any changes that may affect the system's ability to respond to user requests.

One of the first ways to achieve the primary goal is through **elasticity**. This describes the ability to stay responsive under a varying workload, meaning that the throughput of the system should increase automatically when more users start using it and it should decrease automatically when the demand goes down. From the application perspective, this feature enables system responsiveness because at any point in time the system can be expanded without affecting the average latency.

Note that *latency* is the essential characteristic of responsiveness. Without elasticity, growing demand will cause the growth of average latency, which directly affects the responsiveness of the system.

For example, by providing additional computation resources or additional instances, the throughput of our system might be increased. The responsiveness will then increase as a consequence. On the other hand, if demand is low, the system should shrink in terms of resource consumption, thereby reducing business expenses. We may achieve elasticity by employing **scalability,** which might either be horizontal or vertical. However, achieving scalability of the distributed system is a challenge that is typically limited by the introduction of bottlenecks or synchronization points within the system. From the theoretical and practical perspectives, such problems are explained by Amdahl's Law and Gunther's Universal Scalability Model. We will discuss these in `Chapter 6`, *WebFlux Async Non-Blocking Communication*.

Here, the term business expenses refers to the cost of additional cloud instances or extra power consumption in the case of physical machines.

However, building a scalable distributed system without the ability to stay responsive regardless of failures is a challenge. Let's think about a situation in which one part of our system is unavailable. Here, an external payment service goes down, and all user attempts to pay for the goods will fail. This is something that breaks the responsiveness of the system, which may be unacceptable in some cases. For example, if users cannot proceed with their purchases easily, they will probably go to a competitor's web store. To deliver a high-quality user experience, we must care about the system's responsiveness. The acceptance criteria for the system are the ability to stay responsive under failures, or, in other words, to be resilient. This may be achieved by applying isolation between functional components of the system, thereby isolating all internal failures and enabling independence. Let's switch back to the Amazon web store. Amazon has many different functional components such as the order list, payment service, advertising service, comment service, and many others. For example, in the case of a payment service outage, we may accept user orders and then schedule a request auto-retry, thereby protecting the user from undesired failures. Another example might be isolation from the comments service. If the comments service goes down, the purchasing and orders list services should not be affected and should work without any problems.

Another point to emphasize is that elasticity and resilience are tightly coupled, and we achieve a truly responsive system only by enabling both. With scalability, we can have multiple replicas of the component so that, if one fails, we can detect this, minimize its impact on the rest of the system, and switch to another replica.

To learn more about terminology see the following links:

- Elasticity (https://www.reactivemanifesto.org/glossary#Elasticity)
- Failure (https://www.reactivemanifesto.org/glossary#Failure)
- Isolation (https://www.reactivemanifesto.org/glossary#Isolation)
- Component (https://www.reactivemanifesto.org/glossary#Component)

Message-driven communication

The only question that is left unclear is how to connect components in the distributed system and preserve decoupling, isolation, and scalability at the same time. Let's consider communication between components over HTTP. The next code example, doing HTTP communication in Spring Framework 4, represents this concept:

```
@RequestMapping("/resource")                            // (1)
public Object processRequest() {
    RestTemplate template = new RestTemplate();         // (2)

    ExamplesCollection result = template.getForObject(  // (3)
        "http://example.com/api/resource2",             //
        ExamplesCollection.class                         //
    );                                                   //

    ...                                                  // (4)

    processResultFurther(result);                        // (5)
}
```

The previous code is explained as follows:

1. The code at this point is a request handler mapping declaration that uses the @RequestMapping annotation.
2. The code declared in this block shows how we may create the RestTemplate instance. RestTemplate is the most popular web client for doing request-response communication between services in Spring Framework 4.
3. This demonstrates the request's construction and execution. Here, using the RestTemplate API, we construct an HTTP request and execute it right after that. Note that the response will be automatically mapped to the Java object and returned as the result of the execution. The type of response body is defined by the second parameter of the getForObject method. Furthermore, the getXxxXxxxxx prefix means that the HTTP method, in that case, is GET.
4. These are the additional actions that are skipped in the previous example.
5. This is the execution of another processing stage.

In the preceding example, we defined the request handler which will be invoked on users' requests. In turn, each invocation of the handler produces an additional HTTP call to an external service and then subsequently executes another processing stage. Despite the fact that the preceding code may look familiar and transparent in terms of logic, it has some flaws. To understand what is wrong in this example, let's take an overview of the following request's timeline:

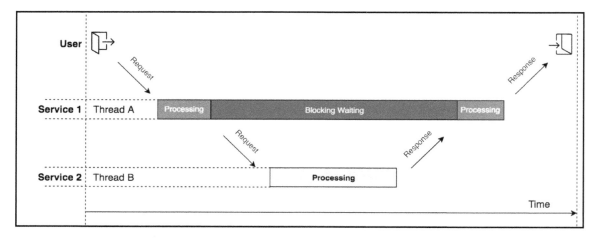

Diagram 1.1. Components interaction timeline

This diagram depicts the actual behavior of the corresponding code. As we may notice, only a small part of the processing time is allocated for effective CPU usage whereas the rest of the time thread is being blocked by the I/O and cannot be used for handling other requests.

 In some languages, such as C#, Go, and Kotlin, the same code might be non-blocking when green threads are used. However, in pure Java, we do not have such features yet. Consequently, the actual thread will be blocked in such cases.

On the other hand, in the Java world, we have thread pools, which may allocate additional threads to increase parallel processing. However, under a high load, such a technique may be extremely inefficient to process the new I/O task simultaneously. We will revisit this problem again during this chapter and also analyze it thoroughly in `Chapter 6`, *WebFlux Async Non-Blocking Communication*.

Nonetheless, we can agree that to achieve better resource utilization in I/O cases, we should use an asynchronous and non-blocking interaction model. In real life, this kind of communication is messaging. When we get a message (SMS, or email), all our time is taken up by reading and responding. Moreover, we do not usually wait for the answer and work on other tasks in the meantime. Unmistakably, in that case, work is optimized and the rest of the time may be utilized efficiently. Take a look at the following diagram:

To learn more about terminology see the following links:

- Non-Blocking (`https://www.reactivemanifesto.org/ glossary#Non-Blocking`)
- Resource (`https://www.reactivemanifesto.org/ glossary#Resource`)

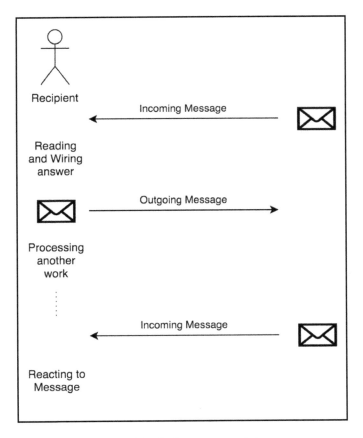

Diagram 1.2. Non-blocking message communication

In general, to achieve efficient resource utilization when communicating between services in a distributed system, we have to embrace the message-driven communication principle. The overall interaction between services may be described as follows—each element awaits the arrival of messages and reacts to them, otherwise lying dormant, and vice versa, a component should be able to send a message in the non-blocking fashion. Moreover, such an approach to communication improves system scalability by enabling location transparency. When we send an email to the recipient, we care about the correctness of the destination address. Then the mail server takes care of delivering that email to one of the available devices of the recipient. This frees us from concerns about the certain device, allowing recipients to use as many devices as they want. Furthermore, it improves failure tolerance since the failure of one of the devices does not prevent recipients from reading an email from another device.

One of the ways to achieve message-driven communication is by employing a **message broker**. In that case, by monitoring the message queue, the system is able to control the load management and elasticity. Moreover, the message communication gives clear flow control and simplifies the overall design. We will not get into specific details of this in this chapter, as we will cover the most popular techniques for achieving message-driven communication in Chapter 8, *Scaling Up with Cloud Streams*.

The phrase **lying dormant** was taken from the following original document, which aims to emphasize message-driven communication: https://www.reactivemanifesto.org/glossary#Message-Driven.

By embracing all of the previous statements, we will get the foundational principles of the reactive system. This is depicted in the following diagram:

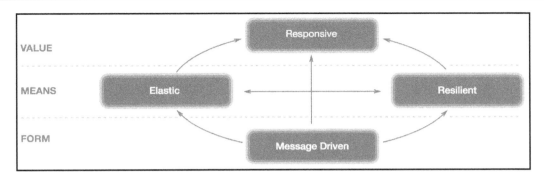

Diagram 1.3. Reactive Manifesto

As we may notice from the diagram, the primary value for any business implemented with a distributed system is responsiveness. Achieving a responsive system means following fundamental techniques such as elasticity and resilience. Finally, one of the fundamental ways to attain a responsive, elastic, and resilient system is by employing message-driven communication. In addition, systems built following such principles are highly maintainable and extensible, since all components in the system are independent and properly isolated.

We will not go all notions defined in the Reactive Manifesto in depth, but it is highly recommended to revisit the glossary provided at the following link: `https://www.reactivemanifesto.org/glossary`.

All those notions are not new and have already been defined in the Reactive Manifesto, which is the glossary that describes the reactive system's concepts. This manifesto was created to ensure that businesses and developers have the same understanding of conventional notions. To emphasize, a reactive system and the Reactive Manifesto are concerned with architecture, and this may be applied to either large distributed applications or small one-node applications.

The importance of the Reactive Manifesto (`https://www.reactivemanifesto.org`) is explained by Jonas Bonér, the Founder and CTO of Lightbend, at the following link: `https://www.lightbend.com/blog/why_do_we_need_a_reactive_manifesto%3F`.

Reactivity use cases

In the previous section, we learned the importance of reactivity and the fundamental principles of the reactive system, and we have seen why message-driven communication is an essential constituent of the reactive ecosystem. Nonetheless, to reinforce what we have learned, it is necessary to touch on real-world examples of its application. First of all, the reactive system is about architecture, and it may be applied anywhere. It may be used in simple websites, in large enterprise solutions, or even in fast-streaming or big-data systems. But let's start with the simplest—consider the example of a web store that we have already seen in the previous section. In this section, we will cover possible improvement and changes in the design that may help in achieving a reactive system. The following diagram helps us get acquainted with the overall architecture of the proposed solution:

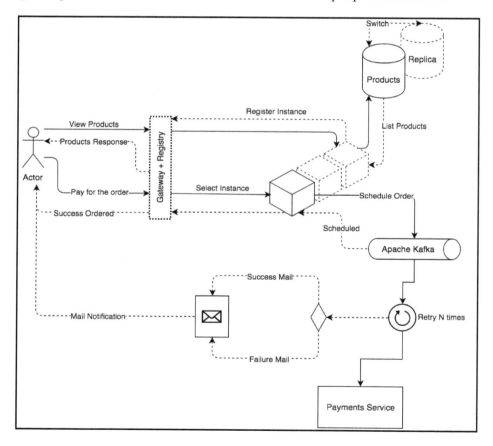

Diagram 1.4. Example of store application architecture

The preceding diagram expands a list of useful practices that allow the reactive system to be achieved. Here, we improved our small web store by applying modern microservice patterns. In that case, we use an API Gateway pattern for achieving location transparency. It provides the identification of a specific resource with no knowledge about particular services that are responsible for handling requests.

 However, it means that the client should know the resource name at least. Once the API Gateway receives the service name as part of a request URI, then it can resolve a specific service address by asking the registry service.

In turn, the responsibility for keeping information about available services up to date is implemented using the service registry pattern and achieved with the support of the client-side discovery pattern. It should be noticed, that in the previous example, the service gateway and service registry are installed on the same machine, which may be useful in the case of a small distributed system. Additionally, the high responsiveness of the system is achieved by applying replication to the service. On the other hand, failure tolerance is attained by properly employed message-driven communication using Apache Kafka and the independent Payment Proxy Service (the point with **Retry N times** description in *Diagram 1.4*), which is responsible for redelivering payment in the case of unavailability of the external system. Also, we use database replication to stay resilient in the case of the outage of one of the replicas. To stay responsive, we return a response about an accepted order immediately and asynchronously process and send the user payment to the payments service. A final notification will be delivered later by one of the supported channels, for example, via email. Finally, that example depicts only one part of the system and in real deployments, the overall diagram may be broader and introduce much more specific techniques for achieving a reactive system.

 Note, we will cover design principles and their pros and cons thoroughly in Chapter 8, *Scaling Up with Cloud Streams*.

To familiarize ourselves with API Gateway, Service Registry, and other patterns for constructing a distributed system, please click on the following link: `http://microservices.io/patterns`.

Along with the plain, small web store example that may seem really complex, let's consider another sophisticated area where a reactive system approach is appropriate. A more complex but exciting example is **analytics**. The term analytics means that the system that is able to handle a huge amount of data, process it in run-time, keep the user up to date with live statistics, and so on. Suppose we are designing a system for monitoring a telecommunication network based on cell site data. Due to the latest statistic report of the number of cell towers, in 2016 there were 308,334 active sites in the USA.

 The statistic report with the number of cell sites in the USA is available at the following link: `https://www.statista.com/statistics/185854/` `monthly-number-of-cell-sites-in-the-united-states-since-june-` `1986/`.

Unfortunately, we can just imagine the real load produced by that number of cell sites. However, we can agree that processing such a huge amount of data and providing real-time monitoring of the telecommunication network state, quality, and traffic is a challenge.

To design this system, we may follow one of the efficient architectural techniques called **streaming**. The following diagram depicts the abstract design of such a streaming system:

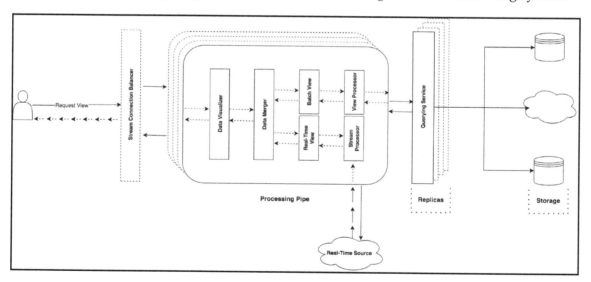

Diagram 1.5. Example of an analytics real-time system architecture

As may be noticed from this diagram, streaming architecture is about the construction of the flow of data processing and transformation. In general, such a system is characterized by low latency and high throughput. In turn, the ability to respond or simply deliver analyzed updates of the telecommunication network state is therefore crucial. Thus, to build such a highly-available system, we have to rely on fundamental principles, as mentioned in the Reactive Manifesto. For example, achieving resilience might be done by enabling backpressure support. Backpressure refers to a sophisticated mechanism of workload management between processing stages in such a way that ensures we do not overwhelm another. Efficient workload management may be achieved by using message-driven communication over a reliable message broker, which may persist messages internally and send messages on demand.

 Note that other techniques for handling backpressure will be covered in `Chapter 3`, *Reactive Streams - the New Streams' Standard*.

Moreover, by properly scaling each component of the system, we will be able to elastically expand or reduce system throughput.

 To learn more about the terminology, see the following link:
Backpressure: `https://www.reactivemanifesto.org/glossary#Back-Pressure`.

In a real-world scenario, the stream of the data may be persisted databases processed in a batch, or partially processed in real-time by applying windowing or machine-learning techniques. Nonetheless, all fundamental principles offered by the Reactive Manifesto are valid here, regardless of the overall domain or business idea.

To summarize, there are a ton of different areas in which to apply the foundational principles of building a reactive system. The area of application of the reactive system is not limited to the previous examples and areas, since all of these principles may be applied to building almost any kind of distributed system oriented to giving users effective, interactive feedback.

Nonetheless, in the next section, we will cover the reasons for moving Spring Framework to reactivity.

Why Reactive Spring?

In the previous section, we looked at a few interesting examples in which reactive system approaches shine. We have also expanded on the usage of fundamentals such as elasticity and resilience, and seen examples of microservice-based systems commonly used to attain a reactive system.

That gave us an understanding of the architectural perspective but nothing about the implementation. However, it is important to emphasize the complexity of the reactive system and the construction of such a system is a challenge. To create a reactive system with ease, we have to analyze frameworks capable of building such things first and then choose one of them. One of the most popular ways to choose a framework is by analyzing its available features, relevance, and community.

In the JVM world, the most commonly known frameworks for building a reactive system has been Akka and Vert.x ecosystems.

On the one hand, Akka is a popular framework with a huge list of features and a big community. However, at the very beginning, Akka was built as part of the Scala ecosystem and for a long time, it showed its power only within solutions written in Scala. Despite the fact that Scala is a JVM-based language, it is noticeably different from Java. A few years ago, Akka provided direct support for Java, but for some reason, it was not as popular in the Java world as it was in Scala.

On the other hand, there is the Vert.x framework which is also a powerful solution for building an efficient reactive system. Vert.x was designed as a non-blocking, event-driven alternative to Node.js that runs on the Java Virtual Machine. However, Vert.x started being competitive only a few years ago and during the last 15 years, the market for frameworks for flexible robust application development has been held by the Spring Framework.

 To get more information about the Java tools landscape, follow this link: https://www.quora.com/Is-it-worth-learning-Java-Spring-MVC-as-of-March-2016/answer/Krishna-Srinivasan-6?srid=xCnf.

The Spring Framework provides wide possibilities for building a web application using a developer-friendly programming model. However, for a long time, it had some limitations in building a robust reactive system.

Reactivity on the service level

Fortunately, the growing demand for reactive systems initiated the creation of a new Spring Project called **Spring Cloud**. The Spring Cloud Framework is a foundation of projects that address particular problems and simplifies the construction of distributed systems. Consequently, the Spring Framework ecosystem may be relevant for us to build reactive systems.

 To learn more about the essential functionality, components, and features of that project please click on the following link: `http://projects.` `spring.io/spring-cloud/`.

We will skip the details of Spring Cloud Framework functionality in this chapter and cover the most important parts that help in the development of the reactive system in `Chapter 8,` *Scaling Up with Cloud Streams*. Nonetheless, it should be noticed that such a solution building a robust, reactive microservices system with minimum effort.

However, the overall design is only one element of constructing the whole reactive system. As may be noticed from the excellent Reactive Manifesto:

> *"Large systems are composed of smaller ones and therefore depend on the Reactive properties of their constituents. This means that Reactive Systems apply design principles so these properties apply at all levels of scale, making them able to be composed".*

Therefore, it is important to provide a reactive design and implementation on the component level as well. In that context, the term design principle refers to a relationship between components and, for example, programming techniques that are used to compound elements. The most popular traditional technique for writing code in Java is **imperative programming**.

To understand whether imperative programming follows reactive system design principles, let's consider the next diagram:

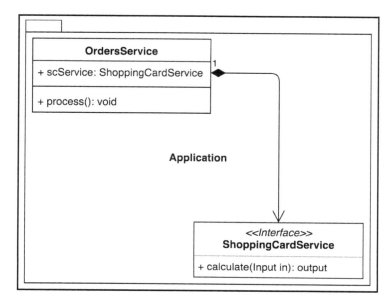

Diagram 1.6. UML Schema of component relationship

Here, we have two components within the web store application. In that case, OrdersService calls ShoppingCardService while processing the user request. Suppose that under the hood ShoppingCardService executes a long-running I/O operation, for example, an HTTP request or database query. To understand the disadvantages of imperative programming let's consider the following example of the most common implementation of the aforementioned interaction between components:

```
interface ShoppingCardService {                              // (1)
    Output calculate(Input value);                           //
}                                                            //

class OrdersService {                                        // (2)
    private final ShoppingCardService scService;            //
                                                            //
    void process() {                                        //
        Input input = ...;                                  //
        Output output = scService.calculate(input);         // (2.1)
        ...                                                 // (2.2)
    }                                                       //
}                                                           //
```

The aforementioned code is explained as follows:

1. This is the `ShoppingCardService` interface declaration. This corresponds to the aforementioned class diagram and has only one `calculate` method, which accepts one argument and returns a response after its processing.
2. This is the `OrderService` declaration. Here, at point `(2.1)` we synchronously call `ShoppingCardService` and receive a result right after its execution. Point `(2.2)` hides the rest of the code responsible for result processing.
3. In turn, in that case our services are tightly coupled in time, or simply the execution of `OrderService` is tightly coupled to the execution of `ShoppingCardService`. Unfortunately, with such a technique, we cannot proceed with any other actions while `ShoppingCardService` is in the processing phase.

As we can understand from the preceding code, in Java world, the execution of `scService.calculate(input)` blocks the `Thread` on which the processing of the `OrdersService` logic takes place. Thus, to run a separate independent processing in `OrderService` we have to allocate an additional `Thread`. As we will see in this chapter, the allocation of an additional `Thread` might be wasteful. Consequently, from the reactive system perspective, such system behavior is unacceptable.

 Blocking communications directly contradicts the message-driven principle, which explicitly offers us non-blocking communication. See the following for more information on this: `https://www.reactivemanifesto.org/#message-driven`.

Nonetheless, in Java, that problem may be solved by applying a callback technique for the purpose of cross-component communication:

```java
interface ShoppingCardService {                           // (1)
    void calculate(Input value, Consumer<Output> c);      //
}                                                         //

class OrdersService {                                     // (2)
    private final ShoppingCardService scService;          //
                                                          //
    void process() {                                      //
        Input input = ...;                                //
        scService.calculate(input, output -> {            // (2.1)
            ...                                           // (2.2)
        });                                               //
    }                                                     //
}                                                         //
```

Each point in the preceding code is explained in the following numbered list:

1. The preceding code is the ShoppingCardService interface declaration. In that case, the calculate method accepts two parameters and returns a void. It means that from the design perspective, the caller may be immediately released from waiting and the result will be sent to the given Consumer<> callback later.
2. This is the OrderService declaration. Here, at point (2.1) we asynchronously call ShoppingCardService and continue processing. In turn, when the ShoppingCardService executes the callback function we will be able to proceed with the actual result processing (2.2).

Now, OrdersService passes the function-callback to react at the end of the operation. This embraces the fact that OrdersService is now decoupled from ShoppingCardService and the first one may be notified via the functional callback where the implementation of the ShoppingCardService#calculate method, which calls the given function, may either be synchronous or asynchronous:

```
class SyncShoppingCardService implements ShoppingCardService {     // (1)
    public void calculate(Input value, Consumer<Output> c) {       //
        Output result = new Output();                              //
        c.accept(result);                                          // (1.1)
    }                                                              //
}                                                                  //

class AsyncShoppingCardService implements ShoppingCardService {    // (2)
    public void calculate(Input value, Consumer<Output> c) {       //
        new Thread(() -> {                                         // (2.1)
            Output result = template.getForObject(...);            // (2.2)
            ...                                                    //
            c.accept(result);                                      // (2.3)
        }).start();                                                // (2.4)
    }                                                              //
}                                                                  //
```

Each point in the preceding code is explained in the following numbered list:

1. This point is the `SyncShoppingCardService` class declaration. This
   implementation assumes the absence of blocking operations. Since we do not
   have an I/O execution, the result may be returned immediately by passing it to
   the callback function `(1.1)`.
2. This point in the preceding code is the `AsyncShoppingCardService` class
   declaration. In the case, when we have blocking I/O as depicted in point `(2.2)`,
   we may wrap it in the separate `Thread` `(2.1)` `(2.4)`. After retrieving the result,
   it will be processed and passed to the callback function.

In that example, we have the sync implementation of `ShoppingCardService`, which keeps
synchronous bounds and offers no benefits from the API perspective. In the async case, we
achieve asynchronous bounds, and a request will be executed in the separate
`Thread`. `OrdersService` is decoupled from the execution process and will be notified of
the completion by the callback execution.

The advantage of that technique is that components are decoupled in time by the callback
function. This means that after calling the `scService.calculate` method, we will be able
to proceed with other operations immediately without waiting for the response in the
blocking fashion from `ShoppingCardService`.

The disadvantage is that callback requires the developer to have a good understanding of
multi-threading to avoid the traps of shared data modifications and callback hell.

 Actually, the phrase *callback hell* is mentioned in relation to
JavaScript: `http://callbackhell.com`, but it is also applicable to Java as
well.

Fortunately, the callback technique is not the only option. Another one is
`java.util.concurrent.Future`, which, to some degree, hides the executional behavior
and decouples components as well:

```
interface ShoppingCardService {                                        // (1)
    Future<Output> calculate(Input value);                             //
}                                                                      //

class OrdersService {                                                   // (2)
    private final ShoppingCardService scService;                       //
                                                                       //
    void process() {                                                   //
        Input input = ...;                                             //
        Future<Output> future = scService.calculate(input);           // (2.1)
```

```
      ...                                         //
      Output output = future.get();              // (2.2)
      ...                                         //
   }                                              //
}                                                 //
```

The numbered points are described in the following:

1. At this point is the `ShoppingCardService` interface declaration. Here, the `calculate` method accepts one parameter and returns `Future`. `Future` is a class wrapper which allows us to check whether there is an available result or blocking to get it.

2. This is the `OrderService` declaration. Here, in point `(2.1)`, we asynchronously call `ShoppingCardService` and receive the `Future` instance. In turn, we are able to continue processing while the result is being processed asynchronously. After some execution, which may be done independently from `ShoppingCardService#calculation`, we get the result. This result may end up waiting in the blocking fashion or it may immediately return the result `(2.2)`.

As we may notice from the previous code, with the `Future` class, we achieve deferred retrieval of the result. With the support of the `Future` class, we avoid callback hell and hide multi-threading complexity behind a specific `Future` implementation. Anyway, to get the result we need, we must potentially block the current `Thread` and synchronize with the external execution that noticeably decreases scalability.

As an improvement, Java 8 offers `CompletionStage` and `CompletableFuture` as a direct implementation for `CompletionStage`. In turn, those classes provide promise-like APIs and make it possible to build code such as the following:

 To learn more about *futures* and *promises*, please see the following link: https://en.wikipedia.org/wiki/Futures_and_promises.

```
interface ShoppingCardService {                       // (1)
    CompletionStage<Output> calculate(Input value);   //
}                                                     //

class OrdersService {                                  // (2)
    private final ComponentB componentB;              //
    void process() {                                  //
        Input input = ...;                            //
        componentB.calculate(input)                   // (2.1)
                .thenApply(out1 -> { ... })           // (2.2)
```

```
                    .thenCombine(out2 -> { ... })            //
                    .thenAccept(out3 -> { ... })             //
        }                                                     //
    }                                                         //
```

The aforementioned code is described in the following:

1. At this point, we have the `ShoppingCardService` interface declaration. In this case, the `calculate` method accepts one parameter and returns `CompletionStage`. `CompletionStage` is a class wrapper that is similar to `Future` but allows processing the returned result in the functional declarative fashion.

2. This is an `OrderService` declaration. Here, at point `(2.1)` we asynchronously call `ShoppingCardService` and receive the `CompletionStage` immediately as the result of the execution. The overall behavior of the `CompletionStage` is similar to `Future`, but `CompletionStage` provides a fluent API which makes it possible to write methods such as `thenAccept` and `thenCombine`. These define transformational operations on the result and `thenAccept`, which defines the final consumers, to handle the transformed result.

With the support of `CompletionStage`, we can write code in the functional and declarative style, which looks clean and processes the result asynchronously. Furthermore, we may omit the awaiting results and provide a function to handle the result when it becomes available. Moreover, all of the previous techniques are valued by Spring teams and have already been implemented within most of the projects within the framework. Even though the `CompletionStage` gives better possibilities for writing efficient and readable code, unfortunately, there are some missing points there. For example, Spring 4 MVC did not support `CompletionStage` for a long time and for that purpose, it provided its own `ListenableFuture`. This happened because Spring 4 aimed to become compatible with older Java versions. Let's take an overview of `AsyncRestTemplate` usage to get an understanding of how to work with Spring's `ListenableFuture`. The following code shows how we may use `ListenableFuture` with `AsyncRestTemplate`:

```
AsyncRestTemplate template = new AsyncRestTemplate();
SuccessCallback onSuccess = r -> { ... };
FailureCallback onFailure = e -> { ... };
ListenableFuture<?> response = template.getForEntity(
    "http://example.com/api/examples",
    ExamplesCollection.class
);
response.addCallback(onSuccess, onFailure);
```

The preceding code shows the callback style for handling an asynchronous call. Essentially, this method of communication is a dirty hack, and Spring Framework wraps blocking network calls in a separate thread under-the-hood. Furthermore, Spring MVC relies on Servlet API, which obligates all implementations to use the thread-per-request model.

 Many things have changed with the release of Spring Framework 5 and the new Reactive WebClient, so with the support of WebClient, all cross-service communication is non-blocking anymore. Also, Servlet 3.0 introduced asynchronous client-server communication, Servlet 3.1 allowed non-blocking writing to I/O, and in general new asynchronous non-blocking features of the Servlet 3 API are well integrated into Spring MVC. However, the only problem was that Spring MVC did not provide an out of the box asynchronous non-blocking client that negates all benefits from improved servlets.

This model is quite non-optimal. To understand why this technique is inefficient, we have to revisit the costs of multi-threading. On the one hand, multi-threading is a complex technique by nature. When we work with multi-threading, we have to think about many things, such as access to shared memory from the different threads, synchronization, error handling, and so on. In turn, the design of multi-threading in Java supposes that a few threads may share a single CPU to run their tasks simultaneously. The fact that CPU time will be shared between several threads introduces the notion of **context switching**. This means that to resume a thread later, it is required to save and load registers, memory maps, and other related elements which in general are computationally-intensive operations. Consequently, its application with a high number of active threads, and few CPUs, will be inefficient.

 To learn more about the cost of context switching, please visit the following link: https://en.wikipedia.org/wiki/Context_switch#Cost.

In turn, a typical Java thread has its overhead in memory consumption. A typical stack size for a thread on a 64-bit Java VM is 1,024 KB. On the one hand, an attempt to handle ~6,4000 simultaneous requests in a thread per connection model may result in about 64 GB of used memory. This might be costly from the business perspective or critical from the application standpoint. On the other hand, by switching to traditional thread pools with a limited size and a pre-configured queue for requests, the client waits too long for a response, which is less reliable, increases the average response timeout, and finally may cause unresponsiveness of the application.

For that purpose, the Reactive Manifesto recommends using a non-blocking operation, and this is an omission in the Spring ecosystem. On the other hand, there is no good integration with reactive servers such as Netty, which solves the problem of context switching.

> To get source information about the average amount of connections, see the following link: `https://stackoverflow.com/questions/2332741/what-is-the-theoretical-maximum-number-of-open-tcp-connections-that-a-modern-lin/2332756#2332756`.
>
> The term *thread* refers to allocated memory for the thread object and allocated memory for the thread stack. See the next link for more information: `http://xmlandmore.blogspot.com/2014/09/jdk-8-thread-stack-size-tuning.html?m=1`.

It is important to note that asynchronous processing is not limited to a plain request-response pattern, and sometimes we have to deal with handling infinitive streams of data, processing it in the manner of an aligned transformation flow with backpressure support:

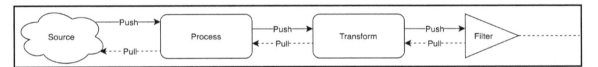

Diagram 1.7. Reactive pipeline example

One of the ways for handling such cases is through reactive programming, which embraces the techniques of asynchronous event processing through chaining transformational stages. Consequently, reactive programming is a good technique which fits the design requirements for a reactive system. We will cover the value of applying reactive programming for building a reactive system in the next chapters.

Unfortunately, the reactive programming technique was not well integrated inside Spring Framework. That put another limitation on building modern applications and decreased the competitiveness of the framework. As a consequence, all the mentioned gaps in the growing hype around reactive systems and reactive programming simply increased the need for dramatic improvements within the framework. Finally, that drastically stimulated the improvement of Spring Framework by adding the support for Reactivity on all levels and providing developers with a powerful tool for reactive system development. Its pivotal developers decided to implement new modules that reveal the whole power of Spring Framework as a reactive system foundation.

Summary

In this chapter, we highlighted the requirements for cost-efficient IT solutions that often arise nowadays. We described why and how big companies such as Amazon failed to force old architectural patterns to work smoothly in current cloud-based distributed environments.

We also established the need for new architectural patterns and programming techniques to fulfill the ever-growing demand for convenient, efficient, and intelligent digital services. With the Reactive Manifesto, we deconstructed and comprehended the term reactivity and also described why and how elasticity, resilience, and message-driven approaches help to achieve responsiveness, probably the primary non-functional system requirement in the digital era. Of course, we gave examples in which the reactive system shines and easily allows businesses to achieve their goals.

In this chapter, we have highlighted a clear distinction between a reactive system as an architectural pattern and reactive programming as a programming technique. We described how and why these two types of reactivity play well together and enable us to create highly efficient die-hard IT solutions.

To go deeper into Reactive Spring 5, we need to gain a solid understanding of the reactive programming basement, learning essential concepts and patterns that determine the technique. Therefore, in the next chapter, we will learn the essentials of reactive programming, its history, and the state of the reactive landscape in the Java world.

Reactive Programming in Spring - Basic Concepts

2

The previous chapter explained why it is important to build reactive systems and how reactive programming helps to do this. In this section, we will look at some toolsets that have already been present in Spring Framework for some time. We will also learn the important basic concepts of reactive programming by exploring the RxJava library, which is the first and most well-known reactive library in the Java world.

In this chapter, we will cover the following topics:

- Observer pattern
- Publish-Subscribe implementation provided by Spring
- Server-sent events
- RxJava history and base concepts
- Marble diagrams
- Business cases implemented by applying reactive programming
- The current landscape of reactive libraries

Early reactive solutions in Spring

We have previously mentioned that there are a lot of patterns and programming techniques that are capable of becoming building blocks for the reactive system. For example, callbacks and `CompletableFuture` are commonly used to implement the message-driven architecture. We also mentioned *reactive programming* as a prominent candidate for such a role. Before we explore this in more detail, we need to look around and find other solutions that we have already been using for years.

In `Chapter 1`, *Why Reactive Spring?*, we saw that Spring 4.x introduced the `ListenableFuture` class, which extends the Java `Future` and makes it possible to leverage the asynchronous execution of operations such as HTTP requests. Unfortunately, only a handful of Spring 4.x components support the newer Java 8 `CompletableFuture`, which introduces some neat methods for asynchronous execution composition.

Nevertheless, Spring Framework provides other bits of infrastructure that will be very useful for building our reactive application. Let's look through some of these features now.

Observer pattern

To move things along, we need to remind ourselves about a particular pretty old and well-known design pattern—the **Observer pattern**. That is one of the twenty-three famous **GoF (Gang of Four)** design patterns. At first glance, it may appear that the Observer pattern is not related to reactive programming. However, as we will see later, with some small modifications, it defines the foundations of reactive programming.

 To read more about GoF design patterns, please refer to *Design Patterns: Elements of Reusable Object-Oriented Software* by Erich Gamma, Richard Helm, Ralph Johnson, and John Vlissides (`https://en.wikipedia.org/wiki/Design_Patterns`).

The Observer pattern involves a **subject** that holds a list of its dependants, called **Observers**. The subject notifies its observers of any state changes, usually by calling one of their methods. This pattern is essential when implementing systems based on event handling. The Observer pattern is a vital part of the **MVC (Model-View-Controller)** pattern. Consequently, almost all UI libraries apply it internally.

To simplify this, let's use an analogy from an everyday situation. We can apply this pattern to the newsletter subscription from one of the technical portals. We have to register our email address somewhere on the site of our interest, and then it will send us notifications in the form of newsletters, as shown in the following diagram:

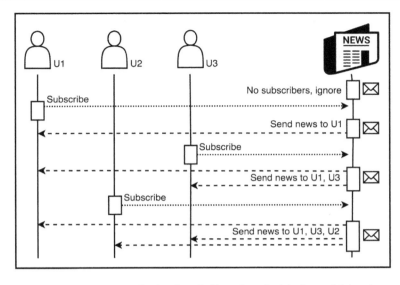

Diagram 2.1 Observer pattern analogy from day-to-day life: newsletter subscription from a technical portal

The Observer pattern makes it possible to register one-to-many dependencies between objects at runtime. At the same time, it does this without knowing anything about the component implementation details (to be type safe, an observer may be aware of a type of incoming event). That gives us the ability to decouple application pieces even though these parts actively interact. Such communication is usually one directional and helps efficiently distribute events through the system, as shown in the following diagram:

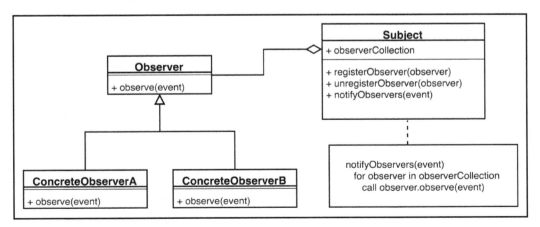

Diagram 2.2 Observer pattern UML class diagram

As the preceding diagram shows, a typical Observer pattern consists of two interfaces, `Subject` and `Observer`. Here, an `Observer` is registered in `Subject` and listens for notifications from it. A `Subject` may generate events on its own or may be called by other components. Let's define a `Subject` interface in Java:

```java
public interface Subject<T> {
    void registerObserver(Observer<T> observer);
    void unregisterObserver(Observer<T> observer);
    void notifyObservers(T event);
}
```

This generic interface is parametrized with the event type `T`, which improves the type safety of our programme. It also contains methods for managing subscriptions (the `registerObserver`, `unregisterObserver`, and `notifyObservers` methods) that trigger an event's broadcasting. In turn, the `Observer` interface may look like the following:

```java
public interface Observer<T> {
    void observe(T event);
}
```

The `Observer` is a generic interface, which parametrized with the `T` type . In turn, it has only one `observe` method in place to handle events. Both the `Observer` and `Subject` do not know about each other more than described in these interfaces.
The `Observer` implementation may be responsible for the subscription procedure, or the `Observer` instance may not be aware of the existence of the `Subject` at all. In the latter case, a third component may be responsible for finding all of the instances of the `Subject` and all registration procedures. For example, such a role may come into play with the Dependency Injection container. This scans the classpath for each `Observer` with the `@EventListener` annotation and the correct signature. After that, it registers the found components to the `Subject`.

 A classic example of a Dependency Injection container is Spring Framework itself. If are not familiar with it, please read the article by Martin Fowler at `https://martinfowler.com/articles/injection.html`.

Now, let's implement two very simple *observers* that simply receive `String` messages and print them to the output stream:

```java
public class ConcreteObserverA implements Observer<String> {
    @Override
    public void observe(String event) {
        System.out.println("Observer A: " + event);
```

```
    }
  }
  public class ConcreteObserverB implements Observer<String> {
    @Override
    public void observe(String event) {
      System.out.println("Observer B: " + event);
    }
  }
```

We also need to write an implementation of the Subject<String>, which produces String events, as shown in the following code:

```
  public class ConcreteSubject implements Subject<String> {
    private final Set<Observer<String>> observers =            // (1)
        new CopyOnWriteArraySet<>();

    public void registerObserver(Observer<String> observer) {
      observers.add(observer);
    }

    public void unregisterObserver(Observer<String> observer) {
      observers.remove(observer);
    }

    public void notifyObservers(String event) {                // (2)
      observers.forEach(observer -> observer.observe(event));   // (2.1)
    }
  }
```

As we can see from the preceding example, the implementation of the Subject holds the Set of observers (1) that are interested in receiving notifications. In turn, a modification (subscription or cancellation of the subscription) of the mentioned Set<Observer> is possible with the support of the registerObserver and unregisterObserver methods. To broadcast events, the Subject has a notifyObservers method (2) that iterates over the list of observers and invokes the observe() method with the actual event (2.1) for each Observer. To be secure in the multithreaded scenario, we use CopyOnWriteArraySet, a thread-safe Set implementation that creates a new copy of its elements each time the update operation happens. It is relatively expensive to update the contents of the CopyOnWriteArraySet, especially when the container holds a lot of elements. However, the list of subscribers does not usually change often, so it is a fairly reasonable option for the thread-safe Subject implementation.

Observer pattern usage example

Now, let's write a simple *JUnit* test that uses our classes and demonstrates how all of them play together. Also, in the following example, we are using the Mockito library (`http://site.mockito.org`) in order to verify expectations with the support of the *Spies Pattern*:

```java
@Test
public void observersHandleEventsFromSubject() {
    // given
    Subject<String> subject = new ConcreteSubject();
    Observer<String> observerA = Mockito.spy(new ConcreteObserverA());
    Observer<String> observerB = Mockito.spy(new ConcreteObserverB());

    // when
    subject.notifyObservers("No listeners");

    subject.registerObserver(observerA);
    subject.notifyObservers("Message for A");

    subject.registerObserver(observerB);
    subject.notifyObservers("Message for A & B");

    subject.unregisterObserver(observerA);
    subject.notifyObservers("Message for B");

    subject.unregisterObserver(observerB);
    subject.notifyObservers("No listeners");

    // then
    Mockito.verify(observerA, times(1)).observe("Message for A");
    Mockito.verify(observerA, times(1)).observe("Message for A & B");
    Mockito.verifyNoMoreInteractions(observerA);

    Mockito.verify(observerB, times(1)).observe("Message for A & B");
    Mockito.verify(observerB, times(1)).observe("Message for B");
    Mockito.verifyNoMoreInteractions(observerB);
}
```

By running the preceding test, the following output is produced. It shows which messages have been received by which `Observer`:

```
Observer A: Message for A
Observer A: Message for A & B
Observer B: Message for A & B
Observer B: Message for B
```

In the case when we do not need to cancel subscriptions, we may leverage Java 8 features and replace the `Observer` implementation classes with *lambdas*. Let's write the corresponding test:

```
@Test
public void subjectLeveragesLambdas() {
    Subject<String> subject = new ConcreteSubject();

    subject.registerObserver(e -> System.out.println("A: " + e));
    subject.registerObserver(e -> System.out.println("B: " + e));
    subject.notifyObservers("This message will receive A & B");
    ...
}
```

It is important to mention that the current `Subject` implementation is based on the `CopyOnWriteArraySet`, which is not the most efficient one. However, that implementation is *thread-safe* at least, which means that we are allowed to use our `Subject` in the multithreaded environment. For example, it may be useful when events are distributed through many independent components, that usually work from multiple threads (it is especially valid nowadays, when most applications are not single threaded). Throughout the course of this book, we will be covering thread safety and other multithreaded concerns.

Do keep in mind that when we have a lot of observers that handle events with some noticeable latency—as introduced by downstream processing—we may parallel message propagation using additional threads or *Thread pool*. This approach may lead to the next implementation of the `notifyObservers` method:

```
private final ExecutorService executorService =
    Executors.newCachedThreadPool();

public void notifyObservers(String event) {
    observers.forEach(observer ->
            executorService.submit(
                    () -> observer.observe(event)
            )
    );
}
```

However, with such **improvements**, we are stepping on the slippery road of homegrown solutions that are usually not the most efficient, and that most likely hide bugs. For example, we may forget to limit the thread pool size, which eventually leads to an `OutOfMemoryError`. A naively configured `ExecutorService` may create a growing number of threads in situations where clients ask to schedule tasks more frequently than the executors can finish their current ones. And because each `Thread` consumes around 1 MB in Java, a typical JVM application has a chance to exhaust all available memory by creating a few thousand threads.

For a more detailed description of experiments with the JVM thread capacity, please refer to Peter Lawrey's article at `http://vanillajava.blogspot.com/2011/07/java-what-is-limit-to-number-of-threads.html`. It is quite old, but not a lot has changed in the JVM memory model since then. To get information about the default stack size of our Java setup, run the following command:

```
java -XX:+PrintFlagsFinal -version | grep ThreadStackSize
```

To prevent excessive resource usage, we may restrict the thread pool size and violate the **liveness** property of the application. Situations such as this arise when all available threads attempt to push some events to the same sluggish `Observer`. Here, we have just scratched the surface of the potential problems that can occur. Also, as stated in the white-paper:

"Improved Multithreaded Unit Testing" (`http://users.ece.utexas.edu/~gligoric/papers/JagannathETAL11IMunit.pdf`), *"Multithreaded code is notoriously hard to develop and test"*.

Consequently, when the multithreaded `Observer` pattern is required, it is better to use battle-proven libraries.

When talking about **liveness**, we are referring to the definition from *Concurrent computing* that describes it as a set of properties that requires a concurrent system in order to make progress, even though its executing components may have to enter critical sections. This was initially defined by Lasley Lamport in *Proving the Correctness of Multiprocess Programs* (`http://citeseerx.ist.psu.edu/viewdoc/download?doi=10.1.1.137.9454&rep=rep1&type=pdf`).

Our overview of the Observer pattern would be incomplete without mentioning how the `Observer` and `Observable` classes form a `java.util` package. These classes were released with JDK 1.0, so they are pretty old. If we look into the source code, we find a pretty straightforward implementation, which is very similar to the one that we made previously in this chapter. Because these classes were introduced before *Java generics*, they operate with events of an `Object` type and consequently are not type safe. Also, this implementation is not very efficient, especially in a multithreaded environment. Taking what we've mentioned into account (all of these issues and some others), these classes are deprecated in Java 9, so it makes no sense to use them for new applications.

 More details about the reasons to deprecate the JDK `Observer` and `Observable` can be found at: https://dzone.com/articles/javas-observer-and-observable-are-deprecated-in-jd.

Of course, when developing applications, we may use hand-crafted implementations of the Observer pattern. This gives us the ability to decouple a source of events and observers. However, it is troublesome to address a lot of aspects that are crucial for modern multithreaded applications. That includes error handling, asynchronous execution, thread-safety, the demand for the highest performance, and so on. We have already seen that event implementation shipped with JDK is not sufficient beyond an educational usage. As a result, it is unquestionably better to use a more mature implementation that is provided by the respectable authority.

Publish-Subscribe pattern with @EventListener

It would be awkward to develop software with the need to re-implement the same software patterns again and again. Luckily, we have Spring Framework, plenty of adorable libraries, and other superb frameworks (Spring is not the only one). As we all know, Spring Framework provides most of the building blocks we could ever need for software development. Of course, for a long time, the framework had its own implementation of the Observer Pattern, and this was widely used for tracking the application's life cycle events. Starting with Spring Framework 4.2, this implementation and concomitant API was extended to be used for the handling of not only application events but also business logic events. In turn, for the event distribution purposes, Spring now provides an `@EventListener` annotation for event handling and the `ApplicationEventPublisher` class for event publishing.

Here we need to clarify that the `@EventListener` and the `ApplicationEventPublisher` implement the **Publish-Subscribe pattern**, which may be seen as a variation of the Observer pattern.

A good description of the Publish-Subscribe pattern can be found at: `http://www.enterpriseintegrationpatterns.com/patterns/messaging/PublishSubscribeChannel.html`.

In contrast to the Observer pattern, in the Publish-Subscribe pattern publishers and subscribers *don't need to know each other,* as is depicted in the following diagram:

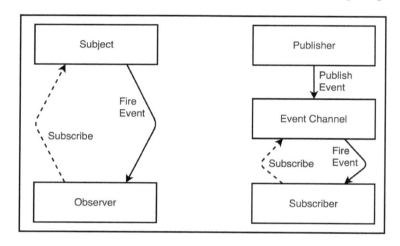

Diagram 2.3 The Observer pattern (on the left) versus the Publish-Subscribe pattern (on the right)

A Publish-Subscribe pattern provides an additional level of indirection between the publishers and subscribers. The subscribers are aware of the event channels that broadcast notifications, but usually do not care about publishers' identities. Also, each event channel may have a few publishers at the same time. The preceding diagram should help to spot the difference between Observer and Publish-Subscribe patterns. The **Event Channel** (also known as a message broker or event bus) may additionally filter incoming messages and distribute them between subscribers. The filtering and routing may happen based on the message content, message topic, or sometimes even both. Consequently, subscribers in a *topic-based system* will receive all messages published to the topics of interest.

The Spring Framework's `@EventListener` annotation makes it possible to apply both topic-based and content-based routing. Message types could play the role of topics; the `condition` attribute enables content-based routing event handling based on the **Spring Expression Language (SpEL)**.

As an alternative to the Spring-based implementation of the Publish-Subscribe pattern, there is a popular open source Java library called **MBassador**. It has the single purpose of providing a light-weight, high-performance event bus that implements the Publish-Subscribe pattern. Authors claim that MBassador preserves resources while delivering high performance. This is because it has almost no dependencies and does not restrict the design of our application. For more details, please refer to the project page on GitHub (`https://github.com/bennidi/mbassador`). Also, the **Guava** library provides **EventBus**, which implements the Publish-Subscribe pattern. The following article describes the API and includes code samples for Guava EventBus: (`https://github.com/google/guava/wiki/EventBusExplained`).

Building applications with @EventListener

To play with the Publish-Subscribe pattern in Spring Framework, let's do an exercise. In turn, assume that we have to implement a simple web service that shows the current temperature in the room. For this purpose, we have a temperature sensor, which sends events with the current temperature in Celsius from time to time. We potentially want to have both mobile and web applications, but for the sake of conciseness, we are implementing only a simple web application. Furthermore, as questions of communication with microcontrollers are out of the scope of this book, we are simulating a temperature sensor using a random number generator.

To make our application following the **reactive design**, we cannot use an old pulling model for data retrieval. Fortunately, nowadays we have some well-adopted protocols for asynchronous message propagation from a server to a client, namely WebSockets and **Server-Sent Events** (**SSE**). In the current example, we will use the last one. The SSE allows a client to receive automatic updates from a server, and is commonly used to send message updates or continuous data streams to a browser. With the inception of HTML5, all modern browsers have a JavaScript API called `EventSource`, which is used by clients who request a particular URL to receive an event stream. The `EventSource` also autoreconnects by default in the case of communication issues. It is important to highlight that SSE is an excellent candidate for fulfilling communication needs between components in the reactive system. On par with WebSocket, SSE is used a lot in this book.

To read more about *Server-Sent Events*, please read the chapter of *High Performance Browser Networking* by Ilya Grigorik at `https://hpbn.co/server-sent-events-sse/`.

Also, the following article by Mark Brown gives a good comparison between WebSockets and Server-Sent Events: `https://www.sitepoint.com/real-time-apps-websockets-server-sent-events/`

Bootstrapping a Spring application

To implement our usecase, we are using the well-known Spring modules Spring Web and Spring Web MVC. Our application will not use the new features of Spring 5, so it will run similarly on Spring Framework 4.x. To simplify our development process and even more, we are leveraging *Spring Boot*, which is described in more detail later. To bootstrap our application, we may configure and download a Gradle project from the Spring Initializer website at `start.spring.io`. For now, we need to select the preferred Spring Boot version and dependency for the web (the actual dependency identifier in Gradle config will be `org.springframework.boot:spring-boot-starter-web`), as shown in the following screenshot:

Diagram 2.4 Web-based Spring Initializer simplifies the bootstrapping of a new Spring Boot application

Alternatively, we may generate a new Spring Boot project using cURL and the HTTP API of the Spring Boot Initializer site. The following command will effectively create and download the same empty project with all the desired dependencies:

```
curl https://start.spring.io/starter.zip \
  -d dependencies=web,actuator \
  -d type=gradle-project \
  -d bootVersion=2.0.2.RELEASE \
  -d groupId=com.example.rpws.chapters \
  -d artifactId=SpringBootAwesome \
  -o SpringBootAwesome.zip
```

Implementing business logic

We may now outline the design of our system in the following diagram:

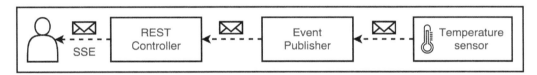

Diagram 2.5 Events flow from a temperature sensor to a user

In this use case, the domain model will consist only of the Temperature class with the only double value inside. For simplicity purposes, it is also used as an event object, as shown in the following code:

```
final class Temperature {
    private final double value;
    // constructor & getter...
}
```

To simulate the sensor, let's implement the TemperatureSensor class and decorate it with a @Component annotation to register the Spring bean, as follows:

```
@Component
public class TemperatureSensor {
    private final ApplicationEventPublisher publisher;           // (1)
    private final Random rnd = new Random();                     // (2)
    private final ScheduledExecutorService executor =            // (3)
            Executors.newSingleThreadScheduledExecutor();

    public TemperatureSensor(ApplicationEventPublisher publisher) {
        this.publisher = publisher;
    }
```

```
    @PostConstruct
    public void startProcessing() {                              // (4)
        this.executor.schedule(this::probe, 1, SECONDS);
    }

    private void probe() {                                       // (5)
        double temperature = 16 + rnd.nextGaussian() * 10;
        publisher.publishEvent(new Temperature(temperature));
        // schedule the next read after some random delay (0-5 seconds)
        executor
          .schedule(this::probe, rnd.nextInt(5000), MILLISECONDS);    //
(5.1)
    }
}
```

So, our simulated temperature sensor only depends on the `ApplicationEventPublisher` class (1), provided by Spring Framework. This class makes it possible to publish events to the system. It is a requirement to have a random generator (2) to contrive temperatures with some random intervals. An event generation process happens in a separate `ScheduledExecutorService` (3), where each event's generation schedules the next round of an event's generation with a random delay (5.1). All that logic is defined in the `probe()` method (5). In turn, the mentioned class has the `startProcessing()` method annotated with `@PostConstruct` (4), which is called by Spring Framework when the bean is ready and triggers the whole sequence of random temperature values.

Asynchronous HTTP with Spring Web MVC

The introduced in Servlet 3.0 asynchronous support expands the ability to process an HTTP request in non-container threads. Such a feature is pretty useful for long-running tasks. With those changes, in Spring Web MVC we can return not only a value of type `T` in `@Controller` but also a `Callable<T>` or a `DeferredResult<T>`. The `Callable<T>` may be run inside a non-container thread, but still, it would be a blocking call. In contrast, `DeferredResult<T>` allows an asynchronous response generation on a non-container thread by calling the `setResult(T result)` method so it could be used within the event-loop.

Starting from version 4.2, Spring Web MVC makes it possible to return `ResponseBodyEmitter`, which behaves similarly to `DeferredResult`, but can be used to send multiple objects, where each object is written separately with an instance of a message converter (defined by the `HttpMessageConverter` interface).

The `SseEmitter` extends `ResponseBodyEmitter` and makes it possible to send many outgoing messages for one incoming request in accordance with SSE's protocol requirements. Alongside `ResponseBodyEmitter` and `SseEmitter`, Spring Web MVC also respects the `StreamingResponseBody` interface. When returned from `@Controller`, it allows us to send raw data (payload bytes) asynchronously. `StreamingResponseBody` may be very handy for streaming large files without blocking Servlet threads.

Exposing the SSE endpoint

The next step requires adding the `TemperatureController` class with the `@RestController` annotation, which means that the component is used for HTTP communication, as shown in the following code:

```
@RestController
public class TemperatureController {
    private final Set<SseEmitter> clients =                    // (1)
        new CopyOnWriteArraySet<>();

    @RequestMapping(
        value = "/temperature-stream",                        // (2)
        method = RequestMethod.GET)
    public SseEmitter events(HttpServletRequest request) {    // (3)
        SseEmitter emitter = new SseEmitter();                // (4)
        clients.add(emitter);                                 // (5)

        // Remove emitter from clients on error or disconnect
        emitter.onTimeout(() -> clients.remove(emitter));     // (6)
        emitter.onCompletion(() -> clients.remove(emitter));  // (7)
        return emitter;                                       // (8)
    }
    @Async                                                    // (9)
    @EventListener                                            // (10)
    public void handleMessage(Temperature temperature) {      // (11)
        List<SseEmitter> deadEmitters = new ArrayList<>();    // (12)
        clients.forEach(emitter -> {
            try {
                emitter.send(temperature, MediaType.APPLICATION_JSON);  // (13)
            } catch (Exception ignore) {
                deadEmitters.add(emitter);                    // (14)
            }
        });
        clients.removeAll(deadEmitters);                      // (15)
    }
}
```

Now, to understand the logic of the `TemperatureController` class, we need to describe the `SseEmitter`. Spring Web MVC provides that class with the sole purpose of sending SSE events. When a request-handling method returns the `SseEmitter` instance, the actual request processing continues until `SseEnitter.complete()`, an error, or a timeout occurs.

The `TemperatureController` provides one request handler (3) for the URI `/temperature-stream` (2) and returns the `SseEmitter` (8). In the case when a client requests that URI, we create and return the new `SseEmitter` instance (4) with its previous registration in the list of the active `clients` (5). Furthermore, the `SseEmitter` constructor may consume the `timeout` parameter.

For the `clients`' collection, we may use the `CopyOnWriteArraySet` class from the `java.util.concurrent` package (1). Such an implementation allows us to modify the list and iterate over it at the same time. When a web client opens a new SSE session, we add a new emitter to the `clients`' collection. The `SseEmitter` removes itself from the `clients`' list when it has finished processing or has reached timeout (6) (7).

Now, having a communication channel with clients means that we need to be able to receive events about temperature changes. For that purpose, our class has a `handleMessage()` method (11). It is decorated with the `@EventListener` annotation (10) in order to receive events from Spring. This framework will invoke the `handleMessage()` method only when receiving `Temperature` events, as this type of method's argument is known as `temperature`. The `@Async` annotation (9) marks a method as a candidate for the **asynchronous** execution, so it is invoked in the manually configured thread pool. The `handleMessage()` method receives a new temperature event and asynchronously sends it to all clients in JSON format in parallel for each event (13). Also, when sending to individual emitters, we track all failing ones (14) and remove them from the list of the active `clients` (15). Such an approach makes it possible to spot clients that are not operational anymore. Unfortunately, `SseEmitter` does not provide any callback for handling errors, and can be done by handling errors thrown by the `send()` method only.

Configuring asynchronous support

To run everything, we need an entry point for our application with the following customized methods:

```
@EnableAsync                                                    // (1)
@SpringBootApplication                                          // (2)
public class Application implements AsyncConfigurer {
```

```
public static void main(String[] args) {
    SpringApplication.run(Application.class, args);
}

@Override
public Executor getAsyncExecutor() {                              // (3)
    ThreadPoolTaskExecutor executor = new ThreadPoolTaskExecutor();// (4)
    executor.setCorePoolSize(2);
    executor.setMaxPoolSize(100);
    executor.setQueueCapacity(5);                                  // (5)
    executor.initialize();
    return executor;
}

@Override
public AsyncUncaughtExceptionHandler getAsyncUncaughtExceptionHandler(){
    return new SimpleAsyncUncaughtExceptionHandler();              // (6)
}
}
```

As we can see, the example is a Spring Boot application (2), with an asynchronous execution enabled by the @EnableAsync annotation (1). Here, we may configure an exception handler for exceptions thrown from the asynchronous execution (6). That is also where we prepare Executor for asynchronous processing. In our case, we use ThreadPoolTaskExecutor with two core threads that may be increased to up to one hundred threads. It is important to note that without a properly configured queue capacity (5), the thread pool is not able to grow. That is because the SynchronousQueue would be used instead, limiting concurrency.

Building a UI with SSE support

The last thing that we need in order to complete our use case is an HTML page with some JavaScript code to communicate with the server. For the sake of conciseness, we will strip all HTML tags and leave only the minimum that is required to achieve a result, as follows:

```
<body>
<ul id="events"></ul>
<script type="application/javascript">
function add(message) {
    const el = document.createElement("li");
    el.innerHTML = message;
    document.getElementById("events").appendChild(el);
}

var eventSource = new EventSource("/temperature-stream");         // (1)
```

```
eventSource.onmessage = e => {                                    // (2)
    const t = JSON.parse(e.data);
    const fixed = Number(t.value).toFixed(2);
    add('Temperature: ' + fixed + ' C');
}
eventSource.onopen = e => add('Connection opened');               // (3)
eventSource.onerror = e => add('Connection closed');              //
</script>
</body>
```

Here, we are using the `EventSource` object pointed at `/temperature-stream` (1). This handles incoming messages by invoking the `onmessage()` function (2), error handling, and reaction to the stream opening, which are done in the same fashion (3). We should save this page as `index.html` and put it in the `src/main/resources/static/` folder of our project. By default, Spring Web MVC serves the content of the folder through HTTP. Such behavior could be changed by providing a configuration that extends the `WebMvcConfigurerAdapter` class.

Verifying application functionality

After rebuilding and completing our application's startup, we should be able to access the mentioned web page in a browser at the following address: `http://localhost:8080` (Spring Web MVC uses port `8080` for the web server as the default one. However, this can be changed in the `application.properties` file using the configuration line `server.port=9090`). After a few seconds, we may see the following output:

```
Connection opened
Temperature: 14.71 C
Temperature: 9.67 C
Temperature: 19.02 C
Connection closed
Connection opened
Temperature: 18.01 C
Temperature: 16.17 C
```

As we can see, our web page reactively receives events, preserving both client and server resources. It also supports autoreconnect in the case of network issues or timeouts. As the current solution is not exclusive to JavaScript, we may connect with other clients for example, `curl`. By running the next command in a terminal, we receive the following stream of raw, but not formatted, events:

```
> curl http://localhost:8080/temperature-stream
data:{"value":22.33210856124129}
data:{"value":13.83133638119636}
```

To explore more about Server-Sent Events technology and its integration with Spring Framework, read an excellent article by Ralph Schaer at `https://golb.hplar.ch/p/Server-Sent-Events-with-Spring`.

Criticism of the solution

At this point, we may praise ourselves for implementing a resilient reactive application using only a few dozen code lines (including HTML and JavaScript). However, the current solution has a few issues. First of all, we are using the Publish-Subscribe infrastructure provided by Spring. In Spring Framework, this mechanism was initially introduced for handling application life cycle events, and was not intended for high-load, high-performance scenarios. What would happen when, instead of one stream of temperature data, we need thousands or even millions of separate streams? Will Spring's implementation be able to handle such a load efficiently?

Furthermore, one significant downside of such an approach lies in the fact that we are using an internal Spring mechanism to define and implement our business logic. This leads to a situation in which some minor changes in the framework may break our application. Besides, it is hard to unit test our business rules without running the application context. As explained in `Chapter 1`, *Why Reactive Spring?*, it is also reasonable to mention an application that has a lot of methods that are decorated with the `@EventListener` annotation, and without an explicit script that describes the whole workflow in one concise piece of code.

Furthermore, `SseEmitter` has a notion for errors and the ends of streams, whereas `@EventListener` does not. So, to signal the end of the stream or error between components, we have to define some special objects or class hierarchies, and it is easy to forget about handling them. Also, such specific markers may have slightly different semantics in different situations, complicating the solution and reducing the attractiveness of the approach.

One more drawback worth highlighting is that we allocate the thread pool to asynchronously broadcast temperature events. In the case of a genuinely asynchronous and reactive approach (framework), we wouldn't have to do this.

Our temperature sensor generates only one stream of events without regard to how many clients are listening. However, it also creates them when nobody listens. That may lead to a waste of resources, especially when creation actions are resource hungry. For example, our component may communicate with real hardware and reduce hardware lifespan at the same time.

To address all of these issues, as well as others, we need a reactive library that is specially designed for such purposes. Fortunately, we have a few of these. We will now look at RxJava, which was the first widely adopted reactive library, and changed the way we build reactive applications using Java.

RxJava as a reactive framework

For some time, there was a **standard** library for reactive programming on Java platforms—namely RxJava 1.x (see `https://github.com/ReactiveX/RxJava` for more details). That library paved the way for reactive programming as we know it in the Java world today. At the moment, it is not the only library of this kind; we also have Akka Streams and Project Reactor. The latter is covered in detail in `Chapter 4`, *Project Reactor - the Foundation for Reactive Apps*. So, currently, we have a few options from which we may choose. Furthermore, RxJava itself has changed a lot with the release of version 2.x. However, to understand the most basic concepts of reactive programming and the reasoning behind them, we will be focusing on the most fundamental part of the RxJava only, on the API, which has not changed since the early versions of the library. All examples in this section should work fine with both RxJava 1.x and RxJava 2.x.

To enable simultaneous usage in one application classpath, RxJava 2.x and RxJava 1.x have different group IDs (`io.reactivex.rxjava2` versus `io.reactivex`) and namespaces (`io.reactivex` versus `rx`).

Even though the end-of-life for RxJava 1.x was in March 2018, it is still used in a handful of libraries and applications, mainly because of long-standing, wide-spread adoption. The following article provides a good description of what was changed in RxJava 2.x in comparison to RxJava 1.x: `https://github.com/ReactiveX/RxJava/wiki/What's-different-in-2.0`.

The RxJava library is a Java VM implementation of **Reactive Extensions** (also known as **ReactiveX**). Reactive Extensions is a set of tools that allows imperative languages to work with data streams, regardless of a stream being synchronous or asynchronous. ReactiveX is often defined as a combination of the Observer pattern, the Iterator pattern, and functional programming. A good starting point to learn more about ReactiveX is at `http://reactivex.io`.

Reactive programming may seem to be difficult, especially when we are approaching it from the imperative world, but the main idea is actually straightforward. Here, we are going to learn the basics of RxJava as the most wide-spread reactive library to date. We are not going to dive into all of the details, but try to walk through all the vital concepts of reactive programming.

Observer plus iterator equals Reactive Stream

In this chapter, we have talked a lot about the Observer pattern, which gives us a clearly separated view of the Producer event and Consumer event. Let's have a recap of the interfaces defined by that pattern, as shown in the following code:

```
public interface Observer<T> {
    void notify(T event);
}

public interface Subject<T> {
    void registerObserver(Observer<T> observer);
    void unregisterObserver(Observer<T> observer);
    void notifyObservers(T event);
}
```

As we saw previously, this approach is charming for infinite streams of data, but it would be great to have the ability to signal the end of the data stream. Also, we do not want the Producer to generate events before the appearance of consumers. In the synchronous world, we have a pattern for that—Iterator pattern. This may be described using the following code:

```
public interface Iterator<T> {
    T next();
    boolean hasNext();
}
```

To retrieve items one by one, `Iterator` provides the `next()` method and also makes it possible to signal the end of the sequence by returning a `false` value as a result of the `hasNext()` call. So what would happen if we tried to mix this idea with an asynchronous execution provided by the Observer pattern? The result would look like the following:

```
public interface RxObserver<T> {
    void onNext(T next);
    void onComplete();
}
```

The RxObserver is pretty similar to the Iterator, but instead of calling the next() method of Iterator, RxObserver would be notified with a new value by the onNext() callback. And instead of checking whether the result of the hasNext() method is positive, RxObserver is informed about the end of the stream through the invoked onComplete() method. That is fine, but what about errors? The Iterator may throw an Exception during the processing of the next() method, and it would be great to have a mechanism for an error propagation from the Producer to RxObserver. Let's add a special callback for that—onError(). So, the final solution will look like the following:

```
public interface RxObserver<T> {
    void onNext(T next);
    void onComplete();
    void onError(Exception e);
}
```

This happened because we have just designed an Observer interface, the foundational concept of RxJava. This interface defines how data flows between every part of a reactive stream. By being the smallest part of the library, the Observer interface is found everywhere. The RxObserver is similar to the Observer from the Observer pattern, as previously described.

The Observable Reactive class is a counterpart to the Subject from the Observer pattern. As a consequence, Observable plays a role as an events source as it emits items. It has hundreds of stream transformation methods, as well as dozens of factory methods to initialize a reactive stream.

A Subscriber abstract class implements the Observer interface and consumes items. It is also used as a base for the actual Subscriber's implementation. The runtime relation between Observable and Subscriber is controlled by a Subscription that makes it possible to check the subscription status and cancel it if needed. This relationship is illustrated in the following diagram:

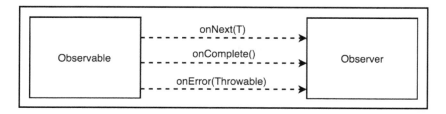

Diagram 2.6 Observable-Observer contract

RxJava defines rules about emitting items. The Observable is allowed to send any number of elements (including zero). Then it signals the end of the execution either by claiming the success or raising an error. So the Observable for each attached Subscriber invokes onNext() any number of times, then calls onComplete() or onError() (but not both). Consequently, it is prohibited for it to call onNext() after onComplete() or onError().

Producing and consuming streams

At this point, we should be familiar enough with the RxJava library to create our first small application. Let's define a stream that is represented by the Observable class. At the moment, we may assume that the Observable is a sort of generator that knows how to propagate events for subscribers as soon as they subscribe:

```
Observable<String> observale = Observable.create(
    new Observable.OnSubscribe<String>() {
        @Override
        public void call(Subscriber<? super String> sub) {        // (1)
            sub.onNext("Hello, reactive world!");                 // (2)
            sub.onCompleted();                                    // (3)
        }
    }
);
```

So, here we create an Observable with a callback that will be applied as soon as the Subscriber appears (1). At that moment, our Observer will produce a one string value (2) and then signal the end of the stream to the subscriber (3). We can also improve this code using the Java 8 lambdas:

```
Observable<String> observable = Observable.create(
    sub -> {
        sub.onNext("Hello, reactive world!");
        sub.onCompleted();
    }
);
```

In contrast with the Java Stream API, Observable is reusable, and each subscriber will receive the Hello, reactive world! event just after the subscription.

 Note that, from RxJava 1.2.7 onward, the Observable creation has been deprecated and treated as unsafe because it may generate too many elements and overload the subscriber. In other words, this approach does not support backpressure, a concept that we are going to examine later in detail. However, that code is still valid for the sake of introduction.

So, now we need a `Subscriber`, as shown in the following code:

```
Subscriber<String> subscriber = new Subscriber<String>() {
    @Override
    public void onNext(String s) {                                    // (1)
        System.out.println(s);
    }

    @Override
    public void onCompleted() {                                       // (2)
        System.out.println("Done!");
    }
    @Override
    public void onError(Throwable e) {                                // (3)
        System.err.println(e);
    }
};
```

As we can see, the `Subscriber` has to implement the `Observer` methods and define the reactions for new events (1), stream completion (2), and errors (3). Now, let's hook the `observable` and `subscriber` instances together:

```
observable.subscribe(subscriber);
```

When running the mentioned code, the program generates the following output:

```
Hello, reactive world!
Done!
```

Hooray! We have just written a small and simple reactive hello-world application! As we may suspect, we may rewrite this example using lambdas, as shown in the following code:

```
Observable.create(
    sub -> {
        sub.onNext("Hello, reactive world!");
        sub.onCompleted();
    }
).subscribe(
    System.out::println,
    System.err::println,
    () -> System.out.println("Done!")
);
```

The RxJava library gives a lot of flexibility in order to create `Observable` and `Subscriber` instances. It is possible to create an `Observable` instance *just* by referencing elements, by using an old-style array, or *from* the `Iterable` collection, as follows:

```
Observable.just("1", "2", "3", "4");
Observable.from(new String[]{"A", "B", "C"});
Observable.from(Collections.emptyList());
```

It is also possible to reference a `Callable` (1) or even a `Future` (2), as shown in the following code:

```
Observable<String> hello = Observable.fromCallable(() -> "Hello ");  // (1)
Future<String> future =
        Executors.newCachedThreadPool().submit(() -> "World");
Observable<String> world = Observable.from(future);                  // (2)
```

Moreover, along with the plain creational functionality, the `Observable` stream may be created by combining other `Observable` instances, which allows for easy implementation of pretty complicated workflows. For example, the `concat()` operator for each of the incoming streams consumes all items by re-sending them to the downstream observer. Incoming streams will then be processed until a terminal operation (`onComplete()`, `onError()`) occurs, and the order of processing is the same as the order of the `concat()` arguments. The following code demonstrates an example of the `concat()` usage:

```
Observable.concat(hello, world, Observable.just("!"))
    .forEach(System.out::print);
```

Here, as part of a straightforward combination of a few `Observable` instances that use different origins, we also iterate through the result with the `Observable.forEach()` method in a way that is similar to the Java 8 Stream API. Such a program generates the following output:

Hello World!

Note that even though it is convenient to not define handlers for exceptions, in the case where an error occurs, the default `Subscriber` implementation throws `rx.exceptions.OnErrorNotImplementedException`.

Generating an asynchronous sequence

RxJava makes it possible to generate not only one event in the future, but an asynchronous sequence of events based, for example, on a time interval, as shown in the following code:

```
Observable.interval(1, TimeUnit.SECONDS)
    .subscribe(e -> System.out.println("Received: " + e));
Thread.sleep(5000);                                          // (1)
```

In that case, the output is as following:

```
Received: 0
Received: 1
Received: 2
Received: 3
Received: 4
```

Also, if we remove `Thread.sleep(...)` (1), our application will exit without any output. This happens because events would be generated and therefore consumed in a separate daemon thread. So, to prevent the main thread from finishing the execution, we may `sleep()` or do some other useful tasks.

Of course, there is something that controls the `Observer-Subscriber` cooperation. This is called `Subscription`, and has the following interface declaration:

```
interface Subscription {
    void unsubscribe();
    boolean isUnsubscribed();
}
```

The `unsubscribe()` method allows the `Subscriber` to inform `Observable` that there is no need to send new events. In other words, the aforementioned code is a subscription cancellation. On the other hand, `Observable` uses `isUnsubscribed()` to check that the `Subscriber` is still waiting for events.

To understand the mentioned unsubscribe functionality, let's consider the case where a subscriber is the only party interested in the events, and consumes them until an external signal is propagated by `CountDawnLatch (1)`. The incoming stream generates a new event every 100 milliseconds, and these events produce the *endless* sequence—0, 1, 2, 3... (3). The following code demonstrates how to get a `Subscription (2)` when defining a reactive stream. It also shows how to unsubscribe from a stream (4):

```
CountDownLatch externalSignal = ...;                          // (1)

Subscription subscription = Observable                        // (2)
        .interval(100, MILLISECONDS)                          // (3)
        .subscribe(System.out::println);

externalSignal.await();
subscription.unsubscribe();                                   // (4)
```

So here, the subscriber receives the events 0, 1, 2, 3, and then the `externalSignal` invocation occurs, which leads to the subscription cancellation.

At this point, we have already learned that reactive programming consists of an `Observable` stream, a `Subscriber`, and some sort of `Subscription` that communicates the intention of the `Subscriber` to receive events from the `Observable` producer. It is now time to transform the data flowing through the reactive streams.

Stream transformation and marble diagrams

Even though `Observable` and `Subscriber` alone make it possible to implement a lot of workflows, the whole power of RxJava is hidden in its operators. Operators are used for tweaking elements of the stream or changing the stream structure itself. RxJava provides a huge amount of operators for almost every potential scenario, but it is out of the scope of this book to study all of them. Let's now look at the most used and foundational operators; most others are just a combination of the basic ones.

Map operator

Unquestioningly, the most used operator in RxJava is `map`, which has the following signature:

```
<R> Observable<R> map(Func1<T, R> func)
```

The preceding method declaration means that the `func` function can transform the `T` object type to the `R` object type, and applying `map` transforms `Observable<T>` into `Observable<R>`. However, a signature does not always describe the operator's behavior well, especially if the operator is doing a complex transformation. For these purposes, **Marble diagrams** were invented. Marble diagrams visually present stream transformations. They are so effective for describing the operator's behavior that almost all RxJava operators contain the image with a marble diagram in Javadoc. The `map` operator is represented by the following diagram:

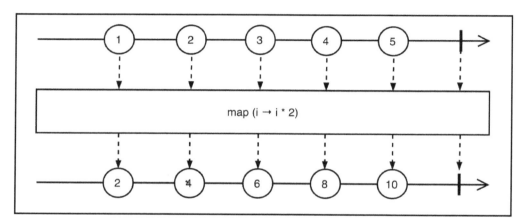

Diagram 2.7 Operator map: transforms the items emitted by an Observable by applying a function to each item

From looking at the preceding diagram, it should be clear that the `map` makes a one-to-one transformation. Furthermore, the output stream has the same number of elements as the input stream.

Filter operator

In contrast with the `map` operator, the `filter` may produce fewer elements than it has received. It only emits those elements that have successfully passed the predicate test, as shown in the following diagram:

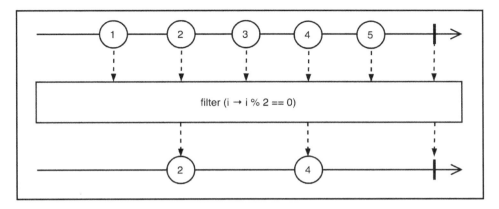

Diagram 2.8 Filter operator: emits only those items from an Observable that pass a predicate test

Count operator

The count operator is pretty descriptive; it emits the only value with the number of elements in the input stream. However, the count emits at the moment when the original stream completes, so, in the case of an endless stream, the count will not ever finish or return anything, as shown in the following diagram:

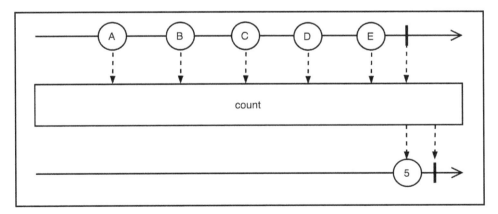

Diagram 2.9 Count operator: counts the number of items emitted by the Observable source and emit only this value

Zip operator

One more operator that we will look at is `zip`. This has a more complex behavior, as it combines values from two parallel streams by applying a `zip` function. It is often used for data enrichment, especially when parts of an expected result are retrieved from different sources, as shown in the following diagram:

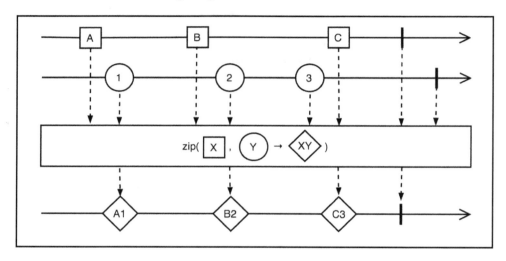

Diagram 2.10 Zip operator: combines the emissions of multiple Observables together via a specified function and emits single items for each combination based on the results of this function

Here, Netflix uses a `zip` operator to combine movie descriptions, movie posters, and movie ratings when streaming a list of recommended videos. However, for the sake of simplicity, let's zip just two streams of string values, as shown in the following code:

```
Observable.zip(
        Observable.just("A", "B", "C"),
        Observable.just("1", "2", "3"),
        (x, y) -> x + y
).forEach(System.out::println);
```

The preceding code joins elements one by one from two streams, as depicted in the preceding diagram, and produces the following console output:

```
A1
B2
C3
```

To learn more about operators that are commonly used in reactive programming (not only in RxJava) visit `http://rxmarbles.com`. This site contains interactive diagrams that reflect actual operator behavior. In turn, the interactive UI allows us to visualize the events' transformation with regards to the order and time in which each event appeared in the streams. Note that the site itself is built with the RxJS library (see `https://github.com/ReactiveX/rxjs` for more details), which is RxJava's counterpart in the JavaScript world.

As previously mentioned, RxJava's `Observable` provides dozens of stream transformation operators that confidently cover a lot of use cases. Of course, RxJava does not only limit developers to operators provided by the library. One can also write a custom operator by implementing a class that is derived from the `Observable.Transformer<T, R>`. Such operator logic could be included in the workflow by applying the `Observable.compose(transformer)` operator. At the moment, we are not going to dive into the operator's building theory or practice; we are going to cover that in later chapters, partially. So far, it will be enough to highlight that RxJava provides a robust set of instruments for building complicated asynchronous workflows that are mainly limited by our imagination, not by the library.

Prerequisites and benefits of RxJava

With RxJava, we have become acquainted with the basics of *reactive programming*. Different reactive libraries may have slightly different APIs and somewhat various implementation details, but the concept remains the same—the subscriber subscribes to an observable stream that in turn triggers an asynchronous process of event generation. Between the producer and subscriber, there usually exists some subscription that makes it possible to break up the producer-consumer relationship. Such an approach is very flexible and enables to have control over the amount of produced and consumed events, decreasing the number of CPU cycles, which are usually wasted on creating data, and will never be used.

To prove that reactive programming offers the ability to save resources, let's assume that we need to implement a simple in-memory search engine service. This should return a collection of URLs to documents that contain the desired phrase. Usually, the client application (a web or mobile app) also passes a limit, for example, the maximum amount of useful results. Without reactive programming, we would probably design such a service using the following API:

```
public interface SearchEngine {
    List<URL> search(String query, int limit);
}
```

As we might note from the interface, our service performs a `search` operation, gathers all results within the `limit`, puts them into a `List`, and returns it to the client. In the preceding scenario, a client of the service receives the whole result set, even if someone picks the first or second result on the page after drawing the result on the UI. In that case, our service did a lot of work, and our client has been waiting for a long time, but the client ignored most of the results. That is undoubtedly a waste of resources.

However, we can do better and process the search result iterating over the result set. So the server will search for the next result items as long as a client continues consuming them. Usually, the server search progression happens not for each row, but rather for some fixed size bucket (let's say 100 items). Such an approach is called **cursor** and is often used by databases. For a client, the resulting cursor is represented in the form of an **iterator**. The following code represents our improved service API:

```
public interface IterableSearchEngine {
    Iterable<URL> search(String query, int limit);
}
```

The only drawback in the case of an iterable is that our client's thread will be blocked when it is actively waiting for a new piece of data. That would be a disaster for the Android UI thread. When the new result arrives, the search service is waiting for the `next()` call. In other words, a client and the service are playing ping-pong through the `Iterable` interface. Nevertheless, the mentioned interaction may be acceptable sometimes, but in most cases, it is not efficient enough to build a high-performance application.

In turn, our search engine may return `CompletableFuture` in order to become an asynchronous service. In that case, our client's thread may do something useful and not bother about the search request, as the service invokes a callback as soon as a result arrives. But here we again receive all or nothing, as `CompletableFuture` may hold only one value, even if it is a list of results, as shown in the following code:

```
public interface FutureSearchEngine {
    CompletableFuture<List<URL>> search(String query, int limit);
}
```

With RxJava, we will improve our solution and get both asynchronous processing and the ability to react to each arriving event. Also, our client may `unsubscribe()` at any moment and reduce the amount of work done by the process of searching a service, as shown in the following code:

```
public interface RxSearchEngine {
    Observable<URL> search(String query);
}
```

By using that approach, we are increasing the *responsiveness* of an application a lot. Even though the client has not received all of the results yet, it may process the pieces that have already arrived. As humans, we do not like to wait for results. Instead, we value *Time To First Byte* or *Critical Rendering Path* metrics. In all of these cases, reactive programming is not worse than conventional approaches, and usually brings better results.

 To read more about *Time To First Byte,* please refer to `https://www.maxcdn.com/one/visual-glossary/time-to-first-byte`. In addition to this, *Critical Rendering Path* is described at `https://developers.google.com/web/fundamentals/performance/critical-rendering-path`.

As we saw earlier, RxJava makes it possible to asynchronously compose data streams in a way that is much more versatile and flexible. Similarly, we may wrap the old-school synchronous code into an asynchronous workflow. To manage the actual execution thread for a slow `Callable`, we may use the `subscriberOn(Scheduler)` operator. This operator defines on which `Scheduler` (reactive counterpart of Java's `ExecutorService`) the stream processing is started. The thread scheduling is covered in detail in Chapter 4, *Project Reactor - the Foundation for Reactive Apps*. The following code demonstrates such a use case:

```
String query = ...;
Observable.fromCallable(() -> doSlowSyncRequest(query))
    .subscribeOn(Schedulers.io())
    .subscribe(this::processResult);
```

Sure, with such an approach we cannot rely on the fact that one thread will process the whole request. Our workflow may start in one thread, migrate to a handful of other threads, and finish processing in a completely different, newly created thread. It is essential to highlight that with this approach, it's hazardous to mutate objects, and the only reasonable strategy is *immutability*. It is not a new concept; it is one of the core principles of *functional programming*. Once an object is created, it may not change. Such a simple rule prevents a whole class of issues in parallel applications.

Before Java 8 introduced lambdas, it was hard to leverage the full power of reactive programming as well as functional programming. Without lambdas, we had to create a lot of anonymous or inner classes that polluted the application code and created more boilerplate than meaningful lines. At the time of RxJava's inception, despite its slow speed, Netflix extensively used Groovy for development purposes, mainly because of lambda support. This leads us to the conclusion that functions as first-class citizens are required for the successful and pleasant usage of reactive programming. Fortunately, this is not a problem for Java anymore, even on the Android platform, where projects such as Retrolambda (`https://github.com/orfjackal/retrolambda`) enable lambda support for old Java versions.

Rebuilding our application with RxJava

To get a feel for RxJava, let's rewrite the previously written temperature sensing application with RxJava. To use the library in the application, let's add the following dependency to the `build.gradle` file:

```
compile('io.reactivex:rxjava:1.3.8')
```

Here, we are using the same value class to represent the current temperature, as shown in the following code:

```
final class Temperature {
    private final double value;
    // constructor & getter
}
```

Implementing business logic

The `TemperatureSensor` class previously sent events to a Spring `ApplicationEventPublisher`, but now it should return a reactive stream with `Temperature` events. The Reactive implementation of `TemperatureSensor` may look like the following:

```
@Component                                                      // (1)
public class TemperatureSensor {
    private final Random rnd = new Random();                    // (2)

    private final Observable<Temperature> dataStream =          // (3)
        Observable
            .range(0, Integer.MAX_VALUE)                        // (4)
            .concatMap(tick -> Observable                       // (5)
                .just(tick)                                     // (6)
                .delay(rnd.nextInt(5000), MILLISECONDS)         // (7)
                .map(tickValue -> this.probe()))               // (8)
            .publish()                                          // (9)
            .refCount();                                        // (10)

    private Temperature probe() {
        return new Temperature(16 + rnd.nextGaussian() * 10);  // (11)
    }

    public Observable<Temperature> temperatureStream() {       // (12)
        return dataStream;
    }
}
```

Here, we register the `TemperatureSensor` as a Spring bean by applying the `@Component` annotation `(1)`, so this bean can be autowired into other beans. The `TemperatureSensor` implementation uses a RxJava API that was not previously explained in detail. Nevertheless, we are trying to clarify the used transformation by exploring the class logic.

Our sensor holds the random number generator `rnd` to simulate actual hardware sensor measurements `(2)`. In a statement, `(3)`, we define a private field called `dataStream`, which is returned by the public method `temperatureStream()` `(12)`. Thus, `dataStream` is the only `Observable` stream defined by the component. This stream generates an effectively endless flow of numbers `(4)` by applying the factory method `range(0, Integer.MAX_VALUE)`. The `range()` method generates a sequence of integers starting from `0` that have `Integer.MAX_VALUE` elements. For each of these values, we apply the transformation `(5)`—`concatMap(tick -> ...)`. The method `concatMap()` receives a function, `f`, that transforms an `tick` item into an observable stream of elements, applies the `f` function to each element of the incoming stream, and joins the resulting streams one by one. In our case, the `f` function makes a sensor measurement after a random delay (to match the behavior of the previous implementation). To probe a sensor, we create a new stream with only one element `tick` `(6)`. To simulate a random delay, we apply the `delay(rnd.nextInt(5000), MILLISECONDS)` `(7)` Operator, which shifts elements forward in time.

For the next step, we probe the sensor and retrieve a temperature value by applying the `map(tickValue -> this.probe())))` transformation `(8)`, which in turn calls the `probe()` method with the same data generation logic as before `(11)`. In that case, we ignore the `tickValue`, as it was required only to generate a one-element stream. So, after applying the `concatMap(tick -> ...)`, we have a stream that returns sensor values with a random interval of up to five seconds between emitted elements.

Actually, we could return a stream without applying operators `(9)` and `(10)`, but in that case, each subscriber (SSE client) would trigger a new subscription for the stream and a new sequence of sensor readings. This means that sensor readings would not be shared among subscribers that could lead to hardware overload and degradation. To prevent this, we use the `publish()` `(9)` operator, which broadcasts events from a source stream to all destination streams. The `publish()` operator returns a special kind of `Observable` called `ConnectableObservable`. The latter provides the `refCount()` `(10)` operator, which creates a subscription to the incoming shared stream only when there is at least one outgoing subscription. In contrast with the Publisher-Subscriber implementation, this one makes it possible not to probe the sensor when nobody listens.

Custom SseEmitter

By using `TemperatureSensor`, which exposes a stream using temperature values, we may subscribe each new `SseEmitter` to the `Observable` stream and send the received `onNext` signals to SSE clients. To handle errors and the closing of a proper HTTP connection, let's write the following `SseEmitter` extension:

```
class RxSeeEmitter extends SseEmitter {
    static final long SSE_SESSION_TIMEOUT = 30 * 60 * 1000L;
    private final Subscriber<Temperature> subscriber;          // (1)

    RxSeeEmitter() {
        super(SSE_SESSION_TIMEOUT);                             // (2)

        this.subscriber = new Subscriber<Temperature>() {      // (3)
            @Override
            public void onNext(Temperature temperature) {
                try {
                    RxSeeEmitter.this.send(temperature);       // (4)
                } catch (IOException e) {
                    unsubscribe();                             // (5)
                }
            }

            @Override
            public void onError(Throwable e) { }               // (6)

            @Override
            public void onCompleted() { }                      // (7)
        };

        onCompletion(subscriber::unsubscribe);                 // (8)
        onTimeout(subscriber::unsubscribe);                    // (9)
    }

    Subscriber<Temperature> getSubscriber() {                  // (10)
        return subscriber;
    }
}
```

The `RxSeeEmitter` extends the well-known `SseEmitter`. It also encapsulates a subscriber for `Temperature` events (1). In the constructor, `RxSeeEmitter` calls the super-class constructor with a necessary SSE session timeout (2) and also creates an instance of the `Subscriber<Temperature>` class (3). This subscriber reacts to the received `onNext` signals by resending them to an SSE client (4). In cases where the data sending fails, the `subscriber` unsubscribes itself from the incoming observable stream (5). In the current implementation, we know that the temperature stream is infinite and cannot produce any errors, so the `onComplete()` and `onError()` handlers are empty (6), (7), but in real applications, it is better to have some handlers there.

Lines (8) and (9) register cleanup actions for SSE session completion or timeout. The `RxSeeEmitter` subscribers should cancel the subscription. To use a subscriber, `RxSeeEmitter` exposes it by utilizing the `getSubscriber()` method (10).

Exposing the SSE endpoint

To expose the SSE endpoint, we need a REST controller that is autowired with the `TemperatureSensor` instance. The following code shows the controller, which utilizes `RxSeeEmitter`:

```
@RestController
public class TemperatureController {
   private final TemperatureSensor temperatureSensor;          // (1)

   public TemperatureController(TemperatureSensor temperatureSensor) {
      this.temperatureSensor = temperatureSensor;
   }

   @RequestMapping(
      value = "/temperature-stream",
      method = RequestMethod.GET)
   public SseEmitter events(HttpServletRequest request) {
      RxSeeEmitter emitter = new RxSeeEmitter();               // (2)

      temperatureSensor.temperatureStream()                    // (3)
         .subscribe(emitter.getSubscriber());                  // (4)

      return emitter;                                          // (5)
   }
}
```

The `TemperatureController` is the same Spring Web MVC `@RestController` as before. It holds a reference to the `TemperatureSensor` bean (1). When a new SSE session is created, the controller instantiates our augmented `RxSeeEmitter` (2) and subscribes to the `RxSeeEmitter` subscribers (4) to the temperature stream referenced from the `TemperatureSensor` instance (3). Then the `RxSeeEmitter` instance is returned to the Servlet container for processing (5).

As we can see with RxJava, the REST controller holds less logic, does not manage the dead `SseEmitter` instances, and does not care about synchronization. In turn, the reactive implementation manages the routine of the `TemperatureSensor`'s values, reading, and publishing. The `RxSeeEmitter` translates reactive streams to outgoing SSE messages, and `TemperatureController` only binds a new SSE session to a new `RxSeeEmitter` that is subscribed to a stream of temperature readings. Furthermore, this implementation does not use Spring's EventBus, so it is more portable and can be tested without initializing a Spring context.

Application configuration

As we do not use the Publish-Subject approach and Spring's `@EventListener` annotation, we do not depend on Async Support, so the application configuration becomes simpler:

```
@SpringBootApplication
public class Application {
    public static void main(String[] args) {
        SpringApplication.run(Application.class, args);
    }
}
```

As we can see, this time we do not need to enable Async Support using the `@EnableAsync` annotation, and we also do not need to configure Spring's `Executor` for event handling. Of course, if required, we may configure a RxJava `Scheduler` for fine-grained thread management when processing reactive streams, but such a configuration would not depend on Spring Framework.

In turn, we do not need to change the code for the UI part of the application; it should work the same way as before. Here, we have to highlight that with the RxJava-based implementation, the temperature sensor is not probed when nobody listens. Such behavior is a natural consequence of the fact that *reactive programming has a notion of active subscription*. The Publish-Subject-based implementations do not have such properties, and as such are more limited.

Brief history of reactive libraries

Now that we are acquainted with RxJava and have even written a few reactive workflows, let's look at its history to recognize the context in which reactive programming was born and the problems it was designed to solve.

Curiously, the RxJava history and the history of reactive programming as we know it today began inside of Microsoft. In 2005, Erik Meijer and his Cloud Programmability Team were experimenting with programming models appropriate for building *large-scale asynchronous and data-intensive internet service architectures*. After some years of experimenting, the first version of the Rx library was born in the summer of 2007. An additional two years were devoted to different aspects of the library, including multithreading and cooperative re-scheduling. The first public version of *Rx.NET* was shipped on November 18, 2009. Later, Microsoft ported the library to different languages, such as JavaScript, C++, Ruby, and Objective-C, and also to the *Windows Phone* platform. As Rx began to gain popularity, Microsoft open sourced Rx.NET in the fall of 2012.

 To read more about the birth of Rx library, please read Erik Meijer's foreword in *Reactive Programming with RxJava* by Tomasz Nurkiewicz and Ben Christensen.

At some point, Rx's ideas spread outside of Microsoft, and Paul Betts with Justin Spahr-Summers from the GitHub Inc. company implemented and released ReactiveCocoa for Objective-C in 2012. At the same time, Ben Christensen from Netflix ported Rx.NET to the Java platform and, in early 2013, open sourced the RxJava library on GitHub.

At that time, Netflix was facing the very complicated problem of handling the tremendous amount of internet traffic generated by streaming media. An asynchronous reactive library called RxJava helped them to build the reactive system that boasted a 37% share of internet traffic in North America in 2015! Now, a huge part of the traffic in the system is handled with RxJava. To withstand all of that enormous load, Netflix had to invent new architecture patterns and implement them in libraries. The most well-known of these are the following:

- **Hystrix**: This is a fault-tolerance library for bulkheads services (`https://github.com/Netflix/Hystrix`)
- **Ribbon**: This is an RPC library with load-balancer support (`https://github.com/Netflix/ribbon`)
- **Zuul**: This is a gateway service that provides dynamic routing, security, resiliency, and monitoring (`https://github.com/Netflix/zuul`)
- **RxNetty**: This is a reactive adapter for *Netty*, an NIO client-server framework (`https://github.com/ReactiveX/RxNetty`)

In all cases, RxJava is a crucial ingredient of named libraries and consequently the whole Netflix ecosystem itself. Netflix's success with microservices and streaming architecture pushed other companies to adopt the same approaches, including RxJava.

Today, RxJava is used natively in some NoSQL Java drivers, such as *Couchbase* (`https://blog.couchbase.com/why-couchbase-chose-rxjava-new-java-sdk/`) and *MongoDB* (`https://mongodb.github.io/mongo-java-driver-rx/`).

It is also important to note that RxJava was welcomed by Android developers and companies such as SoundCloud, Square, NYT, and SeatGeek to implement their mobile applications with RxJava. Such active involvement lead to the appearance of the viral library called *RxAndroid*. This simplifies the process of writing reactive applications in Android quite significantly. On the iOS platform, developers have RxSwift, the Swift variant of the Rx library.

At the moment, it is hard to find a popular programming language without the Rx library ported to it. In the Java world, we have RxScala, RxGroovy, RxClojure, RxKotlin, and RxJRuby, and this list is far from completion. To find an Rx implementation for our favorite language, refer to this web-page at `http://reactivex.io/languages.html`.

It would be unfair to say that RxJava was the first and only pioneer of reactive programming. Importantly, the wide-spread adoption of asynchronous programming created a solid foundation and demand for reactive techniques. Probably the most significant contribution in that direction was conducted by **NodeJS** and its community (`https://nodejs.org`).

Reactive landscape

In the previous sections, we learned how to use pure RxJava and how to combine it with Spring Web MVC. To demonstrate the benefits of this, we have updated our temperature-monitoring application and improved the design by applying RxJava. However, it is worth noting that Spring Framework and RxJava is not the only valid combination. A lot of application servers also value the power of the reactive approach. As such authors of a successful reactive server called *Ratpack* decided to adopt RxJava as well.

Along with callbacks and a promise-based API, Ratpack provides `RxRatpack`, a separate module that allows to convert Ratpack `Promise` to RxJava `Observable` easily, and vice versa, as shown in the following code:

```
Promise<String> promise = get(() -> "hello world");
RxRatpack
    .observe(promise)
    .map(String::toUpperCase)
    .subscribe(context::render);
```

> To find out more about the Ratpack server, please visit the project's official site at `https://ratpack.io/manual/current/all.html`.

Another example that is famous in the Android world is the HTTP client Retrofit, which also creates a RxJava wrapper around its own implementation of Futures and Callbacks. The following example shows that at least four different coding styles may be used in Retrofit:

```
interface MyService {
    @GET("/user")
    Observable<User> getUserWithRx();

    @GET("/user")
    CompletableFuture<User> getUserWithJava8();

    @GET("/user")
    ListenableFuture<User> getUserWithGuava();

    @GET("user")
    Call<User> getUserNatively()
}
```

Even though RxJava may improve any solution, the reactive landscape is not limited to it or its wrappers. In the JVM world, there are a lot of other libraries and servers that created their reactive implementations. For instance, the well-known reactive server Vert.x only used callback based communication for a period of time, but later created its own solution with the `io.vertx.core.streams` package, which harbors the following interfaces:

- `ReadStream<T>`: This interface represents a stream of items that can be read from
- `WriteStream<T>`: This describes a stream of data that can be written to
- `Pump`: This is used for moving data from `ReadStream` to a `WriteStream` and performing flow control

Let's look at the code snippet with the `Vert.x` example:

```
public void vertexExample(HttpClientRequest request, AsyncFile file) {
    request.setChunked(true);
    Pump pump = Pump.pump(file, request);
    file.endHandler(v -> request.end());
    pump.start();
}
```

 Eclipse `Vert.x` is an event-driven application framework that is similar in design to Node.js. It provides a simple concurrency model, primitives for asynchronous programming, and a distributed event bus that penetrates into in-browser JavaScript. If interested in `Vert.x` and its implementation of Reactive Streams, visit this web page: `http://vertx.io/docs/`.

The number of RxJava adoptions and alternative implementations is enormous, and far from being limited to the mentioned solutions. A lot of companies and open source projects around the world have created their own solutions similar to RxJava, or they have extended ones that are already present.

Admittedly, there is nothing wrong with the natural evolution and competition between libraries, but it is evident that problems will occur as soon as we try to compose a few different reactive libraries or frameworks in one Java application. Moreover, we will eventually find that the behavior of reactive libraries is similar in general, but differs slightly in the details. Such a situation may compromise the whole project because of hidden bugs that would be hard to spot and fix. So, with all these API discrepancies, it is not a very good idea to mix a few different reactive libraries (let's say, Vert.x and RxJava) in one application. At this point, it becomes apparent that the whole reactive landscape demands some standard or universal API, which will provide compatibility guarantees between any implementations. Of course, such a standard was designed; it is called **Reactive Streams.** The next chapter will cover this in detail.

Summary

In this chapter, we have revisited a few well-known design patterns by GoF—including Observer, Publish-Subscribe, and Iterator to build the basis of reactive programming. We have written a few implementations to review both the strong and weak sides of the instruments we already have for asynchronous programming. We have also leveraged Spring Framework support for Server-Sent Events, WebSockets, and also played with Event-Bus provided by Spring. Also, we have used Spring Boot and `start.spring.io` for fast application bootstrapping. Even though our examples were pretty simple, they demonstrated the potential issues that arise from immature approaches that are used for asynchronous data processing.

We also looked at reactive programming's history to highlight architectural problems, which reactive programming was invented to fight against. In this context, the success story of Netflix demonstrates that a small library like RxJava may become a starting point toward making a significant success in a very competitive business field. We have also discovered that following RxJava's success, a lot of companies and open source projects re-implemented reactive libraries bearing in mind these considerations, which led to the versatile reactive landscape. This versatility motivated the need for Reactive Standard, which we will talk about in the next chapter.

3
Reactive Streams - the New Streams' Standard

In this chapter, we are going to cover some of the problems mentioned in the previous chapter, along with those that arise when several reactive libraries meet in one project. We will also dig deeper into backpressure control in reactive systems. Here, we are going to oversee solutions proposed by RxJava as well as its limitations. We will explore how the Reactive Streams specification solves those problems, learning the essentials of this specification. We will also cover the reactive landscape changes that come with a new specification. Finally, to reinforce our knowledge, we are going to build a simple application and combine several reactive libraries within it.

In this chapter, the following topics are covered:

- Common API problems
- Backpressure control problems
- Reactive Stream examples
- Technology compatibility problems
- Reactive Streams inside JDK 9
- Advanced concepts of Reactive Streams
- Reinforcement of reactive landscape
- Reactive Streams in action

Reactivity for everyone

In previous chapters, we have learned a lot of exciting things about reactive programming in Spring, as well as the role RxJava plays in its story. We also looked at the need to use reactive programming to implement the reactive system. We have also seen a brief overview of the reactive landscape and available alternatives to RxJava, which makes it possible to quickly start with reactive programming.

The API's inconsistency problem

On the one hand, the extensive list of competitive libraries, such as RxJava and features of the Java Core library, such as `CompletableStage`, give us a choice as to the way in which we write code. For example, we may rely on reaching the API of RxJava in order to write a flow of the items being processed. Consequently, to build an uncomplicated asynchronous request-response interaction, it is more than enough to rely on `CompletableStage`. Alternatively, we may use framework specific classes such as `org.springframework.util.concurrent.ListenableFuture` to build an asynchronous interaction between components and simplify the work with that framework.

On the other hand, the abundance of choices may easily over-complicate the system. For example, the presence of two libraries that rely on an asynchronous non-blocking communication concept but have a different API leads to providing an additional utility class in order to convert one callback into another and vice versa:

```
interface AsyncDatabaseClient {                              // (1)
    <T> CompletionStage<T> store(CompletionStage<T> stage);  //
}                                                            //

final class AsyncAdapters {
    public static <T> CompletionStage<T> toCompletion(       // (2)
                    ListenableFuture<T> future) {            //
                                                             //
        CompletableFuture<T> completableFuture =             // (2.1)
            new CompletableFuture<>();                       //
                                                             //
        future.addCallback(                                  // (2.2)
            completableFuture::complete,                     //
            completableFuture::completeExceptionally         //
        );                                                   //
                                                             //
        return completableFuture;                            //
    }                                                        //
```

```
    public static <T> ListenableFuture<T> toListenable(        // (3)
                    CompletionStage<T> stage) {                 //
        SettableListenableFuture<T> future =                    // (3.1)
            new SettableListenableFuture<>();                   //
                                                                //
        stage.whenComplete((v, t) -> {                          // (3.2)
            if (t == null) {                                    //
                future.set(v);                                  //
            }                                                   //
            else {                                              //
                future.setException(t);                         //
            }                                                   //
        });                                                     //
                                                                //
        return future;                                          //
    }                                                           //
}

@RestController                                                 // (4)
public class MyController {                                     //
    ...                                                         //
    @RequestMapping                                             //
    public ListenableFuture<?> requestData() {                  // (4.1)
        AsyncRestTemplate httpClient = ...;                     //
        AsyncDatabaseClient databaseClient = ...;               //
                                                                //
        CompletionStage<String> completionStage = toCompletion( // (4.2)
            httpClient.execute(...)                             //
        );                                                      //
                                                                //
        return toListenable(                                    // (4.3)
            databaseClient.store(completionStage)               //
        );                                                      //
    }                                                           //
}                                                               //
```

The numbered points in the preceding code are explained in the following:

1. This is the `async` Database client's interface declaration, which is the representative sample of the possible client interface for asynchronous database access.

2. This is the `ListenableFuture` to `CompletionStage` adaptor method implementation. At point (`2.1`), to provide manual control of `CompletionStage`, we create its direct implementation called `CompletableFuture` via the constructor with no arguments. To provide integration with `ListenableFuture`, we have to add callback (`2.2`), where we directly reuse the API of `CompletableFuture`.

3. This is the `CompletionStage` to `ListenableFuture` adapter method implementation. At point (`3.1`) we declare the specific implementation of `ListenableFuture` called `SettableListenableFuture`. This allows us to manually supply the result of the `CompletionStage` execution at point (`3.2`).

4. This is the `RestController`'s class declaration. Here at point (`4.1`), we declare the request handler method, which acts asynchronously and returns `ListenableFuture` to handle the result of the execution in a non-blocking fashion. In turn, to store the result of the execution of `AsyncRestTemplate`, we have to adapt it to the `CompletionStage` (`4.2`). Finally, to satisfy the supported API, we have to adopt the result of storing for `ListenableFuture` again (`4.3`).

As may be noticed from the preceding example, there is no direct integration with Spring Framework 4.x `ListenableFuture` and `CompletionStage`. Moreover, that example is not an exclusion case from the common usage of reactive programming. Many libraries and frameworks provide their own interfaces and classes for asynchronous communication between components, which include plain request-response communication along with the streaming processing frameworks. In many cases, to solve that problem and make several independent libraries compatible, we have to provide our own adaptation and reuse it in a few places. Moreover, our own adaptation may contain bugs and require additional maintenance.

 In Spring Framework 5.x, `ListenableFuture`'s API was extended and an additional method called `completable` was provided to solve that incompatibility. Please see the following link to learn more about that: https://docs.spring.io/spring-framework/docs/current/javadoc-api/org/springframework/util/concurrent/ListenableFuture.html#completable--.

Here, the central problem lies in the fact that there is no single method that allows library vendors to build their aligned API. For example, as we might have seen in Chapter 2, *Reactive Programming in Spring - Basic Concepts*, RxJava was valued by many frameworks such as Vert.x, Ratpack, Retrofit, and so on.

In turn, all of them provided support for RxJava users and introduced additional modules, which allow integrating existing projects easily. At first glance, this was wondrous since the list of projects in which RxJava 1.x was introduced is extensive and includes frameworks for web, desktop, or mobile development. However, behind that support for developer needs, many hidden pitfalls affect library vendors. The first problem that usually happens when several RxJava 1.x compatible libraries meet in one place is rough version incompatibility. Since RxJava 1.x evolved very quickly over time, many library vendors did not get the chance to update their dependency to the new releases. From time to time, updates brought many internal changes that eventually made some versions incompatible. Consequently, having different libraries and frameworks that depend on the different versions of RxJava 1 may cause some unwanted issues. The second problem is similar to the first. Customizations of RxJava are non-standardized. Here, *customization* refers to the ability to provide an additional implementation of `Observable` or a specific transformation stage, which is common during the development of RxJava extensions. Due to non-standardized APIs and rapidly evolving internals, supporting the custom implementation was another challenge.

 An excellent example of significant changes in the version may be found at the following link: `https://github.com/ReactiveX/RxJava/issues/802`.

Pull versus push

Finally, to understand the problem described in the previous section, we have to go back in history and analyze the initial interaction model between a source and its subscribers.

During the early period of the whole reactive landscape evolution, all libraries were designed with the thought that data is pushed from the source to the subscriber. That decision was made because a pure pull model is not efficient enough in some cases. An example of this is when communication over the network appeared in the system with network boundaries. Suppose that we filter a huge list of data but take only the first ten elements from it. By embracing the PULL model for solving such a problem, we are left with the following code:

```
final AsyncDatabaseClient dbClient = ...                          // (1)

public CompletionStage<Queue<Item>> list(int count) {             // (2)
   BlockingQueue<Item> storage = new ArrayBlockingQueue<>(count); //
   CompletableFuture<Queue<Item>> result                         //
      = new CompletableFuture<>();                               //
                                                                  //
```

```
    pull("1", storage, result, count);             // (2.1)
                                                    //
    return result;                                 //
}                                                  //

void pull(                                         // (3)
    String elementId,                              //
    Queue<Item> queue,                             //
    CompletableFuture resultFuture,                //
    int count                                      //
) {                                                //
    dbClient.getNextAfterId(elementId)             //
            .thenAccept(item -> {                  //
                if (isValid(item)) {               // (3.1)
                    queue.offer(item);             //
                                                   //
                    if (queue.size() == count) {   // (3.2)
                        resultFuture.complete(queue); //
                        return;                    //
                    }                              //
                }                                  //
                                                   //
                pull(item.getId(),                 // (3.3)
                    queue,                         //
                    resultFuture,                  //
                    count);                        //
            });                                    //
}                                                  //
```

The annotated code is again explained as follows:

1. This is the `AsyncDatabaseClient` field declaration. Here, using that client, we wire the asynchronous, non-blocking communication with the external database.

2. This is the `list` method declaration. Here we declare an asynchronous contract by returning `CompletionStage` as the result of the calling of the `list` method. In turn, to aggregate the pulling results and asynchronously sent it to the caller, we declare `Queue` and `CompletableFuture` to store received values and then manually send the collected `Queue` later. Here, at point `(2.1)` we start the first call of the `pull` method.

3. This is the `pull` method declaration. Inside that method, we call`AsyncDatabaseClient#getNextAfterId` to execute the query and asynchronously receive the result. Then when the result is received, we filter it at point (`3.1`). In the case of the valid item, we aggregate it into the queue. Additionally, at point (`3.2`), we check whether we collected enough elements, send them to the caller, and exit pulling. If either of the mentioned `if` branches has been bypassed, we recursively call the `pull` method again (`3.3`).

As may be noticed from the preceding code, we use an asynchronous, non-blocking interaction between the service and the database. At first glance, there is nothing wrong here. However, if we look at the following diagram, we see the gap:

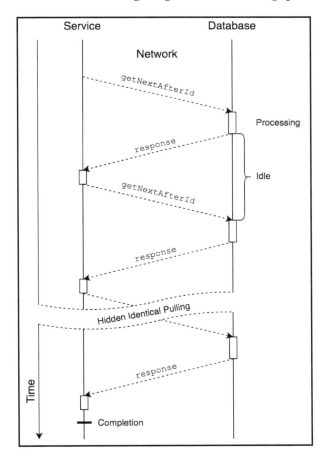

Diagram 3.1. Example of pulling processing flow

As might be noticed from the preceding diagram, asking for the next element one by one results in extra time spent on the request's delivery from *Service* to *Database*. From the service perspective, most of the overall processing time is wasted in the idle state. Even if the resources are not used there, the overall processing time is doubled or even tripled because of the additional network activity. Moreover, the database is not aware of the number of future requests, which means that the database cannot generate data in advance and is therefore in the idle state. It means that the database is waiting for a new request and is inefficient while the response is being delivered to the service and the service is processing the incoming response and then asking for a new portion of data .

To optimize the overall execution and keep the pulling model as the first class citizen, we may combine pulling with batching, as shown in the following modification of the central example:

```
void pull(                                                    // (1)
    String elementId,                                         //
    Queue<Item> queue,                                        //
    CompletableFuture resultFuture,                           //
    int count                                                 //
) {                                                           //

    dbClient.getNextBatchAfterId(elementId, count)            // (2)
            .thenAccept(items -> {                            //
                for(Item item : items) {                      // (2.1)
                    if (isValid(item)) {                      //
                        queue.offer(item);                    //
                                                              //
                        if (queue.size() == count) {          //
                            resultFuture.complete(queue);     //
                            return;                           //
                        }                                     //
                    }                                         //
                }                                             //

                pull(items.get(items.size() - 1)             // (3)
                        .getId(),                             //
                    queue,                                    //
                    resultFuture,                             //
                    count);                                   //
            });                                               //
}
```

Again, the following key explains the code:

1. This is the same `pull` method declaration as in the previous example.
2. This is the `getNextBatchAfterId` execution. As may be noticed, the `AsyncDatabaseClient` method allows asking for a specific number of elements, which are returned as the `List<Item>`. In turn, when the data is available, they are processed in almost the same way, except an additional `for-loop` is created to process each element of the batch separately (`2.1`).
3. This is the recursive `pull` method execution, which is designed to retrieve an additional batch of items in the case of a lack of items from the previous pulling.

On one hand, by asking for a batch of elements we may significantly improve the performance of the `list` method execution and reduce the overall processing time. On the other hand, there are still some gaps in the interaction model, which might be detected by analyzing the following diagram:

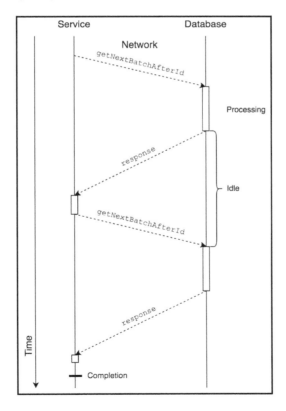

Diagram 3.2. Example of batch-based pulling processing flow

As we may notice, we still have some inefficiency in the processing time. For example, the client is still idle while the database is querying the data. In turn, sending a batch of elements takes a bit more time than sending just one. Finally, an additional request for the whole batch of elements may be effectively redundant. For instance, if only one element remains to finish the processing and the first element from the next batch satisfies the validation, then the rest of the items are going to be skipped and are totally redundant.

To provide the final optimization, we may ask for data once, and the source pushes them asynchronously when they become available. The following modification of the code shows how that might be achieved:

```
public Observable<Item> list(int count) {                          // (1)
    return dbClient.getStreamOfItems()                             // (2)
                    .filter(item -> isValid(item))                 // (2.1)
                    .take(count)                                   // (2.2)
}                                                                  //
```

The annotations are as follows:

1. This is the `list` method declaration. Here, the `Observable<Item>` return type identifies that elements are being *pushed*.
2. This is the *querying the stream* stage. By calling the `AsyncDatabaseClient#getStreamOfItems` method, we subscribe to the database once. Here, at point `(2.1)` we filter elements and, by using the operator, `.take()` takes a specific amount of data, as requested by the caller.

Here, we use RxJava 1.x classes as first-class citizens to receive the *pushed* elements. In turn, once all requirements are met, the cancellation signal is sent, and connection to the database is closed. The current interaction flow is depicted in the following diagram:

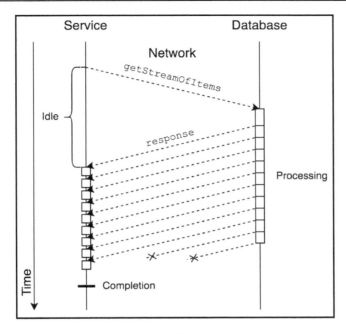

Diagram 3.3. Example of Push processing flow

In the preceding diagram, the overall processing time is optimized again. During the interaction, we have only one big idle when the service is waiting for the first response. After the first element has arrived, the database starts sending subsequent elements as and when they come. In turn, even if processing may be a bit faster than querying the next element, the overall idle of the service is short. However, the database may still generate excess elements that are ignored by the service once the required number of elements have been collected.

The flow control problem

On the one hand, the preceding explanation may have taught us that the central reason to embrace the *PUSH* model was the optimization of the overall processing time by decreasing the amount of asking to the very minimum. That is why the RxJava 1.x and similar libraries were designed for pushing data, and that is why streaming became a valuable technique for communication between components within a distributed system.

On the other hand, in combination with only the *PUSH* model, that technique has its limitations. As we might remember from `Chapter 1`, *Why Reactive Spring?*, the nature of message-driven communication assumes that as a response to the request, the service may receive an asynchronous, potentially infinite stream of messages. That is the tricky part because if a producer disrespects the consumer's throughput possibility it may affect the overall system stability in ways described in the following two sections.

Slow producer and fast consumer

Let's start with the simplest one. Suppose that we have a slow producer and very fast consumer. This situation may arise because of some lean assumptions from the producer's side about an unknown consumer.

On the one hand, such configurations are a particular business assumption. On the other hand, the actual runtime might be different, and the possibilities for the consumer may change dynamically. For example, we may always increase the number of producers by scaling them, thereby increasing the load onto the consumer.

To tackle such a problem, the essential thing that we need is the actual demand. Unfortunately, the pure *push* model can't give us such metrics, and therefore dynamically increasing the system's throughput is impossible.

Fast producer and slow consumer

The second problem is much more complicated. Suppose we have a fast producer and slow consumer. The problem here is that the producer may send much more data than the consumer can process, which may lead to a catastrophic failure of the component under stress.

One intuitive solution for such case is collecting unhandled elements into the queue, which may stay between the producer and consumer or may even reside on the consumer side. Even if the consumer is busy, such a technique makes it possible to handle new data by processing the previous element or portion of data.

One of the critical factors for handling pushed data using the queue is to choose a queue with proper characteristics. In general, there are three common types of queue, which are considered in the following subsections.

Unbounded queue

The first and most obvious solution is to provide a queue that is characterized by unlimited size, or simply an unbounded queue. In that case, all produced elements are stored inside the queue first and then drained by the actual subscriber. The following marble diagram depicts the mentioned interaction (Diagram 3.4):

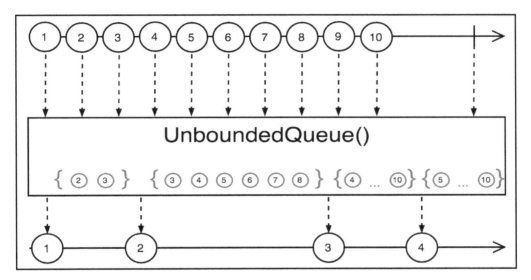

Diagram 3.4.Example of Unbounded Queue

On the one hand, the central benefit that came with handling messages using an unbounded queue is the deliverability of messages, which means that the consumer is going to process all stored elements at some point in time.

On the other hand, by succeeding in the deliverability of messages, the resiliency of the application decreases because there are no unbounded resources. For instance, the whole system may be easily crushed once the memory limit is reached.

Bounded drop queue

Alternatively, to avoid a memory overflow, we may employ a queue that may ignore incoming messages if it is full. The following marble diagram depicts a queue that has a size of 2 elements and is characterized by dropping elements on overflow (Diagram 3.5):

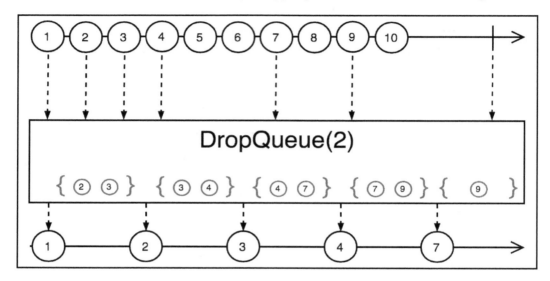

Diagram 3.5. Example of Drop Queue with a capacity of two items

In general, this technique respects the resources' limitations and makes it possible to configure the capacity of the queue based on the resources' capacities. In turn, embracing this kind of queue is a common practice when the importance of the message is low. An example of a business case may be a stream of dataset-changed events. In turn, each event triggers some statistical recalculation which uses the entire dataset aggregation and takes a significant amount of time in comparison with the incoming events quantity. In that case, the only important thing is the fact that the data set changed; it is not vital to known which data has been affected.

 The preceding mentioned example considers the simplest strategy for dropping the newest element. In general, there are a few strategies for choosing the element to drop. For example, dropping by priority, dropping the oldest, and so on.

Bounded blocking queue

On the other hand, this technique may not be acceptable in the case in which each message is significant. For example, in a payment system, each user's submitted payment must be processed, and it is inadmissible to drop some. Consequently, instead of dropping a message and keeping the bounded queue as the method for handling the pushed data, we may block the producer once the limit has been reached. The queues that are characterized by the ability to block the producer are usually called blocking queues. An example of interaction using a blocking queue with the capacity of three elements is depicted in the following marble diagram:

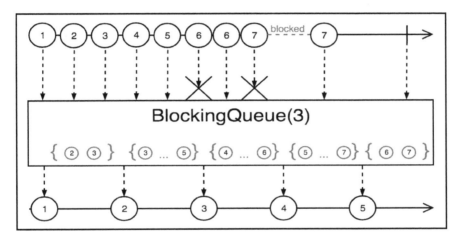

Diagram 3.6.Example of Blocking Queue with a capacity of three items

Unfortunately, this technique negates all of the system's asynchronous behavior. In general, once the producer reaches the queue's limit, it will start being blocked and will be in that state until the consumer has drained an element and free space in the queue became available. We may then conclude that the throughput of the slowest consumer limits the overall throughput of the system. Subsequently, along with negating the asynchronous behavior, that technique also denies the efficient resource utilization. Consequently, none of the cases are acceptable if we want to achieve all three: Resilience, Elasticity, and Responsiveness.

Moreover, the presence of the queues may complicate the overall design of the system and add an additional responsibility of finding a trade-off between the mentioned solutions, which is another challenge.

In general, an uncontrolled semantic of a pure *push* model may cause many undesired situations. This is why the Reactive Manifesto mentions the importance of the mechanism that allows systems to gracefully respond to a load, or in other words the need for the mechanism of backpressure control.

Unfortunately, reactive libraries are similar to RxJava 1.x and do not offer such a standardized feature. There is no explicit API that might allow controlling backpressure out of the box.

 It should be mentioned that in a pure *push* mode, the producing rate can be stabilized using batch processing. RxJava 1.x offers operators such as .window or .buffer which make it possible to collect elements during the specified period to a substream or a collection correspondingly. An example of where such a technique shows a burst in performance is a batch insert or batch update to a database. Unfortunately, not all services support batch operations. Consequently, such a technique is really limited in its application.

The solution

In late 2013, a band of genius engineers from Lightbend, Netflix, and Pivotal gathered to solve the described problem and provide the JVM community with a standard. After a long year of hard work, the world saw the first draft of the Reactive Streams specification. There was nothing extraordinary behind this proposal—the conceptual idea was in the standardization of the familiar reactive programming patterns that we saw in the previous chapter. In the following section, we are going to cover this in detail.

The basics of the Reactive Streams spec

The Reactive Streams specification defines four primary interfaces: Publisher, Subscriber, Subscription, and Processor. Since that initiative grew independently from any organization, it became available as a separate JAR file where all interfaces live within the org.reactivestreams package.

In general, the specified interfaces are similar to what we had earlier (for example, in RxJava 1.x). In a way, these reflect the well-known classes from RxJava. The first two of those interfaces are similar to `Observable-Observer`, which resemble the classic Publisher-Subscriber model. Consequently, the first two were named `Publisher` and `Subscriber`. To check whether these two interfaces are similar to `Observable` and `Observer`, let's consider the declaration of those:

```
package org.reactivestreams;

public interface Publisher<T> {
    void subscribe(Subscriber<? super T> s);
}
```

The preceding code depicts the internals of the `Publisher` interface. As might be noticed, there is only one method that makes it possible to register the `Subscriber`. In comparison with `Observable`, which was designed for providing a useful DSL, `Publisher` stands for a standardized entry point for a straightforward `Publisher` and `Subscriber` connection. As opposed to `Publisher`, the `Subscriber` side is a bit more of a verbose API which is almost identical to what we have in the `Observer` interface from RxJava:

```
package org.reactivestreams;

public interface Subscriber<T> {
    void onSubscribe(Subscription s);
    void onNext(T t);
    void onError(Throwable t);
    void onComplete();
}
```

As we may have noticed, along with three methods that are identical to methods in the RxJava `Observer`, the specification provides us with a new additional method called `onSubscribe`.

The `onSubscribe` method is a conceptually new API method that provides us with a standardized way of notifying the `Subscriber` about a successful subscription. In turn, the incoming parameter of that method introduces us to a new contract called **Subscription.** To understand the idea, let's take a closer look at the interface:

```
package org.reactivestreams;

public interface Subscription {
    void request(long n);
    void cancel();
}
```

As we may have noticed, `Subscription` provides the fundamentals in order to control the elements' production. Similar to RxJava 1.x's `Subscription#unsubscribe()`, here we had the `cancel()` method, allowing us to unsubscribe from a stream or even cancel the publishing completely. However, the most significant improvement that comes along with the cancellation feature is in the new `request` method. The Reactive Stream specification introduced the `request` method to expand the ability of interaction between the `Publisher` and `Subscriber`. Now, to notify the `Publisher` of how much data should be pushed, the `Subscriber` should signal the size of the demand via the `request` method, and may be sure that the number of incoming elements does not exceed the limit. Let's take a look at the following marble diagram to understand the underlying mechanism:

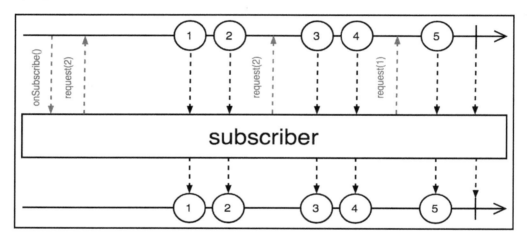

Diagram 3.7. Backpressure mechanism

As may be noticed from the preceding diagram, the `Publisher` now guarantees that the new portion of elements are only sent if the `Subscriber` asked for them. The overall implementation of the `Publisher` is up to the `Publisher`, which may vary from purely blocking waiting, to the sophisticated mechanism of generating data only on the `Subscriber`'s requests. However, we now don't have to pay the cost of additional queues since we have the mentioned guarantees.

Moreover, as opposed to a pure *push* model, the specification provides us with the hybrid *push-pull* model, which allows proper control of the backpressure.

To understand the power of the hybrid model, let's revisit our previous example of streaming from the database and see whether such a technique is as efficient as before:

```
public Publisher<Item> list(int count) {                          // (1)

    Publisher<Item> source = dbClient.getStreamOfItems();         // (2)
    TakeFilterOperator<Item> takeFilter = new TakeFilterOperator<>( // (2.1)
        source,                                                   //
        count,                                                    //
        item -> isValid(item)                                     //
    );                                                            //

    return takeFilter;                                            // (3)
}                                                                 //
```

The key is as follows:

1. This is the list method declaration. Here we follow the Reactive Streams spec and return the `Publisher<>` interface as a first-class citizen for communication.
2. This is the `AsyncDatabaseClient#getStreamOfItems` method execution. Here we use an updated method, which returns `Publisher<>`. At point `(2.1)`, we instantiate a custom implementation of the `Take` and `Filter` operators which accept the number of elements that should be taken. In addition, we pass a custom `Predicate` implementation, which makes it possible to validate the incoming items in the stream.
3. At that point, we return the previously created `TakeFilterOperator` instance. Remember, even though the operator has a different type, it still extends the `Publisher` interface.

In turn, it is essential to get a clear understanding of the internals of our custom `TakeFilterOperator`. The following code expands the internals of that operator:

```
public class TakeFilterOperator<T> implements Publisher<T> {      // (1)
    ...                                                           //

    public void subscribe(Subscriber s) {                         // (2)
        source.subscribe(new TakeFilterInner<>(s, take, predicate)); //
    }                                                             //

    static final class TakeFilterInner<T> implements Subscriber<T>, // (3)
                                          Subscription {          //
        final Subscriber<T> actual;                               //
        final int take;                                           //
        final Predicate<T> predicate;                             //
        final Queue<T> queue;                                     //
```

```
Subscription current;                                      //
int remaining;                                             //
int filtered;                                              //
volatile long requested;                                   //
...                                                        //

TakeFilterInner(                                           // (4)
   Subscriber<T> actual,                                   //
   int take,                                               //
   Predicate<T> predicate                                  //
) { ... }                                                  //

public void onSubscribe(Subscription current) {            // (5)
   ...                                                     //
   current.request(take);                                  // (5.1)
   ...                                                     //
}                                                          //

public void onNext(T element) {                            // (6)
   ...                                                     //
   long r = requested;                                     //
   Subscriber<T> a = actual;                               //
   Subscription s = current;                               //

   if (remaining > 0) {                                    // (7)
      boolean isValid = predicate.test(element);           //
      boolean isEmpty = queue.isEmpty();                   //
      if (isValid && r > 0 && isEmpty) {                   //
         a.onNext(element);                                // (7.1)
         remaining--;                                      //
         ...                                               //
      }                                                    //
      else if (isValid && (r == 0 || !isEmpty)) {          //
         queue.offer(element);                             // (7.2)
         remaining--;                                      //
         ...                                               //
      }                                                    //
      else if (!isValid) {                                 //
         filtered++;                                       // (7.3)
      }                                                    //
   }                                                       //
   else {                                                  // (7.4)
      s.cancel();                                          //
      onComplete();                                        //
   }                                                       //

   if (filtered > 0 && remaining / filtered < 2) {         // (8)
      s.request(take);                                     //
```

```
            filtered = 0;                                  //
        }                                                  //
    }
    ...                                                    // (9)
  }
}
```

The key points of the preceding code are explained in the following list:

1. This is the `TakeFilterOperator` class declaration. This class extends `Publisher<>`. Additionally, behind `...` is hidden the constructor of the class and related fields.

2. This is the `Subscriber#subscribe` method implementation. By considering the implementation, we may conclude that to provide additional logic to the stream, we have to wrap the actual `Subscriber` into an adapter class that extends the same interface.

3. This is the `TakeFilterOperator.TakeFilterInner` class declaration. This class implements the `Subscriber` interface and plays the most important role since it is passed as the actual `Subscriber` to the main source. Once the element is received in `onNext`, it is filtered and transferred to the downstream `Subscriber`. In turn, along with the `Subscriber` interface, the `TakeFilterInner` class implements the `Subscription` interface, making it possible to get transferred to the downstream `Subscriber` and therefore take control of all downstream demands. Note that here, `Queue` is the instance of `ArrayBlockingQueue` which is equal in size to `take`. The technique of creating an inner class that extends the `Subscriber` and `Subscription` interfaces is the classic way of implementing the intermediate transformation stage.

4. This is the constructor declaration. As might be noticed here, along with the `take` and `predicate` parameters, we have the `actual` subscriber instance that has been subscribed to `TakeFilterOperator` by calling the `subscribe()` method.

5. This is the `Subscriber#onSubscribe` method implementation. The most interesting element here is found at point `(5.1)`. Here we have the execution of the first `Subscription#request` to the remote database, which usually happens during the first `onSubscribe` method invocation.

6. This is the `Subscriber#onNext` invocation, which has a list of useful parameters required for the element processing declaration.

7. This is the processing flow of the element declaration. Here, we have four key points in that processing. Once the `remaining` number of elements that should be taken is higher than zero, the actual `Subscriber` has requested the data, the element is valid, and there are no elements in the queue, then we may send that element directly to the downstream `(7.1)`. If the demand has not been shown yet, or there is something in the queue, we have to queue that element (to preserve order) and deliver it later `(7.2)`. In the case in which an element is not valid, we have to increase the number of `filtered` elements `(7.3)`. Finally, if the `remaining` number of elements is zero, then we have to `cancel`, `(7.4)` the `Subscription` and complete the stream.

8. This is the mechanism of an additional data requesting a declaration. Here, if the number of `filtered` elements reaches a limit, we request an additional portion of data from the database without blocking the whole process.

9. This is the rest of the `Subscriber` and `Subscriptions` method's implementation.

In general, when the connection with the database is wired and the `TakeFilterOperator` instance has received the `Subscription`, the first request with the specified number of elements is sent to the database. Right after that, the database starts generating the specified amount of elements and *pushing* them as they come. In turn, the logic of the `TakeFilterOperator` specifies the case in which the additional portion of data should be requested. Once that happens, a new non-blocking request for the next portion of data is sent from the service to the database. It is important to note here that the Reactive Streams specification directly specifies that the calling of the `Subscription#request` should be a non-obstructive execution, which means that blocking operations or any operations that stall the caller's thread of execution within that method are not recommended.

 To get more information about the mentioned behavior, please see the following link: `https://github.com/reactive-streams/reactive-streams-jvm/blob/v1.0.2/README.md#3.4`.

Finally, the following diagram depicts the overall interaction between the service and the database:

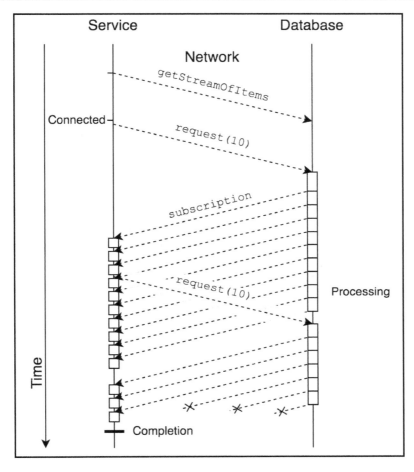

Diagram 3.8. The hybrid Push-Pull processing flow

As might be noticed from the preceding diagram, the first element from the database might arrive a bit later because of the Reactive Streams specification's contract for interaction between the `Publisher` and `Subscriber`. Requesting a new portion of data does not require the interruption or blocking of ongoing elements handling. Consequently, the entire processing time is almost unaffected.

On the other hand, there are some cases in which the pure *push* model is preferable. Fortunately, Reactive Streams is flexible enough. Along with a dynamic *push-pull* model, the specification provides separate *push* and *pull* models as well. According to the documentation, to achieve a pure *push* model we may consider requesting a demand equal to $2^{63}-1$ (`java.lang.Long.MAX_VALUE`).

This number may be considered as unbounded because, with the current or foreseen hardware, it is not feasible to fulfill a demand of 2^{63}-1 within a reasonable amount of time (1 element per nanosecond would take 292 years). Consequently, it is permitted for a Publisher to stop tracking demand beyond this point: https://github.com/reactive-streams/reactive-streams-jvm/blob/v1.0.2/README.md#3.17.

In contrast, to switch to the pure *pull* model, we may request one new element each time the `Subscriber#onNext` has been invoked.

Reactive Streams spec in action

In general, as we might notice from the previous section, even though the interfaces from the Reactive Streams specification are straightforward, the overall concept is complex enough. Thus, we are going to learn the central idea and conceptual behaviors of those three interfaces in an everyday example.

Let's consider as an example a news subscription and how this may become smarter with new Reactive Streams interfaces. Consider the following code for creating a `Publisher` for a news service:

```
NewsServicePublisher newsService = new NewsServicePublisher();
```

Now let's create a `Subscriber` and subscribe it to the `NewsService`:

```
NewsServiceSubscriber subscriber = new NewsServiceSubscriber(5);
newsService.subscribe(subscriber);
...
subscriber.eventuallyReadDigest();
```

By calling `subscribe()` on the `newsService` instance, we show the desire to get the latest news. Usually, before sending any news digests, a high-quality service sends a congratulation letter with the information about the subscription and the subscription's cancellation. This action is absolutely identical to our `Subscriber#onSubscribe()` method, which informs the `Subscriber` about a successful subscription and gives them the ability to unsubscribe. Since our service follows the rules of the Reactive Streams specification, it allows the client to select as many news articles as it can read at once. Only after the client specifies the number of the first portion of digests by calling the `Subscription#request` does the news service starts sending digests over the `Subscriber#onNext` method, and the subscriber can then read the news.

Here, *eventually* means that in real life we may postpone reading the newsletter to the evening or the end of the week, which means that we manually check the inbox with the news. From the subscriber's perspective, that logic is implemented with the support of the `NewsServiceSubscriber#eventuallyReadDigests()`. In general, such behavior means that the user's inbox collects news digests, and a usual service subscription model may easily overflow the subscribers' inboxes. In turn, what usually happens when the news service thoughtlessly sends messages to the subscriber and the subscriber does not read them is that the mail service provider puts the news service email address on the blacklist. Moreover, in that case, the `Subscriber` may miss an important digest. Even if this has not happened, the subscriber would not be happy due to the overflowing mailbox with a bunch of unread digests from the news service. Thus, to preserve the subscriber's happiness, the news service is required to provide a strategy for delivering the news. Suppose that the read state of the newsletter may acknowledge the service. Here, once we have ensured that all messages are read, we may provide some specific logic for sending a new news digest only when the previous one has been read. This mechanism may be easily implemented within the specification. The next piece of code exposes an example of the whole mentioned mechanism:

```
class NewsServiceSubscriber implements Subscriber<NewsLetter> {     // (1)
    final Queue<NewsLetter> mailbox = new ConcurrentLinkedQueue<>();//
    final int take;                                                 //
    final AtomicInteger remaining = new AtomicInteger();            //
    Subscription subscription;                                      //

    public NewsServiceSubscriber(int take) { ... }                  // (2)

    public void onSubscribe(Subscription s) {                       // (3)
        ...                                                         //
        subscription = s;                                           //
        subscription.request(take);                                 // (3.1)
        ...                                                         //
    }                                                               //

    public void onNext(NewsLetter newsLetter) {                     // (4)
        mailbox.offer(newsLetter);                                  //
    }                                                               //

    public void onError(Throwable t) { ... }                        // (5)
    public void onComplete() { ... }                                //

    public Optional<NewsLetter> eventuallyReadDigest() {            // (6)
        NewsLetter letter = mailbox.poll();                         // (6.1)
        if (letter != null) {                                       //
            if (remaining.decrementAndGet() == 0) {                 // (6.2)
                subscription.request(take);                         //
```

```
            remaining.set(take);                    //
        }                                            //
        return Optional.of(letter);                  // (6.3)
    }                                                //
    return Optional.empty();                         // (6.4)
    }                                                //
}                                                    //
```

The key is as follows:

1. This is the NewsServiceSubscriber class declaration which implements Subscriber<NewsLetter>. Here, along with the plain class definition, we have the list of useful fields (such as the mailbox represented by a Queue, or the subscription field) which represents the current subscription; in other words, the agreement between the client and the news service.

2. This is the NewsServiceSubscriber constructor declaration. Here, the constructor accepts one parameter called take which indicates the size of news digests that the user can potentially read at once or at the near time.

3. This is the Subscriber#onSubscribe method implementation. Here, at point (3.1), along with storing the received Subscription, we send the earlier preferenced users' *new reading throughput* to the server.

4. This is the Subscriber#onSubscribe method implementation. The entire logic of new digests handling is straightforward and is just a process of putting messages into the Queue mailbox.

5. This is the Subscriber#onError and Subscriber#onComplete method declaration. Those methods are called on the subscription termination.

6. This is the public eventuallyReadDigest method declaration. First of all, to indicate that the mailbox may be empty, we rely on the Optional. In turn, as the first step, at point (6.1), we try to get the latest unread news digest from the mailbox. If there are no available unread newsletters in the mailbox, we return an Optional.empty(), (6.4). In the case in which there are available digests, we decrease the counter (6.2), which represents the number of unread messages that have previously been requested from the news service. If we are still waiting for some messages, we return the fulfilled Optional. Otherwise, we additionally request a new portion of digests and reset the counter of remaining new messages (6.3).

Due to the specification, the first call invokes `onSubscribe()`, which
stores `Subscription` locally and then notifies `Publisher` about their readiness to receive
newsletters via the `request()` method. In turn, when the first digest comes, it is stored in
the queue for future reading, which is what usually happens in a real mailbox. After all,
when the subscriber has already read all digests from the inbox, the `Publisher` is going to
be notified of that fact and prepare a new portion of the news. In turn, if the news service
changes the subscription policy—which in some cases means the completion of the current
user subscriptions—then the subscriber is going to be notified about that via
the `onComplete` method. The client will then be asked to accept a new policy and
automatically resubscribe to the service. An example of when `onError` may be handled
is (of course) an accidentally dropped database which holds the information about users'
preferences. In that case, it might be counted as a failure, and the subscriber would then
receive an excuse letter and be asked to resubscribe to the service with new preferences.
Finally, the implementation of the `eventuallyReadDigest` is nothing more than a real
user's actions such as opening the mailbox, checking new messages, reading letters and
marking them as read, or just closing the mailbox when there is nothing new to interact
with.

As we might see, Reactive Streams is naturally suitable for and solving problems of
unrelated business cases, at first glance. Just by providing such a mechanism, we can keep
our subscribers happy and not get into the blacklist of the mailbox provider.

The introduction of the Processor notion

We have learned about the primary three interfaces that constitute the Reactive Streams
specification. We have also seen how a proposed mechanism may improve the news service
that sends news digests via email. However, at the beginning of this section, it was
mentioned that there are four core interfaces in the specification. The last one is a
combination of `Publisher` and `Subscriber` and is called the `Processor`. Let's take a look
at the following implementation's code:

```
package org.reactivestreams;

public interface Processor<T, R> extends Subscriber<T>,
                                         Publisher<R> {
}
```

In contrast to the `Publisher` and `Subscriber`, which are *start* and *end* points by definition, `Processor` is designed to add some processing stages between the `Publisher` and `Subscriber`. Since the `Processor` may represent some transformation logic, this makes streaming pipeline behaviors and business logic flows easier to understand. The shining example of the `Processor`'s usage may be any business logic that may be described in a custom operator or it may be to provide additional caching of streaming data, and so on. To get a better understanding of the conceptual application of the `Processor`, let's consider how the `NewsServicePublisher` may be improved with the `Processor` interface.

The most uncomplicated logic that may be hidden behind the `NewsServicePublisher` is database access with newsletter preparation and subsequent multi-casting to all subscribers:

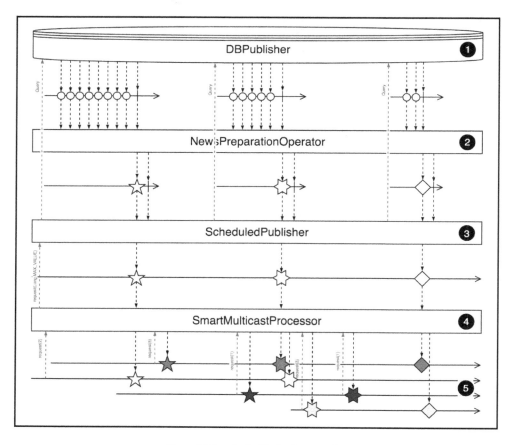

Diagram 3.9. Example of mailing flow for news service

In this example, the `NewsServicePublisher` is split into four additional components:

1. This is the `DBPublisher` stage. Here, `Publisher` is responsible for providing access to the database and returning the newest posts.
2. This is the `NewsPreparationOperator` stage. This stage is an intermediate transformation that is responsible for aggregating all messages and then, when the completion signal is emitted from the main source, combining all news into the digest. Note that this operator always results in one element because of the aggregation nature. Aggregation assumes the presence of storage, which might be either in a queue or any other collection for storing received elements.
3. This is the `ScheduledPublisher` stage. This stage is responsible for scheduling periodic tasks. In the previously mentioned case, a scheduled task is querying a database (`DBPublisher`), processing the result and merging received data to the downstream. Note that `ScheduledPublisher` is effectively an infinite stream and the completion of the merged `Publisher` is ignored. In the case of a lack of requests from the downstream, this `Publisher` throws an exception to the actual `Subscriber` through the `Subscriber#onError` method.
4. This is the `SmartMulticastProcessor` stage. This `Processor` plays a vital role in the flow. First of all, it caches the latest digest. In turn, that stage supports multi-casting, which means that there is no need to create the same flow for each `Subscriber` separately. Also, `SmartMulticastProcessor` includes, as mentioned earlier, a smart mailing tracking mechanism, and only sends newsletters for those who have read the previous digest.
5. These are the actual subscribers, which are effectively `NewsServiceSubscriber`.

In general, the preceding diagram shows what might be hidden behind the plain `NewsServicePublisher`. In turn, that example exposes the real application of the `Processor`. As might be noticed, we have three transformation stages, but only one of those is required to be the `Processor`.

First of all, in cases in which we need just a plain transformation from A to B, we do not need the interface that exposes the `Publisher` and `Subscriber` at the same time. The presence of the `Subscriber` interface means that once the `Processor` has subscribed to the upstream, the elements may start coming to the `Subscriber#onNext` method and may potentially be lost because of the absence of the downstream `Subscriber`. In turn, with such a technique, we have to bear in mind the fact that the `Processor` should be subscribed before it subscribes to the main `Publisher`.

Nevertheless, this over-complicates the business flow and does not allow us to create a reusable operator that fits any case with ease. Moreover, the construction of a `Processor`'s implementation introduces an additional effort on independent (from the main `Publisher`) management of the `Subscriber` and proper backpressure implementation (for example, employing a queue if needed). Subsequently, that may cause degradation in performance or merely decrease the whole stream throughput due to an unreasonably complicated implementation of the `Processor` as a plain operator.

Since we know that we want to transform only A to B, we simply want to start the flow when the actual `Subscriber` calls `Publisher#subscribe`, and we do not want to over—complicate the internal implementation. Consequently, the composition of multiple Publisher instances—which accept upstream as the parameter to the constructor and simply provide the adapter logic—fits the requirements very well.

In turn, the `Processor` shines when we need to multicast elements, regardless of whether there are subscribers or not. It also allows some kind of mutation, since it implements the `Subscriber` interface, which effectively allows mutations such as caching.

Valuing the fact that we have already seen the implementation of the `TakeFilterOperator` operator and `NewsServiceSubscriber`, we may be sure that the internals of most instances of `Publisher`, `Subscriber`, and `Processor` are similar to the mentioned examples. Consequently, we do not get into the details of the internals of each class, and consider only the final composition of all components:

```
Publisher<Subscriber<NewsLetter>> newsLetterSubscribersStream =... // (1)
ScheduledPublisher<NewsLetter> scheduler =                          //
   new ScheduledPublisher<>(                                        //
      () -> new NewsPreparationOperator(new DBPublisher(...), ...),// (1.1)
      1, TimeUnit.DAYS                                              //
   );                                                               //
SmartMulticastProcessor processor = new SmartMulticastProcessor(); //

scheduler.subscribe(processor);                                    // (2)

newsLetterSubscribersStream.subscribe(new Subscriber<>() {         // (3)
   ...                                                             //
   public void onNext(Subscriber<NewsLetter> s) {                 //
      processor.subscribe(s);                                     // (3.1)
   }                                                              //
   ...                                                            //
});                                                               //
```

The key is as follows:

1. This is the publishers, operator, and processor declaration.
   Here, `newsLetterSubscribersStream` represents the infinite stream of users who subscribe to the mailing list. In turn, at point (`1.1`) we declare `Supplier<? extends Publisher<NewsLetter>>`, which supplies the `DBPublisher` wrapped into the `NewsPreparationOperator`.

2. This is the `SmartMulticastProcessor` to the `ScheduledPublisher<NewsLetter>` subscription. That action immediately starts the scheduler, which in turn subscribes to the inner `Publisher`.

3. This is the `newsLetterSubscribersStream` subscription. Here we declare the anonymous class to implement the `Subscriber`. In turn, at point (`3.1`) we subscribe each new incoming `Subscriber` to the processor, which multi-casts the digest among all subscribers.

In this example, we have combined all processors in one chain, sequentially wrapping them into each other or making components subscribe to each other.

 In general, implementation of the `Publisher/Processor` is a challenge. Because of that, we skip the detailed explanation of the implementation of the mentioned operators or sources in that chapter. Nevertheless, to learn more about pitfalls, patterns, and steps required to code our own `Publisher`, please see the following link: `https://medium.com/@olehdokuka/mastering-own-reactive-streams-implementation-part-1-publisher-e8eaf928a78c`.

To summarize, we have covered the basics of the Reactive Streams standard. We have seen the transformation of the idea of reactive programming expressed in libraries such as RxJava to the standard set of interfaces. Along with that, we saw that the mentioned interfaces easily allow us to define an asynchronous and non-blocking interaction model between components within the system. Finally, when embracing the Reactive Streams specification, we are capable of building a reactive system not just on the high architecture level but at the level of smaller components as well.

Reactive Streams technology compatibility kit

While at first glance, Reactive Streams does not seem to be tricky, in reality it does contain a lot of hidden pitfalls. Apart from Java interfaces, the specification includes a lot of documented rules for implementation—perhaps this is the most challenging point. These rules strictly constrain each interface, and it is vital to preserve all of the behaviors mentioned in the specification. This allows further integration of implementations from different vendors, which does not cause any problems. That is the essential point for which these rules were formed. Unfortunately, building a proper test suit that covers all corner cases may take much more time than the proper implementation of interfaces. On the other hand, developers need a common tool that may validate all behaviors and ensure that reactive libraries are standardized and compatible with each other. Luckily, a toolkit has already been implemented by Konrad Malawski for that purpose, and this has the name *Reactive Streams Technology Compatibility Kit* - or simply TCK.

 To learn more about TCK, please see the following link: `https://github.com/reactive-streams/reactive-streams-jvm/tree/master/tck`.

TCK defends all Reactive Streams statements and tests corresponding implementations against specified rules. Essentially, TCK is a bunch of TestNG test-cases, which should be extended and prepared for verification by a corresponding `Publisher` or `Subscriber`. TCK includes a full list of test-classes which aim to cover all of the defined rules in the Reactive Streams specification. Actually, all tests are named to correspond to the specified rules. For instance, one of the sample test-cases which might be found within `org.reactivestreams.tck.PublisherVerification` is the following:

```
...
void
required_spec101_subscriptionRequestMustResultInTheCorrectNumberOfProducedE
lements()
throws Throwable {
    ...
    ManualSubscriber<T> sub = env.newManualSubscriber(pub);          // (1)
    try {
        sub.expectNone(..., pub));                                   // (2)
        sub.request(1);                                              //
        sub.nextElement(..., pub));                                  //
        sub.expectNone(..., pub));                                   //
        sub.request(1);                                              //
        sub.request(2);                                              //
        sub.nextElements(3, ..., pub));                              //
        sub.expectNone(..., pub));                                   //
```

```
    } finally {
        sub.cancel();                                              // (3)
    }
    ...
}
```

The key is as follows:

1. This is the manual subscription to the tested publisher. Reactive Streams' TCK provides its own test classes, which allow the verification of the particular behavior.
2. This is the expectations' declaration. As might be noticed from the preceding code, here we have a particular verification of the given `Publisher`'s behaviors according to rule 1.01. In that case, we verify that the `Publisher` cannot signal more elements than the `Subscriber` has requested.
3. This is the `Subscription`'s cancellation stage. Once the test has passed or failed, to close the opened resource and finalize the interaction, we unsubscribe from the `Publisher` using the `ManualSubscriber` API.

The importance of the mentioned test is hidden behind the verification of the essential guarantee of interaction that any implementation of the `Publisher` should provide. Moreover, all test-cases within the `PublisherVerification` ensure that the given `Publisher` is to some degree compliant to the Reactive Streams specification. Here, *to some degree* means that it is impossible to verify all the rules in the full size. The example of such rules is rule 3.04, which states that the request should not perform heavy computations that cannot be meaningfully tested.

The Publisher verification

Along with the understanding of the importance of the Reactive Streams TCK, it is necessary to get the essential knowledge of the toolkit usage. To acquire a basic knowledge of how this kit works, we are going to verify one of the components of our news service. Since a `Publisher` is an essential part of our system, we are going to start with its analysis. As we remember, TCK provides `org.reactivestreams.tck.PublisherVerification` to check the fundamental behavior of the `Publisher`. In general, `PublisherVerification` is an abstract class which mandates us to extend just two methods. Let's take a look at the following example in order to understand how to write a verification of the previously developed `NewsServicePublisher`:

```
public class NewsServicePublisherTest                              // (1)
    extends PublisherVerification<NewsLetter> ... {                //
```

```
    public StreamPublisherTest() {                              // (2)
        super(new TestEnvironment(...));                        //
    }                                                           //

    @Override                                                   // (3)
    public Publisher<NewsLetter> createPublisher(long elements) {   //
        ...
        prepareItemsInDatabase(elements);                       // (3.1)
        Publisher<NewsLetter> newsServicePublisher =            //
            new NewsServicePublisher(...);                      //
        ...                                                     //
        return newsServicePublisher;                            //
    }                                                           //

    @Override                                                   // (4)
    public Publisher<NewsLetter> createFailedPublisher() {      //
        stopDatabase()                                          // (4.1)
        return new NewsServicePublisher(...);                   //
    }                                                           //

    ...                                                         //
}
```

The key is as follows:

1. This is the `NewsServicePublisherTest` class declaration which extends the `PublisherVerification` class.
2. This is the no-args constructor declaration. It should be noted that `PublisherVerification` does not have the default constructor and mandates the person who implements it to provide the `TestEnvironment` that is responsible for specific configurations for the test, such as configurations of timeouts and debug logs.
3. This is the `createPublisher` method implementation. This method is responsible for generating a `Publisher`, which produces a given number of elements. In turn, in our case, to satisfy the tests' requirements, we have to fill the database with a certain amount of news entries (3.1).
4. This is the `createFailedPublisher` method implementation. Here, in contrast to the `createPublisher` method, we have to provide a failed instance of the `NewsServicePublisher`. One of the options in which we have a failed `Publisher` is when the data source is unavailable, which in our case causes the failure of the `NewsServicePublisher`, (4.1).

The preceding test expands the basic configurations required in order to run the verification of the NewsServicePublisher. It is assumed that the Publisher is flexible enough to be able to provide the given number of elements. In other words, the test can tell the Publisher how many elements it should produce and whether it should fail or work normally. On the other hand, there are a lot of specific cases where the Publisher is limited to only one element. For example, as we might remember, the NewsPreparationOperator responds with only one element, regardless of the number of incoming elements from the upstream.

By simply following the mentioned configurations of the test, we cannot check the accuracy of that Publisher since many test-cases assume the presence of more than one element in the stream. Fortunately, the Reactive Streams TCK respects such corner cases and allows setting up an additional method called maxElementsFromPublisher() which returns a value that indicates the maximum number of produced elements:

```
@Override
public long maxElementsFromPublisher() {
    return 1;
}
```

On the one hand, by overriding that method, the tests that require more than one element are skipped. On the other hand, the coverage of the Reactive Streams rules is decreased and may require implementation of the custom test-cases.

The Subscriber verification

The mentioned configurations are the minimum that are required in order to start testing our producer's behavior. However, along with the instances of Publisher, we have instances of Subscriber that should be tested as well. Fortunately, that group of rules in the Reactive Stream specification is less complex than Publisher's one, but it is still required to satisfy all requirements.

There are two different test suits to test `NewsServiceSubscriber`. The first one is called `org.reactivestreams.tck.SubscriberBlackboxVerification`, which allows verifying the `Subscriber` without knowledge or modification of its internals. Blackbox verification is a useful test kit when the `Subscriber` comes from the external codebase, and there is no legal way to extend the behavior. On the other hand, the Blackbox verification covers only a few rules and does not ensure complete correctness of the implementation. To see how the `NewsServiceSubscriber` may be examined, let's implement the Blackbox verification test first:

```
public class NewsServiceSubscriberTest                          // (1)
    extends SubscriberBlackboxVerification<NewsLetter> {        //

    public NewsServiceSubscriberTest() {                        // (2)
        super(new TestEnvironment());                           //
    }                                                           //

    @Override                                                   // (3)
    public Subscriber<NewsLetter> createSubscriber() {          //
        return new NewsServiceSubscriber(...);                  //
    }                                                           //

    @Override                                                   // (4)
    public NewsLetter createElement(int element) {              //
        return new StubNewsLetter(element);                     //
    }                                                           //

    @Override                                                   // (5)
    public void triggerRequest(Subscriber<? super NewsLetter> s) {  //
        ((NewsServiceSubscriber) s).eventuallyReadDigest();     // (5.1)
    }                                                           //
}
```

The key is as follows:

1. This is the `NewsServiceSubscriberTest` class declaration which extends the `SubscriberBlackboxVerification` tests-suite.
2. This is the default constructor declaration. Here, identically to `PublisherVerification`, we are mandated to provide a certain `TestEnvironment`.
3. This is the `createSubscriber` method implementation. Here, that method returns the `NewsServiceSubscriber` instance, which should be tested against the specification.

4. This is the `createElement` method implementation. Here, we are required to provide an implementation of the method which plays the role of a new element factory and generates a new instance of `NewsLetter` on demand.

5. This is the `triggerRequest` method implementation. Since the Blackbox testing assumes no access to the internals, it means that we do not have direct access to the hidden `Subscription` inside the `Subscriber`. Subsequently, this means that we have to trigger it somehow by manually using the given API (5.1).

The preceding example shows the available API for `Subscriber` verification. Apart from the two required methods, `createSubscriber` and `createElement`, there is an additional method which addresses the handling of the `Subscription#request` method externally. In our case, it is a useful addition that allows us to emulate real user activity.

The second test kit is called `org.reactivestreams.tck.SubscriberWhiteboxVerification`. This is a similar verification to the previous one, but to pass the verification, the `Subscriber` should provide additional interaction with the `WhiteboxSubscriberProbe` :

```java
public class NewsServiceSubscriberWhiteboxTest                    // (1)
    extends SubscriberWhiteboxVerification<NewsLetter> {         //
    ...                                                          //

    @Override                                                    // (2)
    public Subscriber<NewsLetter> createSubscriber(              //
        WhiteboxSubscriberProbe<NewsLetter> probe                //
    ) {                                                          //
        return new NewsServiceSubscriber(...) {                 //
            public void onSubscribe(Subscription s) {           //
                super.onSubscribe(s);                           // (2.1)
                probe.registerOnSubscribe(new SubscriberPuppet() { // (2.2)
                    public void triggerRequest(long elements) { //
                        s.request(elements);                    //
                    }                                           //
                    public void signalCancel() {                //
                        s.cancel();                             //
                    }                                           //
                });                                             //
            }                                                   //
            public void onNext(NewsLetter newsLetter) {         //
                super.onNext(newsLetter);                       //
                probe.registerOnNext(newsLetter);               // (2.3)
            }                                                   //
            public void onError(Throwable t) {                  //
                super.onError(t);                               //
                probe.registerOnError(t);                       // (2.4)
```

```
        }                                                   //
        public void onComplete() {                          //
            super.onComplete();                             //
            probe.registerOnComplete();                     //  (2.5)
        }                                                   //
    };                                                      //
  }                                                         //
  ...                                                       //
}                                                           //
```

The key is as follows:

1. This is the `NewsServiceSubscriberWhiteboxTest` class declaration which extends the `SubscriberWhiteboxVerification` tests-suite.

2. This is the `createSubscriber` method implementation. This method works identically to the Blackbox verification and returns the `Subscriber` instance, but here there is an additional parameter called `WhiteboxSubscriberProbe`. In that case, `WhiteboxSubscriberProbe` represents a mechanism that enables embedded control of the demand and capture of the incoming signals. In comparison to the Blackbox verification, by proper registration of probe hooks inside `NewsServiceSubscriber`, (2.2), (2.3), (2.4), (2.5), the test suite is capable not only of sending the demand but verifying that the demand was satisfied and all elements have been received as well. In turn, the mechanism of demand regulation is more transparent than it previously was. Here, at point (2.2), we implement the `SubscriberPuppet`, which adapts direct access to the received `Subscription`.

As we can see, opposite to the Blackbox verification, the Whitebox requires the extension of the `Subscriber`, providing additional hooks internally. While the Whitebox testing covers a broader number of rules which ensure the correct behavior of the tested `Subscriber`, it may be unacceptable for those cases when we want to make a class final to prevent it from being extended.

The final part of the verification journey is the testing of the `Processor`. For that purpose, TCK provides us with `org.reactivestreams.tck.IdentityProcessorVerification`. This test suite can verify a `Processor`, which receives and produces the same type of elements. In our example, only the `martMulticastProcessor` behaves in such a manner. Since the test kit should verify the behavior of both `Publisher` and `Subscriber`, the `IdentityProcessorVerification` inherits similar configurations as for the `Publisher` and `Subscriber` tests. Consequently, we do not get into the details of the whole test's implementation, but consider additional methods required for the `SmartMulticastProcessor` verification:

```
public class SmartMulticastProcessorTest                        // (1)
    extends IdentityProcessorVerification<NewsLetter> {         //

    public SmartMulticastProcessorTest() {                      // (2)
        super(..., 1);                                          //
    }                                                           //

    @Override                                                   // (3)
    public Processor<Integer, Integer> createIdentityProcessor( //
        int bufferSize                                          //
    ) {                                                         //
        return new SmartMulticastProcessor<>();                 //
    }                                                           //

    @Override                                                   // (4)
    public NewsLetter createElement(int element) {              //
        return new StubNewsLetter(element);                     //
    }                                                           //
}
```

The key is as follows:

1. This is the `SmartMulticastProcessorTest` class definition, which extends `IdentityProcessorVerification`.
2. This is the default constructor definition. As we may notice from the code, (along with the `TestEnvironment` configuration, which is skipped in that example) we pass an additional parameter, which indicates the number of elements that the processor must buffer without dropping. Since we know that our `Processor` supports the buffering of only one element, we have to provide that number manually before starting any verification.

3. This is the `createIdentityProcessor` method implementation, which returns an instance of the tested `Processor`. Here, the `bufferSize` represents the number of elements that the `Processor` must buffer without dropping. We may skip that parameter now, since we know that the internal buffer size is equal to the pre-configured one in the constructor.

4. This is the `createElement` method implementation. Similar to the verification of `Subscriber`, we have to provide the factory method to create new elements.

The preceding example shows the essential configuration for `SmartMulticastProcessor` verification. Since the `IdentityProcessorVerification` extends both `SubscriberWhiteboxVerification` and `PublisherVerification`, the general configurations are merged from each of them.

To generalize, we got an overview of the essential set of tests that help to verify the specified behavior of the implemented Reactive Operators. Here, TCK may be considered as initial integration tests. Nevertheless, we should bear in mind that along with the TCK verification, each operator should carefully test for the desired behavior on its own.

To learn more about verification, please visit the original TCK page `https://github.com/reactive-streams/reactive-streams-jvm/tree/master/tck`.

To look at more examples of TCK usage, visit the following *Ratpack* repository `https://github.com/ratpack/ratpack/tree/master/ratpack-exec/src/test/groovy/ratpack/stream/tck`.

There is also a broader list of TCK usage examples for verification of the RxJava 2 at the following link: `https://github.com/ReactiveX/RxJava/tree/2.x/src/test/java/io/reactivex/tck`.

JDK 9

Likewise, the value of specification was seen by the JDK implementing team too. Not long after the first release of the specification, Doug Lee created a proposal to add the aforementioned interface in JDK 9. The proposal was supported by the fact that the current Stream API offers just a pull model, and a *push model* was a missing point here:

> *"...there is no single best fluent async/parallel API. CompletableFuture/CompletionStage best supports continuation style programming on futures, and java.util.Stream best supports (multi-stage, possibly-parallel) "pull" style operations on the elements of collections. Until now, one missing category was "push" style operations on items as they become available from an active source."*

> - *Doug Lee,* `http://jsr166-concurrency.10961.n7.nabble.com/jdk9-Candidate-classes-Flow-and-SubmissionPublisher-td11967.html`

Note that under the hood, the Java Stream API uses `Spliterator`, which is nothing more than a modified version of `Iterator`, capable of parallel execution. As we might remember, the `Iterator` is not designed for pushing but for pulling over the `Iterator#next` method. Similarly, `Spliterator` has the `tryAdvance` method, which is a combination of the `Iterator`'s `hasNext` and `next` methods. Consequently, we may conclude that in general the Stream API is pulling-based.

The primary goal of the proposal was to specify interfaces for reactive streams inside JDK. According to the proposal, all interfaces defined in the Reactive Streams specification are provided within the `java.util.concurrent.Flow` class as static sub-classes. On the one hand, that improvement is significant because Reactive Streams becomes a JDK standard. On the other hand, many vendors have already relied on the specification provided within the `org.reactivestreams.*` package. Since most vendors (such as RxJava) support several versions of JDK, it is impossible to just implement these interfaces along with the previous ones. Consequently, this improvement manifests an additional requirement to be compatible with JDK 9+ and to somehow convert one specification to another.

Fortunately, the Reactive Streams specification provides an additional module for that purpose, which allows the conversion of Reactive Streams types to JDK `Flow` types:

```
...                                                           // (1)
import org.reactivestreams.Publisher;                         //
import java.util.concurrent.Flow;                             //
...                                                           //
Flow.Publisher jdkPublisher = ...;                            // (2)
Publisher external = FlowAdapters.toPublisher(jdkPublisher)   // (2.1)
Flow.Publisher jdkPublisher2 = FlowAdapters.toFlowPublisher(  //
    external                                                  // (2.2)
);                                                            //
```

The key is as follows:

1. These are the `import` definitions. As might be noticed from the imports' statements, we have the import of the `Publisher` from the original Reactive Streams library and the import of the `Flow`, which is the access point to all interfaces of Reactive Streams, but ported to JDK 9.
2. This is the `Flow.Publisher` instance definition. Here we define the instance of `Publisher` from the JDK 9. In turn, at point (`2.1`), we use the `FlowAdapters.toPublisher` method from the original Reactive Streams library to convert `Flow.Publisher` to `org.reactivestreams.Publisher`. Also, for demo purposes, at line (`2.2`) we use the `FlowAdapters.toFlowPublisher` method to convert `org.reactivestreams.Publisher` back to `Flow.Publisher`.

The preceding example shows how we may easily convert `Flow.Publisher` to `org.reactivestreams.Publisher`. It should be noted that the example is unrelated to the real business use-case because there were no well known reactive libraries written from scratch on top of the JDK 9 Flow API at the time this book was published. Consequently, there was no need to migrate from the Reactive Streams specification as the external library that supports JDK 6 and higher. However, in the future, everything will most likely change, and new iterations of reactive libraries will definitely be written on top of the Reactive Streams specification and ported to JDK 9.

Note that the adapter functionality is delivered as a separate library. To see all available libraries, please see the following link: `http://www.reactive-streams.org/#jvm-interfaces-completed`.

Advanced - async and parallel in Reactive Streams

In the previous sections, we discussed the conceptual behaviors of Reactive Streams. However, there was no mention of asynchronous and non-blocking behaviors of reactive pipes. So, let's dig into the Reactive Streams standard and analyze those behaviors.

On one hand, the Reactive Streams API states, in rules 2.2 and 3.4, that the processing of all signals produced by the `Publisher` and consumed by the `Subscriber` should be non-blocking and non-obstructing. Consequently, we may be sure that we may efficiently utilize one node or one core of the processor, depending on the execution's environment.

On the other hand, the efficient utilization of all processors or cores requires parallelization. The usual understanding of the parallelization notion within the Reactive Streams specification may be interpreted as the parallel invocation of the `Subscriber#onNext` method. Unfortunately, the specification stated in rule 1.3 that the invocation of the `on***` methods *must be signaled in a thread-safe manner and—if performed by multiple threads—use external synchronization*. This assumes a serialized, or simply a sequential, invocation of all `on***` methods. In turn, this means that we cannot create something like `ParallelPublisher` and perform a parallel processing of elements in the stream.

Consequently, the question is: how do we utilize the resources efficiently? To find the answer, we have to analyze the usual stream processing pipe:

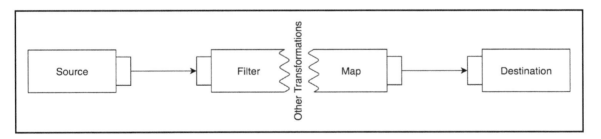

Diagram 3.10. Example of processing flow with some business logic between the Source and Destination

As might be noted, the usual processing pipe—along with a data source and final destination—includes a few processing or transformational stages. In turn, each processing stage may take significant processing time and stall other executions.

In such a case, one of the solutions is asynchronous messages passing between stages. For in-memory stream processing, this means that one part of the execution is bound to one `Thread` and another part to another `Thread`. For example, final element consumption may be a CPU-intensive task, which will be rationally processed on the separate `Thread`:

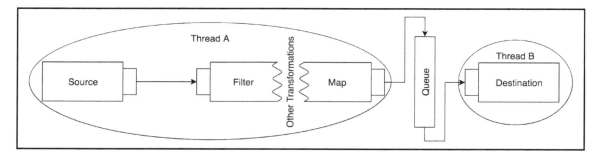

Diagram 3.11. The example of the asynchronous boundary between Source with Processing and Destination

In general, by splitting processing between the two independent `Thread`s, we put the asynchronous boundary between stages. In turn, by doing so, we parallelize the overall processing of elements since both `Thread`s may work independently from each other. To achieve parallelization, we have to apply a data structure, such as `Queue`, to properly decouple the processing. Hence, processing within Thread A independently supplies the items *to*, and the `Subscriber` within Thread B independently consumes items *from*, the same `Queue`.

Splitting the processing between threads leads to the additional overhead in a data structure. Of course, owing to the Reactive Streams specification, such a data structure is always bound. In turn, the number of items in the data structure is usually equal to the size of the batch that a `Subscriber` requests from its `Publisher`, and this depends on the general capacity of the system.

Along with that, the primary question that is addressed to API implementors and developers is *to which async boundary should the flow processing part be attached*? At least three simple choices may arise here. The first case is when a processing flow is attached to the Source resource (Diagram 3.11), and all of the operations occur within the same boundaries as the Source. In that case, all data is processed synchronously one by one, so one item is transformed through all processing stages before it is sent to the processing on the other `Thread`. The second and opposite configuration of asynchronous boundaries to the first case is when the processing is attached to the **Destination**, or the Consumer's `Thread`, and may be used in cases when the elements' production is a CPU-intensive task.

The third case takes place when the production and consumption is a CPU-intensive task. Hence, the most efficient way of running the intermediate transformation is to run it on separate `Thread` objects:

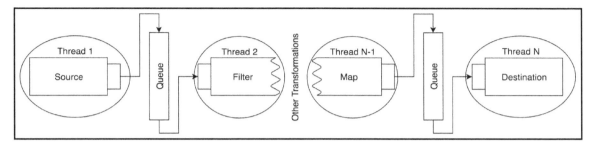

Diagram 3.12. The example of asynchronous boundaries between each component of the pipeline

As we can see in the preceding diagram, each processing stage may be bound to a separate Thread. In general, there are a bunch of ways to configure the processing of the data flow. Each of the cases is relevant in its best-fit conditions. For example, the first example is valid when the Source resource is less loaded than the Destination one. Consequently, the transformation operation is profitable to put within Source boundaries and vice versa, when the Destination consumes fewer resources than the Source, it is logical to process all data in the Destination boundary. Moreover, sometimes transformation may be the highest resource consumable operation. In that case, it is better to separate transformations from the Source and the Destination.

Nevertheless, it is crucial to remember that splitting the processing between different Threads is not free and should be balanced between rational resource consumption to achieve boundaries (`Thread` and additional data structure) and efficient element processing. In turn, achieving such a balance is another challenge, and it is hard to overcome the implementation and management thereof without the library's useful API.

Fortunately, such an API is offered by reactive libraries such as RxJava and Project Reactor. We will not get into the details of the proposed features now, but are going to cover them intensively in `Chapter 4`, *Project Reactor - the Foundation for Reactive Apps*.

Transfiguration of the Reactive Landscape

The fact that JDK 9 includes the Reactive Streams specification enforces its significance, and it has started to change the industry. The leaders in the Open Source Software industry (such as Netflix, Red Hat, Lightbend, MongoDB, Amazon, and others) have started adopting this excellent solution in their products.

RxJava transfiguration

In this way, RxJava provides an additional module that allows us to easily convert one reactive type into another. Let's look at how to convert `Observable<T>` to `Publisher<T>` and adopt `rx.Subscriber<T>` to `org.reactivestreams.Subscriber<T>`.

Suppose we have an application that uses RxJava 1.x and `Observable` as the central communication type between components, as shown in the following example:

```
interface LogService {
    Observable<String> stream();
}
```

However, with the publication of the Reactive Streams specification, we decide to follow the standard and abstract our interfaces from the following particular dependency:

```
interface LogService {
    Publisher<String> stream();
}
```

As might be noticed, we easily replaced the `Observable` with the `Publisher`. However, the refactoring of the implementation may take much more time than just replacing the return type. Fortunately, we may always easily adapt an existing `Observable` to a `Publisher`, as shown in the following example:

```
class RxLogService implements LogService {                          // (1)
    final HttpClient<...> rxClient = HttpClient.newClient(...);     // (1.1)

    @Override
    public Publisher<String> stream() {
        Observable<String> rxStream = rxClient.createGet("/logs")   // (2)
                                        .flatMap(...)               //
                                        .map(Utils::toString);      //

        return RxReactiveStreams.toPublisher(rxStream);             // (3)
    }
}
```

The key is as follows:

1. This is the RxLogService class declaration. That class represents the old Rx-based implementation. At point (1.1) we use the RxNetty HttpClient, which allows interaction with external services in asynchronous, non-blocking fashion using a Netty Client wrapped into an RxJava based API.
2. This is the external request execution. Here, using the created instance of HttpClient, we request the stream of logs from the external service, transforming the incoming elements into String instances.
3. This is the rxStream adaption to the Publisher using the RxReactiveStreams library.

As might be noticed, the developers of RxJava took care of us and provided an additional RxReactiveStreams class, making it possible to convert Observable into a Reactive Streams' Publisher. Moreover, with the appearance of the Reactive Streams specification, RxJava developers have also provided non-standardized support for backpressure, which allows a converted Observable to be compliant with the Reactive Streams specification.

Along with the conversion of Observable to Publisher, we may also convert rx.Subscriber to org.reactivestreams.Subscriber. For example, streams of logs were previously stored in the file. For that purpose, we had the custom Subscriber, which was responsible for I/O interaction. In turn, the transfiguration of the code to migrate to Reactive Streams specification looks like the following:

```
class RxFileService implements FileService {                              // (1)

    @Override                                                             // (2)
    public void writeTo(                                                  //
        String file,                                                      //
        Publisher<String> content                                        //
    ) {                                                                   //

        AsyncFileSubscriber rxSubscriber =                                // (3)
            new AsyncFileSubscriber(file);                                //

        content                                                           // (4)
            .subscribe(RxReactiveStreams.toSubscriber(rxSubscriber));     //
    }
}
```

The key is as follows:

1. This is the `RxFileService` class declaration.
2. This is the `writeTo` method implementation which accepts the `Publisher` as the central type for interaction between components.
3. This is the RxJava-based `AsyncFileSubscriber` instance declaration.
4. This is the `content` subscription. To reuse the RxJava based `Subscriber`, we adapt it using the same `RxReactiveStreams` utility class.

As we can see from the preceding example, the `RxReactiveStreams` provide a broad list of converters, making it possible to convert a RxJava API to the Reactive Streams API.

In the same way, any `Publisher<T>` may be converted back to RxJava `Observable`:

```
Publisher<String> publisher = ...

RxReactiveStreams.toObservable(publisher)
                .subscribe();
```

In general, RxJava started following the Reactive Streams specification in some way. Unfortunately, because of backward compatibility, implementing the specification was not possible, and there are no plans to extend the Reactive Streams specification for RxJava 1.x in the future. Moreover, starting from the 31st of March 2018, there are no plans to support RxJava 1.x anymore.

Fortunately, the second iteration of RxJava brings new hope. Dávid Karnok, the father of the second version of the library, significantly improved the overall library's design and introduced an additional type that is compliant with the Reactive Streams specification. Along with `Observable`, which is left unchanged because of backward compatibility, RxJava 2 offers the new reactive type called `Flowable`.

The `Flowable` reactive type gives the identical API as `Observable` but extends `org.reactivestreams.Publisher` from the beginning. As shown in the next example, in which it is incorporated with the fluent API, `Flowable` may be converted to any common RxJava types and back to a Reactive Streams-compatible type:

```
Flowable.just(1, 2, 3)
        .map(String::valueOf)
        .toObservable()
        .toFlowable(BackpressureStrategy.ERROR)
        .subscribe();
```

As we may notice, the conversion of the `Flowable` to the `Observable` is an uncomplicated application of one operator. However, to convert the `Observable` back to the `Flowable`, it is necessary to provide some of the available backpressure strategies. In RxJava 2, `Observable` was designed as the *push-only* stream. Consequently, it is crucial to keep the converted `Observable` compliant with the Reactive Streams specification.

 `BackpressureStrategy` refers to the strategies that take place when the producer does not respect the consumer's demand. In other words, a `BackpressureStrategy` defines the behavior of the stream when we have a Fast producer and a slow consumer. As we might remember, at the beginning of the chapter, we covered identical cases and considered three central strategies. These strategies included unbounded buffering of elements, dropping elements on the overflow, or blocking the producer based on a lack of demand from the consumer. In general, `BackapressureStrategy` reflects all the described strategies in some way, except the strategy of blocking producers. It also provides strategies such as `BackapressureStrategy.ERROR`, which—upon a lack of demand—sends an error to the consumer and automatically disconnects it. We will not go into detail on each strategy in this chapter but will cover them in `Chapter 4`, *Project Reactor - the Foundation for Reactive Apps.*

Vert.x adjustments

Along with the transformation of RxJava, the rest of the reactive libraries and frameworks vendors have also started adopting the Reactive Streams specification. Following the specification, `Vert.x` included an additional module which provides support for the Reactive Streams API. The following example demonstrates this addition:

```
...                                                       // (1)
.requestHandler(request -> {                              //

    ReactiveReadStream<Buffer> rrs =                      // (2)
        ReactiveReadStream.readStream();                  //
    HttpServerResponse response = request.response();     //

    Flowable<Buffer> logs = Flowable                      // (3)
        .fromPublisher(logsService.stream())              //
        .map(Buffer::buffer)                              //
        .doOnTerminate(response::end);                    //

    logs.subscribe(rrs);                                  // (4)
```

```
        response.setStatusCode(200);                         // (5)
        response.setChunked(true);                           //
        response.putHeader("Content-Type", "text/plain");    //
        response.putHeader("Connection", "keep-alive");      //

        Pump.pump(rrs, response)                             // (6)
            .start();                                        //
    })
    ...
```

The key is as follows:

1. This is the request handler declaration. This is a generic request handler that allows handling any requests sent to the server.
2. This is the `Subscriber` and HTTP response declaration. Here `ReactiveReadStream` implements both `org.reactivestreams.Subscriber` and `ReadStream`, which allows transforming any `Publisher` to the source of data compatible with a `Vert.x` API.
3. This is the processing flow declaration. In that example, we refer to the new Reactive Streams-based `LogsService` interface, and to write a functional transformation of the elements in the stream we use the `Flowable` API from RxJava 2.x.
4. This is the subscription stage. Once the processing flow is declared, we may subscribe `ReactiveReadStream` to the `Flowable`.
5. This is a response preparation stage.
6. This is the final response being sent to the client. Here, the `Pump` class plays an important role in a sophisticated mechanism of backpressure control to prevent the underlying `WriteStream` buffer from getting too full.

As we can see, `Vert.x` does not provide a fluent API for writing a stream of element processing. However, it provides an API that allows converting any `Publisher` to the `Vert.x` API, keeping the sophisticated backpressure management from Reactive Streams in place.

Ratpack improvements

Along with Vert.x, another well-known web framework called Ratpack also provides support for Reactive Streams. In contrast to `Vert.x`, Ratpack offers direct support for Reactive Streams. For example, sending streams of logs in a Ratpack case looks like the following:

```
RatpackServer.start(server ->                                  // (1)
   server.handlers(chain ->                                    //
      chain.all(ctx -> {                                       //

         Publisher<String> logs = logsService.stream();        // (2)

         ServerSentEvents events = serverSentEvents(           // (3)
            logs,                                              //
            event -> event.id(Objects::toString)               // (3.1)
                        .event("log")                          //
                        .data(Function.identity())             //
         );                                                    //

         ctx.render(events);                                   // (4)
      })
   )
);
```

The key is as follows:

1. This is the server start's action and request handler declaration.
2. This is the logs stream declaration.
3. This is the `ServerSentEvents` preparation. Here, the mentioned class plays a role in the mapping stage which converts the elements in the `Publisher` to the Server-Sent Events' representative. As we may have noticed, `ServerSentEvents` mandates the mapper function declaration, which describes how to map an element to the particular `Event`'s fields.
4. This is the rendering of the stream to I/O.

As we may see from the example, Ratpack provides the support for Reactive Streams in the core. Now, the same `LogService#stream` method may be reused without providing an additional type conversion or a requirement for the additional modules to add support for the particular reactive library.

Moreover, in contrast to `Vert.x`, which provides just plain support of the Reactive Streams specification, Ratpack provides its own implementation of the interfaces of the specification. This functionality is available within the `ratpack.stream.Streams` class, which is similar to RxJava API:

```
Publisher<String> logs = logsService.stream();
TransformablePublisher publisher = Streams
    .transformable(logs)
    .filter(this::filterUsersSensitiveLogs)
    .map(this::escape);
```

Here, the Ratpack offers a static factory to convert any `Publisher` to `TransformablePublisher`, which in turn gives the ability to flexibly process a stream of events using familiar operators and transformational stages.

MongoDB Reactive Streams driver

In the previous sections, we took an overview of the support for Reactive Streams from the reactive libraries and framework perspective. However, the area of the specification's application is not limited to frameworks or reactive libraries only. The same rule of interaction between the producer and consumer can be applied to communication with a database via a database driver.

In that way, MongoDB provides a Reactive Streams-based driver along with callback-based and RxJava 1.x drivers. In turn, MongoDB provides additional, fluent API implementation, which gives some sort of querying based on the written transformation. For example, the internal implementation of `DBPublisher` that we might have seen in the news service example potentially may be implemented in the following way:

```
public class DBPublisher implements Publisher<News> {       // (1)
    private final MongoCollection<News> collection;         //
    private final Date publishedOnFrom;                     //

    public DBPublisher(                                      // (2)
        MongoClient client,                                 //
        Date publishedOnFrom                                //
    ) { ... }                                               //
```

```
    @Override                                             // (3)
    public void subscribe(Subscriber<? super News> s) {  //
        FindPublisher<News> findPublisher =               // (3.1)
            collection.find(News.class);                  //
                                                          //
        findPublisher                                     // (3.2)
            .filter(Filters.and(                          //
                Filters.eq("category", query.getCategory()),  //
                Filters.gt("publishedOn", today())        //
            )                                             //
            .sort(Sorts.descending("publishedOn"))        //
            .subscribe(s);                                // (3.3)
    }                                                     //
}
```

The key is as follows:

1. This is the DBPublisher class and related fields declaration. Here, the publishedOnFrom field refers to the date after which the news posts should be searched.
2. This is the constructor declaration. Here, one of the accepted parameters in the DBPublisher's constructor is the configured MongoDB client, which is com.mongodb.reactivestreams.client.MongoClient.
3. This is the Publisher#subscriber method implementation. Here, we simplified the DBPublisher's implementation by using the FindPublisher from the Reactive Streams MongoDB driver at point (3.1) and subscribing to the given Subscriber at point (3.3). As we may have noticed, FindPublisher exposes a fluent API that allows the building of an executable query using a functional programming style.

Along with the support of the Reactive Streams standard, the Reactive Streams-based MongoDB driver provides a simplified means for data querying. We will not go into detail about the implementation and behavior of that driver. Instead, we will cover this in Chapter 7, *Reactive Database Access*.

A composition of reactive technologies in action

To learn more about the technologies' composability, let's try to combine several reactive libraries in one Spring Framework 4-based application. In turn, our application is based on the revisited news service functionality with access to it via a plain REST endpoint. This endpoint is responsible for looking up news from the database and external services:

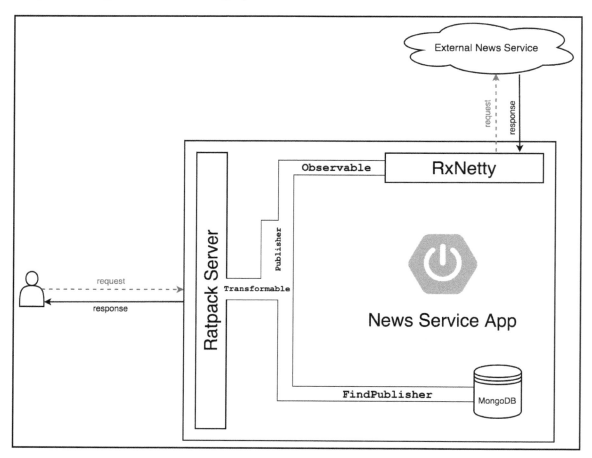

Diagram 3.13. Cross Library communication example inside one application

The preceding diagram introduces three reactive libraries to our system. Here, we use Ratpack as a web server. With the `TransfromablePublisher`, this allows us to easily combine and process results from several sources. In turn, one of the sources is MongoDB, which returns the `FindPublisher` as the result of querying. Finally, here we have access to the external new service and grab a portion of data using the RxNetty HTTP client, which returns the `Observable` and is adapted to the `org.reactivestreams.Publisher` as a result.

To summarize, we have four components in the system, the first of which is Spring Framework 4. The second is Retrofit, which plays the role of the web framework. Finally, the third and fourth are RxNetty and MongoDB, for providing access to the news. We are not going into too much detail on the implementation of the components responsible for communication with the external services, but we are going to cover the implementation of the endpoint instead. This highlights the value of the Reactive Streams specification as the standard for the composability of the independent frameworks and libraries:

```
@SpringBootApplication                                            // (1)
@EnableRatpack                                                    // (1.1)
public class NewsServiceApp {                                     //

    @Bean                                                         // (2)
    MongoClient mongoClient(MongoProperties properties) { ... }   // (2.1)
    @Bean                                                         //
    DatabaseNewsService databaseNews() { ... }                    // (2.2)
    @Bean                                                         //
    HttpNewsService externalNews() { ... }                        // (2.3)

    @Bean                                                         // (3)
    public Action<Chain> home() {                                 //
        return chain -> chain.get(ctx -> {                        // (3.1)

            FindPublisher<News> databasePublisher =               // (4)
                databaseNews().lookupNews();                      //
            Observable<News> httpNewsObservable =                 //
                externalNews().retrieveNews();                    //
            TransformablePublisher<News> stream = Streams.merge(  // (4.1)
                databasePublisher,                                //
                RxReactiveStreams.toPublisher(httpNewsObservable) //
            );                                                    //

            ctx.render(                                           // (5)
                stream.toList()                                   //
                    .map(Jackson::json)                           // (5.1)
            );                                                    //
        })                                                        //
    }                                                             //
```

```
public static void main(String[] args) {                    // (6)
    SpringApplication.run(NewsServiceApp.class, args);       //
}                                                            //
}
```

The key is as follows:

1. This is the `NewsServiceApp` class declaration. This class is annotated with the `@SpringBootApplication` annotation, which assumes the usage of Spring Boot features. In turn, there is an additional `@EnableRatpack` annotation at point (`1.1`) which is part of the `ratpack-spring-boot` module and enables auto-configuration for the Ratpack server.
2. This is the common beans declaration. Here, at point (`2.1`) we configure the `MongoClient` bean. At points (`2.2`) and (`2.3`) there are configurations of services for news retrieval and lookup.
3. This is the request's handler declaration. Here, to create a Ratpack request handler, we have to declare a `Bean` with the `Action<Chain>` type, which allows providing the configuration of the handler at point (`3.1`).
4. This is the services invocation and results aggregation. Here we execute the services' methods and merge the returned streams using Ratpack `Streams` API (`4.1`).
5. This is the rendering of the merged streams stage. Here, we asynchronously reduce all the elements into a list and then transform that list to the specific rendering view such as JSON (`5.1`).
6. This is the main method's implementation. Here we use a common technique for bringing the Spring Boot application to life.

The preceding example shows the power of the Reactive Streams standard in action. Here, using an API of several unrelated libraries, we may easily build one processing flow and return the result to the final user without there being any additional effort for adapting one library to the another. The only exclusion from that rule is `HttpNewsService`, which in the result of the `retrieveNews` method execution returns the `Observable`. Nevertheless, as we might remember, `RxReactiveStreams` offers us a list of useful methods, allowing us to easily convert the RxJava 1.x `Observable` to the `Publisher`.

Summary

As we have learned from the previous example, Reactive Streams drastically increases the composability of reactive libraries. We have also learned that the most useful way to verify the compatibility of the `Publisher` is just to apply Technology Compatibility Test Kits, which are provided with the Reactive Streams specification.

At the same time, the specification brings a *pull-push* communication model for Reactive Streams. This addition solves the backpressure controlling problem and at the same time reinforces communication flexibility by offering a choice of which model to use.

After the Reactive Streams Specification was included in JDK9, its significance skyrocketed. However, as we learned, this improvement brought some overheads in the need for type conversion between two variants of the specification.

As we understood from the previous sections, a Reactive Streams specification allows several means of communication between operators. This flexibility allows different ways of placing asynchronous boundaries. However, it puts an important responsibility on the reactive libraries' vendors since the business needs must justify such decisions. Also, a provided solution should be flexible enough to be configurable for it from the API side.

By changing the behavior of the reactive streams, the specification also changed the reactive landscape. The leaders of open source industries such as Netflix, Redhead, Lightbend, Pivotal, and others have implemented the specification within their reactive libraries. However, for Spring Framework users, the most significant change that has happened in the reactive world is the introduction of the new reactive library called **Project Reactor**.

Project Reactor plays an important role because it is the building block for a new reactive Spring ecosystem. Consequently, before diving deeper into the internal implementation of the new reactive Spring, we should explore Project Reactor and get acquainted with the importance of its role. In the next chapter, we are going to learn the conceptual constituents of Project Reactor and its application by looking at examples.

4
Project Reactor - the Foundation for Reactive Apps

In the previous chapter, we looked at an overview of the Reactive Streams specification and the way it augments reactive libraries by offering common interfaces and a new pull-push model for data exchange.

In this chapter, we are going to dive into Project Reactor, the most famous library in the reactive landscape, which has already become a vital part of the Spring Framework ecosystem. We will explore the most essential, frequently used Project Reactor APIs. The library is so versatile and feature-rich that it deserves a separate book of its own, it being impossible to cover its entire API in one chapter. We will look under the hood of the Reactor library and use its power to build a reactive application.

In this chapter, we are going to cover the following topics:

- The history and motivation behind Project Reactor
- Project Reactor's terminology and API
- Advanced features of Project Reactor
- The most crucial implementation details of Project Reactor
- A comparison of the most frequently used reactive types
- A business case implemented with the Reactor library

A brief history of Project Reactor

As we saw in the previous chapter, the Reactive Streams specification makes reactive libraries compatible with each other and has also resolved the backpressure problem by introducing the pull-push data exchange model. Despite the significant improvements introduced by the Reactive Streams specification, it still only defines APIs and rules, and does not offer a library for everyday use. This chapter covers one of the most popular implementations of the Reactive Streams specification, Project Reactor (or Reactor for short). However, the Reactor library has evolved a lot since its early versions and has now become the most state-of-the-art reactive library. Let's look at its history to see how the Reactive Streams specification has shaped the API and implementation details of the library.

Project Reactor version 1.x

When working on the Reactive Streams specification, developers from the Spring Framework team needed a high-throughput data processing framework, especially for the Spring XD project, the goal of which was to simplify the development of big data applications. To fulfill that need, the Spring team initiated a new project. From the beginning, it was designed with support for asynchronous, non-blocking processing. The team called it **Project Reactor**. Essentially, Reactor version 1.x incorporated best practices for message processing, such as the Reactor Pattern, and functional and reactive programming styles.

 The **Reactor Pattern** is a behavioral pattern that helps with asynchronous event handling and synchronous processing. This means that all events are enqueued and the actual processing of an event happens later by a separate thread. An event is dispatched to all interested parties (event handlers) and processed synchronously. To learn more about the Reactor Pattern, please visit the following link: http://www.dre.vanderbilt.edu/~schmidt/PDF/reactor-siemens.pdf.

By embracing these techniques, Project Reactor version 1.x gives us the ability to write concise code such as the following:

```
Environment env = new Environment();                          // (1)
Reactor reactor = Reactors.reactor()                          // (2)
                       .env(env)                              //
                       .dispatcher(Environment.RING_BUFFER)   // (2.1)
                       .get();                                //

reactor.on($("channel"),                                      // (3)
           event -> System.out.println(event.getData()));     //

Executors.newSingleThreadScheduledExecutor()                  // (4)
        .scheduleAtFixedRate(                                  //
            () -> reactor.notify("channel", Event.wrap("test")), //
            0, 100, TimeUnit.MILLISECONDS                     //
        );                                                    //
```

In the preceding code, there are a couple of conceptual points:

1. Here, we create an Environment instance. The Environment instance is an execution context, which is responsible for creating a particular Dispatcher. This may potentially provide different kinds of dispatchers, ranging from an interprocess dispatcher to distributed ones.
2. An instance of Reactor is created, which is a direct implementation of the Reactor Pattern. In the preceding example code, we use the Reactors class, which is a fluent builder for concrete Reactor instances. At point (2.1), we use the predefined implementation of Dispatcher based on the RingBuffer structure. To learn more about the internals and overall design of RingBuffer-based Dispatcher, please visit the following link: https://martinfowler.com/articles/lmax.html.
3. Here, the declaration of a channel Selector and an Event consumer occurs. At this point, we register an event handler (in this case, a lambda that prints all received events to System.out). The filtering of events happens using the string selector, which indicates the name of the event channel. Selectors.$ provides a broader selection of criteria, so a final expression for event selection may be more complicated.
4. Here, we configure the producer of the Event in the form of a scheduled task. At that point, we use the possibilities of Java's ScheduledExecutorService to schedule periodic tasks that send Event to a specific channel in the previously instantiated Reactor instance.

Under the hood, events are processed by `Dispatcher` and then sent to destination points. Depending on the `Dispatcher` implementation, an event may be processed synchronously or asynchronously. This provides a functional decomposition and generally works in a similar way to the Spring Framework event processing approach. Furthermore, Reactor 1.x provides a bunch of helpful wrappers that allow us to compose events' processing with a clear flow:

```
...                                                            // (1)
Stream<String> stream = Streams.on(reactor, $("channel"));     // (2)
stream.map(s -> "Hello world " + s)                            // (3)
        .distinct()                                            //
        .filter((Predicate<String>) s -> s.length() > 2)       //
        .consume(System.out::println);                         // (3.1)

Deferred<String, Stream<String>> input = Streams.defer(env);   // (4)

Stream<String> compose = input.compose()                       // (5)
compose.map(m -> m + " Hello World")                           // (6)
        .filter(m -> m.contains("1"))                          //
        .map(Event::wrap)                                      //
        .consume(reactor.prepare("channel"));                  // (6.1)

for (int i = 0; i < 1000; i++) {                               // (7)
    input.accept(UUID.randomUUID().toString());               //
}                                                              //
```

Let's break down the preceding code:

1. At this point we have an `Environment` and a `Reactor` creation, as in the previous example.
2. Here we have `Stream` creation. `Stream` allows the building of functional transformation chains. By applying the `Streams.on` method to `Reactor` with a specified `Selector`, we receive a `Stream` object attached to the specified channel in the given `Reactor` instance.
3. Here, the processing flow is created. We apply a few intermediate operations, such as `map`, `filter`, and `consume`. The last of these is a terminal operator (`3.1`).
4. Here, a `Deferred` `Stream` is created. The `Deferred` class is a special wrapper that makes it possible to provide manual events to the `Stream`. In our case, the `Stream.defer` method creates an additional instance of the `Reactor` class.
5. At this point we have a `Stream` instance creation. Here, we retrieve `Stream` from the `Deferred` instance by using the `compose` method on it.

6. At this point we have a reactive processing flow creation. This part of the pipeline composition is similar to what we have at point `(3)`. At point `(6.1)`, we use the `Reactor` API shortcut for the code, as follows—e ->
`reactor.notify("channel", e)`.

7. Here, we supply a random element to the `Deferred` instance.

In the preceding example, we subscribe to the channel and then process all incoming events step by step. In contrast, in that example, we use the reactive programming technique to build a declarative processing flow. Here, we provide two separate processing stages. Furthermore, the code looks like the well-known RxJava API, making it more familiar to RxJava users. At some point, Reactor 1.x had good integration with the Spring Framework. Along with the message processing library, Reactor 1.x provides a bunch of add-ons, such as the add-on for Netty.

To summarize, at that time, Reactor 1.x was good enough at processing events at high speed. With excellent integration with the Spring Framework and composition with Netty, it made it possible to develop high-performance systems that provide asynchronous and non-blocking message processing.

However, Reactor 1.x also has its disadvantages. First of all, the library has no backpressure control. Unfortunately, the event-driven implementation of Reactor 1.x did not offer a way to control backpressure other than blocking the producer thread or skipping events. Furthermore, error handling was quite complicated. Reactor 1.x provides several ways of handling errors and failures. Even though Reactor 1.x was rough around the edges, it was used by the popular Grails web framework. Of course, this significantly influenced the next iteration of the reactive library.

Project Reactor version 2.x

Not long after the first official release of Reactor 1.x, Stephane Maldini was invited to the Reactive Streams Special Interest Group as an expert in high-performance message processing systems and a Project Reactor co-lead. This group, as we may guess, worked on the Reactive Streams specification. After gaining a better understanding of the nature of Reactive Streams and introducing new knowledge to the Rector team, Stephane Maldini and Jon Brisbin announced *Reactor 2.x* in early 2015. Citing Stephane Maldini: *"Reactor 2 was the first shot at Reactive Streams"*.

The most significant change in Reactor design was in extracting the EventBus and Stream features into separate modules. Also, a deep redesign enabled the new Reactor Streams library to become fully compliant with the Reactive Streams specification. The Reactor team dramatically improved the API of Reactor. For example, the new Reactor API had better integration with the Java Collections API.

With the second version, Reactor's Streams API became much more similar to the RxJava API. Along with simple additions to create and consume streams, there were a bunch of useful additions for backpressure management, thread dispatching, and resilience support, as follows:

```
stream
    .retry()                                             // (1)
    .onOverflowBuffer()                                  // (2)
    .onOverflowDrop()                                    //
    .dispatchOn(new RingBufferDispatcher("test"))        // (3)
```

The previous example shows three simple techniques:

1. With the one-line operator `retry`, we introduce resilience into the flow and, in the event of errors, upstream operations should run again.
2. With the `onOverflowBuffer` and `onOverflowDrop` methods, we add backpressure control for when a publisher supports only the push model (and cannot be controlled by consumer demand).
3. At the same time, by applying the `dispatchOn` operator, we dedicated a new Dispatcher to work on that reactive stream. This preserves the ability to process messages asynchronously.

The Reactor EventBus was also improved. First of all, the `Reactor` object, which is responsible for sending messages, was renamed `EventBus`. The module was also redesigned to support the Reactive Streams specification.

Around that time, Stephane Maldini met David Karnok, who was actively working on his dissertation *High resolution and transparent production informatics*. The dissertation reports in-depth research in the field of Reactive Streams, Reactive Programming, and RxJava. In close collaboration, Maldini and Karnok condensed their ideas and experience of RxJava and Project Reactor into a library called `reactive-stream-commons`. A bit later, that library became the foundation of Reactor 2.5, and finally, Reactor 3.x.

The source of the `reactive-streams-commons` library is available for exploration at the following GitHub project page: `https://github.com/reactor/reactive-streams-commons`.

After a year of hard work, Reactor 3.0 was released. At the same time, a pretty *identical* RxJava 2.0 surfaced. The latter has more similarities with Reactor 3.x than with its predecessor, RxJava 1.x. The most notable difference between those libraries is the fact that RxJava targets **Java 6** (including Android support) while Reactor 3 chose **Java 8** as a baseline. Meanwhile, Reactor 3.x shaped a *reactive metamorphosis* of Spring Framework 5. This is why Project Reactor is used extensively in the remaining chapters of this book. Now, we are going to learn about the API of Project Reactor 3.x and how to use it effectively.

Project Reactor essentials

From the beginning, the Reactor library was designed with the aim of omitting **callback hell** and **deeply nested code** when building asynchronous pipelines. We described these phenomena and complications caused by them in `Chapter 1`, *Why Reactive Spring?* In the quest for linear code, the library's authors formulated an analogy using an assembly line: *"You can think of data processed by a reactive application as moving through an assembly line. Reactor is both the conveyor belt and the workstations."*

The primary goal of the library is to improve the **readability** of the code and introduce **composability** to workflows defined with the Reactor library. The Public API is designed to be high-level but very versatile, but at the same time it does not sacrifice performance. The API provides a rich set of operators (the *"workstations"* in the assembly analogy), which provide the biggest added value over the "naked" Reactive Streams specification.

The Reactor API encourages operator chaining, which enables us to build complicated, potentially reusable execution graphs. It is important to note that such an execution graph only defines execution flow, but nothing happens until the subscriber actually creates a subscription, so only **a subscription triggers actual data flow**.

The library is designed for **efficient data manipulation**, both local and retrieved, as a result of asynchronous requests with potentially faulty IO. This is why error handling operators in Project Reactor are very versatile and, as we are going to see later, encourage writing **resilient** code.

As we already know, **backpressure** is an essential property, which the Reactive Streams specification encourages reactive libraries to have, and because Reactor implements the specification, backpressure is a central theme in Reactor itself. So, when talking about Reactive Streams built with Reactor, data travels downstream, from publisher to subscriber. At the same time, subscription and demand control signals are propagated upstream, from a subscriber to a publisher:

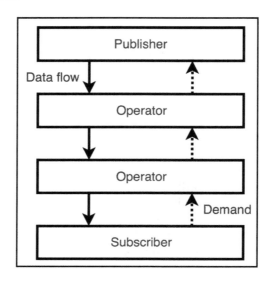

Diagram 4.1 Data flow and subscription/demand signal propagation through a reactive stream

The library supports all common modes of backpressure propagation, as follows:

- **push only**: When a subscriber asks for an effectively infinite number of elements with `subscription.request(Long.MAX_VALUE)`
- **pull only**: When a subscriber requests the next element only after receiving the previous one: `subscription.request(1)`
- **pull-push** (sometimes called **mixed**): When a subscriber has real-time control over the demand and the publisher may adapt to the announced speed of data consumption.

Also, when adapting an old API that doesn't support the pull-push model of operation, Reactor offers lots of *old-school* backpressure mechanisms, namely—buffering, windowing, message dropping, initiating exceptions, and so on. All of these techniques will be covered later in the chapter. In some cases, the aforementioned strategies allow the prefetching of data, even before the actual demand appears, improving the responsiveness of the system. Also, the Reactor API offers enough instruments to smooth out short peaks of user activity and prevent the system from overloading.

Project Reactor is designed to be concurrency agnostic, so it does not enforce any concurrency models. At the same time, it provides a useful set of schedulers to manage execution threads in almost any fashion, and if none of the proposed schedulers fits the requirements, the developer can create their own scheduler with complete low-level control. Thread management in the Reactor library is also covered later in the chapter.

Now, after a brief overview of the Reactor library, let's add it to the project and start investigating its reach API.

Adding Reactor to the project

Here, we assume that the reader is already familiar with the Reactive Streams specification. If not, it is briefly described in the previous chapter. The Reactive Streams specification is essential in the current context, because Project Reactor is built on top of it and `org.reactivestreams:reactive-streams` is the only mandatory dependency of Project Reactor.

Adding Project Reactor as a dependency to our application is as simple as adding the following dependency to the `build.gradle` file:

```
compile("io.projectreactor:reactor-core:3.2.0.RELEASE")
```

At the time of writing, the latest version of the library is `3.2.0.RELEASE`. This version is also used in Spring Framework 5.1.

 The procedure for adding the Project Reactor library to a Maven project is described in the following article: `https://projectreactor.io/docs/core/3.2.0.RELEASE/reference/#_maven_installation`.

It is also often worth adding the following dependency, as this provides the necessary toolset for testing reactive code, which, obviously, we also need to cover with unit tests:

```
testCompile("io.projectreactor:reactor-test:3.2.0.RELEASE")
```

In this chapter, we are going to use some simple testing techniques for Reactive Streams. Additionally, `Chapter 9`, *Testing the Reactive Application*, covers topics regarding reactive code testing in more detail.

Now that we have Reactor in our application classpath, we are ready to experiment with Reactor's reactive types and operators.

Reactive types – Flux and Mono

As we already know, the Reactive Streams specification defines only four interfaces: `Publisher<T>`, `Subscriber<T>`, `Subscription`, and `Processor<T, R>`. More or less, we are going to follow this list and look at the interface implementations provided by the library.

First of all, Project Reactor provides two implementations of the `Publisher<T>` interface: `Flux<T>` and `Mono<T>`. Such an approach adds additional contextual meaning to reactive types. Here, to investigate the behavior of reactive types (`Flux` and `Mono`), we are going to use some reactive operators without a detailed explanation of how these operators work. Operators are covered later in this chapter.

Flux

Let's describe how data flows through the Flux class with the following marble diagram:

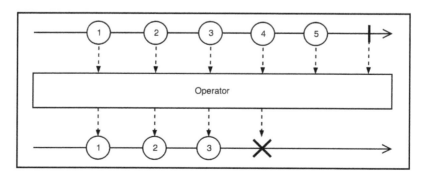

Diagram 4.2 An example of the Flux stream transformed into another Flux stream

`Flux` defines a *usual* reactive stream that can produce **zero, one, or many elements**; even potentially an infinite amount of elements. It has the following formula:

```
onNext x 0..N [onError | onComplete]
```

It is not very common to work with infinite data containers in the imperative world, but it is pretty common with functional programming. The following code may produce a simple *endless* Reactive Stream:

```
Flux.range(1, 5).repeat()
```

This stream repeatedly produces numbers from *1* to *5* (the sequence would look like—*1, 2, 3, 4, 5, 1, 2,...*). This is not a problem and it will not blow up the memory as each element can be transformed and consumed without the need to finish creating the whole stream. Furthermore, the subscriber can cancel the subscription at any time and effectively transform an *endless* stream into a *finite* stream.

Beware: an attempt to collect all elements emitted by an *endless* stream may cause an `OutOfMemoryException`. It is not recommended to do so in production applications, but the simplest way to reproduce such behavior may be with the following code:

```
Flux.range(1, 100)                                        // (1)
    .repeat()                                             // (2)
    .collectList()                                        // (3)
    .block();                                             // (4)
```

In the preceding code, we do the following:

1. The `range` operator creates a sequence of integers starting from *1* up to *100* (inclusive).
2. The `repeat` operator subscribes to the source reactive stream again and again after the source stream finishes. So, the `repeat` operator subscribes to the results of the stream operator, receives elements 1 to 100 and the `onComplete` signal, and then subscribes again, receives elements *1* to *100*, and so on, without stopping.

3. With the `collectList` operator, we are trying to gather all produced elements into a single list. Of course, because the `repeat` operator generates an *endless* stream, elements arrive and increase the size of the list so it consumes all the memory and causes the application to fail with the following error—`java.lang.OutOfMemoryError: Java heap space`. Our application has just run out of free heap memory.

4. The `block` operator triggers an actual subscription and blocks the running thread until the final result arrives, which, in the current case, cannot happen as the reactive stream is endless.

Mono

Now, let's look at how the `Mono` type is different from the `Flux` type:

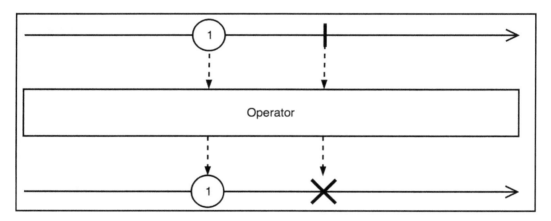

Diagram 4.3 An example of the Mono stream transformed into another Mono stream

In contrast with `Flux`, the `Mono` type defines a stream that can produce **at most one element** and can be described by the following formula:

```
onNext x 0..1 [onError | onComplete]
```

The distinction between `Flux` and `Mono` allows us to not only introduce additional meaning to the method signatures, but also enables more efficient internal implementation of `Mono` due to skipping redundant buffers and costly synchronizations.

`Mono<T>` may be useful in cases when an application API returns one element at most. Consequently, it can easily replace `CompletableFuture<T>`, giving a pretty similar semantic. Of course, these two types have some small semantic differences—`CompletableFuture`, unlike `Mono`, cannot complete normally without emitting a value. Also, `CompletableFuture` starts processing immediately, while `Mono` does nothing until a subscriber appears. The benefit of the `Mono` type lies in providing plenty of reactive operators and the ability to be flawlessly incorporated into a bigger reactive workflow.

Also, `Mono` can be used when it is required to notify a client about a finished action. In such cases, we may return the `Mono<Void>` type and signal `onComplete()` when processing is done or `onError()` in the event of failure. In such a scenario, we don't return any data but signal a notification, which in turn may be used as a trigger for further computation.

`Mono` and `Flux` are not detached types and can easily be "transformed" into each other. For example, `Flux<T>.collectList()` returns `Mono<List<T>>` and `Mono<T>.flux()` returns `Flux<T>`. In addition, the library is smart enough to optimize some transformations that do not change the semantic. For example, let's consider the following transformation (`Mono` -> `Flux` -> `Mono`):

```
Mono.from(Flux.from(mono))
```

When calling the preceding code, it returns the original `mono` instance, as this is conceptually a no-ops conversion.

Reactive types of RxJava 2

Even though the RxJava 2.x library and Project Reactor have the same basis, RxJava 2 has a different set of reactive publishers. As these two libraries implement the same ideas, it is worth describing how RxJava 2 differs, at least regarding reactive types. All other aspects, including reactive operators, thread management, and error handling, are pretty similar. So, being more or less familiar with one of the libraries means being familiar with both of them.

As described in Chapter 2, *Reactive Programming in Spring - Basic Concepts*, RxJava 1.x originally had only one reactive type: Observable. Later, the Single and Completable types were added. In version 2, the library has the following reactive types—Observable, Flowable, Single, Maybe, and Completable. Let's briefly describe the difference between these and compare them to the Flux/Mono tandem.

Observable

RxJava 2's Observable type provides almost the same semantics as in RxJava 1.x, however, it no longer accepts null values. Also, Observable does not support backpressure and does not implement the Publisher interface. So, it is not directly compatible with the Reactive Streams specification. Consequently, be careful when using it for streams with many elements (more than a couple of thousand). On the other hand, the Observable type has less overhead than the Flowable type. It has the toFlowable method that transforms the stream to Flowable by applying the backpressure strategy of the user's choice.

Flowable

The Flowable type is a direct counterpart of Reactor's Flux type. It implements Reactive Streams' Publisher. Consequently, it may be easily used in reactive workflows implemented with Project Reactor, as a well-designed API would consume arguments of the Publisher type instead of a more library-specific Flux.

Single

The Single type represents streams that produce precisely one element. It does not inherit the Publisher interface. It also has the toFlowable method, which, in this case, does not require a backpressure strategy. Single better represents the semantics of CompletableFuture than Reactor's Mono type. However, it still does not start processing before subscription happens.

Maybe

To achieve the same semantics as Reactor's Mono type, RxJava 2.x provides the Maybe type. However, it is not Reactive Streams compliant, as Maybe does not implement the Publisher interface. It has the toFlowable method for that purpose.

Completable

Also, RxJava 2.x has the `Completable` type that may only trigger the `onError` or `onComplete` signals, but cannot produce the `onNext` signal. It does not implement the `Publisher` interface either and has the `toFlowable` method. Semantically, it corresponds to the `Mono<Void>` type, which cannot generate `onNext` signals either.

To summarize, RxJava 2 has more granular semantic distinctions between reactive types. Only the `Flowable` type is a Reactive Streams complaint. `Observable` does the same job but without backpressure support. The `Maybe<T>` type corresponds to Reactor's `Mono<T>`, and RxJava's `Completable` corresponds to Reactor's `Mono<Void>`. The semantics of the `Single` type cannot be directly represented in terms of Project Reactor as none of its types have guarantees about a minimal number of produced events. To integrate with other Reactive Streams complaint code, the RxJava type should be converted to the `Flowable` type.

Creating Flux and Mono sequences

`Flux` and `Mono` provide many factory methods to create Reactive Streams based on data that is already available. For example, we may create `Flux` with object references or from a collection, or we may even create our own lazy range of numbers:

```
Flux<String>  stream1 = Flux.just("Hello", "world");
Flux<Integer> stream2 = Flux.fromArray(new Integer[]{1, 2, 3});
Flux<Integer> stream3 = Flux.fromIterable(Arrays.asList(9, 8, 7));
```

It is easy to generate a stream of integers with the `range` method, where `2010` is a starting point, and `9` is the number of elements in the sequence:

```
Flux<Integer> stream4 = Flux.range(2010, 9);
```

This is a handy way to generate a stream of recent years, so the preceding code generates the following stream of integers:

```
2010, 2011, 2012, 2013, 2014, 2015, 2016, 2017, 2018
```

`Mono` provides similar factory methods, but mainly targets one element. It is also often used in conjunction with nullable and `Optional` types:

```
Mono<String> stream5 = Mono.just("One");
Mono<String> stream6 = Mono.justOrEmpty(null);
Mono<String> stream7 = Mono.justOrEmpty(Optional.empty());
```

Mono may be very useful for wrapping asynchronous operations such as HTTP requests or DB queries. For this purpose, Mono provides these methods—fromCallable(Callable), fromRunnable(Runnable), fromSupplier(Supplier), fromFuture(CompletableFuture), fromCompletionStage(CompletionStage), and others. We can wrap long HTTP requests in Mono with the following line of code:

```
Mono<String> stream8 = Mono.fromCallable(() -> httpRequest());
```

Alternatively, we can rewrite the preceding code to be even shorter with the Java 8 method reference syntax:

```
Mono<String> stream8 = Mono.fromCallable(this::httpRequest);
```

Note that the preceding code not only makes an HTTP request asynchronously (provided with an appropriate Scheduler) but also handles errors that may be propagated as the onError signal.

Both Flux and Mono allow the adaptation of any other Publisher instance with the from(Publisher<T> p) factory method.

Both reactive types have methods for creating handy and commonly used empty streams, as well as streams containing only an error:

```
Flux<String> empty = Flux.empty();
Flux<String> never = Flux.never();
Mono<String> error = Mono.error(new RuntimeException("Unknown id"));
```

Both Flux and Mono have factory methods called empty(), which generate empty instances of Flux or Mono respectively. Similarly, the never() method creates a stream that never signals completion, data, or error.

The error(Throwable) factory method creates a sequence that always propagates an error through the onError(...) method of each subscriber when it subscribes. The error is created during the Flux or Mono declaration and, consequently, each subscriber receives the same Throwable instance.

The defer factory method creates a sequence that decides its behavior at the moment of subscription and, consequently, may generate different data for different subscribers:

```
Mono<User> requestUserData(String sessionId) {
    return Mono.defer(() ->
        isValidSession(sessionId)
            ? Mono.fromCallable(() -> requestUser(sessionId))
            : Mono.error(new RuntimeException("Invalid user session")));
}
```

This code defers `sessionId` validation until the actual subscription happens. In contrast, the following code carries out validation when the `requestUserData(...)` method is called, which may be way before the actual subscription (also, no subscription may happen at all):

```
Mono requestUserData(String sessionId) {
    return isValidSession(sessionId)
        ? Mono.fromCallable(() -> requestUser(sessionId))
        : Mono.error(new RuntimeException("Invalid user session"));
}
```

The first example validates the session each time someone subscribes to the returned `Mono<User>`. The second example carries out session validation, but only when the `requestUserData` method is called. However, no validation happens when a subscription does.

Summing this up, Project Reactor allows the creation of `Flux` and `Mono` sequences just by enumerating elements with the `just` method. We may easily wrap `Optional` into `Mono` with `justOrEmpty`, or wrap `Supplier` into `Mono` with the `fromSupplier` method. We may map `Future` with the `fromFuture` method or `Runnable` with the `fromRunnable` factory method. Also, we may translate an array or an `Iterable` collection to the `Flux` stream with the `fromArray` or `fromIterable` methods. As well as this, Project Reactor allows the creation of more complicated reactive sequences, which we are going to cover later in the chapter. Now, let's learn how to consume elements produced by a reactive stream.

Subscribing to Reactive Streams

As we may guess, `Flux` and `Mono` provide lambda-based overloads of the `subscribe()` method, which simplifies the subscription routine a lot:

```
subscribe();                                            // (1)

subscribe(Consumer<T> dataConsumer);                    // (2)

subscribe(Consumer<T> dataConsumer,                     // (3)
        Consumer<Throwable> errorConsumer);

subscribe(Consumer<T> dataConsumer,                     // (4)
        Consumer<Throwable> errorConsumer,
        Runnable completeConsumer);
```

```
subscribe(Consumer<T> dataConsumer,                          // (5)
          Consumer<Throwable> errorConsumer,
          Runnable completeConsumer,
          Consumer<Subscription> subscriptionConsumer);

subscribe(Subscriber<T> subscriber);                         // (6)
```

Let's explore the options we have for creating subscribers. First of all, all overrides of the subscribe method return an instance of the `Disposable` interface. This can be used to cancel the underlying Subscription. In cases `(1)` to `(4)`, the subscription requests the unbounded demand (`Long.MAX_VALUE`). Now, let's look at the differences:

1. This is the simplest way of subscribing to a stream, as this method ignores all signals. Usually, other variants should be preferred. However, sometimes it may be useful to trigger stream processing that has side effects.
2. The `dataConsumer` is invoked on each value (`onNext` signal). It does not handle `onError` and `onComplete` signals.
3. The same as in option `(2)`; however, this allows handling of the `onError` signal. The `onComplete` signal is ignored.
4. The same as in option `(3)`; however, this also allows handling of the `onComplete` signal.
5. Allows all elements in the Reactive Stream to be consumed, including handle errors and a completion signal. Importantly, this override allows the subscription to be controlled by requesting an adequate amount of data of course, we may still request `Long.MAX_VALUE`).
6. The most generic way of subscribing to the sequence. Here, we may provide our `Subscriber` implementation with the desired behavior. Even though this option is very versatile, it is rarely required.

Let's create a simple Reactive Stream and subscribe to it:

```
Flux.just("A", "B", "C")
   .subscribe(
      data -> log.info("onNext: {}", data),
      err -> { /* ignored */ },
      () -> log.info("onComplete"));
```

The preceding code produces the following console output:

```
onNext: A
onNext: B
onNext: C
onComplete
```

It is worth noting once again that simple subscription request unbound demand options (`Long.MAX_VALUE`) may sometimes force the producer to do a significant amount of work to fulfill the demand. So, if the producer is more suited to handling a bounded demand, it is recommended to control the demand with the subscription object or by applying request limiting operators, which are covered later in the chapter.

Let's subscribe to a Reactive Stream with a manual subscription control:

```
Flux.range(1, 100)                                          // (1)
    .subscribe(                                             // (2)
        data -> log.info("onNext: {}", data),
        err -> { /* ignore */ },
        () -> log.info("onComplete"),
        subscription -> {                                   // (3)
            subscription.request(4);                        // (3.1)
            subscription.cancel();                          // (3.2)
        }
    );
```

The preceding code does the following:

1. At first, we generate *100* values with the `range` operator.
2. We subscribe to the stream in the same way as in the previous example.
3. However, now we control the subscription. At first, we request 4 items (`3.1`) and then immediately cancel the subscription (`3.2`), so other elements should not be generated at all.

When running the preceding code, we receive the following output:

```
onNext: 1
onNext: 2
onNext: 3
onNext: 4
```

Note that, we do not receive an `onComplete` signal because the subscriber canceled the subscription before the stream finished. It is also important to remember that a Reactive Stream may be finished by a producer (with the `onError` or `onComplete` signals) or canceled by a subscriber via a `Subscription` instance. Also, the Disposable instance may also be used for the purposes of cancellation. Usually, it is used not by a subscriber, but by the code one level of abstraction above. For example, let's cancel stream processing by calling `Disposable`:

```
Disposable disposable = Flux.interval(Duration.ofMillis(50))        // (1)
    .subscribe(                                                     // (2)
        data -> log.info("onNext: {}", data)
    );
Thread.sleep(200);                                                  // (3)
disposable.dispose();                                              // (4)
```

The preceding code does the following:

1. The `interval` factory method allows the generation of events with a defined period (every 50 milliseconds). The generated stream is endless.
2. We subscribe by providing only the handler for `onNext` signals.
3. We wait for some time to receive a couple of events (200/50 should allow passing about 4 events).
4. Calls the `dispose` method which internally cancels the subscription.

Implementing custom subscribers

If default `subscribe(...)` methods do not provide the required versatility, we may implement our own `Subscriber`. We can always directly implement the `Subscriber` interface from the Reactive Streams specification and subscribe it to the stream, as follows:

```
Subscriber<String> subscriber = new Subscriber<String>() {
    volatile Subscription subscription;                            // (1)

    public void onSubscribe(Subscription s) {                      // (2)
        subscription = s;                                          // (2.1)
        log.info("initial request for 1 element");                //
        subscription.request(1);                                  // (2.2)
    }

    public void onNext(String s) {                                 // (3)
        log.info("onNext: {}", s);                                //
        log.info("requesting 1 more element");                    //
```

```
        subscription.request(1);                            // (3.1)
    }

    public void onComplete() {
        log.info("onComplete");
    }

    public void onError(Throwable t) {
        log.warn("onError: {}", t.getMessage());
    }
};

Flux<String> stream = Flux.just("Hello", "world", "!");      // (4)
stream.subscribe(subscriber);                                // (5)
```

In our custom `Subscriber` implementation, we do the following:

1. Our subscriber has to hold a reference to a `Subscription` that binds a `Publisher` and our `Subscriber`. As subscription and data processing may happen in different threads, we use the volatile keyword to make sure that all threads will have the correct reference to the `Subscription` instance.
2. When a subscription arrives, our `Subscriber` is informed with the `onSubscribe` callback. Here, we save the subscription `(2.1)` and request the initial demand `(2.2)`. Without that request, a TCK complaint provider will not be allowed to send data and elements processing will not start at all.
3. In the `onNext` callback, we log the received data and request the next element. In this case, we use a straightforward pull model (`subscription.request(1)`) for backpressure management.
4. Here, we generate a simple stream with the `just` factory method.
5. Here, we subscribe our custom subscriber to the Reactive Stream defined in step `(4)`.

The preceding code should produce the following console output:

```
initial request for 1 element
onNext: Hello
requesting 1 more element
onNext: world
requesting 1 more element
onNext: !
requesting 1 more element
onComplete
```

However, the described approach for defining subscription is not right. It breaks the *linear* code flow and is also prone to errors. The hardest part is that we are required to manage backpressure on our own and correctly implement all TCK requirements for a subscriber. Moreover, in the preceding example, we broke a couple of TCK requirements regarding subscription validation and cancelation.

Instead, it is recommended to extend the `BaseSubscriber` class provided by Project Reactor. In this case, our subscriber may look as follows:

```
class MySubscriber<T> extends BaseSubscriber<T> {
    public void hookOnSubscribe(Subscription subscription) {
        log.info("initial request for 1 element");
        request(1);
    }

    public void hookOnNext(T value) {
        log.info("onNext: {}", value);
        log.info("requesting 1 more element");
        request(1);
    }
}
```

Along with the `hookOnSubscribe(Subscription)` and `hookOnNext(T)` methods, we may override
methods such as `hookOnError(Throwable)`, `hookOnCancel()`, `hookOnComplete()`, and a handful of others. The `BaseSubscriber` class provides methods for granular control over the Reactive Stream demands with these methods—`request(long)` and `requestUnbounded()`. Also, with the `BaseSubscriber` class, it is much easier to implement TCK compliant subscribers. Such an approach may be desired when a subscriber itself holds precious resources with attentive life cycle management. For example, a subscriber may wrap a file handler or WebSocket connection to a third-party service.

Transforming reactive sequences with operators

When working with reactive sequences, besides creating and consuming a stream, it is vital to have the ability to transform and manipulate them flawlessly. Only then does reactive programming become a useful technique. Project Reactor provides instruments (methods and factory methods) for almost any required reactive transformation, and in general, we may categorize the features of the libraries as follows:

- Transforming existing sequences
- Methods for peeking at the sequences' processing
- Splitting and joining `Flux` sequences
- Working with time
- Returning data synchronously

Here, we cannot describe all of Reactor's operators and factory methods because it would take too many pages and it is almost impossible to remember all of them. It is also unnecessary given that Project Reactor provides excellent documentation, including a guide to selecting appropriate operators: `http://projectreactor.io/docs/core/release/reference/#which-operator`. Still, in this section, we are going to walk through the most used operators with some code samples.

Note that most operators have many overrides with different options to augment basic behavior. Also, with each version, Project Reactor receives more and more useful operators. So, please refer to Reactor's documentation for the most recent updates regarding operators.

Mapping elements of reactive sequences

The most natural way of transforming a sequence is by mapping every element to some new value. Flux and Mono give the map operator, which behaves similarly to the map operator from the Java Stream API. The function with a map (Function<T, R>) signature allows the processing of elements one by one. Of course, as it changes the type of element from T to R, the whole sequence changes its type, so after the map operator Flux<T> becomes Flux<R>, Mono<T> becomes Mono<R>. The marble diagram for Flux.map() is as follows:

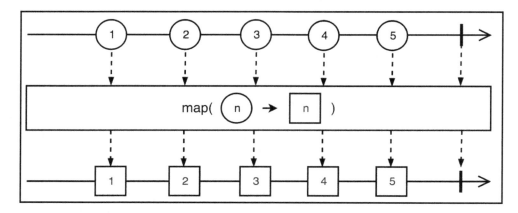

Diagram 4.4 Operator: map

Of course, the map operator of the Mono class behaves similarly. The cast (Class c) operator casts elements of a stream to the target class. The easiest way of implementing the cast (Class c) operator would be through the usage of the map() operator. We can look into the source of the Flux class and find the following code, which proves our assumption:

```
public final <E> Flux<E> cast(Class<E> clazz) {
    return map(clazz::cast);
}
```

The `index` operator allows the enumeration of elements in the sequence. The method has the following signature—`Flux<Tuple2<Long, T>> index()`. So, now we have to work with the `Tuple2` class. This represents the Tuple data structure, which is not present in the standard Java library. The library provides `Tuple2` to `Tuple8` classes, which are often used by the library operators. The `timestamp` operator behaves similarly to the `index` operator, but adds the current timestamp instead of an index. So, the following code should both enumerate elements and attach timestamps to every element in the sequence:

```
Flux.range(2018, 5)                                          // (1)
    .timestamp()                                             // (2)
    .index()                                                 // (3)
    .subscribe(e -> log.info("index: {}, ts: {}, value: {}", // (4)
        e.getT1(),                                           // (4.1)
        Instant.ofEpochMilli(e.getT2().getT1()),             // (4.2)
        e.getT2().getT2()));                                 // (4.3)
```

The preceding code does the following:

1. Here, we generate some data with the `range` operator (2018 to 2022). This operator returns the sequence of type `Flux<Integer>`.
2. With the `timestamp` operator, we attach the current timestamp. Now, the sequence has the `Flux<Tuple2<Long, Integer>>` type.
3. Here, we apply enumeration with the index operator. Now, the sequence has the `Flux<Tuple2<Long, Tuple2<Long, Integer>>>` type.
4. Here, we subscribe to the sequence and log elements. The `e.getT1()` call returns an index `(4.1)`, and the `e.getT2().getT1()` call returns a timestamp, which we output in a human-readable way with the `Instant` class `(4.2)`, while the `e.getT2().getT2()` call returns an actual value `(4.3)`.

After running the previous code snippet, we should receive the following output:

```
index: 0, ts: 2018-09-24T03:00:52.041Z, value: 2018
index: 1, ts: 2018-09-24T03:00:52.061Z, value: 2019
index: 2, ts: 2018-09-24T03:00:52.061Z, value: 2020
index: 3, ts: 2018-09-24T03:00:52.061Z, value: 2021
index: 4, ts: 2018-09-24T03:00:52.062Z, value: 2022
```

Filtering reactive sequences

Of course, Project Reactor contains all kinds of operators for filtering elements, such as:

- The `filter` operator passes only elements that satisfy the condition.
- The `ignoreElements` operator returns `Mono<T>` and filters out all elements. The resulting sequence ends only after the original ends.
- The library allows for the limiting of taken elements with the `take(n)` method, which ignores all elements except the first n.
- `takeLast` returns only the last element of the stream.
- `takeUntil(Predicate)` passes an element until some condition is satisfied.
- `elementAt(n)` allows the taking of only the nth element of the sequence.
- The `single` operator emits a single item from the source and signals the `NoSuchElementException` error for an empty source or `IndexOutOfBoundsException` for a source with more than one element.
- It is possible to take or skip an element not only by an amount but also by `Duration` with the `skip(Duration)` or `take(Duration)` operators.
- Also, we may skip or take an element until some message arrives from another stream—`takeUntilOther(Publisher)` or `skipUntilOther(Publisher)`.

Let's consider a workflow where we have to start and then stop stream processing as a reaction to some events originating from other streams. The code may look like the following:

```
Mono<?> startCommand = ...
Mono<?> stopCommand = ...
Flux<UserEvent> streamOfData = ...

streamOfData
    .skipUntilOther(startCommand)
    .takeUntilOther(stopCommand)
    .subscribe(System.out::println);
```

In this case, we may start and then stop elements processing, but only once. The marble diagram for this use case would be as follows:

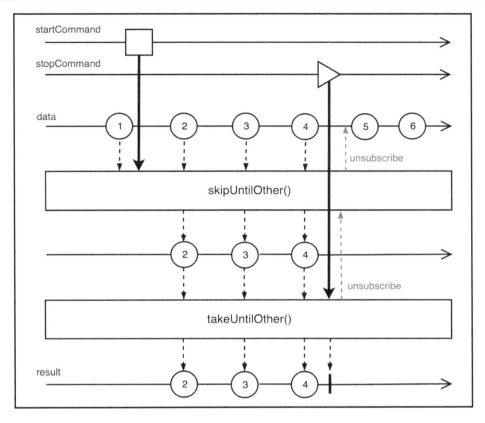

Diagram 4.5 Peeking elements between start-stop commands

Collecting reactive sequences

It is possible to collect all elements in the list and process the resulting collection as a `Mono` stream with `Flux.collectList()` and `Flux.collectSortedList()`. The last one not only collects elements but also sorts them. Consider the following code:

```
Flux.just(1, 6, 2, 8, 3, 1, 5, 1)
    .collectSortedList(Comparator.reverseOrder())
    .subscribe(System.out::println);
```

This produces the following output with one collection containing sorted numbers:

```
[8, 6, 5, 3, 2, 1, 1, 1]
```

 Note that collecting sequence elements in the collection may be resource hungry, especially when a sequence has many elements. Also, it is possible to consume all the available memory when trying to collect on an endless stream.

Project Reactor allows the collection of `Flux` elements not only to `List`, but also to the following:

- Map (`Map<K, T>`) with the `collectMap` operator
- Multi-map (`Map<K, Collection<T>>`) with the `collectMultimap` operator
- Any data structure with a custom `java.util.stream.Collector` and the `Flux.collect(Collector)` operator

Both `Flux` and `Mono` have the `repeat()` and `repeat(times)` methods, which allow for the looping of incoming sequences. We have already used these in the previous section.

One more handy method, called `defaultIfEmpty(T)`, allows the provision of default values for an empty `Flux` or `Mono`.

`Flux.distinct()` passes only the element that has not been encountered in a stream before. However, this method keeps track of all unique elements, so use it carefully, especially with high-cardinality data streams. The `distinct` method has overrides that allow the provision of custom algorithms for duplicate tracking. So, it is sometimes possible to optimize resource usage of the `distinct` operator manually.

 High-cardinality refers to data with elements that are very uncommon or unique. For example, identification numbers or usernames are typically highly-cardinal. At the same time, enum values or values from a small fixed dictionary are not.

The `Flux.distinctUntilChanged()` operator has no such limitation and can be used for endless streams to remove duplicates that appear in an uninterrupted row. The following marble-diagram shows its behavior:

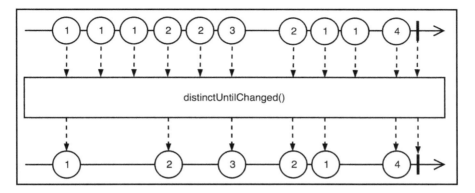

Diagram 4.6. Operator—distinct until changed

Reducing stream elements

Project Reactor makes it possible to `count()` the number of elements in the stream, or check that all elements have required properties with `Flux.all(Predicate)`. It is also easy to check whether at least one element has a desired property with the `Flux.any(Predicate)` operator.

We can check whether a stream has any elements with the `hasElements` operator or whether the stream contains the desired element with the `hasElement` operator. The latter implements the short-circuit logic and completes with `true` as soon as an element matches the value. Also, the `any` operator allows the checking of not only an elements' equality but also any other property by providing a custom `Predicate` instance. Let's check that a sequence has an even number in it:

```
Flux.just(3, 5, 7, 9, 11, 15, 16, 17)
    .any(e -> e % 2 == 0)
    .subscribe(hasEvens -> log.info("Has evens: {}", hasEvens));
```

The `sort` operator allows the sorting of elements in the background and then emits the sorted sequence once the original sequence completes.

The `Flux` class allows the reduction of sequences with a custom logic (sometimes, the procedure is called folding). The `reduce` operator usually requires an initial value and a function that combines the result of the previous step with the element from the current step. Let's sum integer numbers between 1 and 10:

```
Flux.range(1, 5)
    .reduce(0, (acc, elem) -> acc + elem)
    .subscribe(result -> log.info("Result: {}", result));
```

The result would be 15. The `reduce` operator produces only one element with the final result. However, when doing aggregations, it's sometimes handy to send downstream intermediate results. The `Flux.scan()` operator does that. Let's sum integer numbers between 1 and 10 with the `scan` operator:

```
Flux.range(1, 5)
    .scan(0, (acc, elem) -> acc + elem)
    .subscribe(result -> log.info("Result: {}", result));
```

The preceding code produces the following output:

```
Result: 0
Result: 1
Result: 3
Result: 6
Result: 10
Result: 15
```

As we can see, the final result is the same (15). However, we also received all intermediate results. With that said, the `scan` operator may be useful for many applications that need some information about ongoing events. For example, we can calculate the moving average on the stream:

```
int bucketSize = 5;                                              // (1)
Flux.range(1, 500)                                               // (2)
    .index()                                                     // (3)
    .scan(                                                       // (4)
        new int[bucketSize],                                     // (4.1)
        (acc, elem) -> {                                         //
            acc[(int)(elem.getT1() % bucketSize)] = elem.getT2();// (4.2)
            return acc;                                          // (4.3)
        })
    .skip(bucketSize)                                            // (5)
    .map(array -> Arrays.stream(array).sum() * 1.0 / bucketSize) // (6)
    .subscribe(av -> log.info("Running average: {}", av));       // (7)
```

Let's describe this code:

1. Here, we define the size of the moving average window (let's say we are interested in the most recent five events).
2. Let's generate some data with the `range` operator.
3. With the `index` operator, we may attach an index to each of the elements.
4. With the `scan` operator, we collect the latest five elements into a container (`4.1`), where the element's index is used to calculate the position in the container (`4.2`). On every step, we return the same container with the updated content.
5. Here, we skip some elements at the beginning of the stream to gather enough data for the moving average.
6. To calculate the value of the moving average, we divide the sum of the container content on its size.
7. Of course, we have to subscribe for data to receive values.

The `Mono` and `Flux` streams have the `then`, `thenMany`, and `thenEmpty` operators, which complete when the upper stream completes. The operators ignore incoming elements and only replay completion or error signals. These operators can be useful for triggering new streams as soon as the upper stream finishes processing:

```
Flux.just(1, 2, 3)
   .thenMany(Flux.just(4, 5))
   .subscribe(e -> log.info("onNext: {}", e));
```

The lambda in the `subscribe` method receives only 4 and 5, even though 1, 2, and 3 are generated and processed by the stream.

Combining Reactive Streams

Of course, Project Reactor allows the combining of many incoming streams into one outgoing stream. The named operators have many overrides but perform the following transformations:

- The `concat` operator concatenates all sources by forwarding received elements downstream. When the operator concatenates two streams, at first, it consumes and resends all elements of the first stream, then does the same for the second.
- The `merge` operator merges data from upstream sequences into one downstream sequence. Unlike the `concat` operator, upstream sources are subscribed to eagerly (at the same time).

- The `zip` operator subscribes to all upstreams, waits for all sources to emit one element and then combines received elements into an output element. In Chapter 2, *Reactive Programming in Spring - Basic Concepts,* we described how `zip` works in detail. In Reactor, the `zip` operator may operate not only with reactive publishers but also with an `Iterable` container. For that purpose, we can use the `zipWithIterable` operator.
- The `combineLatest` operator works similarly to the zip operator. However, it generates a new value as soon as at least one upstream source emits a value.

Let's concatenate a couple of streams:

```
Flux.concat(
    Flux.range(1, 3),
    Flux.range(4, 2),
    Flux.range(6, 5)
).subscribe(e -> log.info("onNext: {}", e));
```

Obviously, the preceding code in the result generates values from *1* to *10* (*[1, 2 , 3] + [4, 5] + [6, 7, 8, 9, 10]*).

Batching stream elements

Project Reactor supports the batching of stream elements (`Flux<T>`) in a couple of ways:

- **Buffering** elements into containers such as `List`, the result stream has the `Flux<List<T>>`type.
- **Windowing** elements into a stream of streams such as `Flux<Flux<T>>`. Note that, now, the stream signals not values but sub-streams, which we can process.
- **Grouping** elements by some key into a stream that has the type `Flux<GroupedFlux<K, T>>`. Each new key triggers a new `GroupedFlux` instance and all elements with that key are pushed through that instance of the `GroupFlux` class.

Buffering and windowing may happen based on the following:

- The number of processed elements; let's say every 10 elements
- Some time-span; let's say every 5 minutes
- Based on some predicate; let's say cutting before each new even number
- Based on an event arrival from some other `Flux`, which controls the execution

Let's buffer integer elements in lists of size 4:

```
Flux.range(1, 13)
    .buffer(4)
        .subscribe(e -> log.info("onNext: {}", e));
```

The preceding code generates the following output:

```
onNext: [1, 2, 3, 4]
onNext: [5, 6, 7, 8]
onNext: [9, 10, 11, 12]
onNext: [13]
```

In the program's output, we can see that all but the last element are lists of size 4. The last element is a collection of size 1 because it is the modulus of 13 divided by 4. The `buffer` operator gathers many events into a collection of events. That collection itself becomes an event for a downstream operator. The buffer operator is handy for batch processing when it is desirable to make a handful of requests with collections of elements instead of many small requests with only one element. For example, instead of inserting elements into a database one by one, we may buffer items for a couple of seconds and do a batch insert. Of course, this is only if the consistency requirements allow us to do so.

To exercise the `window` operator, let's split the sequence of numbers into windows each time an element is a prime number. For that, we can use the `windowUntil` variant of the `window` operator. It uses a predicate to determine when to make a new slice. The code may look like the following:

```
Flux<Flux<Integer>> windowedFlux = Flux.range(101, 20)       // (1)
    .windowUntil(this::isPrime, true);                       // (2)

windowedFlux.subscribe(window -> window                      // (3)
        .collectList()                                       // (4)
        .subscribe(e -> log.info("window: {}", e)));         // (5)
```

Let's look at the preceding code:

1. At first, we generate 20 integers starting with *101*.
2. Here, we slice a new window with elements each time a number is a prime number. The second argument of the `windowUntil` operator defines whether we cut a new slice before or after satisfying the predicate. In the preceding code, we slice the way that a new prime number begins its window. The resulting stream has the `Flux<Flux<Integer>>` type.

3. Now, we may subscribe to the `windowedFlux` stream. However, each element of the `windowedFlux` stream is itself a Reactive Stream. So, for each `window`, we make another reactive transformation.

4. In our case, for each window, we collect elements with the `collectList` operator so that each window is now reduced to the `Mono<List<Integer>>` type.

5. For each internal `Mono` element, we make a separate subscription and log received events.

The preceding code generates the following output:

```
window: []
window: [101, 102]
window: [103, 104, 105, 106]
window: [107, 108]
window: [109, 110, 111, 112]
window: [113, 114, 115, 116, 117, 118, 119, 120]
```

Note that the first window is empty. This happens because, as soon as we start the original stream, we generate an initial window. Then, the first element arrives (number 101), which is a prime number, which triggers a new window and, consequently, the already-opened window is closed (with the `onComplete` signal) without any elements.

Of course, we could resolve the exercise with the `buffer` operator. Both operators behave pretty similarly. However, `buffer` emits a collection only when a buffer closes, while the `window` operator propagates events as soon as they arrive, making it possible to react sooner and implement more sophisticated workflows.

Also, we may group elements in a Reactive Stream by some criteria with the `groupBy` operator. Let's divide the integer sequence by odd and even numbers and track only the last two elements in each group. The code may look like the following:

```
Flux.range(1, 7)                                         // (1)
    .groupBy(e -> e % 2 == 0 ? "Even" : "Odd")           // (2)
    .subscribe(groupFlux -> groupFlux                    // (3)
        .scan(                                           // (4)
            new LinkedList<>(),                          // (4.1)
            (list, elem) -> {
                list.add(elem);                          // (4.2)
                if (list.size() > 2) {
                    list.remove(0);                      // (4.3)
                }
                return list;
            })
        .filter(arr -> !arr.isEmpty())                   // (5)
```

```
.subscribe(data ->                                    // (6)
    log.info("{}: {}", groupFlux.key(), data)));
```

Let's look at the preceding code:

1. Here, we generate a small sequence of numbers.
2. With the `groupBy` operator, we split the sequence between odd and even numbers based on the division module. The operator returns a stream of type `Flux<GroupedFlux<String, Integer>>`.
3. Here, we subscribe to the main `Flux` and for each of the grouped fluxes, we apply the `scan` operator.
4. The `scan` operator is a seed with the empty list (`4.1`). Each element in the grouped flux is added to the list (`4.2`), and if the list is larger than two elements, the oldest element is removed (`4.3`).
5. The `scan` operator, first of all, propagates the seed and then recalculated values. In that case, the `filter` operator allows us to remove empty data containers from the scan's seed.
6. Finally we subscribe separately for each grouped flux and display what the scan operator sends.

As we expect, the preceding code displays the following output:

```
Odd:  [1]
Even: [2]
Odd:  [1, 3]
Even: [2, 4]
Odd:  [3, 5]
Even: [4, 6]
Odd:  [5, 7]
```

Also, the Project Reactor library supports some advanced techniques such as grouping emitted elements over distinct time windows. For that functionality, please refer to the documentation of the `groupJoin` operator.

The flatMap, concatMap, and flatMapSequential operators

Of course, Project Reactor could not omit the implementation of the `flatMap` operator as it is a crucial transformation in functional programming itself.

The flatMap operator logically consists of two operations—*map* and *flatten* (in terms of Reactor, flatten is similar to the merge operator). The map part of the flatMap operator transforms each incoming element into a Reactive Stream (T -> Flux<R>), and the flatten part merges all generated reactive sequences into a new reactive sequence, through which it passes elements of type R.

The following marble diagram may help us grasp the idea:

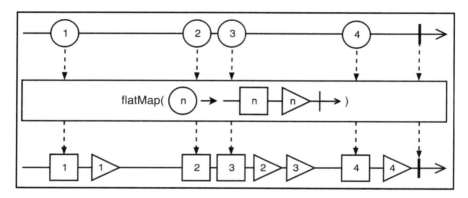

Diagram 4.7. Operator: flatMap

In the preceding diagram, for each *circle(n)*, we generate *square(n)* and then *triangle(n)*. All such subsequences are merged into one downstream.

Project Reactor provides a handful of different variants of the flatMap operator. Besides overrides, the library also gives the flatMapSequential operator and the concatMap operator. These three operators differ in a few dimensions, namely:

- Whether the operator is eagerly subscribing to its inner streams (the flatMap and flatMapSequential operators subscribe eagerly, the concatMap waits for each inner completion before generating the next sub-stream and subscribing to it)
- Whether the operator preserves the order of generated elements (the concatMap naturally preserves the same order as the source elements, the flatMapSequential operator preserves the order by queuing elements received out of order, while the flatMap operator does not necessarily preserve original ordering)

- Whether the operator allows the interleaving of elements from different substreams (the `flatMap` operator allows interleaving, while `concatMap` and `flatMapSequential` do not)

Let's implement a simple algorithm that requests each user's favorite books. A service that provides a user's favorite books may look like the following:

```
public Flux<String> requestBooks(String user) {
    return Flux.range(1, random.nextInt(3) + 1)          // (1)
            .map(i -> "book-" + i)                        // (2)
            .delayElements(Duration.ofMillis(3));         // (3)
}
```

The mock service does the following:

1. The service generates a random amount of integer values
2. Then it maps each number to the book title
3. The service delays each book by an amount of time, which should simulate a communication delay with a database

Now we may combine executions of the `requestBooks` method for a couple of users:

```
Flux.just("user-1", "user-2", "user-3")
    .flatMap(u -> requestBooks(u)
        .map(b -> u + "/" + b))
    .subscribe(r -> log.info("onNext: {}", r));
```

The preceding code generates the following output, which proves the interleaving of elements:

```
[thread: parallel-3] onNext: user-3/book-1
[thread: parallel-1] onNext: user-1/book-1
[thread: parallel-1] onNext: user-2/book-1
[thread: parallel-4] onNext: user-3/book-2
[thread: parallel-5] onNext: user-2/book-2
[thread: parallel-6] onNext: user-1/book-2
[thread: parallel-7] onNext: user-3/book-3
[thread: parallel-8] onNext: user-2/book-3
```

Besides, we can see that the outgoing elements of the `flatMap` operator arrive at the subscriber handlers in **different threads**. However, the Reactive Streams specification guarantees **the happens-before semantics**. So, even when elements may arrive in different threads, none of them ever arrive concurrently. This aspect of Project Reactor is covered in detail in the *Thread scheduling* section.

Also, the library makes it possible to delay `onError` signals with the `flatMapDelayError`, `flatMapSequentialDelayError`, and `concatMapDelayError` operators. Besides this, the `concatMapIterable` operator allows a similar operation when the transformation function generates an iterator for each element instead of a Reactive Stream. In this case, interleaving cannot happen.

The `flatMap` operator (and its variants) is very important both in functional programming and in reactive programming as it allows the implementation of complex workflows with one line of code.

Sampling elements

For a high-throughput scenario, it may make sense to process only a fraction of events by applying the sampling technique. Reactor allows us to do so with the `sample` and `sampleTimeout` operators. So, a sequence may periodically emit an item corresponding to the most recently seen value within a time window. Let's assume the following code:

```
Flux.range(1, 100)
    .delayElements(Duration.ofMillis(1))
    .sample(Duration.ofMillis(20))
    .subscribe(e -> log.info("onNext: {}", e));
```

The preceding code generates the following output:

```
onNext: 13
onNext: 28
onNext: 43
onNext: 58
onNext: 73
onNext: 89
onNext: 100
```

The preceding log shows that, even though we generate items sequentially every millisecond, the subscriber receives only a fraction of events within the desired limit. Through this approach, we may use passive rate limiting in cases where we do not need all incoming events for successful operation.

Transforming reactive sequences into blocking structures

The Project Reactor library provides an API for transforming reactive sequences into blocking structures. Even though any blocking operations should be omitted in a reactive application, sometimes it is required by the upper-level API. So, we have the following options for blocking the stream and producing a result synchronously:

- The `toIterable` method transforms reactive `Flux` into a blocking `Iterable`.
- The `toStream` method transforms reactive `Flux` into a blocking Stream API. As of Reactor 3.2, it uses the `toIterable` method under the hood.
- The `blockFirst` method blocks the current thread until the upstream signals its first value or completes.
- The `blockLast` method blocks the current thread until the upstream signals its last value or completes. In the case of the `onError` signal, it throws the exception in the blocked thread.

It is important to remember that the `blockFirst` and `blockLast` operators have method overrides with a duration for which a thread would be blocked. That should prevent infinitely blocked threads. Also, the `toIterable` and `toStream` methods are able to use a `Queue` to store events that may arrive more quickly than the client code iterates blocking `Iterable` or `Stream`.

Peeking elements while sequence processing

Sometimes it is required to perform an action for each element or a particular signal in the middle of the processing pipeline. To fulfill such requirements, Project Reactor provides the following methods:

- `doOnNext(Consumer<T>)` allows us to execute some action on each element on `Flux` or `Mono`
- `doOnComplete()` and `doOnError(Throwable)` are invoked on corresponding events
- `doOnSubscribe(Consumer<Subscription>)`, `doOnRequest(LongConsumer)`, and `doOnCancel(Runnable)` allow us to react to subscription life-cycle events
- `doOnTerminate(Runnable)` is called when a stream is terminated, no matter what caused the termination

Also, `Flux` and `Mono` provide the `doOnEach(Consumer<Signal>)` method, which handles all signals that represent a Reactive Stream domain—`onError`, `onSubscribe`, `onNext`, `onError`, and `onComplete`.

Let's consider the following code:

```
Flux.just(1, 2, 3)
    .concatWith(Flux.error(new RuntimeException("Conn error")))
.doOnEach(s -> log.info("signal: {}", s))
.subscribe();
```

The preceding code uses the `concatWith` operator, which is a convenient wrapper over the `concat` operator. Also, the preceding code generates the following output:

```
signal: doOnEach_onNext(1)
signal: doOnEach_onNext(2)
signal: doOnEach_onNext(3)
signal: onError(java.lang.RuntimeException: Conn error)
```

In this example, we not only received all `onNext` signals but also the `onError` signal.

Materializing and dematerializing signals

Sometimes, it is useful to process a stream not in terms of data, but in terms of signals. To convert a stream of data into a stream of signals and back again, `Flux` and `Mono` provide the materialize and `dematerialize` methods. An example of this is as follows:

```
Flux.range(1, 3)
    .doOnNext(e -> log.info("data   : {}", e))
    .materialize()
    .doOnNext(e -> log.info("signal: {}", e))
    .dematerialize()
    .collectList()
    .subscribe(r-> log.info("result: {}", r));
```

The preceding code produces the following output:

```
data   : 1
signal: onNext(1)
data   : 2
signal: onNext(2)
data   : 3
signal: onNext(3)
signal: onComplete()
result: [1, 2, 3]
```

Here, when processing the signal stream, the `doOnNext` method receives not only `onNext` events with data but also an `onComplete` event wrapped in the `Signal` class. This approach allows treating the `onNext`, `onError`, and `onCompete` events within one type hierarchy.

If we only want log signals without modifying them, Rector provides the `log` method, which uses the available logger to log all processed signals.

Finding an appropriate operator

Project Reactor provides a very versatile DSL for Reactive Stream processing. However, some practice is required to get used to the library so that selecting an appropriate operator for a task is not a struggle. Reactor's fluent API and well-written documentation help a lot with this process. Also, we recommend reading the *Which operator do I need?* section of the official documentation whenever it is not apparent which operator to use for a concrete problem. The article can be found here: `http://projectreactor.io/docs/core/release/reference/#which-operator`.

Creating streams programmatically

We have already covered how to create Reactive Streams of arrays, futures, and blocking requests. However, sometimes, we need a more complicated way of generating signals within a stream or binding an object's life-cycle to the life-cycle of a Reactive Stream. This section covers what Reactor provides for creating streams programmatically.

Factory methods – push and create

The `push` factory method allows for the programmatical creation of a `Flux` instance by adapting a single-threaded producer. This approach is useful for adapting an async, single-threaded, multi-valued API without worrying about backpressure and cancellation. Both aspects are covered by queueing signals if the subscriber can't handle the load. Let's look at the following code:

```
Flux.push(emitter -> IntStream                          // (1)
        .range(2000, 3000)                              // (1.1)
        .forEach(emitter::next))                        // (1.2)
    .delayElements(Duration.ofMillis(1))               // (2)
    .subscribe(e -> log.info("onNext: {}", e));        // (3)
```

Let's look at the preceding code:

1. Here, we use the `push` factory method to adapt some existing API to the reactive paradigm. For the sake of simplicity, here, we use the Java Stream API to generate 1000 integer elements `(1.1)` and send them to the `emitter` object of the `FluxSink` type `(1.2)`. Inside the push method, we do not care about backpressure and cancellation, as these functionalities are covered by the `push` method itself.

2. Let's delay each element in the stream to simulate a backpressure situation.

3. Here, we subscribe to the `onNext` events.

The `push` factory method can be handy for adapting an asynchronous API with the default backpressure and cancellation strategies.

Also, there is the `create` factory method, which behaves similarly to the `push` factory method. However, this allows forthe sending of events from different threads as it additionally serializes the `FluxSink` instance. Both methods allow for the overriding of the overflow strategy and also enable resource cleanup by registering additional handlers, as in the following code:

```
Flux.create(emitter -> {
    emitter.onDispose(() -> log.info("Disposed"));
    // push events to emitter
})
    .subscribe(e -> log.info("onNext: {}", e));
```

Factory method – generate

The `generate` factory method is designed to allow for the creation of complicated sequences based on an internal forwarded state of the generator. It requires an initial value and a function, which calculates the next internal state based on the previous one and also sends the `onNext` signal to a downstream subscriber. For example, let's create a simple Reactive Stream that produces the Fibonacci sequence (*1, 1, 2, 3, 5, 8, 13, ...*). The code for this task may look as follows:

```
Flux.generate(                                              // (1)
    () -> Tuples.of(0L, 1L),                                // (1.1)
    (state, sink) -> {                                      //
        log.info("generated value: {}", state.getT2());    //
        sink.next(state.getT2());                           // (1.2)
        long newValue = state.getT1() + state.getT2();      //
        return Tuples.of(state.getT2(), newValue);          // (1.3)
    })
```

```
.delayElements(Duration.ofMillis(1))                      // (2)
.take(7)                                                  // (3)
.subscribe(e -> log.info("onNext: {}", e));               // (4)
```

Let's look at the preceding code:

1. With the generate factory method, we may create a custom reactive sequence. We use `Tuples.of(0L, 1L)` as the initial state of the sequence `(1.1)`. In the generation step, we send the `onNext` signal by referencing the second value in the state pair `(1.2)` and recalculate a new state pair based on the next value in the Fibonacci sequence `(1.3)`.
2. With the `delayElements` operator, we introduce some latency between `onNext` signals.
3. Here, we take only the first seven elements for the sake of simplicity.
4. Of course, to trigger sequence generation, we subscribe for events.

The preceding code produces the following output:

```
generated value: 1
onNext: 1
generated value: 1
onNext: 1
generated value: 2
onNext: 2
generated value: 3
onNext: 3
generated value: 5
onNext: 5
generated value: 8
onNext: 8
generated value: 13
onNext: 13
```

As we can see in the logs, each new value is synchronously propagated to the subscriber before generating the next one. This approach may be useful for generating different, complicated reactive sequences that require an intermediate state between emissions.

Wrapping disposable resources into Reactive Streams

The using factory method allows the creation of a stream depending on a disposable resource. It implements the try-with-resources approach in reactive programming. Let's assume that it is a requirement to wrap a blocking API represented with the following, intentionally simplified, Connection class:

```
public class Connection implements AutoCloseable {          // (1)
    private final Random rnd = new Random();

    public Iterable<String> getData() {                     // (2)
        if (rnd.nextInt(10) < 3) {                          // (2.1)
            throw new RuntimeException("Communication error");
        }
        return Arrays.asList("Some", "data");               // (2.2)
    }

    public void close() {                                   // (3)
        log.info("IO Connection closed");
    }

    public static Connection newConnection() {              // (4)
        log.info("IO Connection created");
        return new Connection();
    }
}
```

The preceding code describes the following:

1. The Connection class manages some internal resources and notifies this by implementing the AutoClosable interface.
2. The getData method simulates an IO operation, which may sometimes cause an exception (2.1) or return an Iterable collection with useful data (2.2).
3. The close method may free up internal resources and should always be called, even after an error has happened during getData execution.
4. The static newConnection factory method always returns a new instance of the Connection class.

Usually, connections and connection factories have more complex behaviors, but for the sake of simplicity, we are going to use this simple design.

With the imperative approach, we may receive data from a connection with the following code:

```
try (Connection conn = Connection.newConnection()) {          // (1)
    conn.getData().forEach(                                   // (2)
        data -> log.info("Received data: {}", data)
    );
} catch (Exception e) {                                       // (3)
    log.info("Error: {}", e.getMessage());
}
```

The preceding code follows these steps:

1. Use Java's try-with-resources statement to create a new connection and automatically close it when leaving the current code block.
2. Get and process business data.
3. In the event of an exception, log the appropriate message.

The reactive equivalent of the previous code would look like the following:

```
Flux<String> ioRequestResults = Flux.using(                      // (1)
    Connection::newConnection,                                   // (1.1)
    connection -> Flux.fromIterable(connection.getData()),       // (1.2)
    Connection::close                                            // (1.3)
);

ioRequestResults.subscribe(                                      // (2)
    data -> log.info("Received data: {}", data),                 //
    e -> log.info("Error: {}", e.getMessage()),                  //
    () -> log.info("Stream finished"));                          //
```

The preceding code consists of the following steps:

1. The `using` factory method allows the association of the `Connection` instance life-cycle with the life-cycle of its wrapping stream. The `using` method needs to know how to create a disposable resource; in this case, it is the code that creates a new connection (`1.1`). Then, the method has to know how to transform the resource that was just created into a Reactive Stream. In this case, we call the `fromIterable` method (`1.2`). Last but not least, how do we close the resource? In our case, when the processing is over, the `close` method of the connection instance is called.
2. Of course, to start the actual processing, we need to create a subscription with handles for the `onNext`, `onError`, and `onComplete` signals.

The success path for the preceding code generates the following output:

```
IO Connection created
Received data: Some
Received data: data
IO Connection closed
Stream finished
```

Execution with a simulated error generates the following output:

```
IO Connection created
IO Connection closed
Error: Communication error
```

In both cases, the `using` operator created a new connection at first, then executed a workflow (successfully or not), and then closed the previously created connection. In this case, the life cycle of the connection is bound to the life-cycle of the stream. The operator also makes it possible to choose whether the cleanup action should happen before informing a subscriber about stream termination or after.

Wrapping reactive transactions with the usingWhen factory

Similarly to the `using` operator, the `usingWhen` operator allows us manage resources in the reactive way. However, the `using` operator retrieves the managed resource synchronously (by calling the `Callable` instance). At the same time, the `usingWhen` operator retrieves the managed resource reactively (by subscribing to the instance of `Publisher`). Additionally, the `usingWhen` operator accepts different handlers for the successful and unsuccessful termination of the main processing stream. Those handlers are implemented by publishers. That distinction allows the implementation of completely non-blocking reactive transactions with only one operator.

Let's assume we have an entirely reactive transaction. For demonstration purposes, the code is oversimplified. A reactive transaction implementation may look like the following:

```
public class Transaction {
    private static final Random random = new Random();
    private final int id;

    public Transaction(int id) {
        this.id = id;
        log.info("[T: {}] created", id);
    }
```

```
public static Mono<Transaction> beginTransaction() {              // (1)
    return Mono.defer(() ->
        Mono.just(new Transaction(random.nextInt(1000))));
}

public Flux<String> insertRows(Publisher<String> rows) {          // (2)
    return Flux.from(rows)
        .delayElements(Duration.ofMillis(100))
        .flatMap(r -> {
            if (random.nextInt(10) < 2) {
                return Mono.error(new RuntimeException("Error: " + r));
            } else {
                return Mono.just(r);
            }
        });
}

public Mono<Void> commit() {                                      // (3)
    return Mono.defer(() -> {
        log.info("[T: {}] commit", id);
        if (random.nextBoolean()) {
            return Mono.empty();
        } else {
            return Mono.error(new RuntimeException("Conflict"));
        }
    });
}

public Mono<Void> rollback() {                                    // (4)
    return Mono.defer(() -> {
        log.info("[T: {}] rollback", id);
        if (random.nextBoolean()) {
            return Mono.empty();
        } else {
            return Mono.error(new RuntimeException("Conn error"));
        }
    });
}
}
```

Let's look at the preceding code:

1. This is a static factory that allows the creation of new transactions.
2. Each transaction has a method for saving new rows within the transaction. Sometimes, the process fails due to some internal problems (random behavior). `insertRows` consumes and returns Reactive Streams.
3. This is an asynchronous commit. Sometimes, a transaction may fail to commit.
4. This is an asynchronous rollback. Sometimes, a transaction may fail to roll back.

Now, with the `usingWhen` operator, we can implement a transaction updated with the following code:

```
Flux.usingWhen(
    Transaction.beginTransaction(),                            // (1)
    transaction -> transaction.insertRows(Flux.just("A", "B", "C")), // (2)
    Transaction::commit,                                       // (3)
    Transaction::rollback                                      // (4)
).subscribe(
    d -> log.info("onNext: {}", d),
    e -> log.info("onError: {}", e.getMessage()),
    () -> log.info("onComplete")
);
```

The preceding code uses the `usingWhen` operator for the following:

1. Here, the `beginTransaction` static method returns a new transaction asynchronously by returning the `Mono<Transaction>` type
2. With a given transaction instance, it tries to insert new rows
3. To commit the transaction if step (2) finished successfully
4. To roll back the transaction if step (2) failed

After executing the code in our exercise, we should see the following output for a successful execution:

```
[T: 265] created
onNext: A
onNext: B
onNext: C
[T: 265] commit
onComplete
```

An example of execution with an aborted transaction may look as follows:

```
[T: 582] created
onNext: A
[T: 582] rollback
onError: Error: B
```

With the `usingWhen` operator, it is much easier to manage the resource life cycle in an entirely reactive way. Also, reactive transactions can easily be implemented with it. So, the `usingWhen` operator is an enormous improvement when compared with the `using` operator.

Handling errors

When we design a reactive application that communicates a lot with external services, we have to deal with all kinds of exceptional situations. Fortunately, the `onError` signal is an integral part of the Reactive Stream specification, so an exception should always have a way to propagate to the actor who can handle it. However, if the final subscriber does not define a handler for the `onError` signal, `onError` throws an `UnsupportedOperationException`.

Also, the semantics of Reactive Streams define that `onError` is a terminal operation, after which the reactive sequence stops executions. At that point, we may react differently by applying one of the following strategies:

- Of course, we should define handlers for the `onError` signal in the `subscribe` operator.
- We can catch and replace an error with a default static value or a value calculated from the exception by applying the `onErrorReturn` operator.
- We can catch an exception and execute an alternative workflow by applying the `onErrorResume` operator.
- We can catch and transform an exception into another exception that better represents the situation by applying the `onErrorMap` operator.
- We can define a reactive workflow that, in the event of errors, retries the execution. The `retry` operator resubscribes to the source reactive sequence if it signals an error. It may behave so indefinitely or for a limited amount of time. The `retryBackoff` operator gives out-of-the-box support for the exponential backoff algorithm, which retries the operation with increasing delays.

Also, an empty stream is not what we always want. In that case, we may return a default value with the `defaultIfEmpty` operator or an entirely different reactive stream with the `switchIfEmpty` operator.

One more handy operator, called `timeout`, allows the limiting of the operation waiting time and the throwing of a `TimeoutException` exception, which, in turn, we can process with some other error handling strategy.

Let's demonstrate how we can apply some of the strategies described. We can assume the following unreliable recommendation service:

```
public Flux<String> recommendedBooks(String userId) {
    return Flux.defer(() -> {                                      // (1)
        if (random.nextInt(10) < 7) {
            return Flux.<String>error(new RuntimeException("Err"))  // (2)
                .delaySequence(Duration.ofMillis(100));
        } else {
            return Flux.just("Blue Mars", "The Expanse")           // (3)
                .delayElements(Duration.ofMillis(50));
        }
    }).doOnSubscribe(s -> log.info("Request for {}", userId));      // (4)
}
```

Let's look at the preceding code:

1. We `defer` the calculations until a subscriber arrives.
2. It's highly likely that our unreliable service will return an error. However, we shift all signals in time by applying the `delaySequence` operator.
3. When a client is lucky, they receive their recommendations with some delays.
4. Also, we log each request to the service.

Now, let's implement a client that handles our unreliable service well:

```
Flux.just("user-1")                                      // (1)
    .flatMap(user ->                                     // (2)
        recommendedBooks(user)                           // (2.1)
            .retryBackoff(5, Duration.ofMillis(100))     // (2.2)
            .timeout(Duration.ofSeconds(3))              // (2.3)
            .onErrorResume(e -> Flux.just("The Martian")))  // (2.4)
    .subscribe(                                          // (3)
        b -> log.info("onNext: {}", b),
        e -> log.warn("onError: {}", e.getMessage()),
        () -> log.info("onComplete")
    );
```

The preceding code does the following:

1. Here, we generate a stream of users who request their movie recommendations.
2. For each user, we call our unreliable `recommendedBooks` service (`2.1`). If the call fails, we retry with exponential backoff (no more than 5 retries, starting with a duration of 100 milliseconds) (`2.2`). However, if our retry strategy does not bring any results after three seconds, it causes an error signal (`2.3`). Finally, in the event of any errors, we return a predefined universal set of recommendations with the `onErrorResume` operator (`2.4`).
3. Of course, we need to create a subscriber.

When running, our application may generate the following output:

```
[time: 18:49:29.543] Request for user-1
[time: 18:49:29.693] Request for user-1
[time: 18:49:29.881] Request for user-1
[time: 18:49:30.173] Request for user-1
[time: 18:49:30.972] Request for user-1
[time: 18:49:32.529] onNext: The Martian
[time: 18:49:32.529] onComplete
```

From the logs, we can see that our core tried to get recommendations for `user-1` five times. Also, a retry delay was increased from ~150 milliseconds to ~1.5 seconds. Finally, our code stopped trying to retrieve a result from the `recommendedBooks` method and returned the (`The Martian`) fallback value, and completed the stream.

To summarize, Project Reactor provides a wide range of instruments that help with the handling of exceptional situations and, consequently, improve an application's resilience.

Backpressure handling

Even though the Reactive Stream specification requires backpressure to be built into the communication between the producer and consumer, it is still possible to overflow the consumer. Some consumers may innocently request an unbound demand and then fail to handle the generated load. Some consumers may have hard limitations for the rate of incoming messages. For example, a database client may not insert more than 1,000 records per second. In that case, events batching techniques may help. We covered that approach in the *Batching stream elements* section. Alternatively, we can configure a stream to handle backpressure situations in the following ways:

- The `onBackPressureBuffer` operator requests an unbounded demand and pushes returned elements to a downstream. However, if a downstream consumer cannot keep up, elements are buffered in a queue. The `onBackPressureBuffer` operator has many overrides and exposes many configuration options, which facilitate the tuning of its behavior.
- The `onBackPressureDrop` operator also requests an unbounded demand (`Integer.MAX_VALUE`) and pushes data downstream. If not enough demand is requested from downstream, elements are dropped. It is possible to handle dropped elements with a custom handler.
- The `onBackPressureLast` operator works similarly to `onBackPressureDrop`. However, it remembers the most recently received element and pushes it downstream as soon as the demand appears. It may help to always receive recent data, even in overflow situations.
- The `onBackPressureError` operator requests an unbounded demand while trying to push data downstream. If a downstream consumer cannot keep up, the operator raises an error.

Another way of managing backpressure may be through the rate-limiting technique. The `limitRate(n)` operator splits the downstream demand into smaller batches not bigger than n. In this way, we may protect our delicate producer from an unjustified data request from a downstream consumer. The `limitRequest(n)` operator allows the limiting of the demand (the total requested values) from a downstream consumer. For example, `limitRequest(100)` makes sure that a producer will not be requested for more than *100* elements in total. After sending 100 events, the operator successfully closes the stream.

Hot and cold streams

When talking about reactive publishers, we may distinguish two types of publishers—**hot** and **cold**.

Cold publishers behave in such a way that, whenever a subscriber appears, all of the sequence data is generated for that subscriber. Also, with a cold publisher, no data would be generated without a subscriber. For example, the following code represents the behavior of a cold publisher:

```
Flux<String> coldPublisher = Flux.defer(() -> {
    log.info("Generating new items");
    return Flux.just(UUID.randomUUID().toString());
});

log.info("No data was generated so far");
coldPublisher.subscribe(e -> log.info("onNext: {}", e));
coldPublisher.subscribe(e -> log.info("onNext: {}", e));
log.info("Data was generated twice for two subscribers");
```

The preceding code generates the following output:

```
No data was generated so far
Generating new items
onNext: 63c8d67e-86e2-48fc-80a8-a9c039b3909c
Generating new items
onNext: 52232746-9b19-4b5e-b6b9-b0a2fa76079a
Data was generated twice for two subscribers
```

As we can see, a new sequence is generated whenever a subscriber appears—these semantics may represent HTTP requests. No call is made until no one is interested in the result and each new subscriber triggers an HTTP request.

On the other hand, data generation in hot publishers does not depend on the presence of a subscriber. So, a hot publisher may start producing elements way before the first subscriber. Also, when a subscriber appears, a hot publisher may not send the previously generated values, only new ones. Such semantics represent data broadcast scenarios. For example, a hot publisher may broadcast updates to its subscribers regarding current oil prices, as soon as the prices change. However, when a subscriber arrives, it receives only future updates, not the history of previous prices. Most hot publishers in the Reactor library extend the `Processor` interface. Reactor's processors are covered in the *Processors* section. However, the `just` factory method generates a hot publisher as its values are calculated only once when the publisher is built, and are not recalculated when a new subscriber arrives.

We may transform `just` into a cold publisher by wrapping it in `defer`. That way, even though `just` generates values on its initialization, such an initialization will only happen when a new subscription appears. The latter behavior is dictated by the `defer` factory method.

Multicasting elements of a stream

Of course, we may transform a cold publisher into a hot one by applying a reactive transformation. For example, we may want to share the results of a cold processor between a few subscribers as soon as all of them are ready for data generation. Also, we don't want to regenerate data for each subscriber. Project Reactor has `ConnectableFlux` precisely for such purposes. With `ConnectableFlux`, data is generated to fulfill the most hungry demand and it is also cached so that all other subscribers can process the data at their pace. Of course, the size of the queue and timeouts are configurable via the `publish` and `replay` methods of the class. Also, `ConnectableFlux` can automatically track the number of downstream subscribers to trigger execution when a desired threshold is achieved by using the following methods—connect, `autoConnect(n)`, `refCount(n)`, and `refCount(int, Duration)`.

Let's describe the behavior of `ConnectableFlux` with the following example:

```
Flux<Integer> source = Flux.range(0, 3)
    .doOnSubscribe(s ->
        log.info("new subscription for the cold publisher"));

ConnectableFlux<Integer> conn = source.publish();

conn.subscribe(e -> log.info("[Subscriber 1] onNext: {}", e));
conn.subscribe(e -> log.info("[Subscriber 2] onNext: {}", e));

log.info("all subscribers are ready, connecting");
conn.connect();
```

When running, the preceding code produces the following output:

```
all subscribers are ready, connecting
new subscription for the cold publisher
[Subscriber 1] onNext: 0
[Subscriber 2] onNext: 0
[Subscriber 1] onNext: 1
[Subscriber 2] onNext: 1
[Subscriber 1] onNext: 2
[Subscriber 2] onNext: 2
```

As we can see, our cold publisher received a subscription and consequently only generated items only once. However, both subscribers received a complete set of events.

Caching elements of a stream

With `ConnectableFlux`, it is easy to implement different data caching strategies. However, Reactor already has the API for event caching in the form of the `cache` operator. Internally, the `cache` operator uses `ConnectableFlux`, so the primary added value of it is a fluent and straightforward API. We may tune the amount of data our cache can hold and the expiration time for each cached item. Let's demonstrate how it works with the following example:

```
Flux<Integer> source = Flux.range(0, 2)                              // (1)
    .doOnSubscribe(s ->
        log.info("new subscription for the cold publisher"));

Flux<Integer> cachedSource = source.cache(Duration.ofSeconds(1));    // (2)

cachedSource.subscribe(e -> log.info("[S 1] onNext: {}", e));        // (3)
cachedSource.subscribe(e -> log.info("[S 2] onNext: {}", e));        // (4)

Thread.sleep(1200);                                                  // (5)

cachedSource.subscribe(e -> log.info("[S 3] onNext: {}", e));        // (6)
```

The preceding code does the following:

1. At first, we create a cold publisher that generates a few items.
2. We cache the cold publisher with the cache operator for a duration of 1 second.
3. We connect the first subscriber.
4. Just after the first subscriber, we connect the second subscriber.
5. We wait for some time to allow the cached data to expire.
6. Finally we connect the third subscriber.

Let's look at the program's output:

```
new subscription for the cold publisher
[S 1] onNext: 0
[S 1] onNext: 1
[S 2] onNext: 0
[S 2] onNext: 1
new subscription for the cold publisher
[S 3] onNext: 0
[S 3] onNext: 1
```

Based on the logs, we can conclude that the first two subscribers shared the same cached data of the first subscription. Then, after a delay, the third subscriber was not able to retrieve the cached data, so a new subscription was triggered for the cold publisher. In the end, the third subscriber also received the desired data, even though that data did not arrive from the cache.

Sharing elements of a stream

With `ConnectableFlux`, we multicast events for a couple of subscribers. However, we are waiting for subscribers to appear and only then do we start processing. The `share` operator allows the transformation of a cold publisher into a hot one. The operator behaves in a way that propagates the events that the subscriber has not missed yet for each new subscriber. Let's consider the following use case:

```
Flux<Integer> source = Flux.range(0, 5)
    .delayElements(Duration.ofMillis(100))
    .doOnSubscribe(s ->
        log.info("new subscription for the cold publisher"));

Flux<Integer> cachedSource = source.share();

cachedSource.subscribe(e -> log.info("[S 1] onNext: {}", e));
Thread.sleep(400);
cachedSource.subscribe(e -> log.info("[S 2] onNext: {}", e));
```

In the preceding code, we shared a cold stream that generates events every 100 milliseconds. Then, with some delays, a couple of subscribers subscribe to the shared publisher. Let's look at the application's output:

```
new subscription for the cold publisher
[S 1] onNext: 0
[S 1] onNext: 1
[S 1] onNext: 2
[S 1] onNext: 3
[S 2] onNext: 3
[S 1] onNext: 4
[S 2] onNext: 4
```

From the logs, it is clear that the first subscriber started receiving events starting from the first one, while the second subscriber missed events generated before its appearance (S 2 only received events 3 and 4).

Dealing with time

Reactive programming is asynchronous, so it inherently assumes the presence of the arrow of time.

With Project Reactor, we can generate events based on a duration with the `interval` operator, delay elements with the `delayElements` operator, and delay all signals with the `delaySequence` operator. In this chapter, we have already used a couple of these operators.

We have already discussed how data buffering and windowing can happen based on configured timeouts (the `buffer(Duration)` and `window(Window)` operators). Reactor's API allows you to react to some time-related events, such as with the previously described `timestamp` and `timeout` operators. Similar to `timestamp`, the `elapsed` operator measures the time interval from the previous event. Let's consider the following code:

```
Flux.range(0, 5)
    .delayElements(Duration.ofMillis(100))
    .elapsed()
    .subscribe(e -> log.info("Elapsed {} ms: {}", e.getT1(), e.getT2()));
```

Here, we generate events every *100* milliseconds. Let's look at the log output:

```
Elapsed 151 ms: 0
Elapsed 105 ms: 1
Elapsed 105 ms: 2
Elapsed 103 ms: 3
Elapsed 102 ms: 4
```

From the preceding output, it is evident that events do not arrive precisely within the 100 millisecond interval. This happens because Reactor uses Java's `ScheduledExecutorService` for scheduled events, which itself does not give guarantees about the exact delay. So, we should be careful not to demand too precise time (real-time) intervals from the Reactor library.

Composing and transforming Reactive Streams

When we build complicated reactive workflows, it is often necessary to use the same sequence of operators in a couple of different places. With the transform operator, we can extract such common pieces into separate objects and reuse them whenever required. Previously, we've transformed events within a stream. With the transform operator, we can augment the stream structure itself. Let's assume the following example:

```
Function<Flux<String>, Flux<String>> logUserInfo =          // (1)
    stream -> stream                                          //
        .index()                                              // (1.1)
        .doOnNext(tp ->                                       // (1.2)
            log.info("[{}] User: {}", tp.getT1(), tp.getT2())) //
        .map(Tuple2::getT2);                                  // (1.3)

Flux.range(1000, 3)                                           // (2)
    .map(i -> "user-" + i)                                    //
    .transform(logUserInfo)                                   // (3)
    .subscribe(e -> log.info("onNext: {}", e));
```

Let's look at the preceding code:

1. We define the logUserInfo function with the Function<Flux<String>, Flux<String>> signature. It transforms a Reactive Stream of String values into another Reactive Stream, which also generates String values. In this example, for each onNext signal, our function logs details about a user (1.2), additionally enumerating incoming events with the index operator (1.1). The outgoing stream does not contain any information about enumeration, because we remove it with the map(Tuple2::getT2) call (1.3).
2. Here, we generate some user IDs.
3. We embed the transformation defined by the logUserInfo function by applying the transform operator.

Let's execute the preceding code. The log output is the following:

```
[0] User: user-1000
onNext: user-1000
[1] User: user-1001
onNext: user-1001
[2] User: user-1002
onNext: user-1002
```

In the logs, we see that each element is logged both by the `logUserInfo` function and by the final subscription. However, the `logUserInfo` function also tracks indexes of the events.

The `transform` operator updates the stream behavior only once, at the assembly phase of a stream life-cycle. At the same time, Reactor has the `compose` operator, which does the same stream transformation each time a subscriber arrives. Let's illustrate its behavior with the following code:

```
Function<Flux<String>, Flux<String>> logUserInfo = (stream) -> {      // (1)
    if (random.nextBoolean()) {
        return stream
            .doOnNext(e -> log.info("[path A] User: {}", e));
    } else {
        return stream
            .doOnNext(e -> log.info("[path B] User: {}", e));
    }
};

Flux<String> publisher = Flux.just("1", "2")                          // (2)
    .compose(logUserInfo);                                           // (3)

publisher.subscribe();                                               // (4)
publisher.subscribe();
```

In the preceding code, we do the following:

1. Similar to the previous example, we define a transformation function. In this case, the function randomly chooses the path of a stream transformation each time. Two proposed paths differ only by the log message prefix.
2. Here, we create a publisher that generates some data.
3. With the `compose` operator, we embed the `logUserInfo` function into the execution workflow.
4. Also, we subscribe a couple of times with the hope of observing different behaviors for different subscriptions.

Let's execute the preceding code, it should produce the following output:

```
[path B] User: 1
[path B] User: 2
[path A] User: 1
[path A] User: 2
```

The log messages prove that the first subscription triggered `path B`, while the second triggered `path A`. Of course, the `compose` operator allows the implementation of much more complicated business logic than a random selection of log message prefixes. Both the `transform` and `compose` operators are powerful tools that enable code reuse in reactive applications.

Processors

The Reactive Streams specification defines the `Processor` interface. A `Processor` is a `Publisher` and a `Subscriber` at the same time. So, we can subscribe to a `Processor` instance and also manually send signals (`onNext`, `onError`, `onComplete`) to it. The authors of Reactor recommend omitting processors as they are hard to use and are prone to errors. In most cases, provided processors may be superseded by a combination of operators. Alternatively, a generator factory method (`push`, `create`, `generate`) may fit better for adapting external APIs.

Reactor proposes the following kinds of processors:

- **Direct** processors can only push data through manual user actions by operating with the processor's sink. `DirectProcessor` and `UnicastProcessor` are representatives of this group of processors. `DirectProcessor` does not handle backpressure but may be used to publish events to multiple subscribers. `UnicastProcessor` handles backpressure with an internal queue, however, may serve one `Subscriber` at most.

- **Synchronous** processors (`EmitterProcessor` and `ReplayProcessor`) may push data both manually and by subscribing to an upstream `Publisher`. `EmitterProcessor` may serve multiple subscribers and honor their demands, but may consume data only from one `Publisher` and in a synchronous manner. `ReplayProcessor` behaves similarly to `EmitterProcessor`, however, allows a couple of strategies for caching incoming data.

- **Asynchronous** processors (`WorkQueueProcessor` and `TopicProcessor`) can push downstream data obtained from multiple upstream publishers. To deal with multiple upstream publishers, these processors use the `RingBuffer` data structure. These processors have a dedicated builder API because the number of configuration options makes it hard to initialize them. `TopicProcessor` is Reactive Streams compliant and associates a `Thread` for each downstream `Subscriber` to handle interactions there. Consequently, there is a limit to how many downstream subscribers it can serve. `WorkQueueProcessor` has characteristics similar to `TopicProcessor`. However, it relaxes some of the Reactive Streams' requirements, which allows a reduction in the size of resources it uses at runtime.

Testing and debugging Project Reactor

A versatile testing framework accompanies the Reactor library. The `io.projectreactor:reactor-test` library offers all of the necessary tools for testing reactive workflows implemented with Project Reactor. Chapter 9, *Testing the Reactive Application*, covers testing techniques that are applicable to reactive programming in detail.

Even though reactive code is not so easy to debug, Project Reactor provides techniques to simplify the debugging process if it is required. As in any callback-based framework, stack traces in Project Reactor are not very informative. They do not give the exact location in our code where an exceptional situation had happened. The Reactor library comes with the debugging-oriented capabilities of assembly-time instrumentation. The details of the assembly-time phase of the stream life cycle are covered in the *Project Reactor advanced* section. This feature can be activated with the following code:

```
Hooks.onOperatorDebug();
```

When enabled, this feature begins gathering stack traces for all streams that are going to be assembled, and later this information can extend the stack trace information with the assembly information and, consequently, help spot any problems faster. However, the procedure of creating stack traces is costly. So, it should only be activated in a controlled manner, as a last resort. For more information regarding this feature, please refer to Reactor's documentation.

Also, Project Reactor's `Flux` and `Mono` types provide a handy method called `log`. It logs all signals that are passing through the operator. Many available method's customizations give enough freedom to track the required data, even in a debug situation.

Reactor Addons

Project Reactor is a versatile and feature-rich library. However, it cannot hold all of the useful reactive utilities. So, there are a handful of projects that extend the Reactor's capabilities in a few areas. The official Reactor Addons project (`https://github.com/reactor/reactor-addons`) holds a couple of modules for the Reactor project. At the time of writing, Reactor Addons consists of the following modules—`reactor-adapter`, `reactor-logback`, and `reactor-extra`.

The `reactor-adapter` module brings bridges to RxJava 2 reactive types and schedulers. Also, the module allows integration with Akka.

The `reactor-logback` module provides high-speed, asynchronous logging. It is based on Logback's `AsyncAppender` and LMAX Disruptor's `RingBuffer` via Reactor's `Processor`.

The `reactor-extra` module contains additional utilities for advanced needs. For example, the module contains the `TupleUtils` class, which simplifies code around the `Tuple` class. We explain how to use this class in Chapter 7, *Reactive Database Access*. Also, the module has the `MathFlux` class, which can compute, sum, and average minimum or maximum values from numerical sources. The `ForkJoinPoolScheduler` class adapts Java's `ForkJoinPool` to Reactor's `Scheduler`. We can add the module to our Gradle project with the following imports:

```
compile 'io.projectreactor.addons:reactor-extra:3.2.RELEASE'
```

Also, the Project Reactor ecosystem has reactive drivers for popular asynchronous frameworks and message brokers.

The Reactor RabbitMQ module (`https://github.com/reactor/reactor-rabbitmq`) provides a reactive Java client for RabbitMQ with a familiar Reactor API. The module enables asynchronous non-blocking messaging with backpressure support. Also, the module allows our application to use RabbitMQ as a message bus by using the `Flux` and `Mono` types. The Reactor Kafka module (`https://github.com/reactor/reactor-kafka`) provides similar capabilities for the Kafka message broker.

One more popular Reactor extension is called Reactor Netty (`https://github.com/reactor/reactor-netty`). It adapts Netty's TCP/HTTP/UDP client and server with Reactor's reactive types. The Spring WebFlux module uses Reactor Netty internally for non-blocking web applications. Chapter 6, *WebFlux Async Non-blocking Communication*, covers this topic in more detail.

Advanced Project Reactor

In the previous section, we explored reactive types and reactive operators that allow the implementation of a lot of reactive workflows. Now, we have to go deeper and learn about the life cycle of Reactive Streams, multithreading, and how the internal optimizations are working in Project Reactor.

Reactive Streams life cycle

In order to understand how multithreading works and how many internal optimizations are implemented in Reactor, first, we have to understand the life cycle of reactive types within Reactor.

Assembly-time

The first part of the stream life-cycle is an **assembly-time**. As we may have noticed from the previous sections, Reactor provides us with a fluent API that allows the building of a complex flow of element processing. At first glance, the API offered by Reactor looks like a builder that composes selected operators in the flow. As we may remember, the Builder pattern is mutable and assumes that a terminal operation such as `build` executes the building of another object. In contrast to a common builder pattern, the Reactor API offers immutability. Consequently, each applied operator produces a new object. In reactive libraries, that process of building the execution flow is called **assembling**. In order to understand the assembling approach better, the following pseudocode demonstrates how flow's assembling may look if we do not have the Reactor builder API:

```
Flux<Integer> sourceFlux = new FluxArray(1, 20, 300, 4000);
Flux<String> mapFlux = new FluxMap(sourceFlux, String::valueOf);
Flux<String> filterFlux = new FluxFilter(mapFlux, s -> s.length() > 1)
...
```

The preceding code demonstrates how reactive code may look if we do not have the fluent builder API. It is clear that, under the hood, Fluxes are composed one into each other. After the assembling process, we get a chain of `Publisher`s, where each new `Publisher` wraps the previous one. The following pseudocode demonstrates this:

```
FluxFilter(
  FluxMap(
    FluxArray(1, 2, 3, 40, 500, 6000)
  )
)
```

The preceding code shows how the resulted `Flux` looks after applying a sequence of operators such as `just` -> `map` -> `filter`.

In the streams life cycle, that phase plays an important role since during the streams assembling we can replace operators one on to another by checking the type of the stream. For example, sequence of `concatWith` -> `concatWith` -> `concatWith` operators may be easily compacted to one concatenation. The following code show how it is done in Reactor:

```
public final Flux<T> concatWith(Publisher<? extends T> other) {
    if (this instanceof FluxConcatArray) {
      @SuppressWarnings({ "unchecked" })
      FluxConcatArray<T> fluxConcatArray = (FluxConcatArray<T>) this;

      return fluxConcatArray.concatAdditionalSourceLast(other);
    }
    return concat(this, other);
}
```

As we can see from the preceding code, if current `Flux` is instance `FluxConcatArray`, then, instead of creating `FluxConcatArray(FluxConcatArray(FluxA, FluxB), FluxC)` we create one `FluxConcatArray(FluxA, FluxB, FluxC)` and improve the overall performance of the stream in that way.

In addition, at assemble-time we may provide some `Hooks` to the stream under assembling and enable some additional logging, tracing, metrics' collecting or other important additions that may be useful during debugging or streams monitoring.

To summarize the role of assemble-time phase of Reactive Streams life cycle, during that phase we may manipulate the stream construction and apply different techniques for optimizing, monitoring or better stream debugging which is an inevitable part of building Reactive Systems.

Subscription-time

The second important phase of the execution life cycle in the stream is the **subscription-time**. Subscription happens when we `subscribe` to a given `Publisher`. For example, the following code demonstrates how to `subscribe` to the aforementioned execution flow:

```
...
filteredFlux.subscribe(...);
```

As we may remember from previous sections, in order to build an execution flow, we pass `Publishers` inside each other. So, we have a chain of `Publishers`. Once, we `subscribe` to the top wrapper, we start the subscription process of that chain. The following pseudocode shows how a `Subscriber` is propagated through the chain of `Subscribers` during the subscription time:

```
filterFlux.subscribe(Subscriber) {
  mapFlux.subscribe(new FilterSubscriber(Subscriber)) {
    arrayFlux.subscribe(new MapSubscriber(FilterSubscriber(Subscriber))) {
      // start pushing real elements here
    }
  }
}
```

The preceding code shows what happens during the subscription-time inside the assembled `Flux`. As we can see, execution of the filtered `Flux.subscribe` method subsequently executes the `subscribe` method for each inner `Publisher`. Finally, when execution ends at the line with comment, we will have the following sequence of Subscribers wrapped inside each other:

```
ArraySubscriber(
  MapSubscriber(
    FilterSubscriber(
      Subscriber
    )
  )
)
```

In contrast to the assembled `Flux`s, here, we have the `ArraySubscriber` wrapper at the top of a `Subscribers` pyramid where, in the case of `Flux` pyramid, we have `FluxArray` in the middle (reversed pyramid of wrappers).

The importance of subscription-time phase is in the fact that during that phase we may do the same optimization as during assemble-time phase. Another important thing is that some of the operators that enable multi-threading in Reactor allows changing the worker on which subscription happens. We are going to cover subscription-time optimization and multi-threading in this chapter later and for now switching to explanation of the last phase of the stream execution life cycle.

Runtime

The final step of the stream execution is a runtime phase. During that phase, we have an actual signals' exchange between a `Publisher` and a `Subscriber`. As we may remember from the Reactive Streams specification, the first two signals that `Publisher` and `Subscriber` exchange is the `onSubscribe` signal and the `request` signal. The `onSubscribe` method is called by the top source, which in our case is `ArrayPublisher`. This passes its `Subscription` to the given `Subscriber`. The pseudocode that describes the process of passing `Subscription` through ever `Subscriber`s looks like the following:

```
MapSubscriber(FilterSubscriber(Subscriber)).onSubscribe(
  new ArraySubscription()
) {
  FilterSubscriber(Subscriber).onSubscribe(
    new MapSubscription(ArraySubscription(...))
  ) {
    Subscriber.onSubscribe(
      FilterSubscription(MapSubscription(ArraySubscription(...)))
    ) {
     // request data here
    }
  }
}
```

Once the `Subscription` has passed through all the `Subscriber`s chain and each `Subscriber` in the chain wrapped given `Subscription` into specific representation. So finally we get the pyramid of `Subscription` wrappers as it shown in the following code:

```
FilterSubscription(
  MapSubscription(
    ArraySubscription()
  )
)
```

Finally, the last `Subscriber` receives the chain of `Subscription`s and in order to start receiving elements should call the `Subscription#request` method which initiates the sending of elements. The following pseudocode demonstrates what the process of requesting elements looks like:

```
FilterSubscription(MapSubscription(ArraySubscription(...)))
  .request(10) {
    MapSubscription(ArraySubscription(...))
      .request(10) {
        ArraySubscription(...)
          .request(10) {
```

```
            // start sending data
        }
    }
}
```

Once all of the `Subscriber`s pass the requested demand and `ArraySubscription` receives it, the `ArrayFlux` can start sending elements to the `MapSubscriber(FilterSubscriber(Subscriber))` chain. The following is pseudocode that describes the process of sending elements through all the `Subscriber`s:

```
...
ArraySubscription.request(10) {
  MapSubscriber(FilterSubscriber(Subscriber)).onNext(1) {
    // apply mapper here
    FilterSubscriber(Subscriber).onNext("1") {
      // filter
      // element does not match
      // request and additional element then
      MapSubscription(ArraySubscription(...)).request(1) {...}
    }
  }
  MapSubscriber(FilterSubscriber(Subscriber)).onNext(20) {
    // apply mapper here
    FilterSubscriber(Subscriber).onNext("20") {
      // filter
      // element matches
      // send it downstream Subscriber
      Subscriber.onNext("20") {...}
    }
  }
}
```

As we can see from the preceding code, during runtime, the element from the source goes through the chain of `Subscriber`s, executing different functionality during each of the stages.

The importance of understanding this phase is that during runtime we may apply optimization that may reduce amount of signals exchange. For example, as we are going to see in the next sections, we may reduce the number of `Subscription#request` calls and improve, therefore, performance of the stream.

As we may remember from Chapter 3, *Reactive Streams - the New Streams' Standard*, the invocation of Subscription#request method causes a write to the volatile field that holds demand. Such a write is an expensive operation from computation perspective, so it is better to avoid it if possible.

To summarize our understanding of Stream's life cycle and the execution at each of the phases we may consider the following diagram:

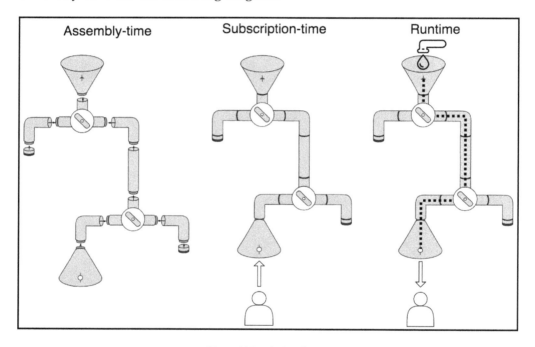

Diagram 4.8. Reactive flow life-cycle

To summarize this, we have covered the central point in the execution life cycle of the Flux and Mono reactive types. In the following sections, we are going to use stream life cycle phases in order to clarify how Reactor provides very efficient implementations for each Reactive Stream.

The thread scheduling model in Reactor

In this section we are going to learn which features Reactor offers for multi-threading execution and what is fundamental difference between available multi-threading operators. In general, there are four operators that allow the switching of execution to different workers. Let's look at these one by one.

The publishOn operator

In a nutshell, the `publishOn` operator allows the moving part of **runtime** execution to a specified **worker**.

We avoid using the word `Thread` here since the underlying mechanism of the `Scheduler` may enqueue work to the same `Thread`, but the execution job may be done by a different *worker* from a `Scheduler` instance perspective.

In order to specify the worker that should process elements at runtime, Reactor introduces a specific abstraction for that purpose, called `Scheduler`. `Scheduler` is an interface that represents a worker or pool of workers in Project Reactor. We are going to cover `Scheduler` later in this chapter, but for now, we will just mention that this interface is used in order to choose a specific worker for the current stream. In order to better understand how we can use the `publishOn` operator, let's consider the following code sample:

```
Scheduler scheduler = ...;        // (1)
                                  //
Flux.range(0, 100)                // (2) ‾|
    .map(String::valueOf)         // (3)  |> Thread Main
    .filter(s -> s.length() > 1)  // (4) _|

    .publishOn(scheduler)         // (5)

    .map(this::calculateHash)     // (6) ‾|
    .map(this::doBusinessLogic)   // (7)  |> Scheduler Thread
    .subscribe()                  // (8) _|
```

As we can see from the preceding code, the operations on elements from step 2 to step 4 take place on the `Thread Main` where the execution after the `publishOn` operator is on a different `Scheduler` worker. This means that the calculation of the hash takes place on `Thread A`, so `calculateHash` and `doBusinessLogic` are executed on a different worker from the `Thread Main` worker. If we look at the `publishOn` operator from an execution model perspective, we can see the following flow:

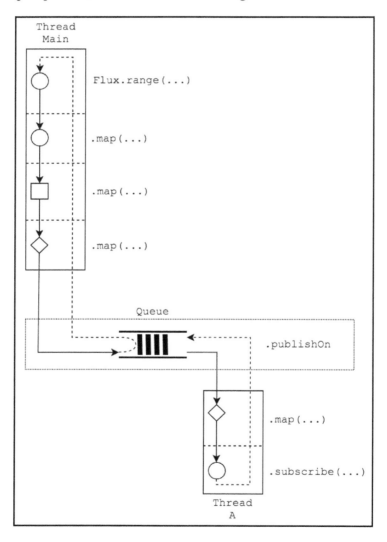

Figure 4.9. Representation of Reactor's publishOn operator internals

As we may notice, the focus of the `publishOn` operator is on runtime execution. Under the hood, the `publishOn` operator keeps a queue to which it supplies new elements so that a dedicated worker can consume messages and process them one by one. In this example, we have shown that work is running on the separate `Thread`, so our execution is split by an asynchronous boundary. So, now, we kind of have two independently processed parts of the flow. One important thing that we need to highlight is that all elements in a Reactive Stream are processed one by one (not concurrently) so that we may always define a strict order for all events. This property is also called **serializability**. This means that, once the element comes to `publishOn`, it will be enqueued, and once its turn has come, it will be dequeued and processed. Note that only one worker is dedicated to processing the queue, so the order of the elements is always predictable.

Parallelization with the publishOn operator

At first glance, the `publishOn` operator does not enable the concurrent processing of the Reactive Stream elements, which we might expect. Nevertheless, the Reactive Programming paradigm enabled by Project Reactor allows fine-grained scaling and parallelizing of the processing flow using the `publishOn` operator. For example, let's first consider the fully synchronous processing depicted in the following diagram:

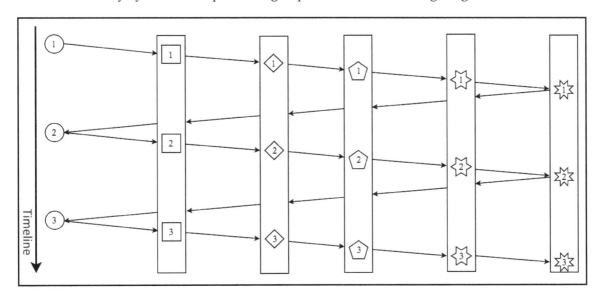

Diagram 4.10 The fully synchronous processing of a Reactive Stream

As we can see from the preceding diagram, we have a processing flow with three elements in it. Due to the nature of the synchronous processing of elements in the stream, we have to move elements one by one through all of the transformation stages. However, in order to start processing the next element, we have to fully process the previous element. In contrast, if we put a `publishOn` in this flow, we can potentially speed up processing. The following shows the same diagram but with a `publishOn` operator included:

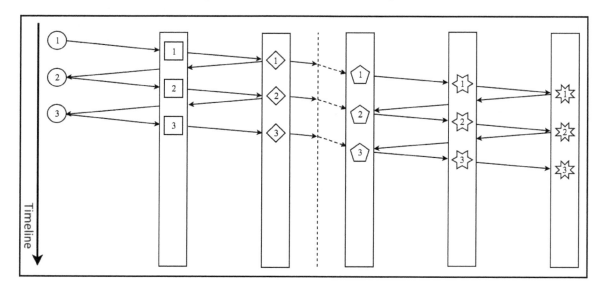

Diagram 4.11 The publishOn operator's effect on stream processing

As we can see from the preceding diagram, keeping the processing time of elements the same, and just by providing an asynchronous boundary (represented by the `publishOn` operator) between processing stages, we can achieve parallel processing. Now, the left-hand side of the processing flow does not need to wait for the completion of the process on the right-hand side. Instead, they can work independently so that parallel processing is achieved properly.

The subscribeOn operator

Another important factor for multithreading in Reactor is through an operator called subscribeOn. In contrast to publishOn, subscribeOn allows you to change the worker on which part of the subscription chain is happening. This operator can be useful when we create a source of the stream from the execution of a function. Usually, such executions take place at subscription time, so a function that provides us with the source of data that executes the .subscribe method is called. For example, let's take a look at the following code sample, which shows how we can supply some information using Mono.fromCallable:

```
ObjectMapper objectMapper = ...
String json = "{ \"color\" : \"Black\", \"type\" : \"BMW\" }";
Mono.fromCallable(() ->
        objectMapper.readValue(json, Car.class)
    )
    ...
```

Here, Mono.fromCallable allows the creation of a Mono from Callable<T> and provides the result of its evaluation to each Subscriber. The Callable instance executes when we call the .subscribe method, so Mono.fromCallable does the following under the hood:

```
public void subscribe(Subscriber actual) {
    ...
    Subscription subscription = ...
    try {
        T t = callable.call();
        if (t == null) {
            subscription.onComplete();
        }
        else {
            subscription.onNext(t);
            subscription.onComplete();
        }
    }
    catch (Throwable e) {
        actual.onError(
            Operators.onOperatorError(e, actual.currentContext()));
    }
}
```

As we can see from the preceding code, execution of the callable happens in the `subscribe` method. This means that we can use `publishOn` to change the worker on which the execution of `Callable` will take place. Fortunately, `subscribeOn` allows us to specify the worker on which the subscription will take place. The following example shows how we can do that:

```
Scheduler scheduler = ...;
Mono.fromCallable(...)
    .subscribeOn(scheduler)
    .subscribe();
```

The preceding example shows how we can execute the given `Mono.fromCallable` on a separate worker. Under the hood, `subscribeOn` executes the subscription to the parent `Publisher` into `Runnable`, which is the scheduler for a specified `Scheduler`. If we compared the execution model of `subscribeOn` and `publishOn`, we would see the following:

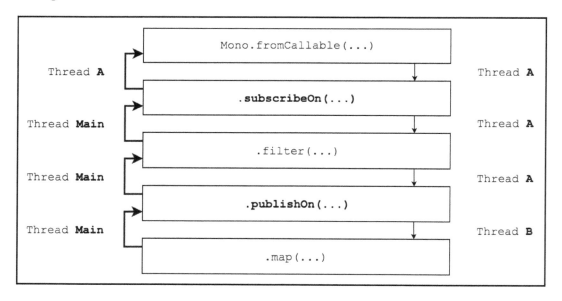

Diagram 4.12 The internals of the .publishOn operator

As we can see from the preceding diagram, `subscribeOn` can partially specify the runtime worker along with the subscription-time worker. This happens because, along with the scheduling of the `subscribe` method's execution, it schedules each call to the `Subscription.request()` method, so it happens on the worker specified by the `Scheduler` instance. According to the Reactive Streams specification, a `Publisher` may start sending data on the caller `Thread`, so the subsequent `Subscriber.onNext()` will be called on the same `Thread` as the initial `Subscription.request()` call. In contrast, `publishOn` can specify the execution behavior only for downstream and cannot affect the upstream execution.

The parallel operator

Along with non-trivial operators for managing threads on which we want to process some part of the execution flow, Reactor offers a familiar technique for work paralleling. For that purpose, Reactor has an operator called `.parallel`, which allows the splitting of the flow on to the parallel substreams and the balancing of elements between them. The following is an example of this operator in use:

```
Flux.range(0, 10000)
    .parallel()
    .runOn(Schedulers.parallel())
    .map()
    .filter()
    .subscribe()
```

As we can see from the preceding example, `.parallel()` is a part of the `Flux` API. One thing that we have noticed here is that, by applying the `parallel` operator, we start operating on a different type of `Flux`, which is called `ParallelFlux`. `ParallelFlux` is an abstraction over a group of Fluxes, between which the elements in the source `Flux` are balanced. Then, by applying the `runOn` operator, we can apply `publishOn` to internal Fluxes and distribute work related to elements being processed between different workers.

Scheduler

Scheduler is an interface that has two central
methods: `Scheduler.schedule` and `Scheduler.createWorker`. The first method makes
it possible to schedule a `Runnable` task, whereas the second one provides us with a
dedicated instance of the `Worker` interface, which can schedule `Runnable` tasks in the same
way. The central difference between the `Scheduler` interface and the `Worker` interface is
that the `Scheduler` interface represents a pool of workers, whereas `Worker` is a dedicated
abstraction over the `Thread` or a resource. By default, Reactor provides three
central `Scheduler` interface implementations, which are listed as follows:

- `SingleScheduler` allows the scheduling of all possible tasks for one dedicated
  worker. It is time-capable, so it can schedule periodical events with a delay. This
  scheduler may be referenced with the `Scheduler.single()` call.

- `ParallelScheduler` works on a fixed size pool of workers (by default, the size
  is bound to the number of CPU cores). Fits well for CPU bound tasks. Also, by
  default, handles time-related scheduled events, for
  example, `Flux.interval(Duration.ofSeconds(1))`. This scheduler may be
  referenced with the `Scheduler.parallel()` call.

- `ElasticScheduler` dynamically creates workers and caches thread pools. The
  maximum number of created thread pools is unbounded, so this scheduler fits
  well when we need a scheduler for IO-intensive operations. This scheduler may
  be referenced with the `Scheduler.elastic()` call.

Also, we can implement our own `Scheduler` with our desired characteristics. Chapter
10, *And, Finally, Release It!* gives an example of how to create a `Scheduler` for Reactor with
extensive monitoring capabilities.

> To learn more about Threading and Schedulers please see the following
> part of Project Reactor documentation [http://projectreactor.io/docs/
> core/release/reference/#schedulers]

Rector Context

Another key feature that comes with Reactor is `Context`. `Context` is an interface that is passed along the stream. The central idea of the `Context` interface is providing access to some contextual information that may be useful to access later at runtime phase. We may wonder why do we need such feature if we have `ThreadLocal` that allows doing the same things. For example, many frameworks uses `ThreadLocal` in order to pass `SecurityContext` along the users requests execution and making it possible to access the authorized user at any point of processing. Unfortunately, such concept works well only when we have a single-threaded processing, so the execution is attache to same `Thread`. If we start using that concept with the asynchronous processing, the `ThreadLocal` will be loosed very fast. For instance, if we have execution as the following, then we will lose the available `ThreadLocal`:

```
class ThreadLocalProblemShowcase {

    public static void main(String[] args) {
        ThreadLocal<Map<Object, Object>> threadLocal =      // (1)
            new ThreadLocal<>();                            //
        threadLocal.set(new HashMap<>());                   // (1.1)

        Flux                                                // (2)
            .range(0, 10)                                   // (2.1)
            .doOnNext(k ->                                  //
               threadLocal                                  //
                  .get()                                    //
                  .put(k, new Random(k).nextGaussian())     // (2.2)
            )                                               //
            .publishOn(Schedulers.parallel())              // (2.3)
            .map(k -> threadLocal.get().get(k))            // (2.4)
            .blockLast();                                  //
    }
}
```

The following is the description to the preceding code:

1. At that point, we have a declaration of the `ThreadLocal` instance. In addition, at point (1.1), we have a setup of that `ThreadLocal`, so we may use it later in the code.
2. Here we have the `Flux` stream declaration, that generate a range of elements from 0 to 9 (2.1). In addition, for each new element in the stream we generate a `randomGaussian` double, where the element is the seed for generated random value. Once the number is generated, we put it in the store in `ThreadLocal` map. Then, at point (2.3) we move execution to a different `Thread`. Finally, at point (2.4) we map the number in the stream to previously stored in the `ThreadLocal` map random gaussian double. At this point, we will get `NullPointerException` because the previously stored map in `Thread Main` is unavailable in a different `Thread`.

As we may notice from the preceding example, the usage of `ThreadLocal` in multi-threading environment is very dangerous and may cause unpredictable behavior. Even though Java API allows to transfer `ThreadLocal` data from `Thread` to `Thread`, it does not guaranty its consistent transferring everywhere.

Fortunately, Reactor Context solves that problem in the following way:

```
Flux.range(0, 10)                                            //
    .flatMap(k ->                                            //
       Mono.subscriberContext()                              // (1)
          .doOnNext(context -> {                             // (1.1)
             Map<Object, Object> map = context.get("randoms"); // (1.2)
             map.put(k, new Random(k).nextGaussian());       //
          })                                                 //
          .thenReturn(k)                                     // (1.3)
    )                                                        //
    .publishOn(Schedulers.parallel())                        //
    .flatMap(k ->                                            //
       Mono.subscriberContext()                              // (2)
          .map(context -> {                                  //
             Map<Object, Object> map = context.get("randoms"); // (2.1)
             return map.get(k);                              // (2.2)
          })                                                 //
    )                                                        //
    .subscriberContext(context ->                            // (3)
       context.put("randoms", new HashMap())                 //
    )                                                        //
    .blockLast();                                            //
```

The following is a description to the preceding code:

1. At this point is an example of how we may access the Reactor's `Context`. As we may see, Reactor provides an access to the instance of `Context` in the current stream using static operator `subscriberContext`. As in the previous sample, once Context is achieved (1.1), we access to stored `Map` (1.2) and put generated value there. Finally, we return the initial parameter of `flatMap`.

2. Here, we access Reactor's `Context` once again, after we switched the `Thread`. Even though this sample is identical to the previous sample where we used `ThreadLocal`, at point (2.1) we will successfully retrieve the stored map and get generated random gaussian double(2.2).

3. Finally, here, in order to make `"randoms"`, key returns a `Map` we populate upstream with a new `Context` instance that contains `Map` under the required key.

What we may see from the preceding example is that `Context` is accessible over the no-arguments `Mono.subscriberContext` operator and can be provided to the stream using the one-argument `subscriberContext(Context)` operator.

Looking at the preceding sample, we may wonder, why do we need to use `Map` in order to transfer data, since the `Context` interface has similar method that the `Map` interface has. By its nature, `Context` designed as an immutable object and once we add new element to it, we achieve new instance of `Context`. Such design decision was made in favor of multi-threading access model which. That means, that the only way to provide `Context` to the stream and dynamically provide some data, that will be available during the whole runtime execution in during the assemble or subscription time. In case, if `Context` is provided during the assemble time, then all subscribers will have share the same static context which may not useful in cases where each `Subscriber` (which may represent user connection) should have its own `Context`. Therefore, the only life-cycle period when each `Subscriber` may be provided with its context is the subscription time.

As we may remember from the previous sections. During the subscription
time Subscriber hoisting from the bottom of the stream to the top through the chain
of Publishers and become wrapped on each stage to a local Subscriber representation
that introduce additional runtime logic. In order to keep that process unchanged and
allows passing an additional Context object through the stream, Reactor uses specific
extension of Subscriber interface called CoreSubscriber. CoreSubscriber allows
transferring Context as its field. The following shows how the CoreSubscriber interface
looks:

```
interface CoreSubscriber<T> extends Subscriber<T> {
    default Context currentContext() {
        return Context.empty();
    }
}
```

As we can see from the preceding code, CoreSubscriber introduces an additional method
called currentContext. Which gives an access to the current Context object. Most of the
operators in Project Reactor, provides an implementation of the CoreSubscriber interface
with referencing to the downstream Context. As we may notice, the only operator that
allows modifying current Context is subscriberContext, which implementation
of CoreSubscriber is held merged Context of downstream and the passed as a
parameter.

Also, such a behavior means that an accessible Context object may be different at the
different point in the stream. For example, the following shows the mentioned behavior:

```
void run() {
    printCurrentContext("top")
    .subscriberContext(Context.of("top", "context"))
    .flatMap(__ -> printCurrentContext("middle"))
    .subscriberContext(Context.of("middle", "context"))
    .flatMap(__ -> printCurrentContext("bottom"))
    .subscriberContext(Context.of("bottom", "context"))
    .flatMap(__ -> printCurrentContext("initial"))
    .block();
}
void print(String id, Context context) {
    ...
}
Mono<Context> printCurrentContext(String id) {
    return Mono
        .subscriberContext()
        .doOnNext(context -> print(id, context));
}
```

The preceding code shows how we may use `Context` during the stream construction. If we run the mentioned code, the following result will appear in the console:

```
top {
   Context3{bottom=context, middle=context, top=context}
}

middle {
   Context2{bottom=context, middle=context}
}

bottom {
   Context1{bottom=context}
}

initial {
   Context0{}
}
```

As we may see from the preceding code, the available `Context` at the top of the stream contains the whole `Context` available in this stream, where the middle can access only to those `Context`, which is defined down the stream, and the context consumer at the very bottom (with id initial) has empty Context at all.

In general, `Context` is a killer feature that push Project Reactor on the next level of tools for building reactive systems. In addition, such feature is useful for many cases where we need to access some contextual data, for instance, at the middle of processing users request. As we are going to see in Chapter 6: *WebFlux Async Non-Blocking Communication*, this feature is extensively used within Spring Framework, especially within reactive Spring Security.

Even though we covered `Context` feature extensively, there is a huge possibilities and use-cases for this Reactor's technique. To learn more about Reactor's `Context`, please see the following section of Project Reactor documentation: `http://projectreactor.io/docs/core/release/reference/#context`.

Internals of Project Reactor

As we saw in the previous section, Reactor is rich in useful operators. Furthermore, we may have noticed that the overall API has similar operators as in RxJava. However, what is the main difference between the old generation of libraries and the new one, which includes Project Reactor 3? What is the most critical breakthrough here? One of the most notable improvements is the **Reactive Stream life-cycle** and **operator fusion**. In the previous section, we have covered the Reactive Streams life cycle; now, let's look at Reactor's operator fusion.

Macro-fusion

Macro-fusion mostly occurs during assemble time and its aim is to replace one operator with another. For example, we have already seen that `Mono` is highly-optimized for processing only one, or zero, elements. At the same time, some parts of operators inside `Flux` are also supposed to process one or zero elements (for instance, the operators `just(T)`, `empty()`, and `error(Throwable)`). In most cases, these simple operators are used along with other transformation flows. Consequently, it is crucial to reduce such overhead. For that purpose, Reactor provides optimization during assembly-time, and if it detects that upstream `Publisher` implements interfaces such as `Callable` or `ScalarCallable`, the upstream `Publisher` will be replaced with an optimized operator. An example where such optimization will be applied is the following code:

```
Flux.just(1)
    .publishOn(...)
    .map(...)
```

The preceding code show a really simple example where the execution on element should be moved to a different worker right after the element is created. In case if no optimization is applied, such execution allocates a queue for keeping elements from the different worker, plus enqueuing and dequeuing elements from such a queue causes a few volatile reads and writes so execution of such plain `Flux` casts too much. Fortunately, we may optimize that flow. Since it does not matter on which worker execution take place and supplying of one element may be represented as a `ScalarCallable#call`, than we may replace `publishOn` operator with `subscribeOn` which does not require creation of an additional queue. Moreover, the execution of the downstream will not be changed because of applied optimizations so we will get the same result from running optimized stream.

The preceding example is one of Macro-fusion optimization hidden in Project Reactor. In *Assembly-time* section of this chapter we mentioned another sample of such optimizations. In general, the purpose of Macro-fusions applied in Project Reactor is optimizing assembled flow and instead of using a powerful tool just to hammer a nail, we can use a more primitive and less costly solutions.

Micro-fusion

Micro-fusion is a more complex optimization and is related to runtime optimization and the reuse of shared resources. One good example of micro-fusion is the conditional operator. To understand this problem, let's take a look at the following diagram:

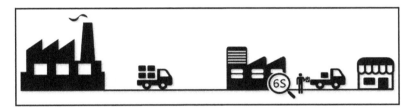

Diagram 4.13. Conditional problem with the truck example

Let's imagine the following situation. The store made an order for n items. After some time, the factory sent the items in a truck to the store. However, to finally arrive at Store B, the truck must go through the Inspection Department and verify that all items are of the expected quality. Unfortunately, some of the items were not carefully packed, and only some of the order arrived at the store. After that, the factory prepared another truck and sent it to the store again. This happened repeatedly until all of the ordered items arrived at the store. Fortunately, the factory realised that they had spent a lot of time and money delivering items through separate Inspection Departments and decided to hire their own local inspector from the Inspection Department (Diagram 4.14):

Diagram 4.14. Solved Conditional overhead with the dedicated inspector on the factory side.

All items can now be verified at the factory and then sent to the store without visiting the Inspection Department.

How does that story correlate with programming? Let's take a look at the following example:

```
Flux.from(factory)
    .filter(inspectionDepartment)
    .subscribe(store);
```

Here, we have a similar situation. The downstream subscriber has requested a certain number of elements from the source. While emitting elements through the chain of operators, elements are moving through the conditional operator, which may reject some of the elements. To satisfy downstream demand, the filter operator for each rejected item must execute an additional `request(1)` call upstream. According to the design of current reactive libraries (such as RxJava or Reactor 3), the `request` operation has its own additional CPU overhead.

 According to David Karnok's research, each *"... call to request() usually ends up in an atomic CAS loop, costing 21-45 cycles for each dropped element."*

This means that conditional operators, such as the `filter` operator, may have a significant impact on the overall performance! For that reason, there is a type of micro-fusion called `ConditionalSubscriber`. This type of optimization allows us to verify the condition right on the source side and send the required amount of elements without additional `request` calls.

The second type of micro-fusion is the most complicated one. This fusion is related to asynchronous boundaries between operators, which were mentioned in Chapter 3, *Reactive Streams - the New Streams' Standard*. To understand the problem, let's imagine an operators chain with a few asynchronous boundaries, as in the following example:

```
Flux.just(1, 2, 3)
    .publishOn(Schedulers.parallel())                       // (1)
    .concatMap(i -> Flux.range(0, i)
                    .publishOn(Schedulers.parallel()))      // (2)
    .subscribe();
```

The previous example shows the Reactor's operators chain. This chain includes two asynchronous boundaries, which means that the queue should appear here. For example, the nature of the concatMap operator is that it may potentially produce *n* elements on each incoming element from the upstream. Thus, it is impossible to predict how many elements will be produced by internal Fluxes. To handle backpressure and avoid overwhelming the consumer, it is necessary to put the result into the queue. The publishOn operator also requires an internal queue to transfer elements in a Reactive Stream from one worker thread to another. As well as the queues overhead, there are more dangerous request() calls through the asynchronous boundaries. These may cause even more significant memory overhead. To understand the problem, let's take a look at the following diagram:

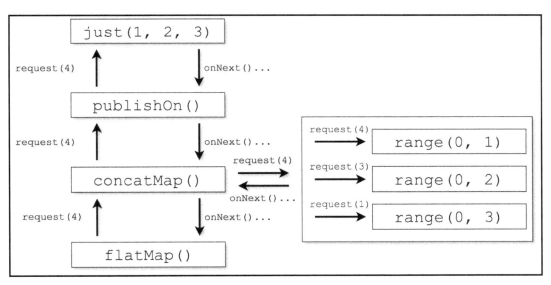

Diagram 4.15. Async boundaries overhead without optimization

The previous example expands the internal behavior of the earlier code snippet. Here, we have a massive overhead in the internals of concatMap, where we are required to send a request for each inner stream until the downstream demand is satisfied. Each operator with a queue has its own CAS loop, which in the event of an inappropriate request model may cause significant performance overhead. For example, request(1) or any other amount of elements that is small enough in comparison to the whole amount of data may be considered an inappropriate request model.

CAS (compare-and-swap) is a single operation that returns a value of 1 or 0 depending on the success of the operation. Since we want the operation to succeed, we repeat CAS operations until it is successful. These repetitive CAS operations are called *CAS loops*.

To prevent memory and performance overhead, we should switch communication protocols, as proposed by the Reactive Streams specification. Supposing that the chain of elements inside the boundary, or boundaries, has a shared queue and switching the whole chain of operators to use the upstream operator as the queue without additional `request` calls may increase the overall performance significantly. Hence, the downstream may drain values from the upstream until it returns `null` if the value is not available to indicate the end of the stream. To notify the downstream that elements are available, the upstream calls the downstream's `onNext` with `null` values as the specific exclusion for that protocol. Also, error cases or completion of the stream will be notified as usual over `onError` or `onComplete`. Thereby, the previous example may be optimized in the following way:

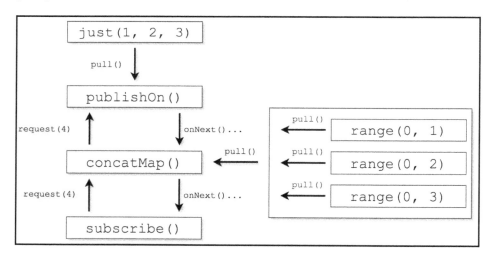

Diagram 4.16. Queue subscription fusion with protocol switching

In this example, the `publishOn` and `concatMap` operators may be significantly optimized. In the first case, there are no intermediate operators, which have to be executed in the main thread. Thus, we may directly use the `just` operator as a queue and `pull` from it on a separate thread. In the case of `concatMap`, all inner streams may also be considered as queues so that each stream may be drained without any additional `request` calls.

We should note that nothing is preventing communication between `publishOn` and `concatMap` using an optimized protocol, but at the time of writing, such optimizations were not implemented, so we decided to expose the communication mechanisms as is.

In summary, as we can see from this section, the internals of the Reactor library are even more complicated than it seems at first glance. With powerful optimizations, Reactor has moved far ahead of RxJava 1.x and thereby provides better performance.

Summary

In this chapter, we covered many topics. We briefly outlined the history of Reactor to ascertain the motivation behind *yet another reactive library*, Project Reactor. We also looked at the most important milestones of this library—milestones that were needed to build such a versatile and powerful tool. Furthermore, we looked at an overview of the main problems with the RxJava 1.x implementation, as well as problems with early Reactor versions. By looking at what has been changed in Project Reactor after the Reactive Streams specification, we highlighted why reactive programming—so efficient and straightforward—requires such a challenging implementation.

We also described the `Mono` and `Flux` reactive types, as well as the different ways to create, transform, and consume Reactive Streams. We looked inside a running stream and controlled backpressure with the pull-push model via the `Subscription` object. We also described how operator fusion improves the performance of Reactive Streams. In summary, the Project Reactor library provides a powerful toolset for reactive programming and asynchronous and IO-intensive applications.

In the following chapters, we are going to cover how the Spring Framework has been improved in order to leverage the power of reactive programming in general and Project Reactor in particular. We will focus on building efficient applications with Spring 5 WebFlux and Reactive Spring Data.

5
Going Reactive with Spring Boot 2

In the previous chapter, we learned the essentials of Project Reactor, as well as the behavior of reactive types and operators and how they help to solve different business problems. Along with the straightforward API, we saw that, under the hood, there are hidden complex mechanisms that allow concurrent, asynchronous, nonblocking message processing. In addition to this, we explored available backpressure controls and related strategies. As we saw in the previous chapter, Project Reactor is more than just a reactive programming library. It also offers add-ons and adapters that make it possible to build reactive systems, even without the Spring Framework. Through this, we saw an integration of Project Reactor with Apache Kafka and Netty.

While Project Reactor may work well without Spring Framework, it is usually not enough to build a feature-rich application. One of the missing elements here is the well-known dependency injection, which gives us decoupling between components. Moreover, the time when we build powerful and customizable applications is when Spring Framework shines more brightly. However, even better applications may be built with Spring Boot.

Consequently, in this chapter, we are going to describe the importance of Spring Boot and the features that it brings. We are also going to see the changes that come with Spring Framework 5 and Spring Boot 2, looking at how the Spring ecosystem adopts the reactive programming approach.

This chapter covers the following topics:

- The problems Spring Boot solves, and how
- The essentials of Spring Boot
- Reactivity in Spring Boot 2.0 and Spring Framework

A fast start as the key to success

Humans have never liked to spend much time on routine work and tasks that are not related to their goals. In business, to achieve the desired result, we are required to learn fast and experiment fast. Reactivity also applies in real life. It is crucial to react to changes in the market, change strategies fast, and achieve new goals as quickly as possible. The faster we prove the concept, the more value it brings to business, and the less money is therefore spent on research.

For this reason, humans have always endeavored to simplify routine work. Developers are not excluded from that rule. We love everything to work out of the box, especially when we are talking about a complex framework such as Spring. Despite a lot of benefits and advantageous features introduced by Spring Framework, it requires a deep understanding of how to work with it, and novice developers may easily fail when they become involved in an area in which they are not experienced. A good example of a possible pitfall is a simple **inversion of control** (**IoC**) container's configuration, which counts at least five possible configuration methods. To understand the problem, let's take a look at the following code sample:

```
public class SpringApp {
    public static void main(String[] args) {
        GenericApplicationContext context =
            new GenericApplicationContext();

        new XmlBeanDefinitionReader(context)
            .loadBeanDefinitions("services.xml");

        new GroovyBeanDefinitionReader(context)
            .loadBeanDefinitions("services.groovy");

        new PropertiesBeanDefinitionReader(context)
            .loadBeanDefinitions("services.properties");

        context.refresh();
    }
}
```

As we can see from the preceding code, the raw Spring Framework has at least three different ways of registering beans in the Spring context.

On the one hand, Spring Framework offers us flexibility in configuring the beans' sources. On the other hand, there are a few problems that come with having such a broad list of options to do this. For example, one of the problems is XML configurations that we *cannot debug* easily. Another issue that makes it harder to work with such configurations is the *inability to validate the correctness of those configurations* without additional tools, such as IntelliJ IDEA or Spring Tool Suite. Finally, the *lack of proper discipline in coding styles and development conventions* may significantly increase the complexity of a large project and decrease its clarity. For example, the lack of proper discipline in the approaches to bean definition may complicate a future project since one individual developer in the team may define beans in the XML and another may do this in properties. Anyone else may do the same in the Java configurations. Consequently, a new developer may easily get confused by that inconsistency and delve into the project for much longer than necessary.

Along with a simple IoC, Spring Frameworks provide much more complex features, such as the Spring Web module or the Spring Data module. Both modules require plenty of configuration just to run the application. Troubles usually arise when the developed application is required to be platform-independent, which means an increasing number of configurations and boilerplate code, and less business-related code.

 Note that here *platform-independent* means being independent of the particular server API, such as the Servlet API. Alternatively, it refers to being unaware of the specific environment and its configurations, as well as other features.

For example, to configure a simple web application and nothing else, we need at least seven lines of boilerplate, as shown in the following code:

```
public class MyWebApplicationInitializer
            implements WebApplicationInitializer {
    @Override
    public void onStartup(ServletContext servletCxt) {
        AnnotationConfigWebApplicationContext cxt =
            new AnnotationConfigWebApplicationContext();
        cxt.register(AppConfig.class);
        cxt.refresh();
        DispatcherServlet servlet = new DispatcherServlet(cxt);
        ServletRegistration.Dynamic registration = servletCxt
            .addServlet("app", servlet);
        registration.setLoadOnStartup(1);
        registration.addMapping("/app/*");
    }
}
```

The preceding code does not include any security configurations or other essential functionalities, such as content rendering. At some point in time, each Spring-based application had similar pieces of code that were quite unoptimized and required additional attention from developers, consequently wasting money for no good reason.

Using Spring Roo to try to develop applications faster

Luckily for us, the Spring team understood the importance of a fast project start. In early 2009, a new project called **Spring Roo** was announced (see `https://projects.spring.io/spring-roo` for more details). This project was aimed at rapid application development. The main idea behind Spring Roo is to use the **convention-over-configuration** approach. For that purpose, Spring Roo provides a command-line user interface that makes it possible to initialize infrastructure and domain models, and create a REST API with a few commands. Spring Roo simplifies the application development process. However, using such a tool for large application development did not seem to work in practice. Here, problems arose when the structure of the project became complicated, or when the technologies used went beyond the scope of the Spring Framework. Finally, Spring Roo was also not too popular for daily use. Consequently, the question of rapid application development remains unanswered.

Note that Spring Roo version 2.0 was released at the time of writing. This contains many improvements that we can learn about at `https://docs.spring.io/spring-roo/docs/current/reference/html`.

Spring Boot as a key to fast-growing applications

In late 2012, Mike Youngstrom raised an issue that influenced the future of Spring Framework. The point that he proposed was to change the entirety of the Spring Architecture and simplify the usage of Spring Framework so developers may start building business logic faster. Even though that proposition was declined, it motivated the Spring team to create a new project that dramatically simplified Spring Framework usage. In mid-2013, the Spring team announced its first prerelease of a project under the name **Spring Boot** (see `https://spring.io/projects/spring-boot` for more details). The main idea behind Spring Boot was to simplify the application development process and allow users to begin a new project without any additional infrastructure configuration.

Along with this, Spring Boot adopts the containerless web application idea and executable **fat** JAR techniques. With this approach, Spring applications could be written on one line and be run with one additional command line. The following code shows a complete Spring Boot web application:

```
@SpringBootApplication
public class MyApplication {
    public static void main(String[] args) {
        SpringApplication.run(MyApplication.class, args);
    }
}
```

The most important part of the preceding example is that there is an annotation called `@SpringBootApplication` that is required to run an IoC container. There is also the MVC server, as well as other application components. Let's dig into this a bit deeper. First of all, Spring Boot is a bunch of modules and additions to modern build tools, such as Gradle or Maven. In general, Spring Boot has two central modules on which it depends. The first one is the `spring-boot` module, which comes with all possible default configurations related to the Spring IoC container. The second one is `spring-boot-autoconfigure`, which brings all possible configurations for all existing Spring projects, such as Spring Data, Spring MVC, Spring WebFlux, and so on. At first glance, it seems that all defined configurations are enabled at once, even if this is not required. However, this is not the case, and all configurations are disabled until a particular dependency is introduced. Spring Boot defines a new notion for modules that usually contain the word `-starter-` in their name. By default, starters do not contain any Java code, but bring all relevant dependencies to activate particular configurations in `spring-boot-autoconfigure`. With Spring Boot, we now have the `-starter-web` and `-starter-data-jpa` modules, which allow the configuration of all required infrastructural parts without additional hassle. The most noticeable difference in the Spring Roo project is its greater flexibility. Along with the default configurations, which may easily be extended, Spring Boot provides a fluent API for building our own starters. This API allows the replacement of default configurations and provides us with our own configurations for particular modules.

 For the purposes of this book, we do not cover the details of Spring Boot. However, *Preview Online Code Files Learning Spring Boot 2.0, Second Edition* by Greg L. Turnquist covers Spring Boot in great detail. We can find it at `https://www.packtpub.com/application-development/learning-spring-boot-20-second-edition`.

Reactive in Spring Boot 2.0

Since this book is about reactive programming, we are not going to go into too much detail regarding Spring Boot. However, as the previous section stated, the ability to bootstrap applications fast is a critical ingredient of a successful framework. Let's figure out how reactivity is reflected in the Spring ecosystem. Since we get no benefits from only changing the programming paradigm to reactive programming because of the blocking nature of Spring MVC and Spring Data modules, the Spring team decided to change the whole paradigm inside those modules as well. For that purpose, the Spring ecosystem brings us a list of reactive modules. In this section, we will very briefly cover all of those modules. However, most of them are covered later in the book in dedicated chapters.

Reactive in Spring Core

The central module of the Spring ecosystem is the **Spring Core** module. One of the noticeable enhancements that were introduced with Spring Framework 5.x was the native support for Reactive Streams and reactive libraries, such as RxJava 1/2 and Project Reactor 3.

Support for reactive types conversion

One of the most comprehensive improvements toward supporting the Reactive Streams specification is the introduction of `ReactiveAdapter` and `ReactiveAdapterRegistry`. The `ReactiveAdapter` class gives two fundamental methods for reactive type conversion, as shown in the following code:

```
class ReactiveAdapter {
   ...

   <T> Publisher<T> toPublisher(@Nullable Object source) { ... }   // (1)

   Object fromPublisher(Publisher<?> publisher) { ... }            // (2)
}
```

In the preceding example, `ReactiveAdapter` introduces two fundamental methods for the conversion of any type to `Publisher<T>` (annotated with `(1)`) and back to `Object`. For example, in order to provide a conversion for the `Maybe` reactive type from RxJava 2, we can create our own `ReactiveAdapter` in the following way:

```
public class MaybeReactiveAdapter extends ReactiveAdapter {          // (1)

    public MaybeReactiveAdapter() {                                  // (2)
        super(
            ReactiveTypeDescriptor                                   // (3)
                .singleOptionalValue(Maybe.class, Maybe::empty),     //
            rawMaybe -> ((Maybe<?>)rawMaybe).toFlowable(),           // (4)
            publisher -> Flowable.fromPublisher(publisher)           // (5)
                                .singleElement()                     //
        );
    }
}
```

In the preceding example, we extend the default `ReactiveAdapter` and provide a custom implementation `(1)`. In turn, we provide a default constructor and hide the details of the implementation behind it `(2)`. The first parameter to the parent constructor `(3)` is a definition of the `ReactiveTypeDescriptor` instance.

The `ReactiveTypeDescriptor` provides information about the reactive type that is used in `ReactiveAdapter`. Finally, the parent constructor requires a definition of conversion functions (lambdas in our case) that transforms a raw object (which is assumed to be `Maybe`) to the `Publisher` `(4)` and transforms any `Publisher` back to `Maybe`.

> Note that `ReactiveAdapter` assumes that, before passing any object to the `toPublisher` method, the object's type compatibility is checked using the `ReactiveAdapter#getReactiveType` method.

To simplify the interaction, there is `ReactiveAdapterRegistry`, which allows us to keep instances of `ReactiveAdapter` in one place, as well as generalizing access to them, as shown in the following code:

```
ReactiveAdapterRegistry
    .getSharedInstance()                                            // (1)
    .registerReactiveType(                                          // (2)
        ReactiveTypeDescriptor
            .singleOptionalValue(Maybe.class, Maybe::empty),
        rawMaybe -> ((Maybe<?>)rawMaybe).toFlowable(),
        publisher -> Flowable.fromPublisher(publisher)
                            .singleElement()
```

```
    );

...

    ReactiveAdapter maybeAdapter = ReactiveAdapterRegistry
        .getSharedInstance()                                      // (1)
        .getAdapter(Maybe.class);                                 // (3)
```

As we can see, the `ReactiveAdapterRegistry` represents a common pool of `ReactiveAdapter` instances for different reactive types. In turn, `ReactiveAdapterRegistry` provides a singleton instance (1) that might be used in many places within the framework or that may be employed in the developed application. Along with that, the registry makes it possible to register an adapter by providing the same list of parameters as in the previous example (2). Finally, we may get an existing adapter by providing the Java class to which the conversion should be done (3).

Reactive I/O

Another dramatic improvement related to reactive support is the reinforcement of the core I/O package. First of all, the Spring Core module introduced an additional abstraction over a buffer of `byte` instances called `DataBuffer`. The main reason to avoid `java.nio.ByteBuffer` is to provide an abstraction that may support different byte buffers without being required to make any additional conversions between them. For example, in order to convert `io.netty.buffer.ByteBuf` to `ByteBuffer`, we have to access the stored bytes that may require pulling them into a heap from the off-heap space. This may break efficient memory usage and buffer recycling (reusing the same buffers of bytes) provided by Netty. Alternatively, Spring `DataBuffer` provides an abstraction of a particular implementation, and allows us to use underlying implementations in a generic way. The additional subinterface, called `PooledDataBuffer`, also enables a reference-counting feature and allows efficient memory management out of the box.

Furthermore, the fifth version of Spring Core introduces an extra `DataBufferUtils` class that permits interaction with I/O (interaction with a network, resources, files, and so on) in the form of Reactive Streams. For example, we may read Shakespeare's *Hamlet* reactively and with backpressure support in the following way:

```
    Flux<DataBuffer> reactiveHamlet = DataBufferUtils
        .read(
            new DefaultResourceLoader().getResource("hamlet.txt"),
            new DefaultDataBufferFactory(),
            1024
        );
```

As we may have noticed, `DataBufferUtils.read` returns a `Flux` of `DataBuffer` instances. Therefore, we may use all of Reactor's functionality in order to read *Hamlet*.

Finally, the last significant and vital feature related to Reactive in Spring Core is **reactive codecs**. Reactive codecs provide a convenient way to convert a stream of `DataBuffer` instances to the stream of objects and back. For that purpose, there are the `Encoder` and `Decoder` interfaces, which provide the following API for encoding/decoding streams of data:

```
interface Encoder<T> {
    ...

    Flux<DataBuffer> encode(Publisher<? extends T> inputStream, ...);
}

interface Decoder<T> {
    ...

    Flux<T> decode(Publisher<DataBuffer> inputStream, ...);

    Mono<T> decodeToMono(Publisher<DataBuffer> inputStream, ...);

}
```

As we can see from the preceding example, both interfaces operate with the Reactive Streams' `Publisher`, and allow the encoding/decoding of a stream of `DataBuffer` instances to objects. The central benefit of using such an API is that it offers a nonblocking way to convert serialized data to Java objects and vice-versa. Furthermore, such a way of encoding/decoding data may decrease the processing latency since the nature of Reactive Streams allows independent element processing so that we do not have to wait for the last byte to start decoding the whole dataset. On the contrary, it is unnecessary to have the complete list of objects in order to start encoding and sending them to the I/O channel so that both directions can improve.

 To learn more about Reactive I/O in Spring Core, please visit `https://docs.spring.io/spring/docs/current/spring-framework-reference/core.html#databuffers`.

To summarize, we can say that we have an excellent foundation for reactive programming in the Spring Framework with the fifth version of Spring Core. In turn, Spring Boot delivers that foundation as a backbone component to any application. It also makes it possible to write reactive applications and at the same time put less effort into inventing ways to convert reactive types, working with I/O in the reactive style, and encoding/decoding data on-the-fly.

Reactive in web

Another critical point that must be mentioned here is the inevitable changes in the Web module. First of all, Spring Boot 2 introduces a new Web starter called WebFlux, which brings new opportunities for a high-throughput and low-latency application. The Spring WebFlux module is built on top of the Reactive Streams adapter and provides integration with server engines such as Netty and Undertow, along with the support of ordinary Servlet-API-3.1-based servers. In this way, Spring WebFlux provides a nonblocking foundation and opens up new possibilities for Reactive Streams as a central abstraction for interaction between a business logic code and a server engine.

 Note that the adapter for Servlet API 3.1 provides purely asynchronous and nonblocking integration that differs from the WebMVC adapter. Of course, the Spring WebMVC module also supports Servlet API 4.0, which enables HTTP/2 support.

In turn, Spring WebFlux extensively uses Reactor 3 as a first-class citizen. Because of this, we can use reactive programming out-of-the-box without any additional effort, and we can also run a web application on top of the built-in integration of Project Reactor with Netty. Finally, the WebFlux module provides built-in backpressure support, so we can be sure that the I/O does not become overwhelmed. Apart from the changes in the interactions on the server-side, Spring WebFlux brings a new `WebClient` class that enables nonblocking, client-side interactions.

Furthermore, as well as the introduction of the WebFlux module, the good old WebMVC module also gained some support for Reactive Streams. Starting with the fifth version of the framework, the Servlet API 3.1 also became a baseline for the WebMVC module. This should mean that WebMVC now supports nonblocking I/O in the form proposed in the Servlet specification. However, the design of the WebMVC module has not changed a lot regarding the nonblocking I/O at the proper level. Nevertheless, the asynchronous behavior of Servlet 3.0 has been properly implemented there for some time. In order to fill the gap in reactive support, Spring WebMVC provides an upgrade for the `ResponseBodyEmitterReturnValueHandler` class. Since the `Publisher` class may be considered an infinite stream of events, the `Emitter` handler is the appropriate place to put the logic for reactive type handling without breaking the whole infrastructure of the WebMVC module. For that purpose, the WebMVC module introduces the `ReactiveTypeHandler` class, which takes care of properly handling reactive types, such as `Flux` and `Mono`.

As well as the changes that support reactive types on the server side, in order to get the non-blocking behavior on the client side, we may use the same WebClient taken from the WebFlux module. At first glance, this may seem to cause a conflict between the two modules. Fortunately, Spring Boot comes to the rescue and provides a sophisticated environment management behavior based on the available classes in the classpath. Consequently, by providing the WebMVC (`spring-boot-starter-web`) module along with WebFlux, we get the WebMVC environment and the nonblocking reactive `WebClient` from the WebFlux module.

Finally, when comparing both modules as reactive pipes, we get the kind of arrangement that is shown in the following diagram:

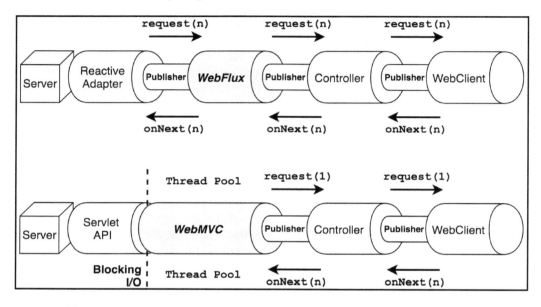

Diagram 5.1. A schematic representation of the reactive WebFlux and partially reactive WebMVC modules in the form of pipes.

As we can see from the preceding diagram, in both cases of WebMVC or WebFlux usage, we get an almost identical Reactive Streams-based programming model. One of the notable differences between the modules is that WebMVC requires the blocking write/read at the point of integration with the Servlet API originating in the old module's design. This flaw leads to degradation in the interaction model within a reactive stream and downgrades it to the plain PULL model. In turn, WebMVC now uses a thread pool internally dedicated to all blocking reads/writes. Consequently, it should be appropriately configured in order to avoid unexpected behavior.

In contrast, the WebFlux communication model depends on the network throughput and underlying transport protocols that may define its own control flow.

To summarize, Spring 5 introduces a powerful tool for building a reactive, nonblocking application using the Reactive Streams specification and Project Reactor. In addition, Spring Boot enables powerful dependency management and autoconfiguration, thereby protecting us from dependency hell. We are not going to go into detail regarding the features of the new Reactive Web, but we will extensively cover the WebFlux module in Chapter 6, *WebFlux Async Non-Blocking Communication.*

Reactive in Spring Data

As well as the changes in the web layer, another vital part of most applications is the data layer that interacts with the storage. For many years, a robust solution that has been simplifying everyday development is the Spring Data project, which provides convenient abstractions for data access via the repository pattern. Since its early days, Spring Data has mostly provided synchronous blocking access to underlying areas of storage. Fortunately, the fifth generation of the Spring Data framework offers new possibilities for reactive and nonblocking access to the database layer. In the new generation, Spring Data offers the `ReactiveCrudRepository` interface, which exposes Project Reactor's reactive types for seamless integration with reactive workflows. Consequently, it allows database connectors to be an efficient part of an utterly reactive application.

As well as the reactive repository, Spring Data provides a couple of modules that integrate with the storage methods by extending the `ReactiveCrudRepository` interface. The following is a list of storage methods that now have a reactive integration in Spring Data:

- **MongoDB via the Spring Data Mongo Reactive module**: This is an entirely reactive and nonblocking interaction with the NoSQL database, and it is also a proper backpressure control.
- **Cassandra via the Spring Data Cassandra Reactive module**: This is an asynchronous and nonblocking interaction with the Cassandra data storage that supports backpressure over the TCP flow control.
- **Redis via the Spring Data Redis Reactive module**: This is a reactive integration with Redis over the Lettuce Java client.
- **Couchbase via the Spring Data Couchbase Reactive module**: This is a reactive Spring Data integration with the Couchbase database over the RxJava-based driver.

Moreover, all of these modules are supported by Spring Boot, which provides additional starter modules that offer smooth integration with their chosen storage method.

Furthermore, as well as NoSQL databases, Spring Data also introduces Spring Data JDBC, a lightweight integration with JDBC that may soon offer Reactive JDBC connectivity. Reactive data access is covered in `Chapter 7`, *Reactive Database Access.*

To summarize, the fifth generation of Spring Data completes the end-to-end reactive data stream from the web endpoints to the reactive database integration, which covers the needs of most applications. In turn, as we will see in the following sections, most of the improvement in the other Spring Framework modules are based either on the reactive capabilities of WebFlux or reactive Spring Data modules.

Reactive in Spring Session

Another significant update in the Spring Framework, which is related to the Spring Web module, is reactive support in the Spring Session module.

Now we get support for the WebFlux module so that we may employ an efficient abstraction for session management. For that purpose, Spring Session introduces ReactiveSessionRepository, which enables asynchronous, nonblocking access to the stored session with the Reactor's Mono type.

Apart from that, Spring Session offers reactive integration with Redis as session storage over reactive Spring Data. In this way, we may achieve a distributed WebSession just by including the following dependencies:

```
compile "org.springframework.session:spring-session-data-redis"
compile "org.springframework.boot:spring-boot-starter-webflux"
compile "org.springframework.boot:spring-boot-starter-data-redis-reactive"
```

As we can see from the preceding Gradle dependencies example, in order to achieve reactive Redis WebSession management, we have to combine those three dependencies in one place. In turn, Spring Boot takes care of providing an exact combination of beans and producing a fitting autoconfiguration in order to run the web application smoothly.

Reactive in Spring Security

In order to enforce the WebFlux module, Spring 5 provides improved reactive support in the Spring Security module. Here, the central enhancement is support for the reactive programming model via Project Reactor. As we might remember, the old Spring Security used ThreadLocal as a storage method for SecurityContext instances. That technique works well in the case of execution within one Thread. At any point in time, we may access a SecurityContext stored inside the ThreadLocal storage. However, problems occur when asynchronous communication comes into force. Here, we have to provide additional effort to transfer the ThreadLocal content into another Thread, and we do this for each instance of switching between Thread instances. Even though Spring Framework simplifies the transfer of SecurityContext between Threads by using an additional ThreadLocal extension, we still may get into trouble when applying a reactive programming paradigm with Project Reactor or similar reactive libraries.

Fortunately, the new generation of Spring Security employs the reactor context feature in order to transfer security context within a `Flux` or `Mono` stream. In this way, we may safely access the security context even in a complicated reactive stream that may operate in different execution threads. The details of how such capability is implemented within a reactive stack are covered in `Chapter 6`, *WebFlux Async Non-Blocking Communication*.

Reactive in Spring Cloud

Even though the Spring Cloud ecosystem is aimed at building reactive systems using the Spring Framework, the reactive programming paradigm did not pass Spring Cloud by. First of all, such changes have affected an entry point of a distributed system, called **gateways**. For a long time, the only Spring module that made it possible to run an application as a gateway was the **Spring Cloud Netflix Zuul** module. As we may know, Netflix Zuul is based on a Servlet API that uses blocking synchronous request routing. The only way to paralyze the process's requests and obtain better performance is through tuning the underlying server thread pool. Unfortunately, such a model does not scale as well as the reactive approach, and the details of why this occurs are covered in `Chapter 6`, *WebFlux Async Non-Blocking Communication*.

Fortunately, Spring Cloud introduces the new Spring Cloud Gateway module, which is built on top of Spring WebFlux and offers asynchronous and nonblocking routing with the support of Project Reactor 3.

 To learn more about Spring Cloud Gateway, please go to `https://cloud.spring.io/spring-cloud-gateway`.

Apart from the new Gateway module, Spring Cloud Streams obtained the support of Project Reactor and also introduced a more fine-grained streaming model. We are going to cover Spring Cloud Streams in `Chapter 8`, *Scaling Up with Cloud Streams*.

Finally, to simplify the development of reactive systems, Spring Cloud introduces a new module called Spring Cloud Function, aimed at providing essential components for building our own **function as a service** (**FaaS**) solutions. As we will see in `Chapter 8`, *Scaling Up with Cloud Streams*, the Spring Cloud Function module cannot be used in ordinary development without proper additional infrastructure. Fortunately, Spring Cloud Data Flow offers such a possibility, and includes part of the Spring Cloud Function's capabilities. We will not go into the details of Spring Cloud Function and Spring Cloud Data Flow here, as they are covered in `Chapter 8`, *Scaling Up with Cloud Streams*.

Reactive in Spring Test

The integral part of any system development process is testing. Therefore, the Spring ecosystem offers the improved Spring Test and Spring Boot Test modules, which expand a list of additional functionalities for testing reactive Spring applications. In this way, Spring Test provides a `WebTestClient` for testing WebFlux-based web applications, and Spring Boot Test takes care of autoconfiguration for test suites using ordinary annotations.

In turn, to test Reactive Streams' `Publisher`, Project Reactor offers the **Reactor-Test** module, which—in combination with the Spring Test and Spring Boot Test modules—makes it possible to write complete verification suites for business logic implemented using Reactive Spring. All the details of reactive testing will be covered in `Chapter 9`, *Testing the Reactive Application*.

Reactive in monitoring

Finally, a production-ready reactive system built on top of Project Reactor and reactive Spring Framework should expose all vital operational metrics. For that purpose, the Spring ecosystem offers a few options with different granularities for application monitoring.

First of all, Project Reactor itself has built-in metrics. It offers the `Flux#metrics()` method that enables the tracking of different events within a reactive stream. However, besides the manually registered monitoring points, an ordinary web application should track a lot of internal processes. It should also somehow report its operational metrics. For that purpose, the Spring Framework ecosystem offers the updated Spring Boot Actuator module that enables the primary metrics for application monitoring and troubleshooting. The new generation of Spring Actuator provides complete integration with WebFlux and uses its asynchronous, nonblocking programming model in order to expose metric endpoints efficiently.

The final option for monitoring and tracking the application is provided by the **Spring Cloud Sleuth** module, which gives out-of-the-box distributed tracing. A noticeable improvement here is the support for reactive programming with Project Reactor, so all reactive workflows within the application are correctly traced.

To summarize, as well as reactive improvements in the core framework, the Spring ecosystem takes care of production-ready features and enables detailed application monitoring, even for reactive solutions. All of these aspects are covered in `Chapter 10`, *And, Finally, Release It!*

Summary

As we have seen in this chapter, Spring Boot was introduced in order to simplify development with Spring Framework. It acts as the glue for Spring components and gives reasonable default configurations based on application dependencies. With version 2, it also provides excellent support for the reactive stack. This chapter skips many details regarding Spring Framework improvements, but instead covers how Spring Boot helps us to obtain all the benefits of reactive with ease.

However, we will go into the features and enhancements introduced in Spring 5.x in depth in the following chapters, starting with an examination of the Spring WebFlux module and comparing this with good old Spring WebMVC.

WebFlux Async Non-Blocking Communication

6

In the previous chapter, we started to take a look at Spring Boot 2.x. We saw that a lot of useful updates and modules have arrived with the fifth version of the Spring Framework, and we also looked at the Spring WebFlux module.

In this chapter, we are going to take a look at that module in detail. We will compare the internal design of WebFlux with good old Web MVC and try to understand the strengths and weaknesses of both. We are also going to build a simple web application with WebFlux.

This chapter covers the following topics:

- A bird's-eye view of Spring WebFlux
- Spring WebFlux versus Spring Web MVC
- A comprehensive design overview of Spring WebFlux

WebFlux as a central reactive server foundation

As we saw in `Chapter 1`, *Why Reactive Spring?*, and `Chapter 4`, *Project Reactor - the Foundation for Reactive Apps*, the new era of application servers has brought new techniques for developers. From the beginning of Spring Framework's evolution in the field of web applications, the decision was made to integrate the Spring Web module with Java EE's Servlet API. The entire infrastructure of the Spring Framework is built around Servlet API and they are tightly coupled. For instance, the entirety of Spring Web MVC is based on the *Front Controller pattern*. That pattern is implemented in Spring Web MVC by the `org.springframework.web.servlet.DispatcherServlet` class, which indirectly extends the `javax.servlet.http.HttpServlet` class.

On the other hand, the Spring Framework does give us a better level of abstraction in the *Spring Web* module, which is a building block for many features, such as annotation-driven controllers. Even though this module partially separates common interfaces from their implementations, the initial design of Spring Web was also based on the synchronous interaction model, and hence blocks the IO. Nevertheless, such separation is a good foundation, so before moving on to looking at the reactive web, let's recap the design of the web module and try to understand what is going on here:

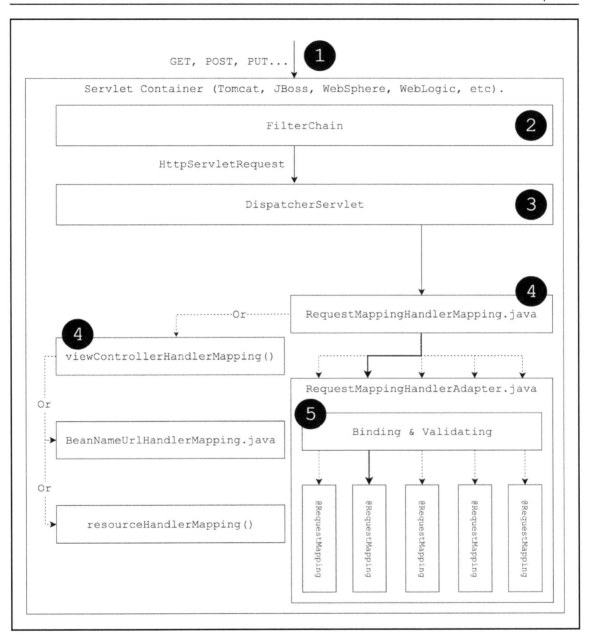

Diagram 6.1. The implementation of the web stack in the Spring WebMVC module

The following is a description of the preceding diagram:

1. The incoming request is handled by the underlying **Servlet Container**. Here, the Servlet Container is responsible for transforming an incoming body into the servlet API's `ServletRequest` interface and preparing the output in the form of the `ServletResponse` interface.

2. The stage of filtering `ServletRequest` through filters is combined in `FilterChain`.

3. The next stage is the `DispatcherServlet` processing stage. Remember that `DispatcherServlet` extends the `Servlet` class. It also holds the list of `HandlerMappings` (**4**), `HandlerAdapters` (**5**), and `ViewResolvers` (which is not depicted in the schema). In the context of the current execution flow, the `DispatcherServlet` class is responsible for searching for a `HandlerMapping` instance and adapting it using a suitable `HandlerAdapter`. It then searches for a `ViewResolver` that can resolve `View` so that `DispatcherServlet` initiates the rendering of the result of `HandlerMapping` and the `HandlerAdapter` execution.

4. After that, we have the `HandlerMapping` stage. `DispatcherServlet` (**3**) searches for all of the `HandlerMapping` beans in the Application Context. During the mapping's initialization process, all instances found during the scanning process are sorted by order. The order number is specified by the `@Order` annotation, or in a case when `HandlerMapping` implements `Ordered` interface. Because of this, the lookup for suitable `HandlerMapping` instances depends on the order that was set up previously. In the preceding diagram, there are a few common `HandlerMapping` instances depicted. The most familiar one is `RequestMappingHandlerMapping`, which enables an annotation-based programming model.

5. Finally, we have the `RequestMappingHandlerAdapter` stage, which takes care of the proper binding of the incoming `ServletRequest` to the `@Controller` annotated object. `RequestMappingHandlerAdapter` also provides request validation, response conversion, and many other helpful things that make the Spring Web MVC framework useful in everyday web development.

As we might have noticed, the overall design relies on the underlying servlet container, which is responsible for handling all mapped servlets inside the container. `DispatchServlet` acts as an integration point between the flexible and highly configurable Spring Web infrastructure and the heavy and complicated Servlet API. A configurable abstraction of `HandlerMapping` helps to separate the final business logic, such as controllers and beans, from the Servlet API.

Spring MVC supports direct interaction with `HttpServletRequest` and `HttpServletResponse`, along with mapping, binding, and validation features. However, when using these classes, we have an additional direct dependency on the Servlet API. This might be considered bad practice, because it may complicate the migration process from Web MVC to WebFlux, or any other web extension for Spring. It is recommended to use `org.springframework.http.RequestEntity` and `org.springframework.http.ResponseEntity` instead. These classes isolate requests and response objects from the web-server implementation.

The Spring Web MVC approach has been a convenient programming model for years. It has proved to be a solid and stable skeleton for web application development. This is why, in 2003, the Spring Framework started on its path to being one of the most popular solutions for building web applications on top of the Servlet API. However, methodologies and techniques of the past do not fit well with the requirements of modern data-intensive systems.

Despite the fact that the Servlet API supports asynchronous, non-blocking communication (starting from version 3.1), the implementation of the Spring MVC module has a lot of gaps and does not allow non-blocking operations throughout the request life cycle. For instance, there is no out-of-the-box non-blocking HTTP client, so any external interaction will most likely cause a blocking IO call. As mentioned in Chapter 5, *Going Reactive with Spring Boot 2*, the Web MVC abstraction does not support all of the features of the non-blocking Servlet API 3.1. Until it does, Spring Web MVC cannot be considered a framework for high-load projects. Another disadvantage of the web abstraction in the old Spring is that there was no flexibility for reusing Spring Web features or programming models for a non-servlet server such as Netty.

That is why the central challenge for the Spring Framework team over the last few years has been to build a new solution that allows the same annotation-based programming model and provides all the benefits of asynchronous non-blocking servers at the same time.

The reactive web core

Let's imagine that we are working on the new asynchronous non-blocking web module for the new Spring ecosystem. How should the new reactive web stack look? First of all, let's analyze the existing solutions and highlight the parts that should be enhanced or eliminated.

It should be noted that, in general, the internal API of Spring MVC is well-designed. The only thing that should be added to the API is a direct dependency on the Servlet API. Therefore, the final solution should have similar interfaces as the Servlet API. The first step toward designing the reactive stack is replacing `javax.servlet.Servlet#service` with an analogical interface and a method that reacts to incoming requests. We also have to change the related interfaces and classes. The Servlet API's way of exchanging a client's request for a server's response should be enhanced and customized as well.

Although the introduction of our own API gives us decoupling from the server engines and concrete APIs, it does not help us set up reactive communication. Hence, all new interfaces should provide access to all data, such as the request body and the session in the reactive format. As we learned from the previous chapters, the Reactive Streams model allows to interact with and process data according to its availability and demand. Since Project Reactor follows the Reactive Streams standard and provides an extensive API from the perspective of functionality, it could be an appropriate tool for building all reactive web APIs on top of it.

Finally, if we combine these things in a real implementation, we come up with the following code:

```
interface ServerHttpRequest {                                    // (1)
   ...                                                           //
   Flux<DataBuffer> getBody();                                   // (1.1)
   ...                                                           //
}                                                                //

interface ServerHttpResponse {                                   // (2)
   ...                                                           //
   Mono<Void> writeWith(Publisher<? extends DataBuffer> body);   // (2.1)
   ...                                                           //
}                                                                //

interface ServerWebExchange {                                    // (3)
   ...                                                           //
   ServerHttpRequest getRequest();                               // (3.1)
   ServerHttpResponse getResponse();                             // (3.2)
   ...                                                           //
   Mono<WebSession> getSession();                                // (3.3)
   ...                                                           //
}                                                                //
```

The preceding code can be explained as follows:

1. This is the draft of the interface that represents an incoming message. As we can see, at point (1.1), the central abstraction that gives access to the incoming bytes is Flux, which means by definition that it has reactive access. As we may remember from Chapter 5, *Going Reactive with Spring Boot 2*, there is a helpful abstraction over the bytes' buffer, which is DataBuffer. This is a convenient way of exchanging data with a particular server implementation. Along with the request's body, any HTTP request usually contains information about incoming headers, paths, cookies, and query parameters, so that information may be expressed as separate methods in either that interface or its sub-interfaces.

2. This is the draft of the response interface, which is a companion interface to the ServerHttpRequest interface. As shown at point (2.1), unlike the ServerHttpRequest#getBody method, the ServerHttpResponse#writeWith method accepts any Publisher<? extends DataBuffer> class. In that case, the Publisher reactive type gives us more flexibility and decouples from that particular reactive library. We may, therefore, use any implementation of the interface and decouple the business logic from the framework. The method returns Mono<Void>, which represents an asynchronous process of sending data to the network. The important point here is that the process of sending data is executed only when we subscribe to the given Mono. Furthermore, the receiving server may control the backpressure, depending on the transport protocol's control flow.

3. This is the ServerWebExchange interface declaration. Here, the interface acts as a container for the HTTP request-response instances (at 3.1 and 3.2). The interface is infrastructural and, as well as the HTTP interaction, may hold information related to the framework. For example, it may contain information about a restored WebSession from the incoming request, as shown at point (3.3). Alternatively, it may provide additional infrastructural methods on top of the request and response interfaces.

In the preceding example, we drafted the potential interfaces for our reactive web stack. In general, those three interfaces are similar to those we have in the Servlet API. For example, ServerHttpRequest and ServerHttpResponse may remind us of ServletRequest and ServletResponse. Essentially, reactive counterparts are aimed at providing almost identical methods from the perspective of the interaction model. However, due to the asynchronous and non-blocking nature of Reactive Streams, we have an out-of-the-box streaming foundation and protection from intricate callback-based APIs. This also protects us from callback hell.

Aside from the central interfaces, to fulfill the whole interaction flow, we have to define the request-response handler and filter API, which may look as follows:

```
interface WebHandler {                                      // (1)
    Mono<Void> handle(ServerWebExchange exchange);          //
}                                                           //

interface WebFilterChain {                                  // (2)
    Mono<Void> filter(ServerWebExchange exchange);          //
}                                                           //

interface WebFilter {                                       // (3)
    Mono<Void> filter(ServerWebExchange exch, WebFilterChain chain);//
}                                                           //
```

The numbered sections in the preceding code can be described as follows:

1. This is the central entry point for any HTTP interaction, called `WebHandler`. Here, our interface plays the role of an abstract `DispatcherServlet`, so we can build any implementation on top of it. Since the responsibility of the interface is to find a request's handler and then compose it with a view's renderer that writes the execution's result to `ServerHttpResponse`, the `DispatcheServlet#handle` method does not have to return any results. However, it might be useful to be notified upon completion of the processing. By relying on a notification signal like this, we may apply a processing timeout so that, if no signal appears within a specified duration, we may cancel execution. For this reason, the method returns `Mono` from `Void`, which allows to wait for the completion of the asynchronous processing without necessarily handling the result.

2. This is the interface that allows to connect a few `WebFilter` instances (3) into a chain, similar to the Servlet API.

3. This is the reactive `Filter` representation.

The preceding interfaces give us a foundation on top of which we may start to build the business logic for the rest of the framework.

We have almost completed the essential elements of the reactive web infrastructure. To finish the abstraction hierarchy, our design requires the lowest-level contract for reactive HTTP request handling. Since we previously defined only the interfaces responsible for data transfer and processing, we have to define an interface that takes responsibility for adapting a server engine to the defined infrastructure. For that purpose, we need an additional level of abstraction that will be responsible for direct interaction with `ServerHttpRequest` and `ServerHttpResponse`.

Moreover, this layer should be responsible for building `ServerWebExchange`. The particular Session storage, the Locale resolvers, and a similar infrastructure are held here:

```
public interface HttpHandler {
    Mono<Void> handle(
        ServerHttpRequest request,
        ServerHttpResponse response);
}
```

Finally, for each server engine, we may have an adaption that calls the middleware's `HttpHandler`, which then composes the given `ServerHttpResponse` and `ServerHttpRequest` to `ServerWebExchange` and passes it to `WebFilterChain` and `WebHandler`. With such a design, it does not matter to Spring WebFlux users how the particular server engine works, since we now have a proper level of abstraction that hides the details of a server engine. We can now move on to the next step and build a high-level reactive abstraction.

The reactive web and MVC frameworks

As we might remember, the key feature of the Spring Web MVC module is its annotation-based programming model. The central challenge, therefore, is providing the same concept for the reactive web stack. If we look at the current Spring Web MVC module, we can see that, in general, the module is designed properly. Instead of building a new reactive MVC infrastructure, we may reuse the existing one and replace synchronous communication with reactive types such as `Flux`, `Mono`, and `Publisher`. For example, two central interfaces for mapping requests and binding contextual information (such as headers, query parameters, attributes, and sessions) to the handler that have been found are `HandlerMapping` and `HandlerAdapter`. In general, we can keep the same chain of `HandlerMapping` and `HandlerAdapter` as in Spring Web MVC, but replace the eager imperative with the reactive interaction using Reactor's types:

```
interface HandlerMapping {                                      // (1)
/* HandlerExecutionChain getHandler(HttpServletRequest request) */ // (1.1)
    Mono<Object>          getHandler(ServerWebExchange exchange); // (1.2)
}                                                               //

interface HandlerAdapter {                                      // (2)
    boolean supports(Object handler);                           //
                                                                //
/* ModelAndView          handle(                                // (2.1)
        HttpServletRequest request, HttpServletResponse response, //
        Object handler                                          //
    ) */                                                        //
```

```
    Mono<HandlerResult> handle(                             // (2.2)
        ServerWebExchange exchange,                         //
        Object handler                                      //
    );                                                      //
}                                                           //
```

The preceding code is explained in the following numbered list:

1. This is the declaration of the reactive `HandlerMapping` interface. Here, to highlight the difference between the old Web MVC implementation and the improved one, the code contains the declarations of both methods. The old implementation, at point `(1.1)`, is commented with `/* ... */` and uses the *italic* font style, while the new interface, at point `(1.2)`, is highlighted in **bold**. As we can see, in general, the methods are very similar. The difference is that the last one returns the `Mono` type, therefore enabling reactive behaviors.

2. This is the reactive `HandlerAdapter` interface version. As we can see here, the reactive version of the `handle` method is a bit more succinct since the `ServerWebExchange` class combines the request and response instances at the same time. At point `(2.2)`, the method returns `Mono` of the `HandlerResult` instead of `ModelAndView` (which is at `2.1`). As we may remember, `ModelAndView` is responsible for providing information such as a status code, `Model`, and `View`. The `HandlerResult` class contains the same information, apart from the status code. `HandlerResult` is better, since it provides the result of the direct execution, so it is easier for `DispatcherHandler` to find a handler. In Web MVC, `View` is responsible for rendering templates as well as objects. It also renders results, so its purpose in Web MVC can be a bit unclear. Unfortunately, such multiple responsibilities cannot be easily adapted to asynchronous result processing. In such cases, when the result is a plain Java object, the `View` lookup is done in `HandlerAdapter`, which is not a direct responsibility of that class. Because of this, it is better to keep the responsibility clear, so the change implemented in the preceding code is an improvement.

Following these steps will give us a reactive interaction model without breaking the whole execution hierarchy, thereby preserving the existing design and potentially reusing existing code with minimal changes.

Finally, by gathering all of the steps that we have taken so far toward achieving a reactive web stack and correcting the processing flow of a request, taking into account the real implementation, we will come up with the following design:

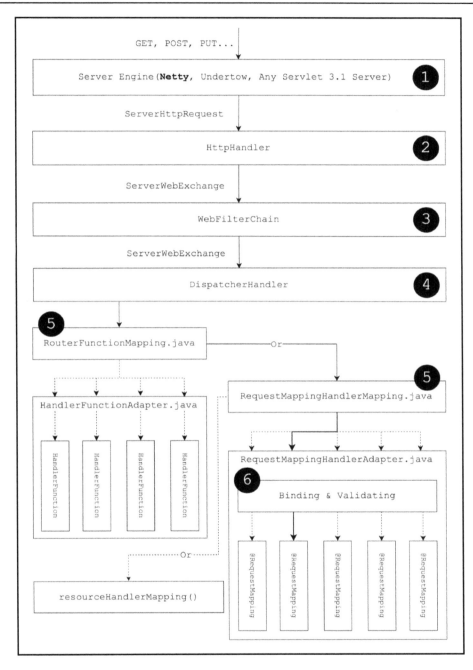

Diagram 6.2. The redesigned reactive web and MVC stack

The preceding diagram may be explained as follows:

1. This is the incoming request, which is handled by the underlying **Server Engine**. As we can see, the list of server engines is not limited to Servlet API-based servers and now includes engines such as *Netty* and *Undertow*. Here, each server engine has its own reactive adapter, which maps the internal representations of HTTP requests and HTTP responses to `ServerHttpRequest` and `ServerHttpResponse`.

2. This is the `HttpHandler` stage, which composes the given `ServerHttpRequest`, the `ServerHttpResponse`, the user's Session, and related information into a `ServerWebExchange` instance.

3. At this point, we have the `WebFilterChain` stage, which composes the defined `WebFilter` into the chain. Then, `WebFilterChain` is responsible for executing the `WebFilter#filter` method of each `WebFilter` instance in this chain, in order to filter the incoming `ServerWebExchange`.

4. If all filter conditions are met, `WebFilterChain` calls the `WebHandler` instance.

5. The next step is to look up instances of `HandlerMapping` and invoke the first suitable one. In this example, we depicted a few `HandlerMapping` instances, such as `RouterFunctionMapping`, the well-known `RequestMappingHandlerMapping`, and the `HandlerMapping` resource. The new `HandlerMapping` instance here is `RouterFunctionMapping`, which is introduced in the WebFlux module and goes beyond purely functional request handling. We will not go into details of that feature here; we will cover this in the following section.

6. This is the `RequestMappingHandlerAdapter` stage, which has the same functionality as it did previously, but now uses Reactive Streams in order to build a reactive interaction flow.

The preceding diagram depicts only a simplified view of the underlying interaction flow in a WebFlux module. It should be noted that in the WebFlux module, the default server engine is Netty. The Netty server is an appropriate default since it is widely used in the reactive space. Also, that server engine provides both client and server asynchronous non-blocking interaction. This means that it's better for the reactive programming paradigm offered by Spring WebFlux. Despite the fact that Netty is a good default server engine, with WebFlux, we have the flexibility to choose our server engine, meaning we can easily switch between various modern server engines such as Undertow, Tomcat, Jetty, or any other Servlet API-based server. As we can see, the WebFlux module mirrors the architecture of the Spring Web MVC module, so it makes it easy to understand for those with experience with the old web framework. Also, the Spring Web Flux module has a lot of hidden gems, which will be covered in the following sections.

Purely functional web with WebFlux

As we might have noticed in the preceding diagram, while it has a lot of similarities to Web MVC, WebFlux also provides a lot of new features. In the era of tiny microservices, Amazon Lambdas, and similar cloud services, it is important to offer functionality that allows developers to create lightweight applications that have almost the same arsenal of framework features. One of the features that made competitor frameworks, such as Vert.x or Ratpack, more attractive was their ability to produce lightweight applications, which was achieved by functional route mapping and a built-in API that allowed us to write complex request routing logic. This is why the Spring Framework team decided to incorporate this feature into the WebFlux module. Moreover, the combination of pure functional routing fits sufficiently with new reactive programming approaches. For example, let's take a look at how to build complex routing using the new functional approach:

```
import static ...RouterFunctions.nest;              // (1)
import static ...RouterFunctions.nest;              //
import static ...RouterFunctions.route;             //
...
import static ...RequestPredicates.GET;             // (2)
import static ...RequestPredicates.POST;            //
import static ...RequestPredicates.accept;          //
import static ...RequestPredicates.contentType;     //
import static ...RequestPredicates.method;          //
import static ...RequestPredicates.path;            //

@SpringBootApplication                              // (3)
public class DemoApplication {                      //
    ...
    @Bean
```

```
    public RouterFunction<ServerResponse> routes(          // (4)
        OrderHandler handler                               // (4.1)
    ) {                                                    //
        return                                             
            nest(path("/orders"),                          // (5)
                nest(accept(APPLICATION_JSON),             //
                    route(GET("/{id}"), handler::get)      //
                    .andRoute(method(HttpMethod.GET), handler::list)  //
                )                                          //
                .andNest(contentType(APPLICATION_JSON),    //
                    route(POST("/"), handler::create)      //
                )                                          //
            );                                             
    }
}
```

The preceding code can be explained as follows:

1. This is a declaration of static imports from the RouterFunctions class. As we can see, the RouterFunctions class provides an extensive list of factory methods that return RouterFunction interfaces with different behaviors.

2. This is a declaration of static imports from the RequestPredicates class. As we can see from the preceding code, the RequestPredicates class allows to check an incoming request from a different perspective. In general, RequestPredicates provides access to a different implementation of the RequestPredicate interface, which is a functional interface and may be extended easily in order to verify incoming requests in a custom way.

3. This is a common declaration of the Spring Boot application, whose class is annotated with @SpringBootApplication.

4. This is a method declaration that initializes the RouterFunction<ServerResponse> bean. In this example, the method is invoked during the bootstrapping of an application.

5. This is a declaration of RouterFunction, expressed with the support of the RouterFunctions and RequestPredicates APIs.

In the preceding example, we used an alternative way of declaring an application's web API. This technique provides a functional method for handler declaration and allows us to keep all routes explicitly defined in one place. In addition, an API such as the one used previously allows us to write our own request predicates easily. For example, the following code shows how to implement a custom `RequestPredicate` and apply it to the routing logic:

```
nest((serverRequest) -> serverRequest.cookies()
                            .containsKey("Redirect-Traffic"),
    route(all(), serverRedirectHandler)
)
```

In the previous example, we created a small `RouterFunction`, which redirects traffic to another server if the `"Redirect-Traffic"` cookie is present.

The new functional web also introduced a new way of dealing with requests and responses. For example, the following code sample shows part of the `OrderHandler` implementation:

```
class OrderHandler {                                           // (1)
    final OrderRepository orderRepository;                     //
    ...
    public Mono<ServerResponse> create(ServerRequest request) {  // (2)
        return request                                         //
            .bodyToMono(Order.class)                           // (2.1)
            .flatMap(orderRepository::save)                    //
            .flatMap(o ->                                      //
                ServerResponse.created(URI.create("/orders/" + o.id))  // (2.2)
                          .build()                             //
            );                                                 //
    }                                                          //
    ...                                                        //
}                                                              //
```

The preceding code can be described as follows:

1. This is the `OrderHandler` class declaration. In this example, we skip the constructor declaration in order to focus on the API of the functional routes.
2. This is the `create` method declaration. As we can see, the method accepts `ServerRequest`, which is specific to the functional routes request type. As we can see at point `(2.1)`, `ServerRequest` exposes the API, which allows the manual mapping of the request body either to `Mono` or `Flux`. In addition, the API allows us to specify the class to which the request body should be mapped. Finally, the functional addition in WebFlux offers an API that allows us to construct a response using the fluent API of the `ServerResponse` class.

As we can see, in addition to the API for functional route declaration, we have a functional API for request and response processing.

Even though the new API gives us a functional approach to declaring the handler and mapping, it does not give us a fully lightweight web application. There are some cases where the whole functionality of the Spring ecosystem may be redundant, therefore decreasing the overall startup time of the application. For example, suppose that we have to build a service that is responsible for matching user passwords. Usually, such a service burns a lot of CPU by hashing the incoming password and then comparing it with the stored password. The only functionality that we need is the `PasswordEncoder` interface from the Spring Security module, which allows us to compare the encoded password with the raw password using the `PasswordEncoder#matchs` method. Therefore, the whole Spring infrastructure with IoC, annotation processing, and autoconfiguration is redundant and makes our application slower in terms of startup time.

Fortunately, the new functional web framework allows us to build a web application without starting the whole Spring infrastructure. Let's consider the following example in order to understand how we can achieve this:

```
class StandaloneApplication {                                    // (1)

    public static void main(String[] args) {                     // (2)
        HttpHandler httpHandler = RouterFunctions.toHttpHandler(  // (2.1)
            routes(new BCryptPasswordEncoder(18))                // (2.2)
        );                                                        //
        ReactorHttpHandlerAdapter reactorHttpHandler =           // (2.3)
            new ReactorHttpHandlerAdapter(httpHandler);          //

        HttpServer.create()                                       // (3)
                .port(8080)                                       // (3.1)
                .handle(reactorHttpHandler)                       // (3.2)
                .bind()                                           // (3.3)
```

```
                .flatMap(DisposableChannel::onDispose)        // (3.4)
                .block();                                      //
    }                                                          //

    static RouterFunction<ServerResponse> routes(             // (4)
        PasswordEncoder passwordEncoder                        //
    ) {                                                        //
        return                                                 //
            route(POST("/check"),                              // (5)
                request -> request                             //
                    .bodyToMono(PasswordDTO.class)             // (5.1)
                    .map(p -> passwordEncoder                  //
                        .matches(p.getRaw(), p.getSecured()))  // (5.2)
                    .flatMap(isMatched -> isMatched            // (5.3)
                        ? ServerResponse                       //
                            .ok()                              //
                            .build()                           //
                        : ServerResponse                       //
                            .status(HttpStatus.EXPECTATION_FAILED)  //
                            .build()                           //
                    )                                          //
            );                                                 //
    }                                                          //
}
```

The following numbered list describes the preceding code sample:

1. This is the declaration of the main application class. As we can see, there is no additional annotation from Spring Boot.
2. Here, we have the declaration of the main method with the initialization of the required variables. At point (2.2), we invoke the `routes` method and then convert `RouterFunction` to `HttpHandler`. Then, at point (2.3), we use the built-in `HttpHandler` adapters called `ReactorHttpHandlerAdapter`.
3. At this point, we create an `HttpServer` instance, which is a part of the Reactor-Netty API. Here, we use a fluent API of the `HttpServer` class in order to set up the server. At point (3.1), we declare the port, put the created instance of `ReactorHttpHandlerAdapter` (at point 3.2), and, by calling `bind` at point (3.3), start the server engine. Finally, in order to keep the application alive, we block the main `Thread` and listen for the disposal event of the created server at point (3.4).
4. This point shows the declaration of the `routes` method.

5. This is the routes mapping logic, which handles a request for any POST methods with the `/check` path. Here, we start with the mapping of incoming requests with the support of the `bodyToMono` method. Then, once the body is converted, we use a `PasswordEncoder` instance in order to check the raw password against the encoded one (in our case, we use a strong BCrypt algorithm with 18 rounds of hashing, which may take a few seconds for encoding/matching) (5.2). Finally, if the password matches the stored one, `ServerResponse` returns with a status of either `OK(200)` or `EXPECTATION_FAILED(417)` if the password does not match the stored one.

The preceding example shows how easily we can set up a web application without having to run the whole Spring Framework infrastructure. The benefit of such a web application is that its startup time is much shorter. The startup time of the application is around ~700 milliseconds, whereas the startup process for the same application with the Spring Framework and Spring Boot infrastructure takes up to ~2 seconds (~2,000 milliseconds), which is approximately three times slower.

Note that startup times may vary, but the overall proportion should be the same.

To summarize the routing declaration technique by switching to a functional route declaration, we maintain all routing configuration in one place and use a reactive approach for incoming request processing. At the same time, such a technique offers almost the same flexibility as the usual annotation-based approach in terms of accessing incoming request parameters, path variables, and other important components of the request. It also provides us with the ability to avoid the whole Spring Framework infrastructure being run and has the same flexibility in terms of route setup, which may decrease the bootstrapping time of the application by up to three times.

Non-blocking cross-service communication with WebClient

In the previous sections, we looked at an overview of the basic design of and changes in the new Spring WebFlux module and learned about new functional approaches with `RoutesFunction`. However, Spring WebFlux also contains other new possibilities. One of the most important introductions is the new non-blocking HTTP client, which is called `WebClient`.

Essentially, WebClient is the reactive replacement for the old RestTemplate. However, in WebClient, we have a functional API that fits better with the reactive approach and offers built-in mapping to Project Reactor types such as Flux or Mono. In order to learn more about WebClient, let's have a look at the following example:

```
WebClient.create("http://localhost/api")                    // (1)
         .get()                                             // (2)
         .uri("/users/{id}", userId)                        // (3)
         .retrieve()                                        // (4)
         .bodyToMono(User.class)                            // (5)
         .map(...)                                          // (6)
         .subscribe();                                      //
```

In the preceding example, we create a WebClient instance using a factory method called create, shown at point 1. Here, the create method allows us to specify the base URI, which is used internally for all future HTTP calls. Then, in order to start building a call to a remote server, we may execute one of the WebClient methods that sounds like an HTTP method. In the previous example, we used WebClient#get, shown at point (2). Once we call the WebClient#get method, we operate on the request builder instance and can specify the relative path in the uri method, shown at point (3). In addition to the relative path, we can specify headers, cookies, and a request body. However, for simplicity, we have omitted those settings in this case and moved on to composing the request by calling the retrieve or exchange methods. In this example, we use the retrieve method, shown at point (4). This option is useful when we are only interested in retrieving the body and performing further processing. Once the request is set up, we may use one of the methods that help us with the conversion of the response body. Here, we use the bodyToMono method, which converts the incoming payload of the User to Mono, shown at point (5). Finally, we can build the processing flow of the incoming response using the Reactor API, and execute the remote call by calling the subscribe method.

 WebClient follows the behavior described in the Reactive Streams specification. This means that only by calling the subscribe method will WebClient wire the connection and start sending the data to the remote server.

Even though, in most cases, the most common response processing is body processing, there are some cases where we need to process the response status, headers, or cookies. For example, let's build a call to our password checking service and process the response status in a custom way using the WebClient API:

```
class DefaultPasswordVerificationService                        // (1)
    implements PasswordVerificationService {                    //

    final WebClient webClient;                                  // (2)
                                                                //
    public DefaultPasswordVerificationService(                  //
       WebClient.Builder webClientBuilder                       //
    ) {                                                         //
       this.webClient = webClientBuilder                        // (2.1)
           .baseUrl("http://localhost:8080")                    //
           .build();                                            //
    }                                                           //

    @Override                                                   // (3)
    public Mono<Void> check(String raw, String encoded) {       //
       return webClient                                         //
           .post()                                              // (3.1)
           .uri("/check")                                       //
           .body(BodyInserters.fromPublisher(                   // (3.2)
              Mono.just(new PasswordDTO(raw, encoded)),         //
              PasswordDTO.class                                 //
           ))                                                   //
           .exchange()                                          // (3.3)
           .flatMap(response -> {                               // (3.4)
              if (response.statusCode().is2xxSuccessful()) {    // (3.5)
                 return Mono.empty();                           //
              }                                                 //
              else if(resposne.statusCode() == EXPECTATION_FAILD) {  //
                 return Mono.error(                             // (3.6)
                    new BadCredentialsException(...)            //
                 );                                             //
              }                                                 //
              return Mono.error(new IllegalStateException());   //
           });                                                  //
    }                                                           //
}                                                               //
```

The following numbered list describes the preceding code sample:

1. This is the implementation of the `PasswordVerificationService` interface.
2. This is the initialization of the `WebClient` instance. It is important to note that we use a `WebClient` instance per class here, so we do not have to initialize a new one on each execution of the `check` method. Such a technique reduces the need to initialize a new instance of `WebClient` and decreases the method's execution time. However, the default implementation of `WebClient` uses the Reactor-Netty `HttpClient`, which in default configurations shares a common pool of resources among all the `HttpClient` instances. Hence, the creation of a new `HttpClient` instance does not cost that much. Once the constructor of `DefaultPasswordVerificationService` is called, we start initializing `webClient` and use a fluent builder, shown at point `(2.1)`, in order to set up the client.
3. This is the implementation of the `check` method. Here, we use the `webClient` instance in order to execute a `post` request, shown at point `(3.1)`. In addition, we send the body, using the `body` method, and prepare to insert it using the `BodyInserters#fromPublisher` factory method, shown in `(3.2)`. We then execute the `exchange` method at point `(3.3)`, which returns `Mono<ClientResponse>`. We may, therefore, process the response using the `flatMap` operator, shown in `(3.4)`. If the password is verified successfully, as shown at point `(3.5)`, the `check` method returns `Mono.empty`. Alternatively, in the case of an `EXPECTATION_FAILED(417)` status code, we may return the `Mono` of `BadCredentialsExeception`, as shown at point `(3.6)`.

As we can see from the previous example, in a case where it is necessary to process the status code, headers, cookies, and other internals of the common HTTP response, the most appropriate method is the `exchange` method, which returns `ClientResponse`.

As mentioned, `DefaultWebClient` uses the Reactor-Netty `HttpClient` in order to provide asynchronous and non-blocking interaction with the remote server. However, `DefaultWebClient` is designed to be able to change the underlying HTTP client easily. For that purpose, there is a low-level reactive abstraction around the HTTP connection, which is called `org.springframework.http.client.reactive.ClientHttpConnector`. By default, `DefaultWebClient` is preconfigured to use `ReactorClientHttpConnector`, which is an implementation of the `ClientHttpConnector` interface. Starting from Spring WebFlux 5.1, there is a `JettyClientHttpConnector` implementation, which uses the reactive `HttpClient` from Jetty. In order to change the underlying HTTP client engine, we may use the `WebClient.Builder#clientConnector` method and pass the desired instance, which might be either a custom implementation or the existing one.

In addition to the useful abstract layer, `ClientHttpConnector` may be used in a raw format. For example, it may be used for downloading large files, on-the-fly processing, or just simple byte scanning. We will not go into details about `ClientHttpConnector`; we will leave this for curious readers to look into themselves.

Reactive WebSocket API

We have now covered most of the new features of the new WebFlux module. However, one of the crucial parts of the modern web is a streaming interaction model, where both the client and server can stream messages to each other. In this section, we will look at one of the most well-known duplex protocols for duplex client-server communication, called **WebSocket**.

Despite the fact that communication over the WebSocket protocol was introduced in the Spring Framework in early 2013 and designed for asynchronous message sending, the actual implementation still has some blocking operations. For instance, both writing data to I/O or reading data from I/O are still blocking operations and therefore both impact on the application's performance. Therefore, the WebFlux module has introduced an improved version of the infrastructure for WebSocket.

WebFlux offers both client and server infrastructure. We are going to start by analyzing the server-side WebSocket and will then cover the client-side possibilities.

Server-side WebSocket API

WebFlux offers `WebSocketHandler` as the central interface for handling WebSocket connections. This interface has a method called `handle`, which accepts `WebSocketSession`. The `WebSocketSession` class represents a successful handshake between the client and server and provides access to information, including information about the handshake, session attributes, and the incoming stream of data. In order to learn how to deal with this information, let's consider the following example of responding to the sender with echo messages:

```
class EchoWebSocketHandler implements WebSocketHandler {          // (1)
    @Override                                                      //
    public Mono<Void> handle(WebSocketSession session) {          // (2)
        return session                                            // (3)
            .receive()                                            // (4)
            .map(WebSocketMessage::getPayloadAsText)              // (5)
            .map(tm -> "Echo: " + tm)                             // (6)
            .map(session::textMessage)                            // (7)
            .as(session::send);                                   // (8)
```

```
    }                                                                    //
}
```

As we can see from the previous example, the new WebSocket API is built on top of the reactive types from Project Reactor. Here, at point (1), we provide an implementation of the `WebSocketHandler` interface and override the handle method at point (2). Then, we use the `WebSocketSession#receive` method at point (3) in order to build the processing flow of the incoming `WebSocketMessage` using the `Flux` API. `WebSocketMessage` is a wrapper around `DataBuffer` and provides additional functionalities, such as translating the payload represented in bytes to text in point (5). Once the incoming message is extracted, we prepend to that text the `"Echo:  "` suffix shown at point (6), wrap the new text message in the `WebSocketMessage`, and send it back to the client using the `WebSocketSession#send` method. Here, the `send` method accepts `Publisher<WebSocketMessage>` and returns `Mono<Void>` as the result. Therefore, using the `as` operator from the Reactor API, we may treat `Flux` as `Mono<Void>` and use `session::send` as a transformation function.

Apart from the `WebSocketHandler` interface implementation, setting up the server-side WebSocket API requires configuring additional `HandlerMapping` and `WebSocketHandlerAdapter` instances. Consider the following code as an example of such a configuration:

```
@Configuration                                                           // (1)
public class WebSocketConfiguration {                                    //

    @Bean                                                                // (2)
    public HandlerMapping handlerMapping() {                             //
        SimpleUrlHandlerMapping mapping =                                //
            new SimpleUrlHandlerMapping();                               // (2.1)
        mapping.setUrlMap(Collections.singletonMap(                      // (2.2)
            "/ws/echo",                                                  //
            new EchoWebSocketHandler()                                   //
        ));                                                              //
        mapping.setOrder(-1);                                           // (2.3)
        return mapping;                                                  //
    }                                                                    //

    @Bean                                                                // (3)
    public HandlerAdapter handlerAdapter() {                             //
        return new WebSocketHandlerAdapter();                           //
    }                                                                    //
}
```

The preceding example can be described as follows:

1. This is the class that is annotated with `@Configuration`.
2. Here, we have the declaration and setup of the `HandlerMapping` bean. At point `(2.1)`, we create `SimpleUrlHandlerMapping`, which allows setup path-based mapping, shown at point `(2.2)`, to `WebSocketHandler`. In order to allow `SimpleUrlHandlerMapping` to be handled prior to other `HandlerMapping` instances, it should be a higher priority.
3. This is the declaration of the `HandlerAdapter` bean, which is `WebSocketHandlerAdapter`. Here, `WebSocketHandlerAdapter` plays the most important role, since it upgrades the HTTP connection to the WebSocket one and then calls the `WebSocketHandler#handle` method.

As we can see, the configuration of the WebSocket API is straightforward.

Client-side WebSocket API

Unlike the WebSocket module (which is based on WebMVC), WebFlux provides us with client-side support too. In order to send a WebSocket connection request, we have the `WebSocketClient` class. `WebSocketClient` has two central methods to execute WebSocket connections, as shown in the following code sample:

```
public interface WebSocketClient {
   Mono<Void> execute(
      URI url,
      WebSocketHandler handler
   );
   Mono<Void> execute(
      URI url,
      HttpHeaders headers,
      WebSocketHandler handler
   );
}
```

As we can see, `WebSocketClient` uses the same `WebSockeHandler` interface in order to process messages from the server and send messages back. There are a few `WebSocketClient` implementations that are related to the server engine, such as the `TomcatWebSocketClient` implementation or the `JettyWebSocketClient` implementation. In the following example, we will look at `ReactorNettyWebSocketClient`:

```
WebSocketClient client = new ReactorNettyWebSocketClient();

client.execute(
    URI.create("http://localhost:8080/ws/echo"),
    session -> Flux
        .interval(Duration.ofMillis(100))
        .map(String::valueOf)
        .map(session::textMessage)
        .as(session::send)
);
```

The preceding example shows how we can use `ReactorNettyWebSocketClient` to wire a `WebSocket` connection and start sending periodic messages to the server.

WebFlux WebSocket versus the Spring WebSocket module

Readers who are familiar with the servlet-based WebSocket module may notice that there are a lot of similarities in the design of both modules. However, there are a lot of differences as well. As we may remember, the main disadvantage of the Spring WebSocket module is its blocking interaction with IO, whereas Spring WebFlux offers fully non-blocking writes and reads. In addition, the WebFlux module offers better streaming abstraction by employing the Reactive Streams specification and Project Reactor. The `WebSocketHandler` interface from the old WebSocket module only allows to process one message at a time. Also, the `WebSocketSession#sendMessage` method only allows sending messages in a synchronous fashion.

However, there are some gaps in the integration of the new Spring WebFlux with WebSocket. One of the critical features of the old Spring WebSocket module was good integration with the Spring Messaging module, which allowed the use of the `@MessageMapping` annotation in order to declare the WebSocket endpoint. The following code shows a simple example of the old, Web MVC-based, WebSocket API with the use of annotation from Spring Messaging:

```
@Controller
```

```
public class GreetingController {

    @MessageMapping("/hello")
    @SendTo("/topic/greetings")
    public Greeting greeting(HelloMessage message) {
        return new Greeting("Hello, " + message.getName() + "!");
    }
}
```

The preceding code shows how we could use the Spring Messaging module to declare a WebSocket endpoint. Unfortunately, such support is missing for WebSocket integration from the WebFlux module, and in order to declare complex handlers, we have to provide our own infrastructure.

In `Chapter 8`, *Scaling Up with Cloud Streams*, we are going to cover another powerful abstraction for duplex messaging between client and server, which may be used ahead of simple browser-server interaction.

Reactive SSE as a lightweight replacement for WebSockets

Along with the heavyweight WebSocket, HTML 5 introduced a new way of creating static (in this case, half-duplex) connections, where the server is capable of pushing events. This technique solves similar problems to WebSocket. For example, we may declare a **Server-sent events (SSE)** stream using the same annotation-based programming model, but return an infinite stream of `ServerSentEvent` objects instead, as shown in the following example:

```
@RestController                                          // (1)
@RequestMapping("/sse/stocks")                           //
class StocksController {                                 //
    final Map<String, StocksService> stocksServiceMap;   //
    ...
    @GetMapping                                          // (2)
    public Flux<ServerSentEvent<?>> streamStocks() {    // (2.1)
        return Flux                                       //
            .fromIterable(stocksServiceMap.values())      //
            .flatMap(StocksService::stream)               // (2.2)
            .<ServerSentEvent<?>>map(item ->              //
                ServerSentEvent                           // (2.3)
                    .builder(item)                        // (2.4)
                    .event("StockItem")                   // (2.5)
                    .id(item.getId())                     // (2.6)
                    .build()                              //
            )                                             //
```

```
            .startWith(                                    //  (2.7)
               ServerSentEvent                             //
                  .builder()                               //
                  .event("Stocks")                         //  (2.8)
                  .data(stocksServiceMap.keySet())         //  (2.9)
                  .build()                                  //
            );                                              //
      }
   }
```

The numbers in the preceding code can be explained as follows:

1. This is the declaration of the @RestController class. In order to simplify the code, we have skipped the constructor and field initialization parts.
2. Here, we have the declaration of the handler method annotated by the familiar @GetMapping. As we can see at point (2.1), the streamStocks method returns the Flux of the ServerSentEvent, which means that the current handler enables event streaming. Then, we merge all available sources of stocks and stream changes to the client, as shown at point (2.2). After that, we apply mapping, which maps each StockItem to a ServerSentEvent, as shown at (2.3), using the static builder method at (2.4). In order to properly set up a ServerSentEvent instance, we provide, in the builder parameters, the event ID (2.6) and the event name (2.5), which allows the messages to be distinguished on the client side. In addition, at point (2.7), we start the Flux with the specific ServerSentEvent instance, shown at point (2.8), which declares the available stock channels to the client (2.9).

As we can see from the preceding example, Spring WebFlux allows to map the streaming nature of the Flux reactive type and send an infinite stream of stock events to the client. In addition, SSE streaming does not require us to change the API or use additional abstractions. It simply requires us to declare a specific return type to help the framework figure out how to deal with the response. We do not have to declare the Flux of the ServerSentEvent either; we can instead provide the content type directly, as shown in the following example:

```
@GetMapping(produces = "text/event-stream")
public Flux<StockItem> streamStocks() {
   ...
}
```

In this case, the WebFlux framework wraps each element of the streams into the ServerSentEvent internally.

As we can see, the central benefit behind the `ServerSentEvent` technique is that the configuration of such a streaming model does not require additional boilerplate code, which we have with WebSocket adoption in WebFlux. This is because SSE is a simple abstraction over HTTP that does not need protocol switching and does not require specific server configuration. As we can see from the preceding example, SSE may be configured using the traditional combination of the `@RestController` and `@XXXMapping` annotations. In the case of WebSocket, however, we need a custom message conversion configuration, such as manually choosing a particular messaging protocol. By contrast, for SSE, Spring WebFlux offers the same message converter configurations as for a typical REST controller.

On the other hand, SSE does not support binary encoding and limits events to UTF-8 encoding. This means that WebSocket may be useful for a smaller message size and for transferring less traffic between the client and the server, therefore having a lower latency.

To summarize, SSE is generally a good alternative to WebSocket. Since SSE is an abstraction over the HTTP protocol, WebFlux supports the same declarative and functional endpoint configurations and message conversion as for typical REST controllers.

 To learn more about the advantages and disadvantages of SSE and how it compares to WebSocket, please see the following post: `https://stackoverflow.com/a/5326159/4891253`.

Reactive template engines

Along with regular API features, one of the most popular parts of modern web applications is the UI. Of course, web application UIs today are based on sophisticated JavaScript rendering and, in most cases, developers prefer client-side rendering rather than server-side. Despite this, a lot of enterprise applications are still using server-side rendering technologies that are relevant to their use cases. Web MVC has support for various technologies, such as JSP, JSTL, FreeMarker, Groovy Markup, Thymeleaf, Apache Tiles, and many others. Unfortunately, with Spring 5.x and the WebFlux module, support for many of these, including Apache Velocity, has been dropped.

Nevertheless, Spring WebFlux has the same technique for view rendering as Web MVC. The following example shows a familiar way of specifying a view for rendering:

```
@RequestMapping("/")
public String index() {
    return "index";
}
```

In the previous example, as a result of the `index` method invocation, we return a `String` with the name of the view. Under the hood, the framework looks up that view in the configured folder and then renders it using an appropriate template engine.

By default, WebFlux only supports the FreeMarker server-side rendering engine. However, it is important to work out how the reactive approach is supported in the template rendering process. To this end, let's consider a case involving the rendering of a large music playlist:

```
@RequestMapping("/play-list-view")
public Mono<String> getPlaylist(final Model model) {          // (1)
   final Flux<Song> playlistStream = ...;                     // (2)
   return playlistStream                                      //
      .collectList()                                          // (3)
      .doOnNext(list -> model.addAttribute("playList", list)) // (4)
      .then(Mono.just("freemarker/play-list-view"));          // (5)
}
```

As we can see from the previous example, we are using a reactive type, `Mono<String>` (shown at point 1), in order to asynchronously return the view name. In addition, our template has a placeholder, `dataSource`, which should be filled by the list of given `Song`, shown at point `(2)`. A common way of providing context-specific data is to define the `Model`, `(1)` and put the required attribute in it, as shown at point `(4)`. Unfortunately, FreeMarker does not support reactive and non-blocking rendering of data, so we have to collect all the songs into a list and put the collected data in the `Model`. Finally, once all entries are collected and stored in the `Model`, we may return the name of the view and start rendering it.

Unfortunately, rendering templates such as these is a CPU-intensive operation. If we have an enormous dataset, this may take some time and memory. Fortunately, Thymeleaf's community decided to support Reactive WebFlux and provide further possibilities for asynchronous and streaming template rendering. Thymeleaf provides similar functionality to FreeMarker and allows to write identical code to render the UI. Thymeleaf also provides us with the ability to use reactive types as a source of data inside the template and render a part of the template when a new element in the stream becomes available. The following example shows how we can use Reactive Streams with Thymeleaf during the handling of a request:

```
@RequestMapping("/play-list-view")
public String view(final Model model) {
   final Flux<Song> playlistStream = ...;
   model.addAttribute(
      "playList",
      new ReactiveDataDriverContextVariable(playlistStream, 1, 1)
```

```
        );
        return "thymeleaf/play-list-view";
    }
```

This example introduces a new data type called `ReactiveDataDriverContextVariable`, which accepts reactive types such as `Publisher`, `Flux`, `Mono`, `Observable`, and other reactive types supported by the `ReactiveAdapterRegistry` class.

Even though reactive support requires an additional class wrapper around streams, the template side does not require any changes. The following example shows how we can work with reactive streams in a similar way as with a normal collection:

```html
<!DOCTYPE html>                                                 // (1)
<html>                                                          //
    ...                                                         //
    <body>                                                      //
        ...                                                     //
        <table>                                                 // (2)
            <thead>                                             //
                ...                                             // (3)
            </thead>                                            //
            <tbody>                                             // (4)
                <tr th:each="e : ${playList}">                  // (5)
                    <td th:text="${e.id}">...</td>              //
                    <td th:text="${e.name}">...</td>            //
                    <td th:text="${e.artist}">...</td>          //
                    <td th:text="${e.album}">...</td>           //
                </tr>                                           //
            </tbody>                                            //
        </table>                                                //
    </body>                                                     //
</html>                                                         //
```

This code demonstrates how to use the markup of Thymeleaf's template, which has a common HTML document declaration, as shown at point 1. It renders a table, shown at point (2), with some headers (point 3) and a body (4). This is filled by the rows constructed from the `playList` of `Song` entries and information about them.

The most valuable advantage here is that Thymeleaf's rendering engine starts streaming data to the client without having to wait for the last element to be emitted. Moreover, it supports the rendering of an infinite stream of elements. This became possible with the addition of support for `Transfer-Encoding: chunked`. Instead of rendering the whole template in memory, Thymeleaf renders the available parts first and then sends the rest of the template asynchronously in chunks, once a new element becomes available.

Unfortunately, at the time of writing, Thymeleaf only supports one reactive data source per template. Nevertheless, this technique returns the first chunk of data much faster than with usual rendering, which requires the whole dataset to be present, and decreases the latency between the request and the first feedback from the server, hence improving the overall user experience.

Reactive web security

One of the most vital parts of modern web applications is security. Since the early years of Spring Web, it has come with a companion module—the Spring Security module. This allows to set up a secure web application and naturally fit the existing Spring Web infrastructure by providing a `Filter` prior to any controller and web handler invocation. For many years, the Spring Security module was coupled with the Web MVC infrastructure and only used the `Filter` abstraction from the Servlet API.

Fortunately, with the introduction of the Reactive WebFlux module, everything has changed. In order to support reactive and non-blocking interaction between components and to provide access in a reactive fashion, Spring Security provides an implementation of a totally new reactive stack that uses the new `WebFilter` infrastructure and relies heavily on Project Reactor's *Context* feature.

Reactive access to SecurityContext

In order to access the `SecurityContext` in the new reactive Spring Security module, we have a new class called `ReactiveSecurityContextHolder`.

`ReactiveSecurityContextHolder` provides access to the current `SecurityContext` in a reactive manner over a static `getContext` method, which returns `Mono<SecurityContext>`. This means that we can write the following code in order to access `SecurityContext` in the application:

```java
@RestController                                         // (1)
@RequestMapping("/api/v1")                              //
public class SecuredProfileController {                 //
    @GetMapping("/profiles")                            // (2)
    @PreAuthorize("hasRole(USER)")                      // (2.1)
    public Mono<Profile> getProfile() {                 // (2.2)
        return ReactiveSecurityContextHolder            // (2.3)
            .getContext()                               // (2.4)
            .map(SecurityContext::getAuthentication)    //
            .flatMap(auth ->                            //
                profileService.getByUser(auth.getName())) // (2.5)
```

```
         );                                         //
      }                                             //
   }
```

The preceding example may be explained as follows:

1. This is the declaration of the REST controller class, with the request mapping equal to `"/api/v1"`.

2. This is the `getProfile` handler method declaration. As we can see, this method returns the `Mono` reactive type, which allows reactive access to the data, as shown at point `(2.2)`. Then, in order to access the current `SecurityContext`, we call `ReactiveSecurityContextHolder.getContext()`, as shown in points `(2.3)` and `(2.4)`. Finally, if `SecurityContext` is present, `flatMap` is handled and we may access the user's profile, as shown at point 2.5. In addition, this method is annotated with `@PreAuthorize`, which in this case checks that the available `Authentication` has the required role. Note that if we have a reactive return type, the invocation of the method will be deferred until the required `Authentication` is resolved and the required authorities are present.

As we can see, the API of the new reactive context holder is somewhat similar to that which we have in a synchronous counterpart of the API. Moreover, with the new generation of Spring Security, we can use the same annotations in order to check the required authorities.

Internally, `ReactiveSecurityContextHolder` relies on the Reactor Context API. The current information about the logged-in user is held within the instance of the `Context` interface. The following example shows how `ReactiveSecurityContextHolder` works under the hood:

```
static final Class<?> SECURITY_CONTEXT_KEY = SecurityContext.class;
...
public static Mono<SecurityContext> getContext() {
   return Mono.subscriberContext()
      .filter(c -> c.hasKey(SECURITY_CONTEXT_KEY))
      .flatMap(c -> c.<Mono<SecurityContext>>get(SECURITY_CONTEXT_KEY));
}
```

As we may remember from Chapter 4, *Project Reactor - the Foundation for Reactive Apps*, in order to access the internal Reactor Context, we can use the dedicated operator of the Mono reactive type, called subscriberContext. Then, once the context is accessed, we filter the current Context and check whether it contains a specific key. The value hidden in that key is a Mono from the SecurityContext, which means that we can access the current SecurityContext in a reactive way. The execution is related to retrieving the stored SecurityContext from, for instance, a database, which is executed only when someone subscribes to the given Mono.

Even though the API of ReactiveSecurityContextHolder looks familiar, it hides a lot of pitfalls. For example, by mistake, we may follow the practice we got used to when working with SecurityContextHolder. Therefore, we might blindly implement the common interaction depicted in the following code sample:

```
ReactiveSecurityContextHolder
    .getContext()
    .map(SecurityContext::getAuthentication)
    .block();
```

Just like we used to retrieve the SecurityContext from ThreadLocal, we may be tempted to try to do the same with ReactiveSecurityContextHolder, as shown in the previous example. Unfortunately, when we make a call to getContext and subscribe to the stream using the block method, an empty context will be configured in the stream. Thus, once the ReactiveSecurityContextHodler class tries to access the inner Context, no available SecurityContext will be found there.

So, the question is, how can the Context be set up and made accessible when we connect the streams properly, as shown at the beginning of the section? The answer lies in the new ReactorContextWebFilter from the fifth generation of the Spring Security module. During the invocation, ReactorContextWebFilter provides a Reactor Context using the subscriberContext method. In addition, the resolution of the SecurityContext is carried out using the ServerSecurityContextRepository. ServerSecurityContextRepository has two methods, called save and load:

```
interface ServerSecurityContextRepository {

    Mono<Void> save(ServerWebExchange exchange, SecurityContext context);

    Mono<SecurityContext> load(ServerWebExchange exchange);
}
```

As we can see in the preceding code, the `save` method allows to associate the `SecurityContext` with a specific `ServerWebExchange` and then restore it using the `load` method from the incoming user request attached to the `ServerWebExchange`.

As we can see, the main advantage of the new generation of Spring Security is full-fledged support for reactive access to `SecurityContext`. Here, reactive access means that the actual `SecurityContext` may be stored in a database, so the resolution of the stored `SecurityContext` does not require blocking operations. The strategy of context resolution is lazy, so the actual call to the underlying storage is executed only when we subscribe to `ReactiveSecurityContextHolder.getContext()`. Finally, the mechanism of the `SecurityContext` transfer allows us to build complex streaming processes easily, paying no attention to the problem of common `ThreadLocal` propagation between `Thread` instances.

Enabling reactive security

The last part that we haven't yet covered is how complex it is to enable security in a reactive web application. Fortunately, the configuration of security in a modern WebFlux-based application requires the declaration of few beans. The following is a reference example of how we may do this:

```
@SpringBootConfiguration                                  // (1)
@EnableReactiveMethodSecurity                             // (1.1)
public class SecurityConfiguration {                      //

   @Bean                                                  // (2)
   public SecurityWebFilterChain securityWebFilterChain(  //
      ServerHttpSecurity http                             // (2.1)
   ) {                                                    //
      return http                                         // (2.2)
         .formLogin()                                     //
         .and()                                           //
         .authorizeExchange()                             //
            .anyExchange().authenticated()                //
         .and()                                           //
         .build();                                        // (2.3)
   }                                                      //

   @Bean                                                  // (3)
   public ReactiveUserDetailsService userDetailsService() { //
      UserDetails user =                                  //
         User.withUsername("user")                        //
            .withDefaultPasswordEncoder()                 // (3.1)
            .password("password")                         //
```

```
            .roles("USER", "ADMIN")                          //
            .build();                                        //
        return new MapReactiveUserDetailsService(user);      // (3.2)
    }                                                        //
}
```

The preceding numbers in the code may be explained as follows:

1. This is the declaration of the configuration class. Here, in order to enable a specific annotated `MethodInterceptor`, we have to add the `@EnableReactiveMethodSecurity` annotation, which imports the configurations required for that, as shown in `(1.1)`.

2. Here, we have the configuration of the `SecurityWebFilterChain` bean. In order to configure the required bean, Spring Security provides us with `ServerHttpSecurity`, which is a builder (shown in `2.3`) with a fluent API (shown in `2.2`).

3. This is the configuration of the `ReactiveUserDetailsService` bean. In order to authenticate a user in the default Spring Security setup, we have to provide an implementation of `ReactiveUserDetailsService`. For demonstration purposes, we provide an in-memory implementation of the interface, as shown at point `(3.2)`, and configure a test user (at `3.1`) in order to log in to the system.

As we may notice in the preceding code, the overall configuration of Spring Security is similar to what we have seen previously. That means that migrating to such a configuration does not take much time.

Support for reactive in the new generation of Spring Security allows us to build a highly protected web application with minimal effort spent on the infrastructure's setup.

Interaction with other reactive libraries

Despite the fact that WebFlux uses Project Reactor 3 as the central building block, WebFlux allows the use of other reactive libraries as well. To enable cross-library interoperability, most operations in WebFlux are based on interfaces from the Reactive Streams specification. In this way, we can easily replace code written in Reactor 3 with RxJava 2 or Akka Streams:

```
import io.reactivex.Observable;                             // (1)
...                                                         //

@RestController                                             // (2)
class AlbomsController {                                    //
```

```
    final ReactiveAdapterRegistry adapterRegistry;          // (2.1)
    ...                                                      //

    @GetMapping("/songs")                                    // (3)
    public Observable<Song> findAlbomByArtists(              // (3.1)
      Flux<Artist> artistsFlux                               // (3.2)
    ) {
      Observable<Artist> observable = adapterRegistry        // (4)
        .getAdapter(Observable.class)                        //
        .fromPublisher(artistsFlux);                         //
      Observable<Song> albomsObservable = ...;               // (4.1)
                                                             //
      return albomsObservable;                               // (4.2)
    }
  }
```

This code is explained in the following list:

1. This is the import declaration, which demonstrates that we import the Observable from RxJava 2.

2. This is the AlbomsController class, which is annotated with the @RestController annotation. We also declare a field of the ReactiveAdapterRegistry type, which is used later in this example.

3. Here, we have a declaration of the request handler method called findAlbumByArtists. As we can see, findAlbumByArtists accepts a Publisher of type Flux<Artist>, as shown at point (3.2), and returns Observable<Song>, as shown at point (3.1).

4. Here, we have the declarations to map artistsFlux to Observable<Artist>, execute business logic (at 4.1), and return the result to the caller.

The preceding example shows how reactive communication might be rewritten using reactive types from RxJava, along with the Project Reactor reactive types. As we may remember from Chapter 5, *Going Reactive with Spring Boot 2,* reactive type conversion is part of the Spring Core module and is supported by org.springframework.core.ReactiveAdapterRegistry and org.springframework.core.ReactiveAdapter. These classes allow conversion both to and from the Reactive Streams Publisher class. Hence, with that support library, we may use almost any reactive library without having to tightly couple it with Project Reactor.

WebFlux versus Web MVC

In the previous sections, we gave a brief overview of the primary components that are included in the new Spring WebFlux. We also looked at the new features that were introduced in the Spring WebFlux module and how they can be used.

However, despite the fact that we now have an understanding of how to use a new API to build a web application, it is still unclear as to why the new WebFlux is better than Web MVC. It would be helpful to understand the principle advantages of WebFlux.

To do this, we have to dig into the theoretical foundations of how to build web servers, understand what the critical characteristics of a fast web server are, and consider what may change the performance of a web server. In the following sections, we are going to analyze the critical characteristics of modern web servers, learn what may cause performance degradation, and think about how to avoid this.

Laws matter when comparing frameworks

Before we move on, let's try to understand the characteristics of the system that we are going to use for our comparison. The central indicators for most web applications are throughput, latency, CPU, and memory usage. The web now has completely different requirements to when it started. Previously, computers were sequential. Users used to be happy to observe simple, static content, and the overall load on the system was low. The primary operations involved generating HTML or simple calculations. Computations fitted into one processor and we did not require more than one server for a web application.

Over time, the rules of the game have changed. The web started counting users by the billion, and content started being dynamic and even real-time. The requirements for throughput and latency have changed substantially. Our web applications have started to be highly distributed on cores and clusters. Understanding how to scale a web application has become critical. An important question is—how does the number of parallel workers change the latency or throughput?

Little's Law

To answer this question, Little's Law comes to the rescue. This law explains how to calculate the number of requests that are processed simultaneously (or simply how many parallel workers there should be) to handle a predefined throughput at a particular latency level. In other words, using this formula, we can calculate the system capacity, or how many computers, nodes, or web application instances running in parallel we need in order to handle the required number of users per second with a stable response time:

$$N = X \times R$$

The preceding formula may be explained as: *the mean number of requests resident (or the number of requests processed simultaneously) in a system or queue (N) is equal to the throughput (or users per second) (X) multiplied by the mean response time or latency (R).*

That means that if our system has an average response time *R* of 0.2 seconds and throughput *X* of 100 requests per second, then it should be able to process 20 requests simultaneously, or 20 users in parallel. We either need 20 workers on one machine, or 20 machines with one worker. That is an ideal case, where there are no intersections between workers or simultaneous requests. This is shown in the following diagram:

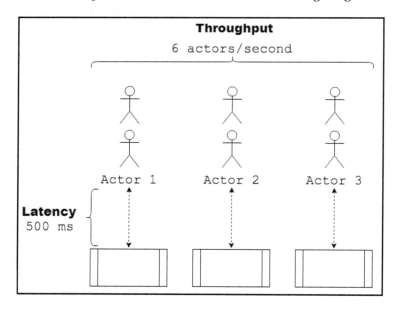

Diagram 6.3. Ideal simultaneous processing

As we can see in the preceding diagram, there are three workers in the system, which can handle six actors or requests per second. In this case, all the actors are *balanced* between the workers, which means that there is no coordination required between them in order to choose the worker.

However, the preceding case is not actually very realistic, because any system, such as a web application, requires concurrent access to shared resources such as CPU or memory. Hence, there is a growing list of amendments to the overall throughput, which is described in *Amdahl's Law* and its extension, the *Universal Scalability Law*.

Amdahl's Law

The first of these laws is about the influence of *serialized access* on the mean response time (or latency), and thereby on throughput. Despite the fact that we may always want to parallelize our work, there may come a point where it cannot be parallelized and we are required to serialize work instead. This might be the case if we have a coordinator worker, or an aggregation or reduction operator in the reactive flow, meaning we have to join all executions. Alternatively, it may be a piece of code that works only in serial mode, so it cannot be executed in parallel. In large microservice systems, this might be the load balancer or orchestration system. Therefore, we can refer to Amdahl's Law in order to calculate the throughput changes using the following formula:

$$X(N) = \frac{X(1) \times N}{1 + \sigma \times (N - 1)}$$

In this formula, *X(1)* is the *initial throughput*, *N* is the parallelization or the number of workers, σ is a *coefficient of contention* (also referred to as the *serialization coefficient*), or in other words, the percentage of the overall time spent on executing code that can't be processed in parallel.

If we do a simple calculation and build a dependency graph of the throughput of parallelization with some random coefficient of contention, $\sigma = 0{,}03$ and initial throughput $X(1) = 50$ requests per second on the range of parallelization $N = 0..500$, then we achieve the following curve:

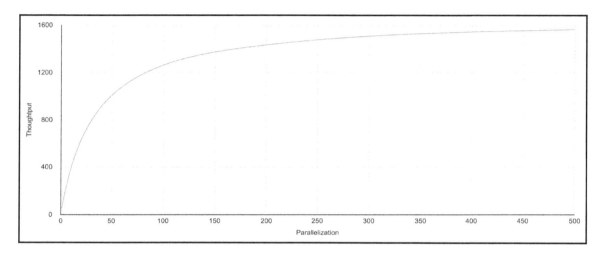

Diagram 6.4. Throughput changes depending on parallelization

As we can observe from the preceding diagram, with an increase in parallelization, the throughput of the system starts becoming slower and slower. Finally, the overall increase in throughput comes to an end and instead follows asymptotical behavior. Amdahl's Law says that the overall work parallelization does not give a linear rise of throughput, because we cannot process results faster than the serialized part of the code. From the perspective of scaling a common web application, this statement means that we do not gain any benefits from increasing the number of cores or nodes in the system if we have a single point of coordination or processing that cannot work faster. Moreover, we lose money by supporting redundant machines, and the overall increase in the throughput is not worth the cost.

From the preceding chart, we can see that the changes in throughput depend on parallelization. However, in many cases, we have to understand how latency changes as dependency on parallelization increases. For this purpose, we may combine the equations from Little's Law and Amdahl's Law. As we may remember, both equations contain the throughput (X). Hence, we have to rewrite Little's Law in order to combine both formulas:

$$X(N) = \frac{N}{R}$$

After the preceding transformation, we may replace $X(N)$ in Amdahl's Law, and derive the following:

$$\frac{N}{R} = \frac{X(1) \times N}{1 + \sigma \times (N - 1)}$$

Finally, in order to derive the latency (R), we have to do the following transformation:

$$\frac{1}{R} = \frac{X(1) \times N}{(1 + \sigma \times (N - 1)) \times N}$$

$$R = \frac{1 + \sigma \times (N - 1)}{X(1)}$$

From the preceding formula, we may conclude that the overall growth is linear. The following diagram shows the latency growth curve depending on the parallelization:

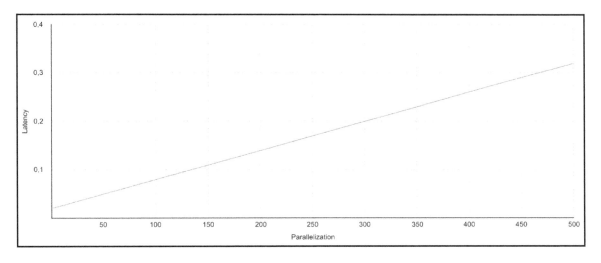

Diagram 6.5. Linear growth of latency depending on parallelization

That means that with an increase in parallelization, the response time decreases.

To conclude, as described by Amdahl's Law, a system that has parallel execution always has points of serialization, which causes additional overhead and does not allow us to reach higher throughput just by increasing the level of parallelization. The following diagram shows this system:

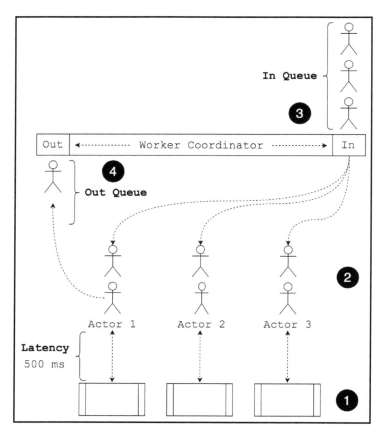

Diagram 6.6. Simultaneous processing example using Amdahl's Law

The previous diagram can be described as follows:

1. This is the worker representation. Note that, even here, the code cannot be split into smaller sub-tasks that can be executed independently, which should also be considered a point of serialization.
2. This is the representation of actors in the queue or user requests.

3. Here is the queue of actors or user requests before they have been assigned to a dedicated worker. The serialization point is coordination and assigning an actor to the worker.

4. Actor coordination may be required in both directions. At this point, the coordinator may carry out some actions to send a response back to the user.

To summarize, Amdahl's Law states that the system has its bottlenecks and, because of this, we can't serve more users or have lower latency.

The Universal Scalability Law

Although Amdahl's Law explains the scalability of any system, real applications show quite different scalability results. After some research in the area, Neil Gunther found that, despite serialization, there is another, more crucial point, which is called **incoherence**.

 Neil Gunther is a computer information systems researcher who is best known internationally for developing the open source performance modelling software Pretty Damn Quick and developing the Guerrilla approach to computer capacity planning and performance analysis. For more information, visit http://www.perfdynamics.com/Bio/njg.html.

Incoherence is a common phenomenon in a concurrent system with shared resources. For instance, from a standard Java web application perspective, such incoherence is exposed in chaotic Thread access to resources such as the CPU. The entire Java threading model is not ideal. In a case with many more Thread instances than actual processors, there is a direct conflict between the different Thread instances for accessing the CPU and for achieving cycles for their computations. This requires additional effort to resolve their redundant coordination and coherence. Each access to the shared memory from a Thread may require additional synchronization and decrease the throughput and latency of the application.

In order to explain such behavior in the system, the **Universal Scalability Law** (**USL**) extension of Amdahl's Law provides the following formula for calculating throughput changes depending on parallelization:

$$X(N) = \frac{X(1) \times N}{1 + \sigma \times (N - 1) + \kappa \times N \times (N - 1)}$$

The preceding formula introduces a coefficient of coherence (k). The most notable thing here is that, from now on, there will be quadratic backward throughput $X(N)$ relation on the parallelization N.

In order to understand the fatal effect of this connection, let's take a look at the following diagram, where we have the same as before—the initial throughput $X(1) = 50$, the coefficient of contention $\sigma = 0,03$, and the coefficient of coherence $k = 0,00007$:

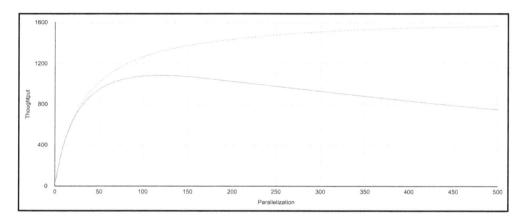

Diagram 6.7 Throughput depending on parallelization. A comparison of Amdahl's Law (dotted line) versus USL (solid line).

From the preceding plot, we can observe that there is a crisis point after which the throughput starts degrading. Moreover, for a better representation of real system scalability, the graph shows both the system scalability as modeled by the USL and the system scalability as modeled by Amdahl's Law. The average response time degradation curve has also changed its behavior. The following diagram shows the latency changes depending on parallelization:

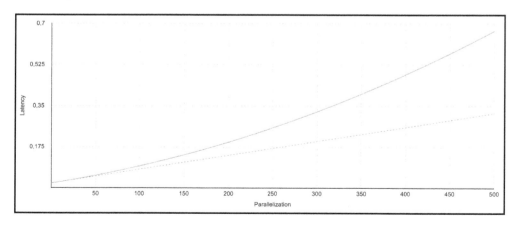

Diagram 6.8 Throughput depending on parallelization. Comparison of Amdahl Law (dotted line) versus the USL (solid line)

Similarly, for the purpose of showing a contrast, the latency change curve modeled by the USL is compared with the same curve modeled by Amdahl's Law. As we can see from the previous plots, the system behaves differently when there are shared points of access, which may be incoherent and require additional synchronization. A schematic example of such a system is depicted in the following diagram:

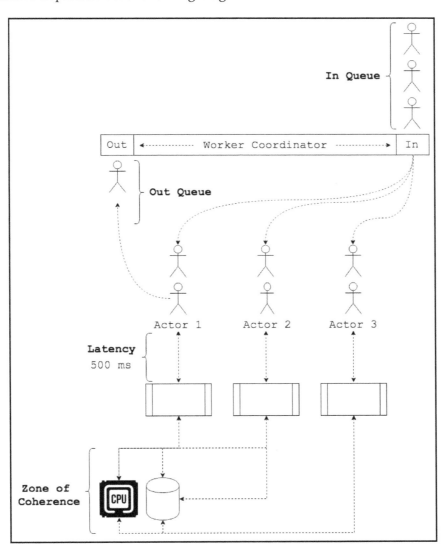

Diagram 6.9. Simultaneous processing example by the USL

As we can see, the whole picture of the system may be much more complex than that which was initially introduced by Little's Law. There are a lot of hidden pitfalls, which may directly impact the scalability of the system.

To conclude these three sections, the overall understanding of these laws plays an important role in modeling a scalable system and planning system capacity. These laws may be applicable to a complex high-load distributed system, as well as to multi-processor nodes with a web application built with the Spring Framework. In addition, understanding what impacts system scalability allows to design the system properly and avoid pitfalls such as incoherence and contention. It also enables to properly analyze WebFlux and Web MVC modules from the laws' perspectives, and predict which scales will perform the best.

Thorough analysis and comparison

From our knowledge of scalability, we know that it is essential to understand the behaviors of frameworks, their architecture, and their resource usage models. Moreover, it is critical to choose the appropriate framework to solve specific problems. In the next few subsections, we are going to compare Web MVC and WebFlux from different perspectives, and finally, learn about which problem areas they are each more suitable for.

Understanding the processing models in WebFlux and Web MVC

First of all, in order to understand the impact of different processing models on system throughput and latency, we will recap how incoming requests are processed in Web MVC and WebFlux.

As mentioned earlier, Web MVC is built on top of blocking I/O. That means that the `Thread` that processes each incoming request may be blocked by reading the incoming body from the I/O:

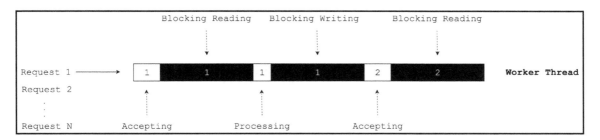

Diagram 6.10. Blocking request and response processing

In the preceding example, all requests are queued and processed sequentially by one `Thread`. The black bars indicate that there is a blocking read/write operation from/to I/O. Also, as we may notice, the actual processing time (white bars) is much smaller than the time spent on blocking operations. From this simple diagram, we can conclude that the `Thread` is inefficient and waiting times may be shared when accepting and processing requests in the queue.

In contrast, WebFlux is built on top of a non-blocking API, which means that no operations require interaction with the I/O block `Thread`. This efficient technique of accepting and processing requests is depicted in the following diagram:

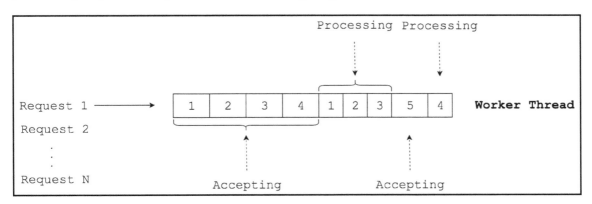

Diagram 6.11. Asynchronous non-blocking request processing

As we can see in the preceding diagram, we have an identical case to the previous blocking I/O case. On the left side of the diagram, there is a queue of requests and, in the middle, there is a processing timeline. In this case, the processing timeline does not have any black bars, which means that even if there are not enough bytes coming from the network in order to continue with the processing of the request, we can always switch to processing another request without blocking the `Thread`. Comparing the preceding asynchronous, non-blocking request processing to the blocking example, we might notice that now, instead of waiting while the request body is collected, the `Thread` is used efficiently to accept new connections. Then, the underlying operating system may notify us that, for example, the request body has been collected and the processor may take it for processing without blocking. In that case, we have optimal CPU utilization. Similarly, writing the response does not require blocking and allows us to write to the I/O in a non-blocking fashion. The only difference is that the system notifies us when it is ready to write a part of the data into the I/O without blocking.

The previous example shows that WebFlux utilizes one `Thread` much more efficiently than Web MVC, and therefore may process many more requests in the same period of time. It is still possible to argue, however, that we still have multi-threading in Java so we can utilize the real processor by having the proper number of `Thread` instances in place. Therefore, to process requests faster and achieve the same CPU utilization with blocking Web MVC, we may use, instead of one `Thread`, several worker threads, or even one `Thread` per connection model:

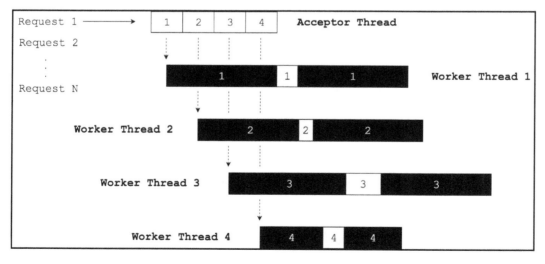

Diagram 6.12. Thread per connection Web MVC model

As we can see from the preceding diagram, the multithreading model allows faster processing of queued requests and gives the illusion that the system accepts, processes, and responds to almost the same number of requests.

However, this design has its flaws. As we learned from the Universal Scalability Law, when the system has shared resources such as CPU or memory, scaling the number of parallel workers may decrease the system's performance. In this case, when the processing of user requests involves too many `Thread` instances, it causes degradation of performance because of incoherence between them.

Impact of processing models on throughput and latency

To verify this statement, let's try to do a simple load test. For this purpose, we are going to use a simple Spring Boot 2.x application with Web MVC or WebFlux (let's call it the middleware). We are also going to simulate I/O activity from the middleware by making a few network calls to a third-party service, which will return an empty successful response with a guaranteed 200 milliseconds of average latency. The communication flow is depicted as follows:

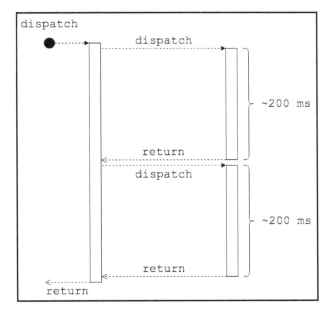

Diagram 6.13. Communication flow for benchmark

To launch our middleware and simulate client activity, we are going to use a Microsoft Azure infrastructure with Ubuntu Server 16.04 installed on each machine. For the middleware, we are going to use D12 v2 VM (4 virtual CPUs and 28 GB RAM). For the client, we are going to use F4 v2 VM (4 virtual CPUs and 8 GB RAM). User activity will be increased sequentially in small steps. We are going to start our load test with four simultaneous users and finish with 20,000 simultaneous users. This will give us a smooth latency curve and throughput change and allow us to create understandable graphics. To produce an appropriate load on the middleware and collect statistics and measurement characteristics correctly, we are going to use a modern HTTP benchmarking tool called **wrk** (https://github.com/wg/wrk).

 Note that these benchmarks are intended to show the *tendency* rather than the system's *stability* over time, and to measure how proper the current implementation of the WebFlux framework is. The following measurements show the advantages of non-blocking and asynchronous communication in WebFlux over blocking synchronous and thread-based communication in Web MVC.

The following is an example of the Web MVC middleware code used for measurements:

```
@RestController                                              // (1)
@SpringBootApplication                                       //
public class BlockingDemoApplication                         //
    implements InitializingBean {                            //
    ...                                                      // (1.1)
    @GetMapping("/")                                         // (2)
    public void get() {                                      //
        restTemplate.getForObject(someUri, String.class);    // (2.1)
        restTemplate.getForObject(someUri, String.class);    // (2.2)
    }                                                        //
    ...                                                      //
}                                                            //
```

The preceding code can be described as follows:

1. This is the declaration of the class, annotated by `@SpringBootApplication`. At the same time, this class is a controller annotated with `@RestController`. To keep this example as simple as possible, we have skipped the initialization process and declared fields in this class, as shown at point (1.1).

2. Here, we have a `get` method with the `@GetMapping` declaration. In order to reduce redundant network traffic and focus only on framework performance, we do not return any content in the response body. According to the flow mentioned in the preceding diagram, we perform two HTTP requests to the remote server, as shown at points (2.1) and (2.2).

As we can see from the previous example and schema, the middleware's average response time should be around 400 milliseconds.

Note that, for this test, we are going to use a Tomcat web server, which is the default for Web MVC. In addition, to see how the performance changes in Web MVC, we are going to set up as many `Thread` instances as simultaneous users. The following `sh` script shows a setup for Tomcat:

```
java -Xss512K -Xmx24G -Xms24G
    -Dserver.tomcat.prestartmin-spare-threads=true
    -Dserver.tomcat.prestart-min-spare-threads=true
    -Dserver.tomcat.max-threads=$1
    -Dserver.tomcat.min-spare-threads=$1
    -Dserver.tomcat.max-connections=100000
    -Dserver.tomcat.accept-count=100000
    -jar ...
```

As we can see from the preceding script, the values of the `max-threads` and `min-spare-threads` parameters are dynamic and are defined by the number of parallel users in the test.

The preceding setup is not production ready and is used only for the purpose of showing the disadvantages of the threading model used in Spring Web MVC, especially the thread-per-connection model.

By launching the test suite against our service, we will get the following result curve:

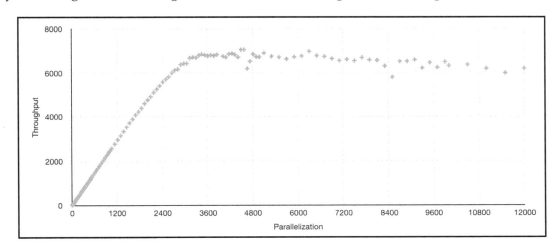

Diagram 6.14. Web MVC throughput measurement results

The preceding diagram shows that, at some point, we start losing throughput, which means that there is contention or incoherence in our application.

In order to compare the performance results of the Web MVC framework, we have to run an identical test for WebFlux as well. The following is the code that we use in order to measure WebFlux-based application performance:

```
@RestController
@SpringBootApplication
public class ReactiveDemoApplication
    implements InitializingBean {
    ...
    @GetMapping("/")
    public Mono<Void> get() {                                    // (1)
        return                                                   //
            webClient                                            //
                .get()                                           // (2)
                .uri(someUri)                                    //
                .retrieve()                                      //
                .bodyToMono(DataBuffer.class)                    //
                .doOnNext(DataBufferUtils::release)              //
            .then(                                               // (3)
                webClient                                        //
                .get()                                           // (4)
                .uri(someUri)                                    //
                .retrieve()                                      //
                .bodyToMono(DataBuffer.class)                    //
                .doOnNext(DataBufferUtils::release)              //
                .then()                                          //
            )                                                    //
            .then();                                             // (5)
    }
    ...
}
```

The preceding code shows that we are now actively using Spring WebFlux and Project Reactor features in order to achieve asynchronous and non-blocking requests and response processing. Just as in the Web MVC case, at point (1), we return a Void result, but it is now wrapped in the reactive type, Mono. Then, we execute a remote call using the WebClient API, and then at point (3), we perform – in the same sequential fashion – the second remote call, shown at point (4). Finally, we skip the result of the execution of both calls and return a Mono<Void> result that notifies the subscriber of the completion of both executions.

Note that, with the Reactor technique, we may improve the execution time without performing both requests in parallel. Since both executions are non-blocking and asynchronous, we do not have to allocate additional `Thread` instances for that. However, in order to maintain the behavior of the system mentioned in *diagram 6.13*, we keep the execution sequential, so the resulting latency should be ~400 milliseconds on average.

By launching the test suite against our WebFlux-based middleware, we will get the following result curve:

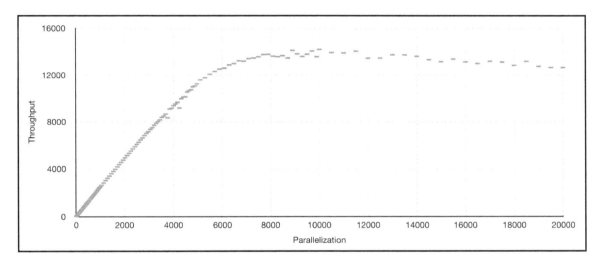

Diagram 6.15. WebFlux throughput measurement results

As we may see from the preceding chart, the tendency of the WebFlux curve is somewhat similar to the WebMVC curve.

In order to compare both curves, let's put them on the same plot:

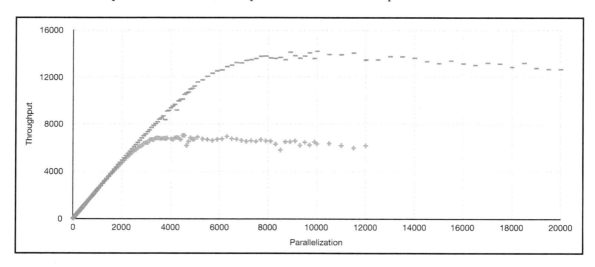

Diagram 6.16. WebFlux versus Web MVC throughput measurement results comparison

In the preceding diagram, the line of + (*plus*) symbols is for Web MVC and the line of − (*dash*) symbols is for WebFlux. In this case, higher means better; as we can see, WebFlux has almost twice the throughput.

Also, it should be noted here that there are no measurements for Web MVC after 12,000 parallel users. The problem is that Tomcat's thread pool takes too much memory and does not fit in the given 28 GB. Therefore, each time Tomcat tries to dedicate more than 12,000 `Thread` instances, the Linux kernel kills that process. This point emphasizes that the *thread-per-connection* model does not fit in cases where we need to handle more than around 10,000 users.

The preceding comparison is a comparison of the *thread-per-connection model* versus the *non-blocking asynchronous processing model*. In the first case, the only way to process requests without significant impact on latency is by dedicating a separate `Thread` for each user. In this way, we minimize the time spent by the user in the queue waiting for an available `Thread`. In contrast, the configuration of WebFlux does not require the allocation of a separate `Thread` per user since we use a non-blocking I/O. In real-world scenarios, the usual configuration of a Tomcat server has a limited size for the thread pool.

Nevertheless, both curves show a similar tendency and have critical points, after which they start degrading in throughput. This may be explained by the fact that many systems have their limitations in terms of open client connections. In addition, the comparison may be a bit unfair since we use different implementations of HTTP clients, with different configurations. For example, the default connection strategy for `RestTemplate` is to allocate a new HTTP connection on each new call. In contrast, the default Netty-based `WebClient` implementation uses a connection pool under the hood. In this case, a connection may be reused. Even though the system may be tuned to reuse opened connections, such a comparison may be misrepresentative.

Therefore, to get a better comparison, we are going to simulate the network activity by providing a 400 millisecond delay. For both cases, the following code is used:

```
Mono.empty()
    .delaySubscription(Duration.ofMillis(200))
    .then(Mono.empty()
            .delaySubscription(Duration.ofMillis(200)))
    .then()
```

For WebFlux, the return type is `Mono<Void>`, and for Web MVC, the execution flow is ended by calling the `.block()` operation, so the `Thread` will be blocked for a specified delay. Here, we use the same code in order to get identical behavior for delay scheduling.

We are also going to use a similar cloud setup. For the middleware, we are going to use E4S V3 VM (four virtual CPUs and 32 GB of RAM) and for the client, B4MS VM (four virtual CPUs and 16 GB RAM).

By running our test suite against the services, the following results can be observed:

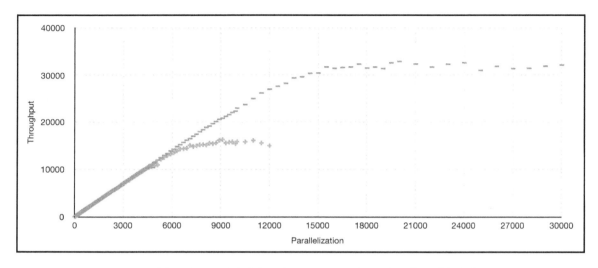

Diagram 6.17. WebFlux versus Web MVC throughput measurement result comparison, without additional I/O

In the preceding diagram, the line of + (*plus*) symbols is for Web MVC and the line of − (*dash*) symbols is for WebFlux. As we can see, the overall results are higher than with real external calls. That means that either a connection pool within the application or a connection policy within the operating system has a huge impact on system performance.

Nevertheless, WebFlux is still showing twice the throughput of Web MVC, which finally proves our assumption about the inefficiency of the thread-per-connection model. WebFlux still behaves as was proposed by Amdahl's Law. However, we should remember that, along with application limitations, there are system limitations, which may alter our interpretation of the final results.

We can also compare both modules with regard to their latency and CPU usage, which are depicted in diagrams *6.18* and *6.19* respectively:

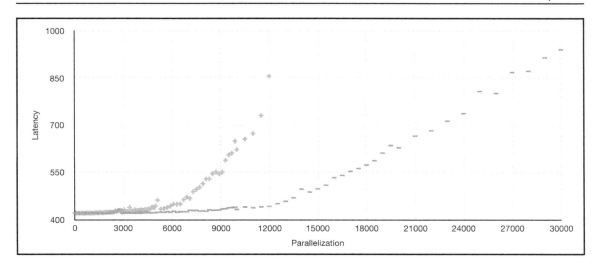

Diagram 6.18. A comparison of the latency of WebFlux and Web MVC without additional I/O

In the preceding diagram, the line of + (*plus*) symbols is for Web MVC and the line of − (*dash*) symbols is for WebFlux. In this case, the lower the result, the better. The preceding diagram depicts a huge degradation in latency for Web MVC. At a parallelization level of 12,000 simultaneous users, WebFlux shows a response time that is around 2.1 times better.

From the perspective of CPU usage, we have the following tendency:

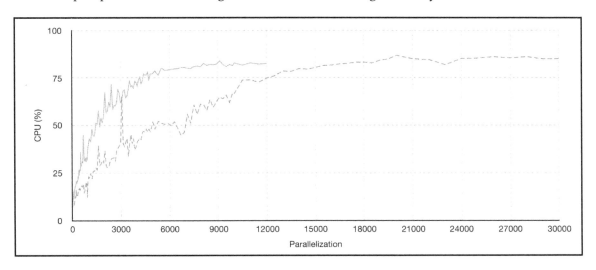

Diagram 6.19. A comparison of the CPU usage of WebFlux and Web MVC without additional I/O

In the preceding diagram, the solid line is for Web MVC and the dashed line is for WebFlux. Again, the lower the result, the better in this case. We can conclude that WebFlux is much more efficient with regard to throughput, latency, and CPU usage. The difference in CPU usage may be explained by the redundant work context switching between different `Thread` instances.

Challenges with the WebFlux processing model

WebFlux is significantly different from Web MVC. Since there is no blocking I/O in the system, we can use only a few `Thread` instances to process all requests. Processing events simultaneously does not require a higher number of `Thread` instances than processors/cores in the system.

 This is because WebFlux is built on top of Netty, where the default number
of `Thread` instances is the `Runtime.getRuntime().availableProcess
ors()` multiplied by two.

Although the use of non-blocking operations allows the processing of results asynchronously (see *diagram 6.11*), so we can scale better, utilize CPUs more efficiently, spend CPU cycles on actual processing, and reduce wastage on context switching, the asynchronous non-blocking processing model has its own pitfalls. First of all, it is important to understand that CPU-intensive tasks should be scheduled on separate `Thread` or `ThreadPool` instances. This problem does not apply to the thread-per-connection model or a similar model in which a thread pool has a high number of workers, because in this case, each connection has already got a dedicated worker. Usually, most developers who have intensive experience with such a model forget about this and execute a CPU-intensive task on the main thread. A mistake like this comes at a high cost and can impact on overall performance. In this case, the main thread is busy with processing and does not have time to accept or process new connections:

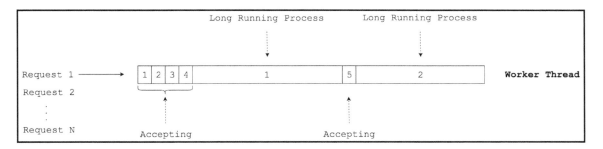

Diagram 6.20. CPU-intensive work in the single-processor environment

As we can see from the preceding diagram, even if the whole request processing line consists of white bars (which means there is no blocking I/O), we may stack the processing by running hard computation that steals processing time from other requests.

To solve this problem, we should delegate long-running work to a separate pool of processors or, in the case of a single-process node, delegate work to a different node. For example, we may organize an efficient event loop (https://en.wikipedia.org/wiki/Event_loop), where one `Thread` accepts connections and then delegates the actual processing to a different pool of workers/nodes:

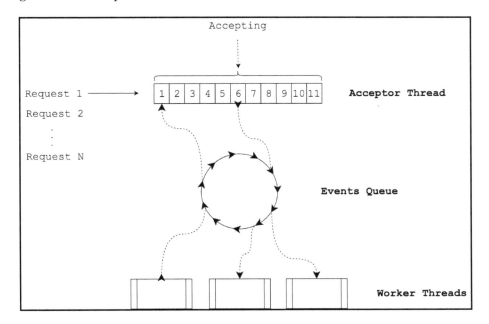

Diagram 6.21. Netty-like non-blocking server architecture

Another common mistake to do with asynchronous, non-blocking programming is blocking the operation usage. One of the tricky parts of web application development is generating a unique UUID:

```
UUID requestUniqueId = java.util.UUID.randomUUID();
```

The problem here is that `#randomUUID()` uses `SecureRandom`. Typical crypto-strength random number generators use a source of entropy that is external to the application. It might be a hardware random number generator, but more commonly it is accumulated **randomness** that is harvested by the operating system in normal operation.

 In this context, the notion of randomness means events such as mouse movements, electrical power changes, and other random events that might be collected by the system at runtime.

The problem is that sources of entropy have a rate limit. If this is exceeded over a period of time, for some of the systems, the syscall to read entropy will stall until enough entropy has been made available. Also, the number of threads has a huge impact on the performance of the generation of UUIDs. That can be explained by looking at the implementation of `SecureRandom#nextBytes(byte[] bytes)`, which generates the random numbers for `UUID.randomUUID()`:

```
synchronized public void nextBytes(byte[] bytes) {
    secureRandomSpi.engineNextBytes(bytes);
}
```

As we can see, `#nextBytes` is synchronized, which leads to significant performance loss when accessed by different threads.

 To learn more about the resolution of `SecureRandom`, please see the following Stack Overflow answer: `https://stackoverflow.com/questions/137212/how-to-solve-slow-java-securerandom`.

As we have learned, WebFlux uses a few threads to process a huge amount of requests asynchronously and in a non-blocking fashion. We have to be careful when using methods that, at first glance, look like they are I/O operations-free but in fact hide some specific interactions with OS. Without proper attention to such methods, we may dramatically decrease the entire system's performance. It is, therefore, crucial to use only non-blocking operations with WebFlux. However, such a requirement puts a lot of limitations on reactive system development. For example, the whole Java Development Kit was designed for imperative, synchronous interaction between components of the Java ecosystem. Therefore, a lot of blocking operations do not have non-blocking, asynchronous analogs, which complicates a lot of non-blocking, reactive system development. While WebFlux gives us a higher throughput and lower latency, we have to pay a lot of attention to all operations and libraries with which we are working.

Also, in cases where complex computations are the central operation of our service, the uncomplicated threading-based processing model is preferable to the non-blocking, asynchronous processing model. Also, if all operations of interaction with the I/O are blocking, we do not have as many benefits as we have with non-blocking I/O. Moreover, the complexity of non-blocking and asynchronous algorithms for event processing may be redundant, so a straightforward threading model in Web MVC would be more efficient than the WebFlux one.

Nevertheless, for cases where there are no such limitations or specific use cases, and we have a lot of I/O interaction, the non-blocking and asynchronous WebFlux will shine brightly.

Impact of different processing models on memory consumption

Another critical component of framework analysis is comparing memory usage. Thinking back to our discussion of the `Thread` per connection model in `Chapter 1`, *Why Reactive Spring?*, we know that, instead of allocating memory for tiny events' objects, we allocate a huge dedicated `Thread` for each new connection. The first thing that we should bear in mind is that a `Thread` keeps some space free for its stack. The actual stack size depends on the OS and JVM configuration. By default, for most common servers running on 64-bit, the VM stack size is 1 MB.

 An event means a signal about changes in the system state, such as an opened connection or data availability.

For the high-load scenario, with this technique, we will have high memory consumption. At most, there will be an unreasonable overhead to keep the whole 1 MB stack along with the request and response body. If a dedicated thread pool is limited, it will lead to the throughput and average latency decreasing. So, in Web MVC, we have to balance the memory usage and the system throughput. In contrast, as we learned from the previous section, WebFlux can use a fixed number of `Thread` instances to process much more requests and at the same time use a predictable amount of memory. To get a full understanding of how memory is used in previous measurements, take a look at the memory usage comparison:

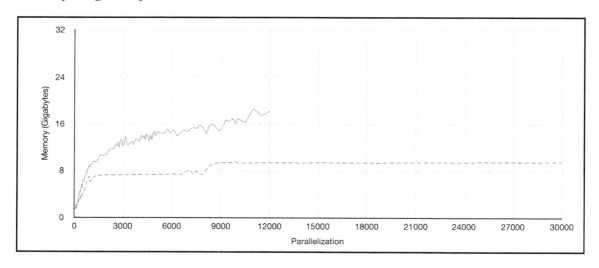

Diagram 6.22. A comparison of the memory usage of WebFlux and Web MVC

In the preceding diagram, the solid line is for Web MVC and the dashed line is for WebFlux. In this case, lower is better. It should be noticed that both applications will be given additional JVM parameters—*Xms26GB* and *Xmx26GB*. This means that both applications have access to the same amount of dedicated memory. However, for Web MVC, memory usage grows with increased parallelization. As mentioned at the beginning of this section, the usual `Thread` stack size is 1 MB. In our case, the `Thread` stack size is set to -Xss512K, so each new thread takes an additional ~512 KB of memory. Hence, for the thread-per-connection model, we have inefficient memory usage.

In contrast, for WebFlux, memory usage is stable in spite of parallelization. This means that WebFlux consumes memory more optimally. In other words, it means that, with WebFlux, we may use cheaper servers.

To make sure this is the right assumption, let's try to run a small experiment, again on the predictability of memory usage and how it might help us in unpredictable situations. For this test, we will try to analyze how much money we will spend on cloud infrastructure using Web MVC and WebFlux.

To measure the upper limit of the system, we will carry out stress testing and verify how many requests our system will be able to handle. In running our web application, we will launch an Amazon EC2 `t2.small` instance, which has one virtual CPU and 2 GB of RAM. The operating system will be Amazon Linux with JDK 1.8.0_144 and VM 25.144-b01. For the first round of measurements, we will use Spring Boot 2.0.x and Web MVC with Tomcat. Also, to simulate network calls and other I/O activity, which are a usual component of the modern system, we will use the following naïve piece of code:

```
@RestController
@SpringBootApplication
public class BlockingDemoApplication {
    ...
    @GetMapping("/endpoint")
    public String get() throws InterruptedException {
        Thread.sleep(1000);
        return "Hello";
    }
}
```

To run our application, we will use the following command:

```
java -Xmx2g
     -Xms1g
     -Dserver.tomcat.max-threads=20000
     -Dserver.tomcat.max-connections=20000
     -Dserver.tomcat.accept-count=20000
     -jar blocking-demo-0.0.1-SNAPSHOT.jar
```

So, with the preceding configuration, we will check whether our system can handle up to 20,000 users without failures. If we run our load test, we will get the following results:

Number of simultaneous requests	Average latency (milliseconds)
100	1,271
1,000	1,429
10,000	`OutOfMemoryError`/Killed

These results may vary over time, but on average they will be identical. As we can see, 2 GB of memory is not enough to handle 10,000 independent threads per connection. Of course, by tuning and playing around with the specific configuration of JVM and Tomcat, we might be able to slightly improve our results, but this does not solve the problem of unreasonable memory wastage. By keeping the same application server and just switching to WebFlux over Servlet 3.1, we may see significant improvements. The new web application looks as follows:

```
@RestController
@SpringBootApplication
public class TomcatNonBlockingDemoApplication {
   ...
   @GetMapping("/endpoint")
   public Mono<String> get() {
      return Mono.just("Hello")
                 .delaySubscription(Duration.ofSeconds(1));
   }
}
```

In this case, the interaction simulation with I/O will be asynchronous and non-blocking, which is easily available with the fluent Reactor 3 API.

 Note that the default server engine for WebFlux is Reactor-Netty. So, in order to switch to the Tomcat web server, we have to exclude `spring-boot-starter-reactor-netty` from WebFlux and provide a dependency on the `spring-boot-starter-tomcat` module.

To run a new stack, we will use the following command:

```
java -Xmx2g
     -Xms1g
     -Dserver.tomcat.accept-count=20000
     -jar non-blocking-demo-tomcat-0.0.1-SNAPSHOT.jar
```

Similarly, we allocate all RAM for our Java application, but in this case, we use the default thread pool size, which is 200 threads. By running the same tests, we will get the following results:

Number of simultaneous requests	Average latency (milliseconds)
100	1,203
1,000	1,407
10,000	9,661

As we can observe, in this case, our application shows much better results. Our results are still not ideal, since some of the users with a high load will have to wait for quite a long time. To improve the outcome, let's check the throughput and latency of a genuinely reactive server, which is Reactor-Netty.

Since the code and command for running the new web application are identical, let's cover just the benchmark results:

Number of simultaneous requests	Average latency (milliseconds)
1,000	1,370
10,000	2,699
20,000	6,310

As we can see, the results are much better. First of all, for Netty, we chose a minimum throughput of 1,000 connections at once. The upper limit was set to 20,000. This is enough to show that Netty as a server gives twice the performance of Tomcat with the same configurations. This comparison alone shows that WebFlux-based solutions may reduce the cost of infrastructure, because now our applications fit on cheaper servers and consume resources in a much more efficient way.

Another bonus that comes with the WebFlux module is the ability to process the incoming request body faster, with less memory consumption. This feature turns on when the incoming body is a collection of elements and our system can process each item separately:

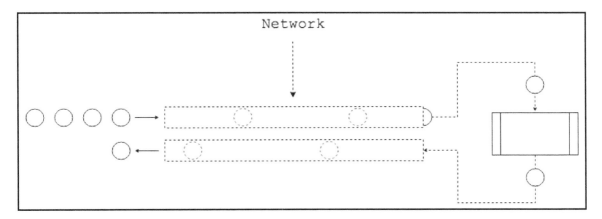

Diagram 6.23. WebFlux processing a large array of data in small chunks

To learn more about reactive message encoding and decoding, please see this link: `https://docs.spring.io/spring/docs/current/spring-framework-reference/web-reactive.html#webflux-codecs`.

As we can see from the preceding diagram, the system requires just a small piece of the request body in order to start processing data. The same may be achieved when we send a response body to the client. We do not have to wait for the whole response body and instead may start writing each element to the network as it comes. The following shows how we may achieve this with WebFlux:

```
@RestController
@RequestMapping("/api/json")
class BigJSONProcessorController {

    @GetMapping(
        value = "/process-json",
        produces = MediaType.APPLICATION_STREAM_JSON_VALUE
    )
    public Flux<ProcessedItem> processOneByOne(Flux<Item> bodyFlux) {
        return bodyFlux
            .map(item -> processItem(item))
            .filter(processedItem -> filterItem(processedItem));
    }
}
```

As we can see from the preceding code, such amazing features are available without hacking the internals of the Spring WebFlux module and may be achieved with the usage of an available API. In addition, the usage of such a processing model allows us to return the first response much faster, since the time between uploading the first item to the network and receiving the response is equal to the following:

$$R = Rnet + Rprocessing + Rnet$$

Note that the technique of *streaming* data processing does not allow us to predict the *content length* of the response body, which may be considered a disadvantage.

By comparison, Web MVC needs to upload the whole request into memory. Only after that can it process the incoming body:

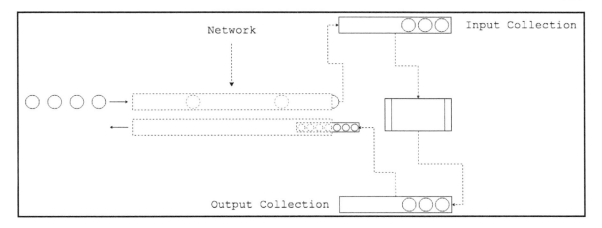

Diagram 6.24. Web MVC processing a large array of data at once

It is impossible to process data reactively, as in WebFlux, since the usual declaration of @Controller looks as follows:

```
@RestController
@RequestMapping("/api/json")
class BigJSONProcessorController {

    @GetMapping("/process-json")
    public List<ProcessedItem> processOneByOne(
        List<Item> bodyList
    ) {
        return bodyList
            .stream()
            .map(item -> processItem(item))
            .filter(processedItem -> filterItem(processedItem))
            .collect(toList());
    }
}
```

Here, the method declaration explicitly requires the full request body to be converted into collections of particular items. From a mathematical perspective, the average processing time is equal to the following:

$$R = N \times (Rnet + Rprocessing) + Rnet$$

Again, returning the first result to the user requires the whole request body to be processed and the results to be aggregated to the collection. Only after that will our system be able to send a response to the client. This means that WebFlux uses much less memory than Web MVC. WebFlux will be able to return the first response much faster than Web MVC and is capable of processing an infinite stream of data.

Impact of processing models on usability

Our comparison between Web MVC and WebFlux should contain some qualitative as well as quantitative indicators. One of the most common qualitative indicators that is measured is the learning curve. Web MVC is a well-known framework with more than ten years of active use in the enterprise arena. It relies on the most simple programming paradigm, which is the imperative programming paradigm. For a business, this means that if we start a new project based on plain Spring 5 and Web MVC, it will be much easier to find skilled developers and much cheaper to teach new ones. In contrast, with WebFlux, the situation will be significantly different. First of all, WebFlux is a new technology, which has not yet sufficiently proved itself and may potentially have a lot of bugs and vulnerabilities. The underlying asynchronous, non-blocking programming paradigm may also be a problem. First of all, it is hard to debug asynchronous, non-blocking code, as demonstrated by Netflix's experience of migrating Zuul to a new programming model.

Asynchronous programming is callback-based and driven by an event loop. The event loop's stack trace is meaningless when trying to follow a request. This is because events and callbacks are processed and there are few tools that can help with debugging. Edge cases, unhandled exceptions, and incorrectly handled state changes create dangling resources, resulting in ByteBuf leaks, file descriptor leaks, lost responses, and more. These types of issues have proven to be quite difficult to debug because it is difficult to know which event wasn't handled properly or cleaned up appropriately. For more information, visit `https://medium.com/netflix-techblog/zuul-2-the-netflix-journey-to-asynchronous-non-blocking-systems-45947377fb5c`.

Also, from a business perspective, it might be unreasonable to search for unbelievably highly-skilled engineers with in-depth knowledge of asynchronous and non-blocking programming, especially using the Netty stack. Teaching new developers from the beginning takes a lot of time and money and there is no guarantee that they will understand fully. Luckily, some parts of this problem are solved by using Reactor 3, which makes building meaningful transformation flows simpler and hides the hardest part of asynchronous programming. Unfortunately, Reactor does not solve all problems and, for businesses, such an unpredictable financial investment in people and risky technology may not be worth it.

Another vital point about qualitative analysis is the migration of an existing solution to a new reactive stack. Despite the fact that, from the very beginning of the framework's development, the Spring team have been doing their best to provide smooth migration, it is still hard to predict all migration cases. For example, those who rely on JSP, Apache Velocity, or similar server-side rendering technologies will be required to migrate the entire UI-related code. Moreover, a lot of modern frameworks rely on `ThreadLocal`, which makes the smooth movement to async, non-blocking programming challenging. Along with this, there are a lot of problems related to databases, which are covered in `Chapter 7`, *Reactive Database Access*.

Application of WebFlux

In the previous sections, we learned about the basics of WebFlux's design and its new features. We also went through a fine-grained comparison of WebFlux and Web MVC. We got an understanding of their advantages and disadvantages from different perspectives. Finally, in this section, we will try to get a clear understanding of the applications of WebFlux.

Microservice-based systems

WebFlux's first obvious application is in microservice systems. The most distinctive feature of typical microservice systems compared to monoliths is the abundance of I/O communication. The presence of I/O, especially blocking I/O, decreases the overall system latency and throughput. Contention and coherence in the thread-per-connection model do not improve system performance significantly. This means that for systems or particular services where inter-service calls are important, WebFlux will be one of the most efficient solutions. An example of such a service is a payment flow orchestration service.

Usually, behind a simple operation, such as money transferring between accounts, there is a hidden, intricate mechanism, which includes a set of retrievals, verifications, and then the actual transfer execution operations. For example, when we send money using PayPal, the first step may be to retrieve the accounts of the sender and the recipient. Then, since PayPal can transfer money from any country to any country, it is important to verify that the transfer will not break the laws of those countries. Each account may have its own limitations and restrictions. Finally, the recipient may have either an internal PayPal account or an external credit or debit card so, depending on the account type, we may have to make an additional call to an external system:

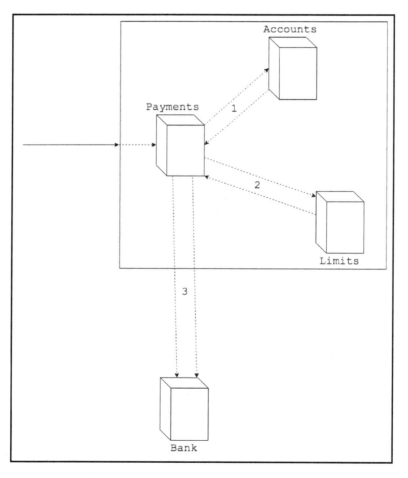

Diagram 6.25. An example implementation of the PayPal payment flow

By configuring non-blocking, asynchronous communication in such a complex flow, we may efficiently process other requests and efficiently utilize computer resources.

Systems that handle clients with slow connections

A second application of WebFlux is in building systems that are intended to work with mobile devices of clients with a slow or unstable network connection. To understand why WebFlux is useful in this area, let's remind ourselves what is going on when we are dealing with a slow connection. The problem is that transferring data from a client to a server may take a significant amount of time and the corresponding response may also take a lot of time. With the use of the thread-per-connection model, there is a higher chance of crashing the system with an increasing number of connected clients. For instance, using a **Denial-of-Service (DoS)** attack, hackers may easily make our server unavailable.

By contrast, WebFlux allows us to accept connections without blocking working threads. In this way, slow connections do not cause any problems. WebFlux will continue to receive other connections without blocking while waiting for an incoming request body. The Reactive Streams abstraction allows us to consume data when it is needed. This means that the server may control event consumption depending on the readiness of the network.

Streaming or real-time systems

Another useful application of WebFlux is with real-time and streaming systems. To understand why WebFlux helps here, let's remind ourselves what real-time and streaming systems are.

First of all, these systems are characterized by low latency and high throughput. For streaming systems, most of the data is outgoing from the server side, so the client side plays the role of a consumer. It is usual for there to be fewer events from the client side than from the server side. However, for real-time systems such as online games, the amount of incoming data is equal to the amount of outgoing data.

Low latency and high throughput can be achieved by using non-blocking communication. As we learned from the previous sections, non-blocking, asynchronous communication allows for efficient resource utilization. The highest throughput and lowest latency were shown by systems based on Netty or similar frameworks. However, such reactive frameworks have their own drawbacks, which are complicated interaction models that use channels and callbacks.

Despite this, reactive programming is an elegant solution for both of these issues. As we learned in Chapter 4, *Project Reactor - the Foundation for Reactive Apps*, reactive programming, especially with reactive libraries such as Reactor 3, helps us build an asynchronous, non-blocking flow with only a small overhead from the underlying code base complexity and an acceptable learning curve. Both solutions are incorporated into WebFlux. Using Spring Framework allows us to build such a system easily.

WebFlux in action

In order to learn how we can use WebFlux in real scenarios, we are going to build a simple web application that connects to the remote Gitter Streams API using WebClient, transforms data using the Project Reactor API, and then broadcasts the transformed messages to the world using SSE. The following diagram shows a schematic representation of the system:

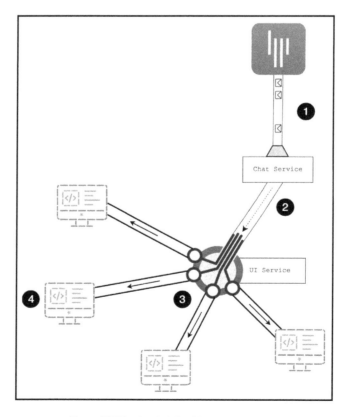

Diagram 6.26. The schematic design of the streaming application

The preceding diagram can be described as follows:

1. This is the point of integration with the Gitter API. As we can see from the preceding diagram, the communication between our server and Gitter is a streaming one. Hence, reactive programming fits naturally there.
2. This is the point in the system where we need to process incoming messages and transform them into a different view.
3. This is the point where we are caching received messages and broadcasting them to each connected client.
4. This is a representation of the connected browsers.

As we can see, the system has four central components in it. In order to build this system, we are going to create the following classes and interfaces:

- `ChatServeice`: This is the interface responsible for wiring communication with a remote server. It provides the ability to listen to messages from that server.
- `GitterService`: This is the implementation of the `ChatService` interface that connects to the Gitter streaming API in order to listen to new messages.
- `InfoResource`: This is the handler class that handles user requests and responds with a stream of messages.

The first step toward implementation of the system is to analyze the `ChatService` interface. The following sample shows the required method:

```
interface ChatService<T> {

    Flux<T> getMessagesStream();

    Mono<List<T>> getMessagesAfter(String messageId);
}
```

The preceding example interface covers the minimal required functionality related to message reading and listening. Here, the `getMessagesStream` method returns an infinite stream of new messages in the chat, whereas `getMessagesAfter` allows us to retrieve a list of messages with a particular message ID.

In both cases, Gitter provides access to its messages over HTTP. That means that we can use a plain `WebClient`. The following is an example of how we can implement `getMessagesAfter` and access the remote server:

```
Mono<List<MessageResponse>> getMessagesAfter(                     //
    String messageId                                             //
) {                                                              //
    ...                                                          //
    return webClient                                            // (1)
        .get()                                                  // (2)
        .uri(...)                                               // (3)
        .retrieve()                                             // (4)
        .bodyToMono(                                            // (5)
            new ParameterizedTypeReference<List<MessageResponse>>() {}//
        )                                                       //
        .timeout(Duration.ofSeconds(1))                        // (6)
        .retryBackoff(Long.MAX_VALUE, Duration.ofMillis(500)); // (7)
}
```

The preceding code sample shows how we can organize plain request-response interaction with the Gitter service. Here, at point (1), we use a `WebClient` instance in order to execute a `GET` HTTP method call (2) to the remote Gitter server (3). We then retrieve the information at point (4) and convert it using the `WebClient` DSL to `Mono` of the `List` of the `MessageResponse` at point (5). Then, in order to provide resilience in communication with the external service, we provide a `timeout` for the call at point (6) and in case of error, retry the call at point (7).

Communicating with the streaming Gitter API is as simple as that. The following shows how we can connect to the JSON streaming (*application/stream+json*) endpoint of the Gitter server:

```
public Flux<MessageResponse> getMessagesStream() {              //
    return webClient                                           //
        .get()                                                 // (1)
        .uri(...)                                              //
        .retrieve()                                            //
        .bodyToFlux(MessageResponse.class)                     // (2)
        .retryBackoff(Long.MAX_VALUE, Duration.ofMillis(500)); //
}                                                              //
```

As we can see in the preceding code, we use the same API as previously, as shown at point (1). The only changes that we have made are in the URI, which is hidden, and the fact that we are mapping to `Flux`, instead of `Mono`, as shown at point (2). Under the hood, `WebClient` uses the `Decoder` available in the container. If we have an infinite stream, this allows us to convert the elements on the fly, without waiting for the end of the stream.

Finally, in order to combine both streams into one and cache them, we may implement the following code, which provides an implementation for the InfoResource handler:

```
@RestController                                                      // (1)
@RequestMapping("/api/v1/info")                                     //
public class InfoResource {                                          //

    final ReplayProcessor<MessageVM> messagesStream                 // (2)
        = ReplayProcessor.create(50);                               //

    public InfoResource(                                            // (3)
        ChatService<MessageResponse> chatService                    //
    ) {                                                             //
      Flux.mergeSequential(                                         // (3.1)
            chatService.getMessageAfter(null)                       // (3.2)
                      .flatMapIterable(Function.identity())          //
            chatService.getMessagesStream()                         // (3.3)
        )                                                           //
        .map(...)                                                   // (3.4)
        .subscribe(messagesStream);                                 // (3.5)
    }

    @GetMapping(produces = MediaType.TEXT_EVENT_STREAM_VALUE)        // (4)
    public Flux<MessageResponse> stream() {                         //
        return messagesStream;                                      // (4.1)
    }                                                               //
}                                                                   //
```

The preceding code can be explained as follows:

1. This is the declaration of the class annotated with @RestController.
2. This is the ReplayProcessor field declaration. As we may remember from Chapter 4, *Project Reactor - the Foundation for Reactive Apps*, ReplayProcessor allows us to cache a predefined number of elements and replay the latest elements to each new subscriber.

3. Here, we have a declaration of the constructor of the `InfoResource` class. Within the constructor, we build a processing flow, which merges the stream of the latest messages from Gitter (shown at points `3.1` and `3.2`). In the case of a null ID, Gitter returns the 30 latest messages. The processing flow also listens to the stream of new messages in near real-time, as shown at point `(3.3)`. Then, all messages are mapped to the view-model, as shown at point `(3.4)`, and the stream is immediately subscribed to by the `ReplayProcessor`. This means that once the `InfoResource` bean has been constructed, we connect to the Gitter service, cache the latest messages, and start listening for updates. Note that `mergeSequential` subscribes to both streams simultaneously, but starts sending messages from the second, but only when the first stream has been completed. Since the first stream is a finite one, we receive the latest messages and start sending the queued messages from the `getMessagesStream Flux`.

4. This is a handler method declaration, which is invoked on each new connection to the specified endpoint. Here, we may just return the `ReplayProcessor` instance, shown at point `(4.1)`, so it will share the latest cached messages and send new messages once they are available.

As we can see in the preceding example, providing complex functionality such as merging streams in the proper order, or caching the latest 50 messages and dynamically broadcasting them to all subscribers, does not require a lot of effort or written code. Reactor and WebFlux cover the hardest parts and allow us just to write business logic. This enables efficient non-blocking interaction with I/O. Therefore, we may achieve a high-throughput and low-latency system by using this powerful toolkit.

Summary

In this chapter, we learned that WebFlux is an efficient replacement for the good old Web MVC framework. We also learned that WebFlux uses the same techniques for request handler declarations (using the well-known `@RestController` and `@Controller`). In addition to the standard handler declaration, WebFlux introduces a lightweight, functional endpoint declaration using `RouterFunction`. For a long time, modern reactive web servers, such as Netty, and non-blocking Undertow features were unavailable to users of the Spring Framework. With the WebFlux web framework, these technologies have become available using the same, familiar API. Since WebFlux is based on asynchronous non-blocking communication, this framework depends on Reactor 3, which is the core component of the module.

We also explored changes that have been introduced with the new WebFlux module. These include changes to communication between the user and the server, based on Reactor 3 Reactive Types; changes to communication between the server and external services, in particular with the new `WebClient` technology; and a new `WebSocketClient`, which allows client-server communication over WebSocket. Also, WebFlux is a cross-library framework, which means that any Reactive Streams-based library is supported here and may replace the default Reactor 3 library or any other preferred library.

After that, this chapter introduced a detailed comparison of WebFlux and Web MVC from different perspectives. To summarize, in most cases, WebFlux is the right solution for high-load web servers, and in all performance results, it performs twice as well as Web MVC. We looked at business gains of using the WebFlux module and considered how WebFlux simplifies work. We also looked at the pitfalls of this technology.

Finally, we learned about a few use cases in which WebFlux is the most appropriate solution. Those cases were microservice systems, real-time streaming systems, online games, and other similar application areas, where the important characteristics include low latency, high throughput, low memory footprint, and efficient CPU utilization.

Although we have learned about the core aspects of the web application, there is another even more important part, which is interaction with databases. In the next chapter, we will go through the main features of reactive communication with databases, which databases support reactive communication, and what we should do when there is no reactive support.

Reactive Database Access

The previous chapter introduced a new addition to the Spring Framework family—Spring WebFlux. This addition brings reactive programming to the application front and enables non-blocking processing of HTTP requests of all kinds.

In this chapter, we will learn how to access data in a reactive manner using *Spring Data* modules. This ability is vital for the creation of an entirely reactive and responsive application that leverages all available computing resources most efficiently, delivering the maximum business value and also requiring a minimal operational cost at the same time.

Even if our database of choice does not provide a reactive or asynchronous driver, it is still possible to build a reactive application around it using a dedicated thread pool—this chapter covers how to do this. However, blocking I/O is always discouraged in reactive applications.

In this chapter, we cover the following topics:

- Patterns of data storage and data processing in the modern world
- Pros and cons of synchronous data access
- How Spring Data allows reactive data access and how to use this in reactive applications
- What reactive connectors are available at the moment
- How to adapt blocking I/O to the reactive programming model

Data handling patterns in the modern world

Even though monolithic software systems still exist, operating on and supporting a lot of our everyday activities, most new systems are designed for—or at least at some point are transitioned to—microservices. Microservices is now probably the most dominant architectural style for modern applications, especially *cloud-native applications*. In most cases, this approach allows a rapid development cycle for a software product. At the same time, it also provides an opportunity for more cost-effective underlying infrastructure (servers, networking, backups, and so on), especially when relying on cloud providers such as AWS, Google Cloud Platform, or Pivotal Cloud Foundry.

 For more information about cloud-native applications, see the **Cloud Native Computing Foundation** (**CNCF**) Charter at https://cncf.io/about/charter. More pros and cons of cloud-native applications in the context of reactive programming are covered in Chapter 10, *And, Finally, Release It!*

We will now take a look at an overview of the basics of data storing in the context of microservices, possible strategies, implementation approaches, and some recommendations related to data persistence.

Domain-driven design

Domain-driven design (**DDD**) by Eric Evans (Addison-Wesley, 2004) should occupy an honored place on every software engineer's bookshelf. This is because it defines and formalizes an important theoretical basis for a successful microservices architecture. DDD establishes a common vocabulary (namely, context, domain, model, and ubiquitous language) and formulates a set of principles for maintaining model integrity. One of the most important consequences of DDD is that individual **bounded contexts** defined in terms of DDD are usually mapped into separate microservices, demonstrated as follows:

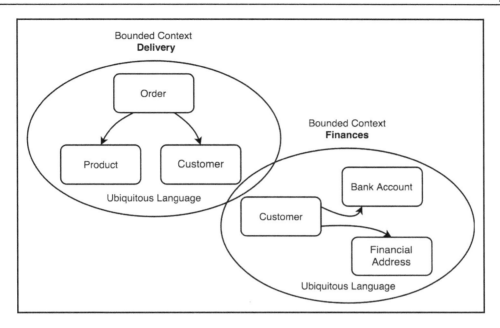

Diagram 7.1 Bounded contexts (good candidates for microservices) as depicted by Vaughn Vernon, the author of *Implementing Domain-Driven Design* and *Domain-Driven Design Distilled*

Since DDD is very focused on the business **core domain**, especially on artifacts to express, create, and retrieve domain models, the following objects will often be referenced during this chapter—*entity, value objects, aggregate, repository*.

To learn more about DDD concepts, please read the following article: `http://dddcommunity.org/resources/ddd_terms`.

During application implementation with DDD in mind, the preceding objects should be mapped to the application persistence layer if such a layer is present in the service. Such a domain model formulates the basis for logical and physical data models.

Data stores in the era of microservices

Probably the leading persistence-related change introduced by the microservices architecture is strong encouragement to not share data stores between services. This means that each logical service owns and manages its database (if it requires a database at all) and ideally no other service can access the data in a way that is different from a service API call.

It is out of this book's scope to explain all the reasons for such separation, but the most important ones are as follows:

- The ability to evolve different services separately, without tight coupling on a database schema
- The potential for more precise resource management
- The chance of horizontal scalability
- The possibility to use the best fit persistence implementation

Consider the following diagram:

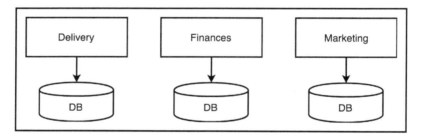

Diagram 7.2 Separate database per service

At the physical level, storage separation can be implemented in a few different ways. The simplest way is to have one database server and one database for all services, but to divide them using separate schemas (*schema per microservice*). Such a configuration can be easily implemented, requires a minimal amount of server resources, and does not require much administration in production, so it is pretty attractive in the first stages of application development. Data separation could be enforced with the database access control rules. Such an approach is easy to implement, but at the same time, it is easy to break. As data is stored in the same database, it is sometimes tempting for developers to write a single query that may retrieve or update data belonging to more than one service. It is also easier to compromise the security of the whole system by compromising only one service. The following diagram shows the design of the mentioned system:

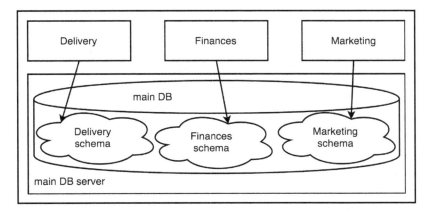

Diagram 7.3 Schema per service

Services may share a single database server but have different databases with different access credentials. Such an approach improves data separation as it is much harder to write a single query capable of accessing external data. However, this also complicates backup routines a little. The following diagram depicts this:

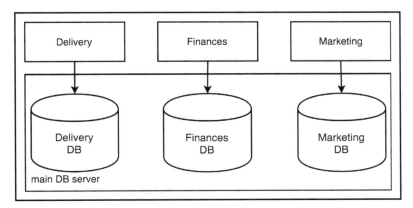

Diagram 7.4 Database per service

Each service may have its database server. Such an approach requires a lot more administration but provides a good starting point for fine-grained tuning of the database server to meet the needs of the concrete service. Also, in this case, it is possible to only vertically and horizontally scale the databases that require such scalability. The following diagram shows this:

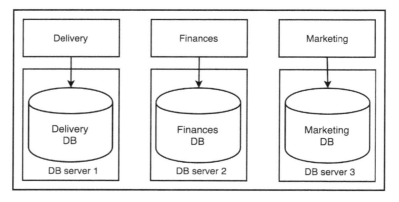

Diagram 7.5 Database server per service

When implementing a software system, all of the previously mentioned techniques could easily be used simultaneously in different proportions depending on the actual demands of the system. The following schema shows the design of such a system:

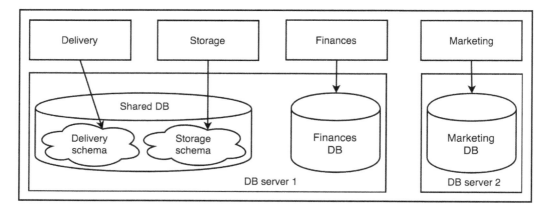

Diagram 7.6 Mixed combinations of persistence strategies

Furthermore, it is possible to have different database server instances, and we can now use different database engines together (SQL and NoSQL) to achieve the best results. This approach is called **polyglot persistence**.

Polyglot persistence

In 2006, *Neal Ford* proposed the term **polyglot programming**. This expresses the idea that software systems may be written with a mix of different languages to get the most significant boost from the best-fit language in a business or technical context. After that, a lot of new programming languages were introduced with the intention of being the best in a specific area, or good in multiple areas.

At the same time, another similar mind-shift happened in the area of data persistence. This caused people to question what would happen if different application parts used different persistence techniques depending on business or technical requirements. For example, storing HTTP sessions for distributed web applications and storing a graph of friends on a social network require different operational characteristics, and consequently require different databases. Nowadays, it is pretty standard for a system to have two or more different database technologies at the same time.

Historically, most **Relational Database Management Systems** (**RDBMSes**) are built on the same ACID principles and offer pretty similar SQL dialects for communicating with storage. RDBMSes, in general, are suitable for a wide range of applications, but they rarely have the best performance and operational features for a lot of common use cases (for example, storing graphs, in-memory storage, and distributed storage). In contrast, **NoSQL databases** that have appeared recently have a broader spectrum of foundational principles, which results in better features for common use cases, even though most NoSQL databases cannot efficiently serve as universal data storage. The following diagram depicts this:

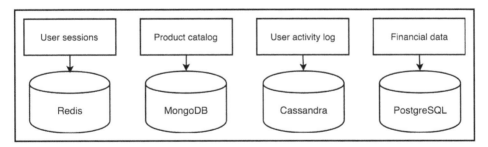

Diagram 7.7 Each service uses the persistence technology that best fits its needs

Also, polyglot persistence comes at the additional cost of complexity. Each new storage mechanism introduces new APIs and paradigms to be learned, new client libraries to be developed or adopted, and a new set of standard issues to address in development and production. Also, incorrect use of a NoSQL database may mean a complete redesign of the service. Using the **right** persistence technology (SQL or NoSQL) should make this more comfortable, but the challenge does not go away.

Spring Framework has separate sub-projects dedicated to data persistence called Spring Data (`http://projects.spring.io/spring-data`). The rest of this chapter describes different design approaches and database connectors available in Spring Data, especially targeting reactive programming patterns and how they change the way applications access the data stored within a polyglot persistence layer.

Database as a Service

In a properly designed microservice architecture, all services are stateless, and all the states are stored in special services that know how to manage data persistence. In a cloud environment, stateless services enable efficient scalability and high availability. However, it is much harder to manage and scale database servers efficiently, especially ones that were not designed for a cloud. Most cloud providers offer to address that problem by using their **Database as a Service (DBaaS)** solutions. Such storage solutions might be customized versions of ordinary databases (MySQL, PostgreSQL, and Redis) or designed from scratch to operate only in the cloud (AWS Redshift, Google BigTable, and Microsoft CosmosDB).

Usually, an algorithm of cloud storage or database usage works in the following way:

1. A client issues a request for an access to the database or file storage (via admin page or API).
2. The cloud provider grants access to the API or server resource, which can be used for data persistence. At the same time, the client does not know or even care about how the provided API is implemented.
3. The client uses a storage API or a database driver providing access credentials.
4. The cloud provider charges the client depending on a client subscription plan, stored data size, query frequency, concurrent connections, or other characteristics.

Usually, such an approach allows a client (in our case a software developer) and a cloud provider to focus on their primary objectives. The cloud provider implements the most efficient way of storing and processing client data, minimizing spending on the underlying infrastructure. At the same time, the client focuses on the primary business objectives of the application and does not spend time configuring database servers, replication, or backups. Such a separation of concerns is not always the most profitable for a client, and it may not even be possible at all. However, when relevant, it sometimes allows us to build successful and widely-used applications with only a handful of engineers.

 Among other use cases, Foursquare, whose applications are used by more than 50 million people per month, is primarily built with an AWS technology stack, namely Amazon EC2 for cloud hosting, Amazon S3 for storing images and other data, and Amazon Redshift as a database.

Some of the most well-known cloud-native data storage and DB services are as follows:

- **AWS S3** provides key-value storage through web service interfaces (REST API or AWS SDK). This is designed for storing files, images, backups, or any other information that could be represented as a bucket of bytes.
- **AWS DynamoDB** is a fully managed proprietary NoSQL database that provides synchronous replication across multiple data centers.
- **AWS Redshift** is a data warehouse built on top of technology for parallel processing (MPP). This enables analytics workloads on big data.
- **Heroku PostgreSQL as a Service** is a PostgreSQL database that is fully managed by the Heroku cloud provider, allowing shared and exclusive database servers for applications deployed to the Heroku cluster.
- **Google Cloud SQL** is a fully-managed PostgreSQL and MySQL database provided by Google.
- **Google BigTable** is compressed, high performance, and proprietary data storage designed to handle massive workloads at a consistent low latency and high throughput.
- **Azure Cosmos DB** is Microsoft's proprietary globally distributed multi-model database with a few different APIs, including MongoDB driver-level protocol support.

Sharing data across microservices

In real business systems, it is often required to query data owned by two or more services in order to process a client request. For example, a client may want to see all their orders and the payment statuses corresponding to their orders. Before the microservices architecture, this could be implemented with a single join query, but now this is against best practices. To handle a multi-service request, it is required to implement an adapter service that queries both order and payment services, applies all required transformations, and returns an aggregated result to the client. Also, it is quite evident that if two services communicate a lot or highly depend on each other, they may be the right candidates for merging into one service (if such service merging does not harm the domain-driven design). The following diagram depicts this:

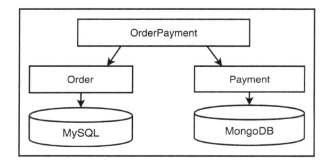

Diagram 7.8 An adapter service that aggregates data from an Order service and a Payment service

The reading strategy is pretty simple, but it is much harder to implement and update a strategy that requires a few services at once. Let's say a client wants to place an order, but it is only possible to have the appropriate inventory balance and payment information validated. Every service has its own database, so within a workflow, two or more microservices and databases are involved in a business transaction. There are a few approaches to tackling such a problem, but the two most popular are **distributed transactions** and **event-driven architecture**.

Distributed transactions

A distributed transaction is a transaction that updates data on two or more networked computer systems. In other words, a few services together in one accord agree whether a certain action happened or not. In practice, most database systems use strong, strict, and two-phase locking to ensure global serializability.

Distributed transactions are often used by services to update data stores atomically. They were frequently used in monolithic applications to ensure reliable action on different data stores. This facilitated proper recovery from failures at the same time. However, the usage of distributed transactions is discouraged nowadays between multiple microservices. There are a few reasons for this, but the most important ones are as follows:

- A service that allows distributed transactions requires an API that supports two-phase commit and is not very trivial to implement
- Microservices that are involved in a distributed transaction are tightly coupled, which is always discouraged in a microservices architecture
- Distributed transactions do not scale, limiting system bandwidth and consequently reducing the scalability of the system

Event-driven architecture

The best way to implement a distributed business transaction in a microservice environment is through an event-driven architecture, which we have explored a few times throughout this book so far.

If it is required to change the state of the system, the first service changes its data in its own database, and the same inner transaction publishes an event to a message broker. So, even if transactions are involved, they do not cross the boundary of the service. The second service, which registers the subscription to the required type of events, receives events and changes its storage accordingly, as well as possibly sending an event. The services are not blocked together and do not depend on each other; the only coupling present in the system is on the messages that they exchange. In contrast, with distributed transactions, the event-driven architecture allows a system to progress even if the second service is not running at the time when the first service acts. This characteristic is very important as it directly impacts the resilience of the system. A distributed transaction demands that all concerned components (microservices) have to be available and have to operate correctly during the whole duration of a transaction in order for it to progress. The more microservices a system has, or the broader the microservices' involvement during distributed transactions, the harder it is for the system to progress.

In the same way as before, when two services communicate a lot in a chatty fashion, they may be considered for merging. Also, adapter services making multiple updates to a few services may be implemented using events.

Eventual consistency

Let's look back for a second and analyze what functions distributed transactions play in a software system. It is evident that we use distributed transactions to be sure about the system state, or in other words, we eliminate the uncertainty that some state across the system may be inconsistent. However, this elimination of uncertainty is a very restrictive demand. Vaughn Vernon, the author of *Implementing Domain-Driven Design*, proposes to *embed uncertainty into the domain model*. According to him, if it is tough to protect the system from inconsistent state and inconsistency still occurs no matter how hard we fight against it, it may be beneficial to accept the uncertainty and embed it as part of a regular business workflow.

For example, our system may still create an order without verified payment information by introducing a new state called **verifying payment info**. This new event converts an uncertain situation (payment information may be valid or invalid) into a separate business step that may be occupied for a finite time (until payment information is validated). With this approach, we do not require our system to be consistent all of the time. Instead, it is required to ensure that the system has a consistent vision about the state of each business transaction. Such future consistency is called **eventual consistency**. The following diagram depicts this:

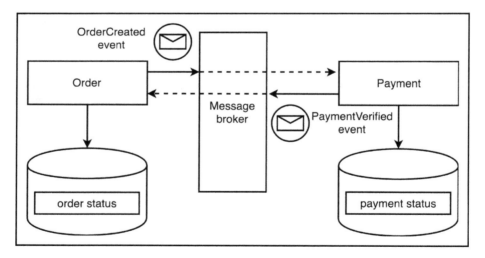

Diagram 7.9 The Order and Payment services both update private databases and communicate the workflow state via messages

Usually, eventual consistency guarantees are enough to build a sound system that successfully progresses its operation. Moreover, any distributed system has to deal with eventual consistency in order to be available (processing user requests) and to be partition tolerant (survive network outages between components).

The SAGA pattern

One of the most popular patterns for distributed transactions, especially in a microservice world, is called the **SAGA pattern**. This was introduced in 1987 to manage long-lived transactions in databases.

A saga consists of a few small transactions, each of which is local to its microservice. Here, an external request initiates the saga, and in turn, it starts the first small transaction, which upon successful completion triggers the second transaction, and so on. If a transaction fails to succeed in the middle, it triggers a compensation action for the previous transactions. The are two main ways to implement the pattern—*events-based choreography* and *orchestration via a coordinator service*.

Event sourcing

To handle events flowing through the microservice application, microservices may use the **event sourcing** pattern. Event sourcing persists the state of a business entity as a sequence of state-changing events. For example, a bank account may be represented as an initial amount of money and a sequence of deposit/withdraw operations. Having this information not only allows us to calculate the current account state by replaying update events, it also gives a reliable audit log of the entity changes and allows queries to determine the state of an entity at any point in the past. Usually, services that implement event sourcing provide APIs that allow other services to subscribe to entities updates.

To optimize the time required to calculate the current state, an application can periodically build and save snapshots. To reduce the storage size, events before the selected snapshot may be deleted. In this case, it is clear that a part of the entire history of updated events is lost.

Bank Account 111-11 event log:

Date	Action	Amount
2018-06-04 22:00:01	create	$0
2018-06-05 00:05:00	deposit	$50
2018-06-05 09:30:00	withdraw	$10
2018-06-05 14:00:30	deposit	$20
2018-06-06 15:00:30	deposit	$115
2018-06-07 10:10:00	withdraw	$40

Current balance: $135

Despite its simplicity, event sourcing is not used frequently due to its unfamiliar and slightly alien programming approach, as well as its learning curve. Also, because of the constant state recalculation, event sourcing does not allow efficient querying, especially when queries are complicated. In this case, Command Query Responsibility Segregation may help.

Command Query Responsibility Segregation

Command Query Responsibility Segregation (**CQRS**) is often used alongside event sourcing. CQRS consists of two parts:

- The **writing** part receives state-update commands and stores them in an underlying event store, but does not return an entity state.
- The **reading** part does not change the state and returns it for a requested query type. State representations for distinct queries are stored in views, which are recalculated asynchronously after update events are received as commands.

The way in which the CQRS pattern works is as follows:

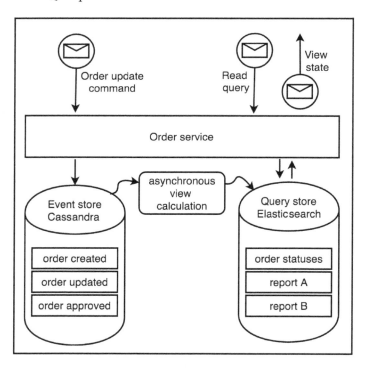

Diagram 7.10 A CQRS implementation for the Order service. The write part stores update commands, and the read part asynchronously calculates views for expected queries

The CQRS pattern allows software systems to process huge volumes of data in a streaming manner and, at the same time, it makes it possible to respond quickly to various queries regarding the current system state.

Conflict-free replicated data types

The bigger our application becomes, the more data it has to process, even for a single microservice with a well-defined scope. As we mentioned previously, transactions do not scale well, and with application growth, it is harder to keep the global state consistent even within boundaries of one microservice. So, for the sake of performance and system scalability, we may allow data to be updated concurrently by different service instances without a global lock or transactional consistency. Such an approach is called **optimistic replication** and allows data replicas to evolve **in parallel** with possible inconsistencies that should be **resolved** later. In such scenarios, consistency between replicas is re-established when replicas are merged. At that point, conflicts have to be resolved, but this usually means that some changes have to be reverted, which may be unacceptable from a user's standpoint. However, there are also data structures with mathematical properties that ensure the merge process always succeeds. Such data structures are called **Conflict-Free Replicated Data Types** (**CRDT**).

CRDT describes data types that can be replicated across multiple computation units, updated concurrently without any coordination, and then merged to get a consistent state. This concept was described by Marc Shapiro, Nuno Preguica, Marek Zawirski, and Carlos Baquero in 2011. At the time of writing, CRDT has a handful of data types, such as a Grow-only Counter, a Grow-only Set, a Two-Phase Set, a Last-Write-Wins-Element Set, and a few other sets that can only cover a subset of typical business workflows. However, CRDT is still proven to be very useful for collaborative text editing, online chats, and online gambling. The SoundCloud audio distribution platform uses CRDT, and a Phoenix web framework employs CRDT to enable real-time multi-node information sharing, while Microsoft's Cosmos DB uses CRDT for writing multi-master data. The Redis database also has built-in support for CRDT in the form of a **Conflict-Free Replicated Database** (**CRDB**).

Messaging system as a data store

Building on the idea of event sourcing, we may conclude that a *message broker with persistence storage for messages may diminish the need for a dedicated database* for individual microservices. Indeed, if all entity update events (including entity snapshots) are stored in the message broker for a sufficient period of time and can be re-read at any moment, the entire state of the system may be defined only by that event. During startup, each service may read recent event history (up to the last snapshot) and recalculate an entity's state in memory. So, a service may function by merely processing new update commands and read queries, and generating and sending entity snapshots to the broker from time to time.

Apache Kafka is a popular distributed message broker with a reliable persistence layer that could be used as a primary and potentially the only data store in the system.

As we can see, nowadays the polyglot persistence and the event-driven architecture based on message brokers are often used in tandem to implement reliable complex workflows in a highly volatile, scalable, ever-changing software system. The rest of the chapter is focused on the persistence mechanisms provided by Spring Framework, while Chapter 8, *Scaling Up with Cloud Streams*, reveals what techniques are available in the Spring ecosystem for implementing efficient applications based on event-driven architecture.

Synchronous model for data retrieval

To understand all the benefits and pitfalls of reactive persistence, first we have to recap on how applications have been implementing data access in the pre-reactive era. We also have to learn how a client and a database communicate when issuing and processing queries, what parts of such communication could be done asynchronously, and what parts could benefit from applying reactive programming patterns. As database persistence consists of a few layers of abstraction, we are going to go through all of these layers, describing them and trying on the reactive outfit.

Wire protocol for database access

There are types of databases called **embedded databases**. Such databases run inside the application process itself and do not require any communication over the network. For embedded databases, there is no hard requirement to have a wire protocol, even though some have or may run both as an embedded mode or as a separate service. Later in the chapter, we are going to use the H2 embedded database in a few examples.

However, most software uses databases that run in separate processes on separate servers (or in separate containers). An application uses a specialized client library called a **database driver** to communicate with an external database. Furthermore, the wire protocol defines how the database driver and the database itself communicates. It defines the format of the order of messages sent between a client and the database. In most cases, a wire protocol is language independent so that a Java application can query a database written in C++.

As wire protocols are usually designed to work over TCP/IP, there is no need for the wire protocol to be blocking. As with the synchronous HTTP communication, the protocol itself is not blocking, and it is a client that decides to be blocked while waiting for results. Moreover, TCP is an asynchronous protocol that supports backpressure via the flow control implemented by the sliding window. However, the sliding window approach is tuned for sending chunks of bytes over the network and may not reflect the needs of the application's backpressure in the best way. For example, when receiving rows from a database, it's more natural to request the next portion of data processing in the number of rows rather than relying on the system settings that define network buffer size. Of course, the wire protocol may intentionally use another mechanism or even a combination of mechanisms for backpressure implementation, but it is essential to remember that TCP mechanisms also work under the hood all the time.

It is also possible to use a more high-level protocol as a basis for the database wire protocol. For example, we may use HTTP2, WebSockets, gRPC, or RSocket. Chapter 8, *Scaling Up with Cloud Streams*, makes a brief comparison of the RSocket and gRPC protocols.

Aside from the backpressure concerns, there are different approaches for communicating big datasets between the client and the database. For example, a client inserts tens of thousands of rows of data, or an analytical query result contains millions of rows. For the sake of simplicity, let's consider only the latter use case. In general, there are a few approaches for communicating such a result set:

- Calculate the **entire result set** on the database side, putting the data into a container and sending the container entirely as soon as the query finishes. This approach does not imply any logical backpressure and requires huge buffers on the database side (and also potentially on the client side). Furthermore, the client receives its first results only after the whole query is executed. Such an approach is easy to implement. Furthermore, the query execution process does not last too long and may cause less contention with updated queries happening at the same time.

- Send **result set in chunks** as the client requests them. The query may be executed entirely, and results may be stored in a buffer. Alternatively, the database may execute the query only to the point where it fills one or a few requested chunks and continues execution only after it has communicated the client's demand. This way of operating may require fewer memory buffers, returns the first rows when the query is still running, and makes it possible to propagate logical backpressure or query cancelation.
- Send **results as a stream** as soon as such results are obtained during the query execution. On top of that, the client may also inform the database about the demand and propagate logical backpressure that may, in turn, impact the query execution process. Such an approach requires almost no additional buffers, and the client receives the first row of the result as soon as it is possible. However, this way of communicating may under-utilize the network and CPU due to a very **chatty** manner of communication and frequent system calls.

The following diagram shows the interaction flow for a chunked result flow:

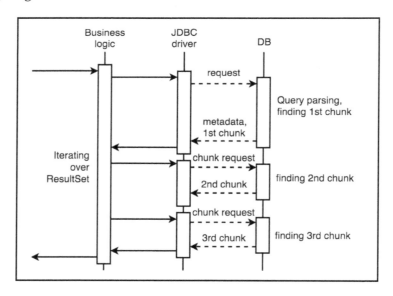

Diagram 7.11 Iterating over the query results using chunks

In general, different databases implement one or more of the approaches in their wire protocols. For example, MySQL knows how to send data as a whole or as a stream, row by row. At the same time, PostgreSQL databases have a concept called **portal**, which allows the client to propagate as many rows of data as they are ready to receive. The preceding diagram depicts how a Java application may use such an approach.

At this level, a well-designed database wire protocol may already have all the characteristics required to be reactive. At the same time, even the most straightforward protocol may potentially be wrapped with a reactive driver that may use TCP control flow for backpressure propagation.

Database driver

The database driver is a library that adapts the database wire protocol to language constructs such as method calls, callbacks, or potentially Reactive Streams. In the case of relational databases, drivers usually implement a language-level API such as DB-API for Python or JDBC for Java.

It is not a surprise that software written in a synchronous blocking manner uses the same approach for data access. Moreover, usually, communication with an external database through the driver is no different from communication with an external HTTP service. For example, the Apache Phoenix JDBC driver is based on the Avatica component of the Apache Calcite framework and uses JSON or Protocol Buffer over HTTP. Consequently, in theory, we may also apply reactive design to database communication protocols and gain pretty similar benefits, as with the reactive `WebClient` from the Spring WebFlux module. The following diagram shows that an HTTP request and database query are pretty similar from a network communications standpoint:

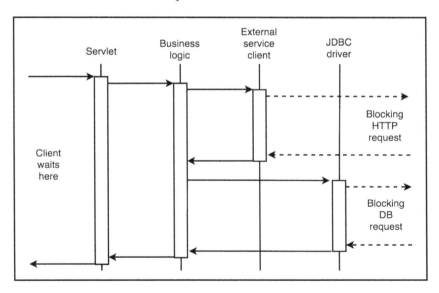

Diagram 7.12 Similar blocking IO behavior of the blocking HTTP request and the database request

Usually, the blocking nature of database drivers is dictated by the upper-level API, and not by the wire protocol. Consequently, it should not be tough to implement a reactive database driver that has an appropriate language-level API. The candidates for such an API are covered later in this chapter. At the same time, the NoSQL database driver has no established language-level API to implement, so it is free to implement its own API asynchronously or reactively. For example, MongoDB, Cassandra, and Couchbase decided to take this route, and they now provide either asynchronous or reactive drivers.

JDBC

Released for the first time in 1997, **Java Database Connectivity** (**JDBC**) has since been defining how applications communicate with databases (primary relational), providing a unified API for data access on a Java platform. The latest API revision, 4.3, was released in 2017 and was included in Java SE 9.

JDBC allows multiple database client drivers to exist and be used by the same application. JDBC Driver Manager is responsible for correct registration, loading, and usage of required driver implementation. When the driver is loaded, the client may create a connection with appropriate access credentials. JDBC connections make it possible to initialize and execute statements such as SQL's `SELECT`, `CREATE`, `INSERT`, `UPDATE`, and `DELETE`. Statements that update the state of the database as an execution result return a number of affected rows, and query statements return `java.sql.ResultSet`, which is an iterator over the rows of the result. `ResultSet` was designed long ago and has a strange API. For example, an index that enumerates columns in a row starts from `1`, not from `0`.

The `ResultSet` interface is designed for backward iteration, and even random access, but that level of compatibility requires the driver to load all the rows before allowing any processing. For the sake of simplicity, we assume that `ResultSet` resembles a simple iterator over the rows of the result. This assumption allows an underlying implementation to operate over a chunked result set and load batches from the database on demand. Any underlying asynchronous implementation has to be wrapped into synchronous blocking calls at the level of JDBC.

In the area of performance, JDBC allows batching for non-select queries. This should allow communicating with the database in fewer network requests. However, because JDBC is designed to be synchronous and blocking, that does not help when processing big datasets.

Even though JDBC was designed as a business-logic level API, it operates with tables, rows, and columns, instead of *entities* and *aggregates* as domain-driven design recommends. Consequently, nowadays, JDBC is considered to be too low-level for direct use. For such purposes, the Spring ecosystem has the Spring Data JDBC and Spring Data JPA modules. There are also a lot of well-established libraries that wrap JDBC and provide a more pleasant API to use. One example of such a library is `Jdbi`. It proposes not only a fluent API but also has excellent integration with the Spring ecosystem.

Connection management

Modern applications rarely create a JDBC connection directly. More often, **connection pools** are used. The reason behind this is pretty simple—establishing a new connection is costly. Consequently, it is wise to have a cache of connections managed in the way that allows reuse. The cost of creating a connection may come from two areas. First of all, the connection initiation process may require client authentication and authorization, and this takes up precious time. Secondly, a new connection may cost a database a fortune. For example, PostgreSQL creates a whole new process (not a thread!) whenever a new connection is established, which itself may take hundreds of milliseconds on a powerful Linux machine. At the time of writing, the most commonly-used connection pools for the Java platform are Apache Commons DBCP2, C3P0, Tomcat JDBC, and HikariCP. HikariCP is considered to be the fastest connection pool in the Java world.

Note that even though connection pooling is widely used for JDBC connectivity, it is not an inherent part of database communication. For example, the Oracle database driver allows connection multiplexing, which allows us to **funnel** multiple logical connections through a single network connection. Of course, such support is enabled not only by the driver but by the wire protocol and the database implementation itself.

Making relational database access reactive

As JDBC is the primary language-level API for data access in the Java world (at least for relational data sources), it shapes the behavior of all abstraction levels built on top of it. Previously, we showed that blocking APIs are not recommended for use in reactive applications as they limit the application's scalability. Consequently, it is crucial for us to have a proper language-level database access API to be used in reactive applications. Unfortunately, there are no easy solutions that might tweak JDBC slightly for that purpose. At the moment, two promising API drafts may fit this niche, and we are going to look at them later in this chapter. The following diagram depicts what is required for making a reactive JDBC API:

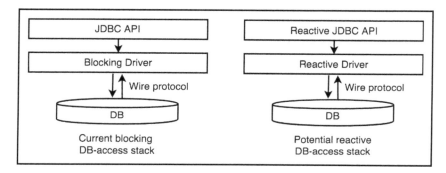

Diagram 7.13 The current JDBC stack and a potential reactive replacement

Spring JDBC

To simplify the hassle surrounding raw JDBC, Spring provides the Spring JDBC module, which is pretty old but well described. This module offers a few versions of the `JdbcTemplate` class that helps to execute queries and maps relational rows into entities. It also handles the creation and release of resources, helping to omit common errors such as forgetting to close a prepared statement or connection. `JdbcTemplate` also catches JDBC exceptions and translates them to generic `org.springframework.dao` exceptions.

Let's say we have a collection of books in an SQL database and the entity is represented by the following Java class:

```
class Book {
    private int id;
    private String title;

    public Book() { }
```

```
    public Book(int id, String title) {
        this.id = id;
        this.title = title;
    }
    //getters and setters ...
}
```

With `JdbcTemplate` and a generic `BeanPropertyRowMapper`, we may create a Spring repository in the following way:

```
@Repository
class BookJdbcRepository {

    @Autowired
    JdbcTemplate jdbcTemplate;

    public Book findById(int id) {
        return jdbcTemplate.queryForObject(
            "SELECT * FROM book WHERE id=?",
            new Object[] { id },
            new BeanPropertyRowMapper<>(Book.class));
    }
}
```

Alternatively, we may provide our own mapper class to instruct Spring on how a `ResultSet` should be translated into a domain entity:

```
class BookMapper implements RowMapper<Book> {
    @Override
    public Book mapRow(ResultSet rs, int rowNum) throws SQLException {
        return new Book(rs.getInt("id"), rs.getString("title"));
    }
}
```

Let's implement the `BookJdbcRepository.findAll()` method using the `BookMapper` class:

```
public List<Book> findAll() {
    return jdbcTemplate.query("SELECT * FROM book", new BookMapper());
}
```

One more improvement over `JdbcTemplate` is implemented by the `NamedParameterJdbcTemplate` class. This adds support for passing JDBC parameters using human-readable names as opposed to `?` placeholders. Consequently, a prepared SQL query and its corresponding Java code may look like this:

```
SELECT * FROM book WHERE title = :searchtitle
```

Here is a classic prepared SQL statement:

```
SELECT * FROM book WHERE title = ?
```

This may only seem to be a minor improvement, but named parameters give better readability for code than indexes, especially when a query requires half a dozen parameters.

In summary, the Spring JDBC module consists of utilities, helper classes, and tools used by higher-level abstractions. Higher-level APIs do not limit the Spring JDBC module, so it can absorb the required reactive support relatively easily given that the underlying API also supports it.

Spring Data JDBC

Spring Data JDBC is a pretty new module in the Spring Data family. It aims to simplify the implementation of JDBC-based repositories. Spring Data repositories, including JDBC-based ones, are inspired by the repository described in *Domain-Driven Design* by Eric Evans. This means that we are recommended to have a repository per Aggregate Root. Spring Data JDBC features CRUD operations for simple aggregates, supporting @Query annotations and entity life cycle events.

 Be attentive—*Spring Data JDBC* and *Spring JDBC* are different modules!

To use Spring Data JDBC we have to modify the Book entity and apply the org.springframework.data.annotation.Id annotation to the id field. The repository requires an entity to have a unique identifier, so the Book entity refactored for use in repository looks like the following:

```
class Book {
    @Id
    private int id;
    private String title;

    // other parts are unchanged
}
```

Now let's define the `BookRepository` interface, deriving it from `CrudRepository<Book, Integer>`:

```
@Repository
public interface BookSpringDataJdbcRepository
    extends CrudRepository<Book, Integer> {                        // (1)

    @Query("SELECT * FROM book WHERE LENGTH(title) = " +           // (2)
            "(SELECT MAX(LENGTH(title)) FROM book)")
    List<Book> findByLongestTitle();                               // (2.1)

    @Query("SELECT * FROM book WHERE LENGTH(title) = " +
            "(SELECT MIN(LENGTH(title)) FROM book)")
    Stream<Book> findByShortestTitle();                            // (3)

    @Async                                                         // (4)
    @Query("SELECT * FROM book b " +
        "WHERE b.title = :title")
    CompletableFuture<Book> findBookByTitleAsync(                  // (4.1)
        @Param("title") String title);

    @Async                                                         // (5)
    @Query("SELECT * FROM book b " +
        "WHERE b.id > :fromId AND b.id < :toId")
    CompletableFuture<Stream<Book>> findBooksByIdBetweenAsync(     // (5.1)
        @Param("fromId") Integer from,
        @Param("toId") Integer to);
}
```

The preceding code is doing the following things:

1. By extending `CrudRepository`, our book repository received a dozen methods for basic CRUD operations, such as `save(...)`, `saveAll(...)`, `findById(...)`, `deleteAll()`.

2. It registers a custom method to find books with the longest title by providing a custom SQL defined in a `@Query` annotation. However, in contrast to *Spring JDBC*, we do not see any `ResultSet` transformations. `JdbcTemplate` is not required, and the only thing we have to write is an *interface*. Spring Framework generates the implementation, taking care of many pitfalls. As a result of the `findByLongestTitle` method `(2.1)`, the repository returns a `List` container, so the client is only unblocked when the whole query result arrives.

3. Alternatively, the repository may return a `Stream` of books, so when a client calls the `findByShortestTitle` method (`3.1`), depending on the underlying implementation, an API may allow processing the first element while the database still executes the query. Of course, this is only the case when the underlying implementation and the database itself supports this mode of operation.
4. With the `findBookByTitleAsync` method (`4.1`), the repository leverages the asynchronous support of the Spring Framework. The method returns `CompletableFuture` so the client's thread won't be blocked while waiting for results. Unfortunately, an underlying thread still has to be locked due to the blocking manner of JDBC.
5. Also, it is possible to combine `CompletableFuture` and `Stream` as done in the `findBooksByIdBetweenAsync` method (`5.1`). That way, the client's thread should not be blocked until the first rows arrive, and then the result set may be traversed in chunks. Unfortunately, for the first part of the execution, an underlying thread has to be blocked and the client's thread is later blocked when retrieving the next chunks of data. Such behavior is the best we can achieve with JDBC and without reactive support.

To inform Spring about the need to generate `BookRepository` implementation with Spring Data JDBC, we have to add the next dependency to our Spring Boot application:

```
compile('org.springframework.data:spring-data-jdbc:1.0.0.RELEASE')
```

It is also necessary to add the `@EnableJdbcRepositories` annotation to the application configuration. Under the hood, *Spring Data JDBC* uses *Spring JDBC* and `NamedParameterJdbcTemplate`, which was discussed previously.

Spring Data JDBC is a pretty small module that gives a convenient way to build a simple persistence layer for a small microservice. However, it is intentionally designed to be simple and not target ORM aspects such as caching, lazy-loading of entities, and complex entity relationships. For these purposes, the Java ecosystem has a separate specification called the **Java Persistence API (JPA)**.

Making Spring Data JDBC reactive

Spring Data JDBC is part of a larger project, Spring Data Relational. Spring Data JDBC requires JDBC which is a fully blocking API that isn't suitable in fully reactive stacks. At the moment of writing, the Spring Data team develops the R2DBC specification that allows drivers to provide a fully reactive and non-blocking integration with databases. These efforts are likely to be adopted in a Spring Data R2DBC module that will be part of the Spring Data Relational project. The following diagram shows the potential reactive stacks of Spring Data Relational:

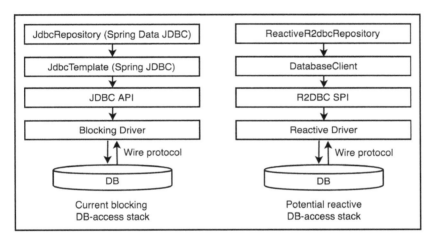

Diagram 7.14 The current Spring Data JDBC stack and a potential reactive replacement

JPA

JPA first appeared in 2006 (the latest version, 2.2, was released in 2013, and sometimes it is called JPA2), and it aims to describe relational data management in Java applications. Nowadays, JPA is a standard that defines how applications organize a persistence layer. It consists of the API itself and **Java Persistence Query Language** (**JPQL**). JPQL is an SQL-like platform-independent language that queries JPA entity objects through repositories instead of databases.

In contrast with JDBC, which is a standard for database access, JPA is a standard for **Object Relational Mapping** (**ORM**), which allows mapping objects in code to tables in a database. ORM usually uses JDBC and on-flight generated SQL queries under the hood, but this mechanic is mostly hidden from application developers. JPA allows mapping not only entities but also entity relationships in order to easily load associated objects.

The most used JPA implementations are Hibernate (`http://hibernate.org`) and EclipseLink (`http://www.eclipse.org/eclipselink`). Both of these implement JPA 2.2 and are interchangeable. As well as implementing the JPA standard, both projects propose an additional set of features that are not defined in the specification but may be handy in some cases. For example, EclipseLink makes it possible to handle database change events and describe the mapping of entities to tables in multiple databases. On the other hand, Hibernate proposes better support for timestamps and natural IDs. Both libraries support multi-tenancy. However, we should understand that when using exclusive features, these libraries stop being interchangeable.

Another reason to use JPA implementation instead of pure JDBC is due to the caching features provided by Hibernate and EclipseLink. Both libraries allow us to minimize the number of actual database requests caching entities in a first-level session cache, or even in a second-level external cache. This feature alone may have a notable impact on application performance.

Making JPA reactive

At the time of writing, it's not known whether there are any attempts to make JPA asynchronous or reactive. Such work requires an established asynchronous or reactive replacement for JDBC, on which JPA is also built. Furthermore, JPA is designed with many assumptions that are not true anymore in reactive programming. Moreover, the huge code base of JPA providers is not an easy target for reactive refactoring. Consequently, most likely, there won't be reactive JPA support any time soon.

Spring Data JPA

Spring Data JPA similarly allows us to build repositories like Spring Data JDBC does, but internally it uses a much more powerful JPA-based implementation. Spring Data JPA has excellent support for both Hibernate and EclipseLink. On the fly, Spring Data JPA generates JPA queries based on the method name convention, providing an implementation for the Generic DAO pattern and adding support for the Querydsl library (`http://www.querydsl.com`), which enables elegant, type-safe, Java-based queries.

Now, let's create a straightforward application to demonstrate the basics of Spring Data JPA. The following dependency gets all the required modules for a Spring Boot application:

```
compile('org.springframework.boot:spring-boot-starter-data-jpa')
```

Spring Boot is smart enough to deduce that Spring Data JPA is being used, so it is not even required to add the `@EnableJpaRepositories` annotation (but we may do so if we wish).

The `Book` entity should look as follows:

```
@Entity
@Table(name = "book")
public class Book {
    @Id
    private int id;
    private String title;

    // Constructors, getters, setters...
}
```

The `Book` entity marked with the `javax.persistence.Entity` annotation allows setting the entity name used in JPQL queries. The `javax.persistence.Table` annotation defines coordinates of the table and also may define constraints and indexes. It is important to note that instead of the `org.springframework.data.annotation.Id` annotation, we have to use the `javax.persistence.Id` annotation.

Now, let's define a CRUD repository with a custom method that uses a naming convention for query generation, as well as another method that uses a JPQL query:

```
@Repository
interface BookJpaRepository
    extends CrudRepository<Book, Integer> {

    Iterable<Book> findByIdBetween(int lower, int upper);

    @Query("SELECT b FROM Book b WHERE LENGTH(b.title) = " +
            "(SELECT MIN(LENGTH(b2.title)) FROM Book b2)")
    Iterable<Book> findShortestTitle();
}
```

A JDBC driver in the classpath, one Spring Boot dependency, the `Book` entity class, and the `BookJpaRepository` interface are enough to provide a basic but very versatile persistence layer based on the next stack of technologies—Spring Data JPA, JPA, JPQL, Hibernate, and JDBC.

Making Spring Data JPA reactive

Unfortunately, the reactive variant of the Spring Data JPA module would require all its underlying layers to also be reactive, including JDBC, JPA, and the JPA provider. Consequently, it's highly unlikely that this will happen during the next few years.

Spring Data NoSQL

Spring Data JPA and Spring Data JDBC are both excellent solutions for connecting to relational databases that at least provide JDBC driver, but most NoSQL databases do not do this. In such cases, the Spring Data project has a couple of separate modules that target popular NoSQL databases one by one. The Spring team actively develops modules for MongoDB, Redis, Apache Cassandra, Apache Solr, Gemfire, Geode, and LDAP. At the same time, the community develops modules for the following databases and storage—Aerospike, ArangoDB, Couchbase, Azure Cosmos DB, DynamoDB, Elasticsearch, Neo4j, Google Cloud Spanner, Hazelcast, and Vault.

It is worth mentioning that both EclipseLink and Hibernate support NoSQL databases. EclipseLink supports MongoDB, Oracle NoSQL, Cassandra, Google BigTable, and Couch DB. The following article describes NoSQL support in EclipseLink: https://wiki.eclipse.org/EclipseLink/Examples/JPA/NoSQL. Furthermore, Hibernate has a sub-project called Hibernate OGM (http://hibernate.org/ogm), which targets NoSQL support, namely Infinispan, MongoDB, Neo4j, and so on. However, since JPA is an inherently relational API, such solutions, in contrast to specialized Spring Data modules, lack NoSQL-related features. Additionally, JPA with its relational assumptions may lead application design in the wrong direction when applied over a NoSQL data store.

The code to use MongoDB would be almost the same as in the Spring Data JDBC example. To use a MongoDB repository, we have to add the following dependency:

```
compile('org.springframework.boot:spring-boot-starter-data-mongodb')
```

Let's imagine that we have to implement an online book catalog. The solution should be based on MongoDB and the Spring Framework. For that purpose, we may define the Book entity with the following Java class:

```
@Document(collection = "book")                                    // (1)
public class Book {
    @Id                                                           // (2)
    private ObjectId id;                                          // (3)

    @Indexed                                                      // (4)
    private String title;

    @Indexed                                                      // (5)
    private List<String> authors;
```

```
    @Field("pubYear")                                              // (6)
    private int publishingYear;

    // constructors, getters and setters
    // ...
}
```

Here, instead of a JPA `@Entity`, we use the `@Document` annotation (1) from the `org.springframework.data.mongodb.core.mapping` package. This annotation is specific to MongoDB and makes it possible to reference the correct database collection. Furthermore, to define an internal ID for the entity, we use a MongoDB specific type, `org.bson.types.ObjectId` (3), in conjunction with the Spring Data annotation `org.springframework.data.annotation.Id` (2). Our entity and consequently our database document would contain a `title` field, which would also be indexed by MongoDB. To do that, we decorate the field with the `@Indexed` annotation (4). This annotation provides a few configuration options regarding indexing details. In addition, a book may have one or more authors, and we represent this by declaring a type of the `authors` field to be `List<String>` (5). The `authors` field is also indexed. Note, here we do not create a reference to a separate `author` table with many-to-many relations, as it would most likely be implemented with a relational database, but instead we embed author names as a sub-document into the `book` entity. Finally, we define the `publishingYear` field. The field names in the entity and the database are different. The `@Field` annotation allows custom mappings for such cases (6).

In the database, such a `book` entity would be represented by the following JSON document:

```
{
    "_id" : ObjectId("5b1c0908eb696eddfadc0b1b"),                  /*(1)*/
    "title" : "The Expanse: Leviathan Wakes",
    "pubYear" : 2011,                                             /*(2)*/
    "authors" : [                                                 /*(3)*/
        "Daniel Abraham",                                        /*   */
        "Ty Franck"                                              /*   */
    ],
    "_class" : "org.rpis5.chapters.chapter_07.mongo_repo.Book"    /*(4)*/
}
```

As we can see, MongoDB uses the specially designed data type to represent a document's ID (1). In this case, the `publishingYear` is mapped to the `pubYear` field (2), and `authors` are represented by an array (3). Also, Spring Data MongoDB adds the supporting `_class` field, which describes a Java class used for Object-Document Mapping.

With MongoDB, a repository interface should extend the
`org.springframework.data.mongodb.repository.MongoRepository` interface (1),
which in turn extends the `CrudRepository`, which we already used in the previous
examples:

```
@Repository
public interface BookSpringDataMongoRepository
    extends MongoRepository<Book, Integer> {                           // (1)

    Iterable<Book> findByAuthorsOrderByPublishingYearDesc(             // (2)
        String... authors
    );

    @Query("{ 'authors.1': { $exists: true } }")                      // (3)
    Iterable<Book> booksWithFewAuthors();
}
```

Of course, a MongoDB repository supports query generation based on naming conventions,
so the `findByAuthorsOrderByPublishingYearDesc` method searches books by their
authors and returns a result sorted by the publishing year beginning with the most recent
publications. Also, the `org.springframework.data.mongodb.repository.Query`
annotation allows us to write MongoDB-specific queries. For example, the preceding query
(3) cleverly searches for books with more than one author.

The rest of the application should work the same way as in cases with Spring Data JDBC or
Spring Data JPA.

Even though we have touched on the main approaches for data persistence with Spring, we
have barely scratched the surface of this area. We have entirely omitted transaction
management, database initialization, and migration (Liquibase, Flyway), which are the best
practices of entity mapping, caching, and performance tuning. All of these areas could fill
more than one book, but we have to move forward and investigate how to do persistence
reactively.

Achieving reactive support for a NoSQL database with the Spring Framework requires the
whole underlying infrastructure to provide a reactive or asynchronous API. In general,
NoSQL databases have appeared relatively recently and evolved fast, so not a lot of
infrastructure is heavily bounded by the synchronous blocking API. Consequently, it
should be easier to achieve reactive persistence with NoSQL databases than with
relational databases with JDBC drivers. So far, Spring Data has a few reactive data
connectors, and MongoDB is among them. This is covered later in the *Reactive data access
with Spring Data* section.

Limitations of the synchronous model

During the investigation of persistence options with Spring Framework or even Java in general, we have looked through JDBC, JPA, Hibernate, EclipseLink, Spring Data JDBC, and Spring Data JDBC, and all these API and libraries are inherently synchronous and blocking. Even though they are almost always used for data retrieval from external services involving network calls, they do not permit non-blocking interactions. Consequently, all previously mentioned APIs and libraries conflict with the reactive paradigm. A Java thread that issues a query to the database is doomed to be blocked until the first piece of data arrives or a timeout occurs, and this is pretty wasteful from the perspective of resource management in a reactive application. As described in `Chapter 6`, *WebFlux Async Non-Blocking Communication,* this approach massively limits the throughput of the application and requires many more server resources and, therefore, more money.

It is wasteful to make IO requests in a blocking manner no matter whether this is an HTTP request or a database request. Also, JDBC-based communication usually uses a whole pool of connections to execute queries in parallel. In contrast, the widely used HTTP2 protocol allows using the same TCP connection to send and receive multiple resources at the same time. This approach decreases the number of occupied TCP sockets and allows greater concurrency both for client and server (in our case, this is the database). Consider the following diagram:

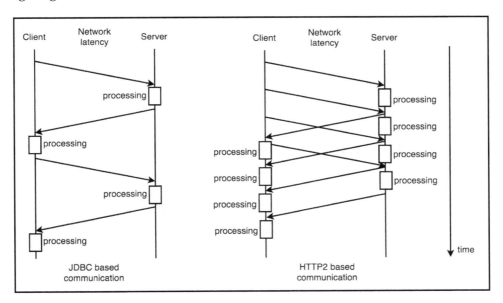

Diagram 7.15 Comparison between usual database communication and a communication protocol that allows multiplexing, such as HTTP2

Of course, connection pools exist to save time when opening new connections. It is also possible to implement a communication layer beneath JDBC in order to leverage multiplexing like in HTTP2, but still, the code preceding the JDBC level has to be synchronous and blocking.

Likewise, when processing large query results that occupy few batches, communication with the database cursor (a control structure that enables iteration over the query result records) looks like the left side of the preceding diagram. Chapter 3, *Reactive Streams - the New Streams' Standard*, analyzes the difference between the communication options in detail from the perspective of Reactive Streams, but the same arguments apply to network interactions.

Even if a database provides an asynchronous non-blocking driver capable of communicating efficiently and leveraging connection multiplexing, we are not able to get the full potential of it when using JDBC, JPA, or Spring Data JPA. Consequently, to build an entirely reactive application, we have to abandon synchronous techniques and make an API using reactive types.

To summarize this section, conventional and well-established JDBC and JPA implementations may become a bottleneck in a modern reactive application. JDBC and JPA are most likely to use too many threads and too much memory at runtime, at the same time requiring aggressive caching to limit lengthy synchronous requests and blocking IO.

It is not the synchronous model that is bad; it just does not fit well within a reactive application and most likely becomes a limiting factor. However, these models may successfully coexist. Both synchronous and reactive approaches have their pros and cons. For example, so far, the reactive persistence approach cannot propose any ORM solutions that are even close to JPA in terms of features.

Advantages of the synchronous model

Even though synchronous data access is not the most efficient way of spending server resources when implementing a persistence layer, it is still a highly valuable approach, primarily when used for building blocking web applications. JDBC, while probably being the most popular and versatile API for accessing data, almost entirely hides the complexity of client-server communications between an application and a database. Spring Data JDBC and Spring Data JPA give even more high-level instruments for data persistence, hiding the tremendous complexity of query translation and transaction management. All of this is battle-tested and considerably simplifies the way in which modern applications have developed.

The synchronous data access is simple, easy to debug, and easy to test. It is also easy to track resource usage by monitoring thread pools. The synchronous approach provides a massive set of instruments (such as JPA and Spring Data connectors) that do not require any backpressure support and still may be efficient when using iterators and synchronous streams. Moreover, most modern databases internally use a blocking model, so it is natural to use blocking drivers for interactions. This synchronous approach has excellent support for local and distributed transactions. It is also easy to implement a wrapper over a native driver written in C or C++.

The only downside of synchronous data access lies in the blocking manner of execution, which is poorly compatible with reactive web applications built with the reactive paradigm (Netty, Reactor, WebFlux).

After a short recap of synchronous data access techniques, we may move towards the exploration of reactive data persistence and see how Spring Data's reactive connectors fulfill the promise of high performance without compromising the versatility of Spring Data repositories.

Reactive data access with Spring Data

So, to build an entirely reactive application, we need a repository that operates not with collections of entities, but rather a repository that operates with reactive streams of entities. A reactive repository should be able to save, update, or delete entities by consuming not only an `Entity` itself but also by consuming a reactive `Publisher<Entity>`. It should also return data through reactive types. Ideally, when querying the database, we would like to operate with data repositories in a similar way to `WebClient` in the Spring WebFlux module. Indeed, the Spring Data Commons module provides the `ReactiveCrudRepository` interface with such a contract.

Now, let's discuss what benefits we may expect when using a reactive data access layer instead of a usual blocking one. `Chapter 3`, *Reactive Streams - the New Streams' Standard*, compares synchronous and reactive models of data retrieval, so, by employing an ideal reactive data access layer, our application may receive all of the following benefits:

- **Effective thread management**, since no thread is required to ever block on IO operations. This usually means that fewer threads are created, there's less overhead on thread scheduling, there's less memory footprint allocated for the `Thread` object's stack, and consequently, it's able to handle a massive amount of concurrent connections.

- **Smaller latency to the first results** of a query. These may become available even before the query finishes. It may be convenient for search engines and interactive UI components that target low latency operation.

- **Lower memory footprint**. This is useful as less data is required to be buffered when processing a query for outgoing or incoming traffic. Also, the client may unsubscribe from a reactive stream and reduce the amount of data sent over the network as soon as it has enough data to fulfill its needs.

- **Backpressure propagation** informs the client about a database's ability to consume new data. Also, it permits informing the database server about the client's ability to process query results. In this case, more urgent work may be done instead.

- One more benefit may come from the fact that reactive clients are not thread bound, so sending a query and different data processing operations may happen in different threads. In turn, underlying queries and connection objects have to be tolerant to such modes of operation. As no threads hold exclusive rights over query objects and no client code is ever blocked, it is possible to **share a single wire connection to the database** and forget about connection pooling. If a database supports a **smart** connection mode, query results may be transported via a single physical network connection and routed to correct reactive subscribers.

- Last but not least, **smooth integration of the persistence layer with a fluent reactive code** of the reactive application is backed by the Reactive Streams specification.

The more *reactive* a database access stack is, the more benefits an application may have. However, it is possible to gain some of the benefits mentioned previously by applying an asynchronous driver or even a blocking driver wrapped into a proper reactive adapter. An application may lose its ability to propagate backpressure, but it still may use less memory and have proper thread management. Now, it is time to play with a reactive code in a Spring Boot application.

To enable reactive persistence in a Spring Boot application, we have to use one of the databases that have reactive connectors. At the time of writing, the Spring Data project provides reactive connectivity for MongoDB, Cassandra, Redis, and Couchbase. This list may seem to be limited, but at the moment the reactive persistence is still a novelty headed towards widespread acceptance. Plus, the primary constraining factor that limits the Spring team in reactively supporting more databases is a lack of reactive and asynchronous drivers for databases. Now, let's investigate how a reactive CRUD repository works in the example of MongoDB.

Using MongoDB reactive repository

To use the reactive data access for MongoDB instead of its synchronous counterpart, we have to add the following dependency to our Gradle project:

```
compile 'org.springframework.boot:spring-boot-starter-data-mongodb-
reactive'
```

Let's say we want to refactor our simple MongoDB application from the previous section to become reactive. In this case, we may leave the `Book` entity as is, without making any modifications. All the annotations associated with MongoDB Object-Document Mapping are the same for both synchronous and reactive MongoDB modules. However, in the repository, we now have to replace ordinary types with reactive types:

```
public interface ReactiveSpringDataMongoBookRepository
    extends ReactiveMongoRepository<Book, Integer> {          // (1)

    @Meta(maxScanDocuments = 3)                               // (2)
    Flux<Book> findByAuthorsOrderByPublishingYearDesc(        // (3)
        Flux<String> authors
    );

    @Query("{ 'authors.1': { $exists: true } }")             // (4)
    Flux<Book> booksWithFewAuthors();
}
```

So, our repository now extends the `ReactiveMongoRepository` interface (1) instead of `MongoRepository`. In turn, `ReactiveMongoRepository` extends the `ReactiveCrudRepository` interface, the common interface for all reactive connectors.

> While there is no `RxJava2MongoRepository`, we can still use all reactive Spring Data repositories with RxJava2 by just extending from `RxJava2CrudRepository`. Spring Data handles the adoption of Project Reactor types to RxJava2 and vice versa so to provide a native RxJava 2 experience.

The `ReactiveCrudRepository` interface is the reactive equivalent of the `CrudRepository` interface from synchronous Spring Data. Reactive Spring Data Repositories use the same annotations and support the majority of synchronously provided features. So, the reactive Mongo repository supports queries by the method name convention (3), the `@Query` annotation with hand-written MongoDB queries (4), and the `@Meta` annotation with some addition query-tuning abilities (2). It also supports constructs for running **Query by Example** (**QBE**) requests. However, in contrast to the synchronous `MongoRepository`, `ReactiveMongoRepository` extends the `ReactiveSortingRepository` interface, which provides the ability to request the specific order of results but does not provide pagination support. The question of data pagination is covered in the *Pagination support* section.

As usual, we may inject a bean of the `ReactiveSpringDataMongoBookRepository` type in our application and Spring Data would then provide the desired bean. The following code shows how to insert a few books into MongoDB using a reactive repository:

```
@Autowired
private ReactiveSpringDataMongoBookRepository rxBookRepository;        // (1)
...
Flux<Book> books = Flux.just(                                          // (2)
    new Book("The Martian", 2011, "Andy Weir"),
    new Book("Blue Mars", 1996, "Kim Stanley Robinson")
);

rxBookRepository
    .saveAll(books)                                                    // (3)
    .then()                                                            // (4)
    .doOnSuccess(ignore -> log.info("Books saved in DB"))              // (5)
    .subscribe();                                                      // (6)
```

Let's understand what the preceding code is doing here:

1. Injecting a bean with the `BookSpringDataMongoRxRepository` interface.
2. Preparing a reactive stream with `Book` that has to be inserted into the database.
3. Saving entities using the `saveAll` method that consumes a `Publisher<Book>`. As usual, no saving happens until an actual subscriber subscribes. `ReactiveCrudRepository` also has the `saveAll` method override that consumes the `Iterable` interface. These two methods have different semantics, but we are going to cover this topic later.

4. The `saveAll` method returns a `Flux<Book>` with saved entities, but as we are not interested in that level of detail, with the `then` method, we transform a stream in such a way that only `onComplete` or `onError` events are propagated.

5. We report a corresponding log message when the reactive stream is complete and all books are saved.

6. As always, with a reactive stream, there should be a subscriber. Here, for the sake of simplicity, we subscribe without any handlers. However, in a real application, there should be real subscribers, such as a subscription from a WebFlux exchange that processes a response.

Now, let's query MongoDB using Reactive Streams. To print query results that flow through a reactive stream, we can use the following convenient helper method:

```
private void reportResults(String message, Flux<Book> books) {      // (1)
    books
        .map(Book::toString)                                         // (2)
        .reduce(                                                     // (3)
            new StringBuilder(),                                     // (3.1)
            (sb, b) -> sb.append(" - ")                             // (3.2)
                .append(b)
                .append("\n"))
        .doOnNext(sb -> log.info(message + "\n{}", sb))             // (5)
        .subscribe();                                               // (6)
}
```

Let's understand what the preceding code is doing here:

1. This is a method that prints a human-readable list of books as a one log message with the desired message prefix.

2. For each book in the stream, it calls its `toString` method and propagates its string representation.

3. The `Flux.reduce` method is used to collect all book representations into one message. Note that this approach may not work if the amount of books is significant, as each new book increases the size of the stored buffer and may cause high memory consumption. To store intermediate results, we use the `StringBuilder` class (`3.1`). Keep in mind that `StringBuilder` is not thread-safe and the `onNext` method may call different threads, but the Reactive Streams Specification guarantees the happens-before relation. So, even if different threads push different entities, it is safe to work to concatenate them together with `StringBuilder` as memory barriers guarantee the latest state of the `StringBuilder` object while it is updated inside one reactive stream. At point (`3.2`) a book representation appends to the single buffer.

5. As the `reduce` method emits its `onNext` event only after processing of all incoming `onNext` events, we are safe to log the final message with all books.

6. To start processing, we have to `subscribe`. For the sake of simplicity, we assume that no errors are possible here. However, in production code, there should be some logic for handling errors.

Now, let's read and report all the books in the database:

```
Flux<Book> allBooks = rxBookRepository.findAll();
reportResults("All books in DB:", allBooks);
```

The following code searches for all books by Andy Weir using the method naming convention:

```
Flux<Book> andyWeirBooks = rxBookRepository
    .findByAuthorsOrderByPublishingYearDesc(Mono.just("Andy Weir"));
reportResults("All books by Andy Weir:", andyWeirBooks);
```

Furthermore, the preceding code passes the search criteria using the `Mono<String>` type and starts an actual database query only when that `Mono` produces an `onNext` event. So, the reactive repository becomes a natural part of a reactive stream, where incoming and outgoing streams are reactive.

Combining repository operations

Now, let's implement a slightly more complicated business use case. We may want to update a publication year for a book, and we only have the book's title. So, first, we have to find the desired book instance, then update the year of publishing, and save the book to the database. To make our use case even more complicated, let's assume that both the title and year values are retrieved asynchronously with some delay and are delivered by the `Mono` type. Also, we want to know whether our updated request was successful or not. So far, we do not require the update to be atomic and assume that there is always no more than one book with the same title. So, with those requirements we may design the following business method API:

```
public Mono<Book> updatedBookYearByTitle(                          // (1)
                    Mono<String> title,                            // (2)
                    Mono<Integer> newPublishingYear)               // (3)
```

The preceding code does the following:

1. The `updatedBookYearByTitle` method returns an updated book entity (or nothing, if no book is found).
2. The title value is referenced via the `Mono<String>` type.
3. The new publishing year value is referenced via the `Mono<Integer>` type.

We may now create a testing scenario to check how our implementation of the `updatedBookYearByTitle` works:

```
Instant start = now();                                          // (1)
Mono<String> title = Mono.delay(Duration.ofSeconds(1))          // (2)
    .thenReturn("Artemis")                                      //
    .doOnSubscribe(s -> log.info("Subscribed for title"))       //
    .doOnNext(t ->                                              //
       log.info("Book title resolved: {}" , t));                // (2.1)

Mono<Integer> publishingYear = Mono.delay(Duration.ofSeconds(2)) // (3)
    .thenReturn(2017)                                           //
    .doOnSubscribe(s -> log.info("Subscribed for publishing year")) //
    .doOnNext(t ->                                              //
       log.info("New publishing year resolved: {}" , t));       // (3.1)

updatedBookYearByTitle(title, publishingYear)                   // (4)
    .doOnNext(b ->                                              //
       log.info("Publishing year updated for book: {}", b))      // (4.1)
    .hasElement()                                               // (4.2)
    .doOnSuccess(status ->                                      //
       log.info("Updated finished {}, took: {}",                // (5)
            status ? "successfully" : "unsuccessfully",          //
            between(start, now()))))                             // (5.1)
    .subscribe();                                               // (6)
```

The preceding code does the following:

1. Tracks running time, storing the start time of the test.
2. Resolves the title with a simulated delay of one second, logging it as soon as the value is ready (`2.1`).
3. Resolves the new publishing year value with a simulated delay of two seconds, logging it as soon as the value is ready (`2.1`).
4. Calls our business method, logging it when the update notification arrives, if any (`4.1`). To check the presence of `onNext` events (meaning the actual book update), the `Mono.hasElement` method that returns `Mono<Boolean>` is called.

5. When the stream completes, the code logs whether an update was successful and reports the total execution time.

6. As always, someone has to subscribe in order to start the reactive workflow.

From the previous code, we may conclude that the workflow cannot run faster than two seconds, as this is the time required to resolve the publishing year. However, it may run for longer. Let's do the first iteration of the implementation:

```
private Mono<Book> updatedBookYearByTitle(              /* First Iteration */
    Mono<String> title,
    Mono<Integer> newPublishingYear
) {
    return rxBookRepository.findOneByTitle(title)              // (1)
        .flatMap(book -> newPublishingYear                    // (2)
            .flatMap(year -> {                                // (3)
                book.setPublishingYear(year);                 // (4)
                return rxBookRepository.save(book);           // (5)
            }));
}
```

With this approach, right at the start of the method, we call the repository with the provided reactive reference to the `title` (1). As soon as the `Book` entity is found (2), we subscribe to the new publishing year value. Then, as soon as the new publishing year value arrives, we update the `Book` entity (4) and call the `save` method for the repository. This code produces the following output:

```
Subscribed for title
Book title resolved: Artemis
Subscribed for publishing year
New publishing year resolved: 2017
Publishing year updated for book: Book(publishingYear=2017...
Updated finished successfully, took: PT3.027S
```

So, the book was updated, but as we can see from the logs, we subscribed to the new publishing year only after receiving the title, so in total the method spent more than three seconds calculating the result. We can do better. We have to subscribe to both streams at the beginning of the workflow in order to start concurrent retrieval processes. The following code depicts how to do this using the `zip` method:

```
private Mono<Book> updatedBookYearByTitle(             /* Second Iteration */
    Mono<String> title,
    Mono<Integer> newPublishingYear
) {
    return Mono.zip(title, newPublishingYear)                 // (1)
        .flatMap((Tuple2<String, Integer> data) -> {         // (2)
            String titleVal = data.getT1();                  // (2.1)
```

```
      Integer yearVal = data.getT2();                       // (2.2)
      return rxBookRepository
         .findOneByTitle(Mono.just(titleVal))               // (3)
         .flatMap(book -> {
            book.setPublishingYear(yearVal);                // (3.1)
            return rxBookRepository.save(book);             // (3.2)
         });
   });
}
```

Here, we `zip` two values and subscribe to them at the same time `(1)`. As soon as both values are ready, our stream receives a `Tuple2<String, Integer>` container with the values of interest `(2)`. Now we have to unpack values `(2.1)` and `(2.2)` using the `data.getT1()` and `data.getT2()` calls. At point `(3)`, we query the `Book` entity, and as soon as it arrives, we update the publishing year and save the entity to the database. After the second iteration, our application shows the following output:

```
Subscribed for title
Subscribed for publishing year
Book title resolved: Artemis
New publishing year resolved: 2017
Publishing year updated for the book: Book(publishingYear=2017...
Updated finished successfully, took: PT2.032S
```

Now, we may see that we subscribe to both streams at first, and as both values arrive, we update the book entity. In the second approach, we spend roughly two seconds executing the operation instead of three seconds. It is faster but requires working with the `Tuple2` type, which requires extra lines of code as well as making transformations. To improve readability and to remove the `getT1()` and `getT2()` calls we may add the *Reactor Addons* module, which provides some syntactic sugar for such cases.

With the following new dependency, we can improve the previous code sample:

```
compile('io.projectreactor.addons:reactor-extra')
```

This is how we can improve it:

```
private Mono<Book> updatedBookYearByTitle(              /* Third Iteration */
   Mono<String> title,
   Mono<Integer> newPublishingYear
) {
   return Mono.zip(title, newPublishingYear)
      .flatMap(
         TupleUtils.function((titleValue, yearValue) ->   // (1)
            rxBookRepository
               .findOneByTitle(Mono.just(titleValue))      // (2)
```

```
                    .flatMap(book -> {
                        book.setPublishingYear(yearValue);
                        return rxBookRepository.save(book);
                    })));
    }
```

Here, at point (1), we may replace the manual deconstruction of the `Tuple2` object with the `function` method from the `TupleUtils` class and work with already deconstructed values. Due to the fact that the `function` method is static, the resulting code is pretty fluent and verbose:

```
return Mono.zip(title, newPublishingYear)
    .flatMap(function((titleValue, yearValue) -> { ... }));
```

Furthermore, at point (2), we take `titleValue` and wrap it again into the `Mono` object. We could use the original `title` object that already has the correct type, but in that case, we would subscribe twice for the `title` stream and would receive the following output. Note that we trigger the title resolving code twice:

```
Subscribed for title
Subscribed for publishing year
Book title resolved: Artemis
New publishing year resolved: 2017
Subscribed for title
Book title resolved: Artemis
Publishing year updated for the book: Book(publishingYear=2017...
Updated finished successfully, took: PT3.029S
```

One more point is that in the third iteration we issue a database request to load the book only after receiving both title and new publishing values. However, we might start loading the book entity when the publishing year request is still in flight but the title value is already present. The fourth iteration shows how to build this reactive workflow:

```
private Mono<Book> updatedBookYearByTitle(          /* Forth Iteration */
    Mono<String> title,
    Mono<Integer> newPublishingYear
) {
    return Mono.zip(                                     // (1)
        newPublishingYear,                               // (1.1)
        rxBookRepository.findOneByTitle(title)           // (1.2)
    ).flatMap(function((yearValue, bookValue) -> {       // (2)
        bookValue.setPublishingYear(yearValue);          //
        return rxBookRepository.save(bookValue);         // (2.1)
    }));
}
```

Here, with the `zip` operator `(1)` we subscribe to the new publishing year values `(1.1)` and the book entity `(1.2)` at the same time. When both values arrive `(2)`, we update the publishing year of the entity and request the book saving procedure `(2.1)`. Moreover, as in all previous iterations of this business use case, even though the workflow takes at least two seconds to complete, no threads are ever blocked. Consequently, this code uses computation resources very efficiently.

The point of this exercise is to demonstrate that with Reactive Streams' capabilities and the versatility of the Project Reactor API, it is easy to build different asynchronous workflows involving even the data persistence layer. With just a few reactive operators, we may completely change the way data flows through the system. However, not all such alternatives of reactive flows are equal. Some may run faster while others may run slower, and in many cases, the most obvious solution is not the most appropriate one. So, when writing reactive pipelines, please consider alternative combinations of reactive operators and do not choose the first that comes to mind but the option that is best for the business request.

How reactive repositories work

Now, let's dive into the details of how reactive repositories work. A reactive repository in Spring Data works by adapting underlying database driver capabilities. Underneath there could be a Reactive Streams-compliant driver or an asynchronous driver that could be wrapped into a reactive API. Here we are going to look how the reactive MongoDB repository uses the Reactive Streams-compliant MongoDB driver, as well as how the reactive Cassandra repository is built on the asynchronous driver.

First of all, the `ReactiveMongoRepository` interface extends more generic interfaces—`ReactiveSortingRepository` and `ReactiveQueryByExampleExecutor`. The `ReactiveQueryByExampleExecutor` interface allows the execution of queries with the QBE language. The `ReactiveSortingRepository` interface extends the more generic `ReactiveCrudRepository` interface and adds the `findAll` method, which allows requesting the sorting order of the query result.

As a lot of reactive connectors use the `ReactiveCrudRepository` interface, let's look at it closely. `ReactiveCrudRepository` declares methods for saving, finding, and deleting entities. The `Mono<T> save(T entity)` method saves the `entity` and then returns the saved entity for further operations. Note that the save operation might change the entity object entirely. The `Mono<T> findById(ID id)` operation consumes the entity's `id` and returns results wrapped into `Mono`. The `findAllById` method has two overrides, one of each consumes IDs in the form of the `Iterable<ID>` collection, and the other in the form of `Publisher<ID>`. The only notable difference between `ReactiveCrudRepository` and `CrudRepository` besides the reactive approach is in the fact that `ReactiveCrudRepository` does not have pagination support and does not allow transactional operations. Transactional support for reactive persistence with Spring Data is covered later in this chapter. However, now it is the developer's responsibility to implement a pagination strategy.

Pagination support

It is important to note that the Spring Data team intentionally omitted pagination support as the implementation used in synchronous repositories does not fit the reactive paradigm. To calculate the parameters of the next page, we need to know the number of returned records for the previous result. Also, to calculate the total amount of pages using that approach, we need to query for the total amount of records. Both aspects do not fit the reactive non-blocking paradigm. Additionally, querying the database to count all rows is rather expensive, and increases the lag before actual data processing. However, it is still possible to fetch chunks of data by passing the `Pageable` object to the repository as follows:

```
public interface ReactiveBookRepository
    extends ReactiveSortingRepository<Book, Long> {

    Flux<Book> findByAuthor(String author, Pageable pageable);
}
```

So, now we may request the second page of the result (note, the indexes start from 0), where each page contains five elements:

```
Flux<Book> result = reactiveBookRepository
    .findByAuthor('Andy Weir', PageRequest.of(1, 5));
```

ReactiveMongoRepository implementation details

The Spring Data MongoDB Reactive module has only one implementation of the
`ReactiveMongoRepository` interface, namely the `SimpleReactiveMongoRepository`
class. It provides implementations for all methods of `ReactiveMongoRepository` and
uses the `ReactiveMongoOperations` interface for handling all the operations at the lower
level.

Let's look at the `findAllById(Publisher<ID> ids)` method implementation:

```
public Flux<T> findAllById(Publisher<ID> ids) {
    return Flux.from(ids).buffer().flatMap(this::findAllById);
}
```

It is evident that this method gathers all the `ids` with the `buffer` operation and then makes
one request using the `findAllById(Iterable<ID> ids)` override of the method. That
method, in turn, formulates the `Query` object and calls `findAll(Query query)`, which
invokes the `ReactiveMongoOperations`
instance, `mongoOperations.find(query,...)`.

Another interesting observation is that the `insert(Iterable<S> entities)` method
inserts entities in a one batch query. At the same time, the `insert(Publisher<S>
entities)` method generates many queries inside the `flatMap` operator as follows:

```
public <S extends T> Flux<S> insert(Publisher<S> entities) {
    return Flux.from(entities)
        .flatMap(entity -> mongoOperations.insert(entity,...));
}
```

In this case, two overrides of the `findAllById` method behave in the same way and
generate only one database query. Now, let's look at the `saveAll` method. The method
override that consumes a `Publisher` issues a query per entity. The method override, that
consumes an `Iterable`, issues one query in the case when all entities are new, but issues a
query per entity in other cases. The `deleteAll(Iterable<? extends T> entities)`
method always issues a query per entity even though all the entities are available in the
`Iterable` container and there is no need to wait for elements to appear asynchronously.

As we can see, different overrides of the same method may behave in different ways and
may generate different amount of database queries. Also, such behavior has no strong
correlation with whether the method consumes some synchronous iterator or reactive
`Publisher`. So, we recommend checking method implementation of the repository method
to understand how many queries it issues to the database.

In cases when we use `ReactiveCrudRepository` methods with implementations generated on-the-fly, it is harder to look at the actual query. However, in that case, query generation behaves in the ways similar to ordinary synchronous `CrudRepository`. `RepositoryFactorySupport` generates an appropriate proxy for the `ReactiveCrudRepository`. The `ReactiveStringBasedMongoQuery` class is used for generating queries when the method is decorated with the `@Query` annotation. The `ReactivePartTreeMongoQuery` class is used for query generation based on method name conventions. Of course, setting the `DEBUG` level for the `ReactiveMongoTemplate`'s logger allows tracking all queries sent to MongoDB.

Using ReactiveMongoTemplate

Even though the `ReactiveMongoTemplate` is used as a building block of a reactive repository, the class itself is very versatile. Sometimes it allows working with the database more efficiently than the higher-level repository does.

For example, let's implement a simple service that uses `ReactiveMongoTemplate` to find books by title using a regular expression. The implementation may look as follows:

```
public class RxMongoTemplateQueryService {
    private final ReactiveMongoOperations mongoOperations;           // (1)
    // Constructor...

    public Flux<Book> findBooksByTitle(String titleRegExp) {        // (2)
        Query query = Query.query(new Criteria("title")             // (3)
            .regex(titleRegExp)))
            .limit(100);
        return mongoOperations
            .find(query, Book.class, "book");                       // (4)
    }
}
```

Let's describe the main points of the `RxMongoTemplateQueryService` class:

1. We have to reference the instance of the `ReactiveMongoOperations` interface. `ReactiveMongoTemplate` implements that interface and is present in the Spring context when the MongoDB data source is configured.
2. The service defines the `findBooksByTitle` method and consumes regular expressions as search criteria and returns a `Flux` with results.

3. The MongoDB connector's `Query` and `Criteria` classes are used to build an actual query with the regular expression. Also, we limit the number of results to `100` by applying the `Query.limit` method.

4. Here, we are asking `mongoOperations` to execute the previously built query. Query results should be mapped to entities of the `Book` class. Also, we have to tell what collection we are using for the query. In the preceding example, we query a collection called `book`.

 Note that we may achieve the same behavior (except for the query limit) with an ordinary reactive repository by providing the following method signature, which follows the naming convention:
`Flux<Book> findManyByTitleRegex(String regex);`

Under the hood, `ReactiveMongoTemplate` uses the `ReactiveMongoDatabaseFactory` interface to get an instance of reactive MongoDB connections. Also, it uses an instance of the `MongoConverter` interface to convert entities to documents and vice versa. `MongoConverter` is also used in a synchronous `MongoTemplate`. Let's look at how `ReactiveMongoTemplate` implements its contract. For example, the `find(Query query, ...)` method maps the `org.springframework.data.mongodb.core.query.Query` instance to an instance of the `org.bson.Document` class, with which the MongoDB client is capable of working. Then `ReactiveMongoTemplate` invokes the database client with the converted query. The `com.mongodb.reactivestreams.client.MongoClient` class gives an entry point to the reactive MongoDB driver. It is Reactive Streams-compliant and returns data through reactive publishers.

Using reactive drivers (MongoDB)

Reactive MongoDB connectivity in Spring Data is built on MongoDB Reactive Streams Java Driver (`https://github.com/mongodb/mongo-java-driver-reactivestreams`). The driver provides asynchronous stream processing with non-blocking backpressure. In turn, the reactive driver is built on top of MongoDB Async Java Driver (`http://mongodb.github.io/mongo-java-driver/3.8/driver-async`). The asynchronous driver is low level and has a callback-based API, so it is not as easy to use as the more high-level Reactive Streams driver. We have to note that along with the MongoDB Reactive Streams Java Driver there is also MongoDB RxJava Driver (`http://mongodb.github.io/mongo-java-driver-rx`), which is also built on top of the same asynchronous MongoDB driver. So, for MongoDB connectivity, the Java ecosystem has one synchronous, one asynchronous, and two reactive drivers.

Of course, if we need more control over the query process than ReactiveMongoTemplate gives us, we may use the reactive driver directly. With that approach, the previous example with the pure reactive driver is as follows:

```
public class RxMongoDriverQueryService {
    private final MongoClient mongoClient;                              // (1)

    public Flux<Book> findBooksByTitleRegex(String regex) {            // (2)
        return Flux.defer(() -> {                                      // (3)
            Bson query = Filters.regex(titleRegex);                   // (3.1)
            return mongoClient                                         //
                .getDatabase("test-database")                         // (3.2)
                .getCollection("book")                               // (3.3)
                .find(query);                                        // (3.4)
        })
            .map(doc -> new Book(                                     // (4)
                doc.getObjectId("id"),
                doc.getString("title"),
                doc.getInteger("pubYear"),
                // ... other mapping routine
            ));
    }
}
```

Let's look at the preceding code:

1. The service refers to the instance of the com.mongodb.reactivestreams.client.MongoClient interface. This instance should be accessible as a Spring bean when the data source is configured correctly.

2. The service defines the findBooksByTitleRegex method, which returns a Flux with Book entities.

3. We have to return a new Flux instance, which defers the execution until the time when the actual subscription happens. Inside that lambda, we define a new query with the org.bson.conversions.Bson type using the com.mongodb.client.model.Filters helper class. Then we reference the database (3.2) as well as the collection (3.3) by names. No communication with the database happens unless we send the previously prepared query (3.4) with the find method.

4. As soon as results start coming back, we may transfer MongoDB documents into domain entities, if that is required at all.

Even though in the preceding example we work at the database driver level, it is still pretty comfortable as we operate with Reactive Streams. Besides, we do not need to handle backpressure manually as the MongoDB Reactive Streams Java Driver already supports it. Reactive MongoDB connectivity uses backpressure demand based on batch size. This approach is a sane default but can generate many roundtrips when using small demand increments. The following diagram highlights all the abstraction layers required for a reactive MongoDB repository:

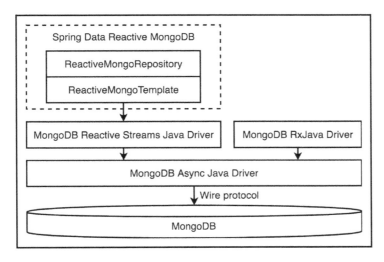

Diagram 7.16 Reactive MongoDB stack with Spring Data

Using asynchronous drivers (Cassandra)

We have described how the reactive Mongo repository is built on top of the reactive driver. Now, let's look at how the reactive Cassandra repository adapts the asynchronous driver.

Similarly to `ReactiveMongoRepository`, reactive Casandra connector gives us the `ReactiveCassandraRepository` interface, which also extends the more generic `ReactiveCrudRepository`. The `ReactiveCassandraRepository` interface is implemented by `SimpleReactiveCassandraRepository`, which, in turn, uses the `ReactiveCassandraOperations` interface for low-level operations. `ReactiveCassandraOperations` is implemented by the `ReactiveCassandraTemplate` class. Of course, `ReactiveCassandraTemplate` may be used directly in the application, similar to `ReactiveMongoTemplate`.

The ReactiveCassandraTemplate class internally uses ReactiveCqlOperations. ReactiveCassandraTemplate operates with Spring Data entities such as org.springframework.data.cassandra.core.query.Query, while ReactiveCqlOperations operates with CQL statements (represented by String) recognizable by the Cassandra driver. The ReactiveCqlOperations interface is implemented by the ReactiveCqlTemplate class. In turn, ReactiveCqlTemplate uses the ReactiveSession interface for actual database querying. ReactiveSession is implemented by the DefaultBridgedReactiveSession class, which bridges asynchronous Session methods, provided by the driver, to reactive execution patterns.

Let's go deeper and look at how the DefaultBridgedReactiveSession class adapts the asynchronous API into the reactive API. The execute method receives a Statement (for example, a SELECT statement) and reactively returns results. The execute method and its adaptFuture helper method look as follows:

```
public Mono<ReactiveResultSet> execute(Statement statement) {     // (1)
  return Mono.create(sink -> {                                     // (2)
    try {
      ListenableFuture<ResultSet> future = this.session            // (3)
          .executeAsync(statement);
      ListenableFuture<ReactiveResultSet> resultSetFuture =
          Futures.transform(                                       // (4)
            future, DefaultReactiveResultSet::new);
      adaptFuture(resultSetFuture, sink);                          // (5)
    } catch (Exception cause) {
      sink.error(cause);                                           // (6)
    }
  });
}

<T> void adaptFuture(                                              // (7)
    ListenableFuture<T> future, MonoSink<T> sink
) {
  future.addListener(() -> {                                       // (7.1)
    if (future.isDone()) {
      try {
        sink.success(future.get());                                // (7.2)
      } catch (Exception cause) {
        sink.error(cause);                                         // (7.3)
      }
    }
  }, Runnable::run);
}
```

Let's go through the preceding code:

1. First of all, the `execute` method does not return a `Flux` with results, but rather a `Mono` with an instance of `ReactiveResultSet`. `ReactiveResultSet` wraps asynchronous `com.datastax.driver.core.ResultSet`, which supports pagination so that the first page of the result is fetched when a `ResultSet` instance is returned and the next page fetched only after all the results of the first one have been consumed. `ReactiveResultSet` adapts that behavior with the following method signature—`Flux<Row> rows()`.

2. We create a new `Mono` instance with the `create` method, which defers operations to the moment of subscription.

3. This is an asynchronous query execution on a driver's asynchronous `Session` instance. Note that the Cassandra driver used Guava's `ListenableFuture` for returning results.

4. The asynchronous `ResultSet` is wrapped into a reactive counterpart called `ReactiveResultSet`.

5. Here, we're calling the `adaptFuture` helper method, which maps `ListenableFuture` to `Mono`.

6. If there are any errors, we have to inform our reactive subscriber.

7. The `adaptFuture` method simply adds a new listener to the future `(7.1)`, so when a result appears, it generates a reactive `onNext` signal `(7.2)`. It also informs the subscriber about execution errors, if any `(7.3)`.

It is important to note that the multi-page `ResultSet` allows calling the `fetchMoreResults` method to get the subsequent page of data asynchronously. `ReactiveResultSet` is doing that internally inside the `Flux<Row> rows()` method. Even though this approach works, it is considered an intermediate solution until Casandra receives an entirely reactive driver.

The following diagram shows the internal architecture of the reactive Spring Data Cassandra module:

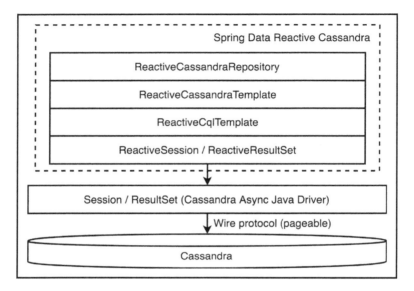

Diagram 7.17 Reactive Cassandra stack with Spring Data

Reactive transactions

A transaction is a marker for a database that defines the boundaries of a single unit with many logical operations that should be performed atomically. So, we have a point in time when a transaction is initialized, then some operations are happening with regard to the transaction object, then a decision moment happens. At that moment, the client and the database decide whether a transaction should be successfully committed or rolled back.

In the synchronous world, a transaction object is often held in the ThreadLocal container. However, ThreadLocal isn't suitable for associating data with a reactive flow as the user has no control over thread switching. A transaction requires binding of the underlying resource to the materialized flow. With Project Reactor, this is achieved best by leveraging the Reactor Context, described in Chapter 4, *Project Reactor - the Foundation for Reactive Apps*.

Reactive transactions with MongoDB 4

Starting with version 4.0, MongoDB supports *multi-document transactions*. This allows us to experiment with reactive transactions in the new version of MongoDB. Previously, Spring Data only had reactive connectors to databases that did not support transactions. Now, the situation has changed. As reactive transactions are a novelty in the reactive persistence area, which itself is pretty new, all the following claims and code examples should be treated as some of the possibilities of how reactive transactions could be implemented in the future. At the time of writing, Spring Data does not have any features that apply reactive transactions at the service or repository levels. However, we may operate with transactions at the level of `ReactiveMongoOperations` implemented by `ReactiveMongoTemplate`.

First of all, the multi-document transaction is a new feature for MongoDB. It works only for a non-sharded replica set with the WiredTiger storage engine. No other configuration supports multi-document transactions as of MongoDB 4.0.

Also, some MongoDB features are not available inside a transaction. It is not allowed to issue meta commands, or create collections or indices. Also, the implicit creation of collections does not work inside a transaction. So, it is required to set up required database structures to prevent errors. Besides, some commands may behave differently, so please check the documentation regarding multi-document transactions.

Previously, MongoDB allowed atomic updates only for one document, even if that document contained embedded documents. With multi-document transactions, it is possible to get all-or-nothing semantics across many operations, documents, and collections. Multi-document transactions guarantee a globally consistent view of data. When a transaction is committed, all the changes made within the transaction are saved. However, when any action within the transaction fails, the whole transaction aborts and all the changes are discarded. Also, no data updates are visible outside the transaction until the transaction is committed.

Now, let's demonstrate that reactive transactions may be used for storing documents to MongoDB. For that purpose, we may use a well-known classical example. Let's say we have to implement a wallet service that transfers money between the users' accounts. Each user has their own account with a non-negative balance. A user may transfer any arbitrary sum to another user only when they have enough funds. Transfers may happen in parallel, but the system is not allowed to lose or gain any money while doing transfers. Consequently, a withdraw operation for sender's wallet and a deposit operation for receiver's wallet has to happen simultaneously and atomically. Multi-document transactions should help here.

Without transactions we may face the following issues:

- A client makes a few transfers at the same time with more funds than they have on their account. Hence, there is a chance that simultaneous transfers may impact the consistency of the system and illegally *create* money.
- A user receives a few deposits simultaneously. Some updates may rewrite the wallet state, and the user may *lose* money forever.

There are a few approaches that may describe the algorithm of money transfer, but here we stick with the most simple one. To transfer an `amount` of money from `account` A to `account` B, we should do the following:

1. Open a new transaction.
2. Load the wallet of `account` A.
3. Load the wallet of `account` B.
4. Check that the wallet of `account` A has sufficient funds.
5. Calculate the new balance of `account` A by withdrawing the `amount`.
6. Calculate the new balance of `account` B by depositing the `amount`.
7. Save the wallet of `account` A.
8. Save the wallet of `account` B.
9. Commit the transaction.

As a result of that algorithm, we would either get the new consistent state of the wallets or see no changes at all.

Let's describe the `Wallet` entity class that is mapped to a MongoDB document and has some handy utility methods:

```
@Document(collection = "wallet")                                    // (1)
public class Wallet {
    @Id private ObjectId id;                                        // (2)
    private String owner;
    private int balance;

    // Constructors, getters, and setters are omitted...

    public boolean hasEnoughFunds(int amount) {                     // (3)
        return balance >= amount;
    }

    public void withdraw(int amount) {                              // (4)
        if (!hasEnoughFunds(amount)) {
            throw new IllegalStateException("Not enough funds!");
```

```
        }
        this.balance = this.balance - amount;
    }

    public void deposit(int amount) {                               // (5)
        this.balance = this.balance + amount;
    }
}
```

Let's describe the preceding code:

1. The `Wallet` entity class is mapped to the `wallet` collection in MongoDB.
2. The `org.bson.types.ObjectId` class is used as an entity identifier. The `ObjectId` class has great integration with MongoDB and is often used for entity identification.
3. The `hasEnoughFunds` method checks whether the wallet has enough funds for an operation.
4. The `withdraw` method decreases the wallet's balance by the requested amount.
5. The `deposit` method increases the wallet's balance by the requested amount.

To store and load wallets from a database, we need a repository:

```
public interface WalletRepository
        extends ReactiveMongoRepository<Wallet, ObjectId> {        // (1)
    Mono<Wallet> findByOwner(Mono<String> owner);                  // (2)
}
```

Let's describe the `WalletRepository` interface in more detail:

1. Our `WalletRepository` interface extends the `ReactiveMongoRepository` interface.
2. Also, we define an additional method called `findByOwner` to retrieve a wallet if we have the owner's name. The generated implementation of the interface knows how to execute an actual query as the `findByOwner` method follows the Spring Data naming convention.

Now, let's define an interface for `WalletService`:

```
public interface WalletService {

    Mono<TxResult> transferMoney(                                   // (1)
        Mono<String> fromOwner,
        Mono<String> toOwner,
        Mono<Integer> amount);
```

```
    Mono<Statistics> reportAllWallets();                              // (2)
    enum TxResult {                                                   // (3)
        SUCCESS,
        NOT_ENOUGH_FUNDS,
        TX_CONFLICT
    }
    class Statistics {                                                // (4)
        // Implementation is omitted ...
    }
}
```

Here, the numbered points mean the following:

1. The transferMoney method transfers the amount of money from the wallet of fromOwner to the wallet of toOwner. Note that the method consumes reactive types, so at the moment of the method call, the actual transaction participants may still be unknown. Of course, the method could equally accept primitives or Mono<MoneyTransferRequest>. However, here, we intentionally use three distinct Mono instances to exercise the zip operator and TupleUtils.

2. The reportAllWallets method sums up the data of all registered wallets and checks the total balance.

3. The transferMoney method returns a result of the TxResult type. The TxResult enum describes three potential outcomes of a transfer operation: SUCCESS, NOT_ENOUGH_FUNDS, and TX_CONFLICT. The SUCCESS and NOT_ENOUGH_FUNDS operations are self-describing. TX_CONFLICT describes a situation when the transaction has failed because some other concurrent transactions succeed, updating one or both of the involved wallets.

4. The Statistics class represents the aggregated state of all wallets in the system, which is useful for integrity checks. The implementation details are omitted for the sake of simplicity.

Now that we have the WalletService interface defined we can write a unit test with a simulation. With the desired parallelism, the simulation chooses two random owners and tries to transfer a random amount of money. With some insignificant parts omitted, the simulation may look as follows:

```
public Mono<OperationStats> runSimulation() {
    return Flux.range(0, iterations)                                  // (1)
        .flatMap(i -> Mono
            .delay(Duration.ofMillis(rnd.nextInt(10)))               // (2)
            .publishOn(simulationScheduler)                          // (3)
            .flatMap(_i -> {
                String fromOwner = randomOwner();                    // (4)
                String toOwner = randomOwnerExcept(fromOwner);        //
```

```
            int amount = randomTransferAmount();           //
            return walletService.transferMoney(            // (5)
                Mono.just(fromOwner),
                Mono.just(toOwner),
                Mono.just(amount));
        }))
    .reduce(                                                // (6)
        OperationStats.start(),
        OperationStats::countTxResult);
}
```

The preceding code consists of the following steps:

1. Use the `Flux.range` method to simulate the desired amount of transfer iterations.
2. Apply a small random delay in order to stimulate random transaction contentions.
3. Transactions are running on `simulationScheduler`. Its parallelism defines how many concurrent transactions may happen. We may create a schedule with this code—`Schedulers.newParallel("name", parallelism)`.
4. Select random wallet owners and the amount of money to be transferred.
5. Make the `transferMoney` service request.
6. As the `transferMoney` call may result in one of `TxResult` states, the `reduce` method helps to track the simulation statistics. Note that the `OperationStats` class tracks how many operations were successful, how many were rejected due to insufficient funds, and how many failed due to transaction conflicts. On the other hand, the `WalletService.Statistics` class tracks the total amount of funds.

With a correct implementation of `WalletService`, we expect that a test simulation leads to a system state where the total amount of money in the system does not change. At the same time, we expect that money transfer requests are successfully executed when a sender has enough funds for a transaction. Otherwise, we may face system integrity issues that may lead to an actual financial loss.

Now, let's implement the `WalletService` service using reactive transaction support provided by MongoDB 4 and Spring Data. An implementation represented by the `TransactionalWalletService` class may look like this:

```
public class TransactionalWalletService implements WalletService {
    private final ReactiveMongoTemplate mongoTemplate;         // (1)

    @Override
```

```
    public Mono<TxResult> transferMoney(                            // (2)
        Mono<String> fromOwner,                                     //
        Mono<String> toOwner,                                       //
        Mono<Integer> requestAmount                                 //
    ) {                                                             //
        return Mono.zip(fromOwner, toOwner, requestAmount)         // (2.1)
            .flatMap(function((from, to, amount) -> {              // (2.2)
                return doTransferMoney(from, to, amount)           // (2.3)
                    .retryBackoff(                                 // (2.4)
                        20, Duration.ofMillis(1),                 //
                        Duration.ofMillis(500), 0.1               //
                    )                                              //
                    .onErrorReturn(TxResult.c);                    // (2.5)
            }));                                                   //
    }

    private Mono<TxResult> doTransferMoney(                         // (3)
        String from, String to, Integer amount                     // (3.1)
    ) {                                                             //
        return mongoTemplate.inTransaction().execute(session ->    // (3.2)
            session                                                //
                .findOne(queryForOwner(from), Wallet.class)        // (3.3)
                .flatMap(fromWallet -> session                     //
                    .findOne(queryForOwner(to), Wallet.class)      // (3.4)
                    .flatMap(toWallet -> {                         //
                        if (fromWallet.hasEnoughFunds(amount)) {   // (3.5)
                            fromWallet.withdraw(amount);           // (3.6)
                            toWallet.deposit(amount);              // (3.7)
                            return session.save(fromWallet)        // (3.8)
                                .then(session.save(toWallet))      // (3.9)
                                .then(Mono.just(TxResult.SUCCESS)); // (3.10)
                        } else {                                   //
                            return Mono.just(TxResult.NOT_ENOUGH_FUNDS); // (3.11)
                        }                                          //
                    })))                                           //
            .onErrorResume(e ->                                    // (3.12)
                Mono.error(new RuntimeException("Conflict")))      //
            .last();                                               // (3.13)
    }

    private Query queryForOwner(String owner) {                    // (4)
        return Query.query(new Criteria("owner").is(owner));      // (4.1)
    }
}
```

As the preceding code may seem to be non-trivial, let's describe it piece by piece:

1. First of all, we have to use the `ReactiveMongoTemplate` class, because, at the time of writing, Reactive MongoDB connector does not support transactions at the level of repositories, only at the level of the MongoDB template.

2. The implementation of the `transferMoney` method is defined here. With the `zip` operation, it subscribes to all method arguments (`2.1`), and when all the arguments are resolved, it uses the `TupleUtils.function` static helper function in order to decompose `Tuple3<String, String, Integer>` into its constituents (`2.2`) for code fluency. At point (`2.3`) we call the `doTransferMoney` method, which does the actual money transfer. However, the `doTransferMoney` method may return the `onError` signal that indicates a transaction conflict. In that case, we can retry the operation with the convenient `retryBackoff` method (`2.4`). The `retryBackoff` method needs to know the number of retries (20), the initial retry delay (1 millisecond), the maximum retry delay (500 milliseconds), and the jitter value (0.1), which configures how fast the retry delay increases. In cases when we fail to process the transaction even after all retries, we should return the `TX_CONFLICT` status to the client.

3. The `doTransferMoney` method tries to make an actual money transfer. It is called with the already resolved arguments—`form`, `to`, and `amount` (`3.1`). By calling the `mongoTemplate.inTransaction().execute(...)` method, we define the boundaries of a new transaction (`3.2`). Inside the `execute` method, we are given the `session` instance of the `ReactiveMongoOperations` class. The `session` object is bound to a MongoDB transaction. Now, within the transaction, we search for the wallet of the sender (`3.3`) and then search for the wallet of the receiver (`3.4`). With both wallets resolved, we check whether the sender has enough funds (`3.5`). Then we withdraw the correct amount of money from the sender's wallet (`3.6`) and deposit the same amount of money in the receiver's wallet (`3.7`). At this point, the changes are not saved to the database yet. Now, we save the updated wallet of the sender (`3.8`) and then the updated wallet of the receiver (`3.9`). If the database does not reject the changes, we return the `SUCCESS` status and automatically commit the transaction (`3.10`). If the sender does not have enough funds, we return the `NOT_ENOUGH_FUNDS` status (3.11). If there are any errors while communicating with the database, we propagate the `onError` signal (`3.12`), which in turn should trigger the retry logic described at point (`2.4`).

4. At points (`3.3`) and (`3.4`) we used the `queryForOwner` method, which uses the Criteria API to build MongoDB queries.

Referencing the correct session with the transaction is implemented using the Reactor Context. The `ReactiveMongoTemplate.inTransaction` method starts a new transaction and puts it into the context. Consequently, it is possible to get the session with the transaction represented by the `com.mongodb.reactivestreams.client.ClientSession` interface anywhere within the reactive flow. The `ReactiveMongoContext.getSession()` helper method allows us to get the session instance.

Of course, we may improve the `TransactionalWalletService` class by loading both wallets in one query as well as updating both wallets in one query. Changes such as these should decrease the number of database requests, speed up money transfers, and also decrease the rate of transaction conflicts. However, these improvements are left as an exercise for the reader.

Now, we may run the previously described test scenario with a different number of wallets, money transfer iterations, and parallelism. If we implemented all the business logic in the `TransactionalWalletService` class correctly, we should receive the output of the test as follows:

```
The number of accounts in the system: 500
The total balance of the system before the simulation: 500,000$
Running the money transferring simulation (10,000 iterations)
...
The simulation is finished
Transfer operations statistic:
  - successful transfer operations: 6,238
  - not enough funds: 3,762
  - conflicts: 0
All wallet operations:
  - total withdraw operations: 6,238
  - total deposit operations: 6,238
The total balance of the system after the simulation: 500,000$
```

So, in the preceding simulation, we performed `10,000` transfer operations, `6,238` of which succeeded, and `3,762` of which failed due to insufficient funds. Also, our retry strategy allowed to resolve all transaction conflicts as none of the transactions were finished with the `TX_CONFLICT` status. As is evident from the logs, the system preserved the invariance of the total balance—the total amount of money in the system before and after the simulation is the same. Consequently, we have achieved system integrity while doing concurrent money transfers by applying reactive transactions with MongoDB.

The support for multi-document transactions for replica sets now allows the whole new set of applications to be implemented with MongoDB as primary data storage. Of course, future versions of MongoDB may allow transactions across sharded deployments and provide various isolation levels for dealing with transactions. However, we should note that multi-document transactions incur greater performance costs and longer response latencies compared with simple document writes.

Even though reactive transactions is not a widely used technique yet, these examples clearly show that it is possible to apply transactions in the reactive fashion. Reactive transactions will be in high demand when applying reactive persistence to relational databases such as PostgreSQL. However, that topic requires a reactive language-level API for database access, which, at the time of writing, is not present yet.

Distributed transactions with the SAGA pattern

As it was stated previously in this chapter, distributed transactions may be implemented in different ways. Of course, this statement is also true for persistence layers implemented with the reactive paradigm. However, given that Spring Data supports reactive transactions only for MongoDB 4 and that aforementioned transactional support is not compatible with **Java Transaction API** (**JTA**), the only viable option for implementing distributed transactions within reactive microservices would be the SAGA pattern, which was described earlier in this chapter. Additionally, the SAGA pattern has good scalability characteristics and suites better for Reactive Systems than alternative patterns that require distributed transactions.

Spring Data reactive connectors

At the time of writing, Spring Data 2.1 has database connectors for four NoSQL databases, namely MongoDB, Cassandra, Couchbase, and Redis. It's likely that Spring Data will support other data stores as well, especially the ones that communicate over HTTP by leveraging Spring WebFlux WebClient.

Here, we will not cover all the features of the Spring Data reactive connectors or their implementation details. In the previous sections, we covered a lot of that for MongoDB and Cassandra. However, let's highlight the main distinctive features for each of the reactive connectors.

Reactive MongoDB connector

As described previously in this chapter, Spring Data has excellent support for MongoDB. The Spring Data Reactive MongoDB module may be enabled with the `spring-boot-starter-data-mongodb-reactive` Spring Boot starter module. Reactive MongoDB support provides a reactive repository. The `ReactiveMongoRepository` interface defines the basic repository contract. The repository inherits all the features of `ReactiveCrudRepository` and adds support for QBE. Also, the MongoDB repository supports custom queries with the `@Query` annotation and additional query configuration with the `@Meta` annotation. The MongoDB repository supports query generation from a method name if it follows the naming convention.

Another distinct feature of the MongoDB repository is support for tailable cursors. By default, the database automatically closes a query cursor when all results are consumed. However, MongoDB has **capped collections**, which are fixed-size and support high-throughput operations. Document retrieval is based on the insertion order. Capped collections work similarly to circular buffers. Also, capped collections support a **tailable cursor**. This cursor remains open after the client consumes all results in the initial query and when someone inserts new documents into the capped collection, the tailable cursor will return the new documents. In `ReactiveMongoRepository` the method marked with the `@Tailable` annotation returns a tailable cursor represented by the `Flux<Entity>` type.

One level lower, the `ReactiveMongoOperations` interface and its implementation class, `ReactiveMongoTemplate`, give more granular access to the MongoDB communication. Among other things, `ReactiveMongoTemplate` enables multi-document transactions with MongoDB. This feature works only for a non-sharded replica set with the WiredTiger storage engine. This capability is described in the *Reactive transactions with MongoDB 4* section.

The reactive Spring Data MongoDB module is built on top of Reactive Streams MongoDB Driver, which implements the Reactive Stream specification and uses Project Reactor internally. In turn, MongoDB Reactive Streams Java Driver is built on top of MongoDB Async Java Driver. The *How reactive repositories work* section describes how `ReactiveMongoRepository` works in further detail.

Reactive Cassandra connector

The Spring Data Reactive Cassandra module may be enabled by importing the `spring-boot-starter-data-cassandra-reactive` starter module. Cassandra also has support for reactive repositories. The `ReactiveCassandraRepository` interface extends `ReactiveCrudRepository` and defines the capabilities of the Cassandra bases data access layer. The `@Query` annotation allows defining CQL3 queries manually. The `@Consistency` annotation can configure the desired consistency level applied to the query.

The `ReactiveCassandraOperations` interface and the `ReactiveCassandraTemplate` class give access to lower-level operations on the Cassandra database.

As of Spring Data 2.1, the reactive Cassandra connector wraps the asynchronous Cassandra driver. The *Using asynchronous drivers (Cassandra)* section describes how the asynchronous communication is wrapped into the reactive client.

Reactive Couchbase connector

The Spring Data Reactive Couchbase module may be enabled with the `spring-boot-starter-data-couchbase-reactive` starter module. It enables the reactive access for Couchbase (`https://www.couchbase.com`). The `ReactiveCouchbaseRepository` interface extends basic `ReactiveCrudRepository`, additionally requiring the type of entity ID to extend the `Serializable` interface.

The default implementation of the `ReactiveCouchbaseRepository` interface is built on top of the `RxJavaCouchbaseOperations` interface. The `RxJavaCouchbaseTemplate` class implements `RxJavaCouchbaseOperations`. At this point, it should be evident that the reactive Couchbase connector uses the RxJava library for `RxJavaCouchbaseOperations`. As the `ReactiveCouchbaseRepository` methods return the `Mono` and `Flux` types and the `RxJavaCouchbaseOperations` methods return the `Observable` type, reactive type conversion is required. It happens at the level of the repository implementation.

The reactive Couchbase connector is built on top of the reactive Couchbase driver. The latest Couchbase driver 2.6.2 uses RxJava version 1.3.8, the last release of the 1.x branch. Consequently, backpressure support may be limited with the Couchbase connector. However, it has an entirely non-blocking stack through the Netty framework and the RxJava library, so it should not waste any application resources.

Reactive Redis connector

The Spring Data Reactive Redis module may be enabled by importing the `spring-boot-starter-data-redis-reactive` starter. In contrast to other reactive connectors, the Redis connector does not provide a reactive repository. Consequently, the `ReactiveRedisTemplate` class becomes the central abstraction for reactive Redis data access. `ReactiveRedisTemplate` implements the API defined by the `ReactiveRedisOperations` interface and provides all necessary serialization-deserialization routines. At the same time, `ReactiveRedisConnection` allows working with raw byte buffers when communicating with Redis.

Along with the ordinary operations for storing and retrieving objects and managing Redis data structures, the template allows subscription to Pub-Sub channels. For example, the `convertAndSend(String destination, V message)` method publishes the given message to the given channel and returns the number of clients that received the message. The `listenToChannel(String... channels)` method returns a `Flux` with messages from the channels of interest. This way, the reactive Redis connector enables not only reactive data storage but also provides a messaging mechanism. `Chapter 8`, *Scaling Up with Cloud Streams*, describes more how messaging improves the scalability and elasticity of a reactive application.

Spring Data Redis currently integrates with the Lettuce driver (`https://github.com/lettuce-io/lettuce-core`). It is the only reactive Java connector for Redis. Lettuce version 4.x used RxJava for underlying implementation. However, the 5.x branch of the library switched to Project Reactor.

All reactive connectors except for Couchbase have reactive health indicators. Consequently, database health checks also should not waste any server resources. More on that is covered in `Chapter 10`, *And, Finally, Release It!*

We are sure that, with time, Spring Data will add more reactive connectors to its ecosystem.

Limitations and anticipated improvements

As the area of reactive connectivity is relatively new, there are some limitations that prohibit using the approach in many applications:

- The **lack of reactive drivers** for popular databases used in large part of modern projects. So far, we have reactive or asynchronous drivers for MongoDB, Cassandra, Redis, and Couchbase. Consequently, these databases have reactive connectors in the Spring Data ecosystem. Also, we have a few options for reactive access to PostgreSQL. At the same time, there is some work going on to enable reactive access for MySQL and MariaDB. Even though the few databases with reactive support cover many use cases, this list is still limiting. To become a trendy development technique, the reactive data access should have connectors for most widespread relational databases, such as PostgreSQL, MySQL, Oracle, MS SQL, for popular search engines such as ElasticSearch and Apache Solr, as well as for cloud databases such as Google Big Query, Amazon Redshift, and Microsoft CosmosDB.

- The **lack of reactive JPA**. Currently, the reactive persistence operates at a pretty low level. We can not easily work with entities in the ways proposed by ordinary JPA. With the current reactive connectors, we have no support for entity relationship mappings, for entity caching, or for lazy loading. However, it would be odd to demand such capabilities even before consenting to any low-level API for the reactive data access.

- The **lack of a language-level reactive API for data access**. As was described previously in this chapter, at the time of writing, the Java platform has only JDBC API for data access, which is synchronous and blocking, and, consequently, cannot smoothly be used with a reactive application.

However, we may see that the increasing number of NoSQL solutions provide reactive drivers or at least asynchronous drivers that are easy to wrap into the reactive API. Also, serious improvements are currently being made in the area of a language-level APIs for data access in Java. At the time of writing, there are two prominent proposals to fulfill that niche, namely ADBA and R2DBC. Now, let's look at them more closely.

Asynchronous Database Access

Asynchronous Database Access (**ADBA**) defines a non-blocking database access API for Java platform. At the time of writing, it is still a draft, and JDBC Expert Group is discussing what it should look like. ADBA was announced at the JavaOne 2016 conference and has been under discussion for a couple of years now. ADBA is intended to complement the current JDBC API and propose an asynchronous alternative (not a replacement) geared toward high-throughput programs. ADBA is designed to support the fluent programming style and provide a builder pattern for composing database queries. ADBA is not an extension to JDBC and has no dependencies on it. When ready, most likely, ADBA will live in the `java.sql2` package.

ADBA it is an asynchronous API, so no method calls should block while doing a network call. All potentially blocking actions are represented as separate ADBA operations. A client application builds and submits one ADBA operation or a graph of ADBA operations. A driver that implements ADBA asynchronously executes the operation and reports the result via `java.util.concurrent.CompletionStage` or callbacks. When ready, an asynchronous SQL that requests issues over ADBA may look as follows:

```
CompletionStage<List<String>> employeeNames =                      // (1)
connection
  .<Integer>rowOperation("select * from employee")                 // (2)
  .onError(this::userDefinedErrorHandler)                          // (3)
  .collect(Collector.of(                                           // (4)
     () -> new ArrayList<String>(),
     (ArrayList<String> cont, Result.RowColumn row) ->
        cont = cont.add(row.at("name").get(String.class)),
     (l, r) -> l,
     container -> container))
  .submit()                                                        // (5)
  .getCompletionStage();                                           // (6)
```

Note that the preceding code is still based on an ADBA draft so that the API may change at any time. However, the numbered lines mean the following:

1. The query returns result in `CompletionStage`. In our case, we return a list of employees' names.
2. This initiates a new row operation by calling the `rowOperation` method of the database `connection`.
3. The operation allows registering error handlers by invoking the `onError` method. Error handling happens in our custom `userDefinedErrorHandler` method.

4. The `collect` method allows gathering results using Java Stream API collectors.

5. The `submit` method starts processing the operation.

6. The `getCompletionStage` method gives the user an instance of `CompletionStage` that will hold the result when the processing is finished.

Of course, ADBA is going to provide the ability to write and execute more complex database queries, including conditional, parallel, and dependent operations. ADBA has support for transactions. However, in contrast with JDBC, ADBA is not intended to be used directly by business code (even though it is possible), but rather intended to provide an asynchronous basis for more high-level libraries and frameworks.

At the time of writing, ADBA has only one implementation, called **AoJ**. AoJ (`https://gitlab.com/asyncjdbc/asyncjdbc/tree/master`) is an experimental library that implements a subset of the ADBA API by invoking the standard JDBC on a separate thread pool. AoJ is not suitable for production use, but provides the ability to play with ADBA without the need to implement a full-blown asynchronous driver.

There are some conversations regarding ADBA's ability to return results not only with `CompletionStage` but also with a reactive `Publisher` from the Java Flow API. However, it is not clear how the Flow API would be integrated into ADBA or whether ADBA would expose a reactive API at all. At the time of writing, this topic is still the subject of hot debate.

At this point, we have to claim again that asynchronous behavior represented by Java's `CompletionStage` may always be substituted by a reactive `Publisher` implementation. However, this statement is not valid for the reverse situation. Reactive behavior may be represented with `CompletionStage` or `CompletableFuture` only with some compromises, namely by dropping backpressure propagation. Also, with `CompletionStage<List<T>>`, there is no actual data streaming semantic as clients are required to wait for the complete result set. Leveraging the Collector API for streaming doesn't really seem to be an option here. Besides, `CompletableFuture` begins its execution as soon as it is submitted, while `Publisher` begins execution only when it receives a subscription. A reactive API for database access would fulfill the needs for both a reactive language-level API and an asynchronous language-level API. It is because any reactive API could be quickly turned to an asynchronous API without any semantic compromises. However, an asynchronous API, in most cases, may become a reactive API only with some compromises. That is why, from the standpoint of the authors of this book, ADBA with Reactive Streams support seems to be more beneficial than asynchronous-only ADBA.

The alternative candidate for the next-generation data-access API in Java is called R2DBC. It has more to offer than the entirely asynchronous ADBA and proves that a reactive API for relational data access has huge potential. So, let's look at it more closely.

Reactive Relational Database Connectivity

Reactive Relational Database Connectivity (R2DBC) (`https://github.com/r2dbc`) is an initiative to explore what an entirely reactive database API may look like. The Spring Data team leads the R2DBC initiative and uses it to probe and verify ideas in the context of reactive data access within reactive applications. R2DBC was publicly announced at the Spring OnePlatform 2018 conference. R2DBC has the aim of defining a reactive database access API with backpressure support. The Spring Data team gained some excellent experience with reactive NoSQL persistence, so they decided to propose their vision of what a genuinely reactive language-level data access API may look like. Also, R2DBC may become an underlying API for the relational reactive repositories in Spring Data. At the time of writing, R2DBC is still experimental, and it is unclear whether or when it may become a production-ready software.

The R2DBC project consists of the following parts:

- **R2DBC Service Provider Interface (SPI)** defines the minimalistic API for driver implementations. The API is concise in order to drastically trim down the API that driver implementors had to conform to. The SPI is not intended for direct use from the application code. Instead, a dedicated client library is required for that purpose.

- **R2DBC Client** offers a human-friendly API and helper classes that translate user requests to the SPI level. This separate level of abstraction adds some comfort when using R2DBC directly. The authors highlight that R2DBC Client does for R2DBC SPI the same things as the Jdbi library does for JDBC. However, anyone is free to use SPI directly or implement their own client library over R2DBC SPI.

- **R2DBC PostgreSQL Implementation** provides a R2DBC driver for PostgreSQL. It uses the Netty framework for asynchronous communication via the PostgreSQL wire protocol. Backpressure may be achieved either by TCP Flow Control or by a PostgreSQL feature called **portal**, which is effectively a cursor into a query. The portal translates perfectly to Reactive Streams. It is important to note that not all relational databases have the wire protocol features required for a proper backpressure propagation. However, at least TCP Flow Control is available in all cases.

R2DBC Client allows working with the PostgreSQL database as follows:

```
PostgresqlConnectionFactory pgConnectionFactory =                    // (1)
    PostgresqlConnectionConfiguration.builder()
        .host("<host>")
        .database("<database>")
        .username("<username>")
        .password("<password>")
```

```
        .build();

R2dbc r2dbc = new R2dbc(pgConnectionFactory);               // (2)

r2dbc.inTransaction(handle ->                               // (3)
    handle
        .execute("insert into book (id, title, publishing_year) " +  // (3.1)
                "values ($1, $2, $3)",
                20, "The Sands of Mars", 1951)
        .doOnNext(n -> log.info("{} rows inserted", n))    // (3.2)
).thenMany(r2dbc.inTransaction(handle ->                    // (4)
        handle.select("SELECT title FROM book")            // (4.1)
            .mapResult(result ->                           // (4.2)
                result.map((row, rowMetadata) ->           // (4.3)
                    row.get("title", String.class)))))     // (4.4)
    .subscribe(elem -> log.info(" - Title: {}", elem));    // (5)
```

Let's describe the preceding code:

1. First of all, we have to configure a connection factory represented by the `PostgresqlConnectionFactory` class. The configuration is trivial.

2. We have to create an instance of the `R2dbc` class, which provides the reactive API.

3. `R2dbc` allows us to create a transaction by applying the `inTransaction` method. A `handle` wraps an instance of the reactive connection and provides additional convenience APIs. Here, we may execute an SQL statement, for example, insert a new row. The `execute` method receives an SQL query and its parameters, if any (`3.1`). In turn, the `execute` method returns the number of affected rows. In the preceding code, we log the number of updated rows (`3.2`).

4. After inserting a row, we start another transaction to select all book titles (`4.1`). When the result arrives, we map individual rows (`4.2`) by applying the `map` function (`4.3`), which know about the row structure. In our case, we retrieve the `title` of the `String` type (`4.4`). The `mapResult` method returns the `Flux<String>` type.

5. We log all `onNext` signals reactively. Each signal holds a book title, including the one inserted at step (`3`).

As we can see, R2DBC Client provides a fluent API with the reactive style. This API feels very natural in the code base of reactive applications.

Using R2DBC with Spring Data R2DBC

Of course, the Spring Data team could not resist the appeal of implementing the ReactiveCrudRepository interface on top of R2DBC. At the moment of writing, this implementation lives in the Spring Data JDBC module, which has already been described in this chapter. However, it is going to obtain its own module called **Spring Data R2DBC**. The SimpleR2dbcRepository class implements the ReactiveCrudRepository interface using R2DBC. It is worth noting that the SimpleR2dbcRepository class does not use the default R2DBC Client but defines its own client to work with R2DBC SPI.

Before Spring Data R2DBC kick-off, reactive support in the Spring Data JDBC module lives in the r2dbc Git branch of the project and, consequently, is not yet ready for production. However, the Spring Data JDBC module with R2DBC support demonstrates the vast potential of using ReactiveCrudRepository for relational data manipulation. So, let's define our first ReactiveCrudRepository for PostgreSQL. It may look as follows:

```
public interface BookRepository
    extends ReactiveCrudRepository<Book, Integer> {

    @Query("SELECT * FROM book WHERE publishing_year = " +
        "(SELECT MAX(publishing_year) FROM book)")
    Flux<Book> findTheLatestBooks();
}
```

So far, the Spring Data JDBC module does not have auto-configuration, so we have to create an instance of the BookRepository interface manually:

```
BookRepository createRepository(PostgresqlConnectionFactory fct) {   // (1)
    TransactionalDatabaseClient txClient =                           // (2)
        TransactionalDatabaseClient.create(fct);
    RelationalMappingContext cnt = new RelationalMappingContext();   // (3)
    return new R2dbcRepositoryFactory(txClient, cnt)                 // (4)
        .getRepository(BookRepository.class);                       // (5)
}
```

In the preceding code, we do the following steps:

1. We need a reference to PostgresqlConnectionFactory, which was created in the previous example.
2. TransactionalDatabaseClient enables basic support for transactions.
3. We have to create a simple RelationalMappingContext in order to map rows to entities and vice versa.

4. We create an appropriate repository factory. The `R2dbcRepositoryFactory` class knows how to create `ReactiveCrudRepository`.

5. The factory generates the instance of the `BookRepository` interface.

Now, we may use our entirely reactive `BookRepository` in a normal reactive workflow, as follows:

```
bookRepository.findTheLatestBooks()
    .doOnNext(book -> log.info("Book: {}", book))
    .count()
    .doOnSuccess(count -> log.info("DB contains {} latest books", count))
    .subscribe();
```

Even though the R2DBC project is still experimental, as well as its support in Spring Data JDBC, we may see that genuinely reactive data access is not very far away. Besides, the problem of backpressure is resolved at the R2DBC SPI level.

At this point, it is unclear whether ADBA will receive reactive support or whether R2DBC will become a reactive alternative to ADBA. However, in both cases, there is confidence that the reactive relational data access will become a real thing very soon, at least for databases with either ADBA- or R2DBC-compliant drivers.

Transforming a synchronous repository into reactive

Although Spring Data provides reactive connectors for popular NoSQL databases, a reactive application sometimes needs to query a database that does not have reactive connectivity. Wrapping any blocking communication into a reactive API is possible. However, all blocking communication should happen on an appropriate thread pool. If not, we may block the event loop of the application and stop it entirely. Note, a small thread pool (with a bounded queue) is likely to be exhausted at some point. A full queue turns into blocking mode at some point and the whole point of making it non-blocking is gone. Such solutions are not as efficient as their entirely reactive counterparts. However, the approach with a dedicated thread pool for blocking requests is often acceptable in a reactive application.

Let's assume that we have to implement a reactive microservice that issues requests to a relational database from time to time. That database has a JDBC driver but does not have any asynchronous or reactive drivers. In this case, the only option would be to build a reactive adapter that hides blocking requests behind a reactive API.

As was previously stated, all blocking requests should happen on a dedicated scheduler. The underlying thread pool of the scheduler defines the level of parallelism for blocking actions. For example, when running blocking actions on `Schedulers.elastic()`, the amount of *concurrent* requests is not limited because the `elastic` scheduler does not bind the maximum number of created thread pools. At the same time, `Scheduler.newParallel("jdbc", 10)` defines the number of pooled workers, so no more than 10 concurrent requests will happen simultaneously. This approach works well when a communication with the database happens through the connection pool of a fixed size. In most cases, it makes little sense to set the size of the thread pool bigger than the size of the connection pool. For example, with a scheduler that operates over an unlimited thread pool, when the connection pool is exhausted, a new task and its running thread will be blocked not by the network communication but at the stage of connection retrieval from the connection pool.

When choosing the appropriate blocking API, there are a few options. Each option has its pros and cons. Here, we are going to cover the `rxjava2-jdbc` library and see how to wrap a pre-existing blocking repository.

Using the rxjava2-jdbc library

David Moten's `rxjava2-jdbc` library (`https://github.com/davidmoten/rxjava2-jdbc`) was created to wrap a JDBC driver in a way that does not block a reactive application. The library is built on RxJava 2 and uses a dedicated thread pool and the concept of the non-blocking connection pool. Consequently, a request does not block a thread while waiting for a free connection. As soon as a connection is available, the query starts executing on the connection and blocks the thread. The application may not manage a dedicated scheduler for blocking requests because the library does this. Additionally, the library has a fluent DSL that allows us to issue SQL statements and receive results as Reactive Streams. Let's define the `Book` entity and annotate it properly for use with `rxjava2-jdbc`:

```
@Query("select id, title, publishing_year " +                        // (3)
       "from book order by publishing_year")
public interface Book {                                              // (1)
   @Column String id();                                             // (2)
   @Column String title();
   @Column Integer publishing_year();
}
```

In the preceding code, we can see the following:

1. We define the `Book` interface. Note that with Spring Data, we usually define an entity as a class.
2. Accessor methods are decorated with the `@Column` annotation. The annotation helps to map row columns to entity fields.
3. With the `@Query` annotation, we define the SQL statement used for the entity retrieval.

Now let's define a simple repository that finds books published during a certain period:

```
public class RxBookRepository {
    private static final String SELECT_BY_YEAR_BETWEEN =        // (1)
        "select * from book where " +
        "publishing_year >= :from and publishing_year <= :to";

    private final String url = "jdbc:h2:mem:db";
    private final int poolSize = 25;
    private final Database database = Database.from(url, poolSize);// (2)

    public Flowable<Book> findByYearBetween(                    // (3)
      Single<Integer> from,
      Single<Integer> to
    ) {
      return Single
        .zip(from, to, Tuple2::new)                            // (3.1)
        .flatMapPublisher(tuple -> database                    //
          .select(SELECT_BY_YEAR_BETWEEN)                      // (3.2)
          .parameter("from", tuple._1())                       // (3.3)
          .parameter("to", tuple._2())                         //
          .autoMap(Book.class));                               // (3.5)
    }
}
```

Let's describe the implementation of the `RxBookRepository` class as follows:

1. As the library cannot generate queries automatically, we have to provide the SQL query that searches required books. Named parameters are allowed in an SQL query.
2. Database initialization requires a JDBC URL and the pool size. In our case, no more than 25 concurrent queries may run at the same time.

3. The `findByYearBetween` method uses reactive types from the RxJava 2 library (`Flowable` and `Single`), not from Project Reactor. This is because the `rxjava2-jdbc` library internally uses RxJava 2.x and exposes RxJava types through its API. However, it is easy to convert RxJava types to types from Project Reactor. At point (`3.1`) we subscribe to the stream that resolves request arguments. Then we call the `select` method (`3.2`) and fill the query parameters (`3.3`). The `autoMap` method translates a JDBC row into a `Book` entity. The `autoMap` method returns the `Flowable<Book>`, which is equivalent to Project Reactor's `Flux<Book>`.

The `rxjava2-jdbc` library supports most JDBC drivers. Also, the library has some support for transactions. All the operations inside a transaction have to be executed on the same connection. The commit/rollback of the transaction happens automatically.

The `rxjava2-jdbc` library is neat, reduces some potential thread blocks, and makes it possible to work with relational databases reactively. However, so far, it is still new and may not handle complex reactive workflows, especially those that involve transactions. The `rxjava2-jdbc` library also needs definitions for all SQL queries.

Wrapping a synchronous CrudRepository

Sometimes we may already have a `CrudRepository` instance with all the required mechanics for data access (no manual queries or entity mappings needed). However, we cannot directly use this in a reactive application. In this case, it is easy to write our own reactive adapter that would behave similarly to the `rxjava2-jdbc` library but at the repository level. Be cautious with JPA when applying this approach. We can quickly run into proxy issues when using lazy loading. So, let's assume that we have the following `Book` entity defined by JPA:

```
@Entity
@Table(name = "book")
public class Book {
    @Id
    @GeneratedValue(strategy = GenerationType.IDENTITY)
    private Integer id;
    private String title;
    private Integer publishingYear;
    // Constructors, getters, setters...
}
```

Also, we have the following Spring Data JPA repository:

```
@Repository
public interface BookJpaRepository
    extends CrudRepository<Book, Integer> {                         // (1)

    Iterable<Book> findByIdBetween(int lower, int upper);           // (2)

    @Query("SELECT b FROM Book b WHERE " +
        "LENGTH(b.title)=(SELECT MIN(LENGTH(b2.title)) FROM Book b2)") // (3)
    Iterable<Book> findShortestTitle();
}
```

The `BookJpaRepository` has the following characteristics:

1. It extends the `CrudRepository` interface and inherits all the methods for data access.
2. The `BookJpaRepository` defines a method that generates a query based on the naming convention.
3. The `BookJpaRepository` defines a method with a custom SQL.

The `BookJpaRepository` interface works fine with blocking JPA infrastructure. All the methods of the `BookJpaRepository` repository return non-reactive types. To wrap the `BookJpaRepository` interface into a reactive API and receive most of its capabilities, we may define an abstract adapter and extend it with additional methods to map the `findByIdBetween` and `findShortestTitle` method. The abstract adapter may be reused for adapting any `CrudRepository` instance. The adapter may look as follows:

```
public abstract class
    ReactiveCrudRepositoryAdapter
            <T, ID, I extends CrudRepository<T, ID>>          // (1)
    implements ReactiveCrudRepository<T, ID> {                //

    protected final I delegate;                               // (2)
    protected final Scheduler scheduler;                      //

    // Constructor...

    @Override
    public <S extends T> Mono<S> save(S entity) {             // (3)
        return Mono                                           //
            .fromCallable(() -> delegate.save(entity))        // (3.1)
            .subscribeOn(scheduler);                          // (3.2)
    }

    @Override
```

```
    public Mono<T> findById(Publisher<ID> id) {           // (4)
       return Mono.from(id)                               // (4.1)
          .flatMap(actualId ->                            // (4.2)
             delegate.findById(actualId)                  // (4.3)
                .map(Mono::just)                          // (4.4)
                .orElseGet(Mono::empty))                  // (4.5)
          .subscribeOn(scheduler);                        // (4.6)
    }

    @Override
    public Mono<Void> deleteAll(Publisher<? extends T> entities) {  // (5)
       return Flux.from(entities)                         // (5.1)
          .flatMap(entity -> Mono                         //
             .fromRunnable(() -> delegate.delete(entity)) // (5.2)
             .subscribeOn(scheduler))                     // (5.3)
          .then();                                        // (5.4)
    }
    // All other methods of ReactiveCrudRepository...
}
```

Let's describe the preceding code:

1. ReactiveCrudRepositoryAdapter is an abstract class that implements the
   ReactiveCrudRepository interface and has the same generic types as the
   delegate repository.

2. ReactiveCrudRepositoryAdapter uses the underlying delegate of
   the CrudRepository type. Furthermore, the adapter requires the Scheduler
   instance to offload requests from the event loop. The parallelism of the scheduler
   defines the number of concurrent requests, so it is natural to use the same
   number as we use for connection pool configuration. However, the best mapping
   is not always one to one. If the connection pool is used for other purposes, the
   number of available connections may be less than available threads, and some
   threads may be blocked while waiting for a connection (rxjava2-jdbc handles
   such a scenario better).

3. Here is a reactive wrapper method for the blocking save method. The blocking
   call is wrapped into the Mono.fromCallable operator (3.1) and offloaded to
   the dedicated scheduler (3.2).

4. Here is a reactive adapter for the findById method. At first, the method
   subscribes to the id stream (4.1). If the value arrives (4.2), the delegate
   instance is called (4.3). The CrudRepository.findById method returns
   Optional, so it is required to map the value to a Mono instance (4.4). In case of
   receiving an empty Optional, return empty Mono (4.5). Of course, the
   execution is offloaded to the dedicated scheduler.

5. Here is a reactive adapter for the `deleteAll` method. As the `deleteAll(Publisher<T> entities)` and `deleteAll(Iterator<T> entities)` methods have different semantics, we cannot map one reactive call directly into one blocking call. For example, the stream of entities is endless, and consequently no items are ever deleted. So, the `deleteAll` method subscribes to entities (`5.1`) and issues a separate `delegate.delete(T entity)` request (`5.2`) for each of them. As a delete request may run in parallel, each request has its own `subscribeOn` call to receive a worker from the `scheduler` (`5.3`). The `deleteAll` method returns an output stream that completes when the incoming stream is terminated and all the delete operations are completed. All methods of the `ReactiveCrudRepository` interface should be mapped in this way.

Now, let's define the missing custom methods in the concrete reactive repository implementation:

```
public class RxBookRepository extends
    ReactiveCrudRepositoryAdapter<Book, Integer, BookJpaRepository> {

    public RxBookRepository(
        BookJpaRepository delegate,
        Scheduler scheduler
    ) {
        super(delegate, scheduler);
    }
    public Flux<Book> findByIdBetween(                          // (1)
        Publisher<Integer> lowerPublisher,                      //
        Publisher<Integer> upperPublisher                       //
    ) {                                                         //
        return Mono.zip(                                        // (1.1)
            Mono.from(lowerPublisher),                          //
            Mono.from(upperPublisher)                           //
        ).flatMapMany(                                          //
            function((low, upp) ->                              // (1.2)
                Flux                                            //
                    .fromIterable(delegate.findByIdBetween(low, upp))  // (1.3)
                    .subscribeOn(scheduler)                     // (1.4)
            ))                                                  //
            .subscribeOn(scheduler);                            // (1.5)
    }

    public Flux<Book> findShortestTitle() {                     // (2)
        return Mono.fromCallable(delegate::findShortestTitle)   // (2.1)
            .subscribeOn(scheduler)                             // (2.2)
            .flatMapMany(Flux::fromIterable);                   // (2.3)
    }
}
```

The RxBookRepository class extends the abstract ReactiveCrudRepositoryAdapter class, references the BookJpaRepository and Scheduler instances, and defines the following methods:

1. The findByIdBetween method receives two Reactive Streams and subscribes to them with the zip operation (1.1). When both values are ready (1.2), the corresponding method is called on the delegate instance (1.3) and the blocking execution is offloaded to the dedicated scheduler. However, it is also possible to offload the resolution of the lowerPublisher and upperPublisher stream so that the event loop would not spend resources there (1.5). Be careful with such an approach because it may fight for resources with actual database requests and reduce the throughput.

2. The findShortestTitle method calls the corresponding method (2.1) on the dedicated scheduler (2.2) and maps Iterable to Flux (2.3).

Now, we may finally wrap blocking BookJpaRepository into reactive RxBookRepository with the following code:

```
Scheduler scheduler = Schedulers.newParallel("JPA", 10);
BookJpaRepository jpaRepository = getBlockingRepository(...);

RxBookRepository rxRepository =
    new RxBookRepository(jpaRepository, scheduler);

Flux<Book> books = rxRepository
    .findByIdBetween(Mono.just(17), Mono.just(22));

books
    .subscribe(b -> log.info("Book: {}", b));
```

Not all blocking features may be mapped so easily. For example, JPA lazy loading would most likely be broken with the described approach. Also, the support of transactions would require an additional effort similar to that in the rxjava2-jdbc library. Alternatively, we would need to wrap synchronous operations at the granularity where no transaction expands beyond one blocking call.

The approach described here does not magically transform the blocking request into a reactive non-blocking execution. Some threads that form the JPA scheduler will still be blocked. However, detailed monitoring of the scheduler and wise pool management should help to create an acceptable balance between the application's performance and resource usage.

Reactive Spring Data in action

To finish this chapter and highlight the benefits of the reactive persistence, let's create a data-intensive reactive application that has to communicate with a database frequently. For example, let's revisit the example from `Chapter 6`, *WebFlux Async Non-Blocking Communication*. There, we implemented an alternative read-only web frontend application for the Gitter service (`https://gitter.im`). The application connects to a predefined chat room and re-streams all the messages to all connected users through **Server-Sent Events** (**SSE**). Now, with new requirements, our application has to collect statistics about the most active and the most referenced users in the chat room. Our chat application may use MongoDB to store messages and user profiles. This information may also be used for statistic recalculation purposes. The following diagram depicts the application design:

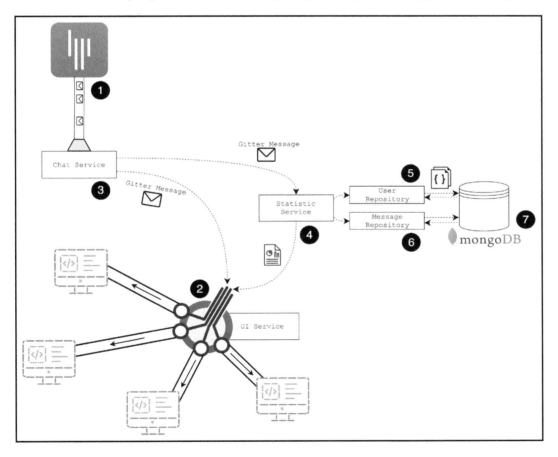

Diagram 7.18 The chat application with reactive Spring Data for MongoDB access

In the preceding diagram, the numbered points are as follows:

1. This is a Gitter server that may stream messages from the particular chat room through SSE. This is an external system from which our application receives all data.

2. This is the **UI Service**, which is a part of our application. That component streams messages from Gitter and recent statistics to the clients, which are web applications running in browsers. The **UI Service** uses the WebFlux module for data streaming via SSE in a reactive fashion.

3. This is the **Chat Service**, which uses a reactive `WebClient` to listen for incoming messages from the Gitter server. Received messages are broadcast to `WebClient` through the **UI Service** and also streamed to the **Statistics Service**.

4. The **Statistics Service** continually tracks the most active and the most mentioned users. The statistics are constantly streamed to the web clients via the **UI Service**.

5. The **User Repository** is a reactive repository that communicates with MongoDB to store and retrieve information about chat participants. It is built with the Spring Data MongoDB Reactive module.

6. The **Message Repository** is a reactive repository that allows storing and searching for chat messages. It is also built with Spring Data MongoDB Reactive.

7. We choose MongoDB to be our storage as it fits the application needs and also has a reactive driver and good reactive support in Spring Data.

So, the flow of data in the application is constant and does not require any blocking calls. Here, the Chat Service broadcasts messages through the UI Service, the Statistics Service receives chat messages, and after recalculating the statistic, it sends messages to the UI Service with statistics. The WebFlux module is responsible for all network communications, and Spring Data makes it possible to plug MongoDB interactions without breaking the reactive flows. Here, we omit most of the implementation details. However, let's look at the Statistics Service. This may look as follows:

```
public class StatisticService {
    private static final UserVM EMPTY_USER = new UserVM("", "");

    private final UserRepository userRepository;              // (1)
    private final MessageRepository messageRepository;        //

    // Constructor...

    public Flux<UsersStatistic> updateStatistic(             // (2)
        Flux<ChatMessage> messagesFlux                        // (2.1)
    ) {
        return messagesFlux
            .map(MessageMapper::toDomainUnit)                 // (2.2)
```

```
        .transform(messageRepository::saveAll)                  // (2.3)
        .retryBackoff(Long.MAX_VALUE, Duration.ofMillis(500))   // (2.4)
        .onBackpressureLatest()                                 // (2.5)
        .concatMap(e -> this.doGetUserStatistic(), 1)           // (2.6)
        .errorStrategyContinue((t, e) -> {});                   // (2.7)
    }

    private Mono<UsersStatistic> doGetUserStatistic() {         // (3)
        Mono<UserVM> topActiveUserMono = userRepository
            .findMostActive()                                   // (3.1)
            .map(UserMapper::toViewModelUnits)                  // (3.2)
            .defaultIfEmpty(EMPTY_USER);                        // (3.3)

        Mono<UserVM> topMentionedUserMono = userRepository
            .findMostPopular()                                  // (3.4)
            .map(UserMapper::toViewModelUnits)                  // (3.5)
            .defaultIfEmpty(EMPTY_USER);                        // (3.6)

        return Mono.zip(                                        // (3.7)
            topActiveUserMono,
            topMentionedUserMono,
            UsersStatistic::new
        ).timeout(Duration.ofSeconds(2));                       // (3.8)
    }
}
```

Let's analyze the implementation of the StatisticService class:

1. The StatisticService class has references to the UserRepository and MessageRepository, which provide reactive communication with MongoDB collections.
2. The updateStatistic method streams statistic events that are represented by the UsersStatistic view-model objects. At the same time, the method requires an incoming stream of chat messages represented by the messagesFlux method argument (2.1). The method subscribes to a Flux of ChatMessage objects, transforming them into the desired representation (2.2), and saving them to MongoDB with messageRepository (2.3). The retryBackoff operator helps to overcome potential MongoDB communication issues (2.4). Also, if a subscriber cannot handle all the events, we drop old messages (2.5). By applying the concatMap operator, we start the process of statistic revaluation by calling the doGetUserStatistic method inside (2.6).

We use `concatMap` for this, as it guarantees the correct order of statistic results. This is because the operator waits for the inner sub-stream to complete before generating the next sub-stream. Also, in the statistics recalculation, we ignore all errors by applying the `errorStrategyContinue` operator (2.7) because this part of the application is not critical and tolerates some temporary issues.

3. The `doGetUserStatistic` helper method calculates the top users. To calculate the most active user, we call the `findMostActive` method on the `userRepository` (3.1), map the result to the correct type (3.2), and, in a case in which no user is found, we return the predefined `EMPTY_USER` (3.3). Similarly, to get the most popular user, we call the `findMostPopular` method on the repository (3.4), map the result (3.5), and set the default value if required (3.6). The `Mono.zip` operator helps to merge those two reactive requests and produce a new instance of the `UsersStatistic` class. The `timeout` operator sets the maximum time budget available for statistics recalculation.

With this elegant code, we have easily blended the incoming stream of messages originating from a `WebClient` object, the outgoing stream of SSE events handled by the WebFlux module. Naturally, we also included MongoDB query processing into our reactive pipeline through reactive Spring Data. Moreover, we have not blocked any threads anywhere in this pipeline. As a result, our application utilizes server resources very efficiently.

Summary

In this chapter, we have learned a lot about data persistence in modern applications. We have described the challenges of data access within with microservice architecture and how polyglot persistence helps to build services with the desired characteristics. We have also had an overview of the available options for implementing distributed transactions. This chapter covered the pros and cons of blocking and reactive approaches for data persistence, as well as missing reactive alternatives for each of the modern blocking data access levels.

In this chapter, we described how the Spring Data project gracefully brings reactive data access into modern Spring applications. We have investigated the features and implementation details of the reactive MongoDB connector and the Cassandra connector. We have also covered the support for multi-document transactions with MongoDB 4. This chapter revealed the available options for the next-gen language-level reactive database APIs, namely ADBA and R2DBC. We have explored the pitfalls and benefits of both approaches to this and investigated how Spring Data may support reactive repositories for relational databases with the new Spring Data JDBC module.

We have also covered the current options for integrating blocking drivers or repositories into a reactive application—we have learned a lot! However, we have only scratched the surface of data persistence as this is a vast topic that cannot possibly be covered within one chapter.

At the beginning of this chapter, we mentioned the dual nature of databases—static data storage and streams of messages with data updates. The next chapter explores reactive systems and reactive programming in the context of messaging systems such as Kafka and RabbitMQ.

Scaling Up with Cloud Streams

8

The previous chapters taught us how a reactive programming paradigm can become a pleasure to work with when using Reactor 3. So far, we have learned how to build a reactive web application using Spring WebFlux and Spring Data Reactive. This robust combination makes it possible to build an application that is capable of handling a high load while also providing the efficient resource utilization, a low memory footprint, low latency, and high throughput.

However, this is not the end of the possibilities that come with the Spring ecosystem. In this chapter, we are going to learn how to improve our application using the features offered by the Spring Cloud ecosystem as well as learning how to build a complete reactive system using **Spring Cloud Streams**. In addition, we are going to see what the RSocket library is and how it can help us develop fast streaming systems. Finally, this chapter also covers the **Spring Cloud Function** module, which simplifies the construction of a cloud-native reactive system based on reactive programming and backpressure support.

In this chapter, we will cover the following topics:

- The role of message brokers in reactive systems
- The role of Spring Cloud Streams in reactive systems with Spring Framework
- Serverless reactive systems with Spring Cloud Function
- RSocket as an application protocol for asynchronous, low-latency message passing

Message brokers as the key to message-driven systems

If we remember from Chapter 1, *Why Reactive Spring?*, the essence of reactive systems is in message-driven communication. Moreover, the previous chapters made it clear that by applying reactive programming techniques, we can write async interactions for interprocess/cross-service communication. In addition, by using the Reactive Streams specification, we are equipped to manage backpressure as well as failures in an asynchronous manner. Gathering all these features, we are capable of building a high-grained reactive application within one computer. Unfortunately, a one-node application has its constraints, which are expressed in hardware limitations. First of all, it is impossible to provide new computation resources such as additional CPU, RAM, and hard drive/SSD without shutting down the whole system. No benefit is gained from doing this, since users can be distributed over the world, so the overall user experience is different.

 Here, *different user experiences* refers to the different latency distribution that directly depends on the distance between the application's server location and the user's location.

Such restrictions may be solved by splitting a monolithic application into microservices. The central idea of this technique is aimed at reaching an elastic system with straightforward location transparency. However, this way of building applications exposes a new horizon of problems, such as service management, monitoring, and painless scaling.

Server-side load balancing

In the earliest stages of distributed system development, one of the ways to achieve location transparency and elasticity was to use external load balancers, such as HAProxy/Nginx, as an entry point on top of the group of replicas or as a central load balancer for the whole system. Consider the following diagram:

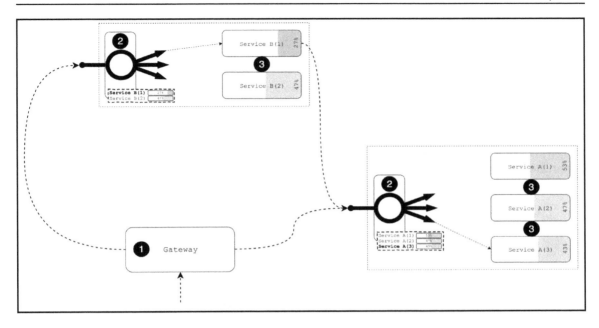

Diagram 8.1 Example of load balancing with external service

Each section of the numbered diagram is explained as follows:

1. Here, we have a service that plays the role of the gateway and orchestrates all users' requests. As we may see, the gateway makes two calls to **Service A** and **Service B**. Suppose that **Service A** plays the role of access control if the first call verifies that the given access token is correct or checks the presence of the valid authorization to access the gateway. Once the access is checked, the second call is performed, and that may include an execution of business logic on **Service B**, which may require an additional permission check as a result, therefore calling access control again.

2. This is the schematic representation of the load balancer. To enable auto-scaling, the load balancer may collect metrics such as the number of open connections, which may give the state of the overall load on that service. Alternatively, the load balancer may collect response latencies and make some additional assumptions about the service's health status based on that. Combining this information with additional periodical health checking, the load balancer may invoke a third-party mechanism for allocating additional resources on spikes in the load or de-allocating redundant nodes when the load decreases.

3. This demonstrates the particular instances of the services grouped under a dedicated load balancer **(2)**. Here, each service may work independently on separate nodes or machines.

As we can see from the diagram, the load balancer plays the role of the registry of available instances. For each group of services, there is a dedicated load balancer that manages the load among all instances. In turn, the load balancer may initiate a scaling process based on the overall group load and available metrics. For example, when there is a spike in user activity, new instances may be dynamically added to the group, so the increased load is handled. In turn, when the load decreases, the load balancer (as the metrics holder) may send a notification stating that there are redundant instances in the group.

 Note that, for the purpose of this book, we are going to skip autoscaling techniques. However, we will cover the monitoring and health-checking features that Spring Framework 5 offers in `Chapter 10`, *And, Finally, Release It.*

However, there are a few known issues with that solution. First of all, under a high load, the load balancer might become a hotspot in the system. Recalling Amdahl's Law, we might remember that the load balancer becomes a point of contention, and the underlying group of services cannot handle more requests than the load balancer can. In turn, the cost of serving the load balancer might be high, since each dedicated load balancer requires a separate powerful machine or virtual machine. Moreover, it might require an additional backup machine with the load balancer installed. Finally, the load balancer should also be managed and monitored. This may result in some extra expenses for infrastructure administration.

 In general, server-side load balancing is a technique that has been verified by time and may be used for many cases. Although it has its limitations, it is a reliable solution nowadays. To learn more about techniques and use-cases, just check out the following link: `https://aws.amazon.com/ru/blogs/devops/introducing-application-load-balancer-unlocking-and-optimizing-architectures/`.

Client-side load balancing with Spring Cloud and Ribbon

Fortunately, the Spring Cloud ecosystem comes to the rescue and tries to address the issue when a server-side load balancer becomes a hot-point in a system. Instead of providing a workaround for the external load balancer, the Spring team decided to follow Netflix's best practices of building distributed systems. One of the ways of achieving scalability and location transparency is through client-side load balancing.

The idea of client-side load balancing is straightforward and means that a service communicates through a sophisticated client that is aware of the available instances of a target service so that it may balance the load among them easily:

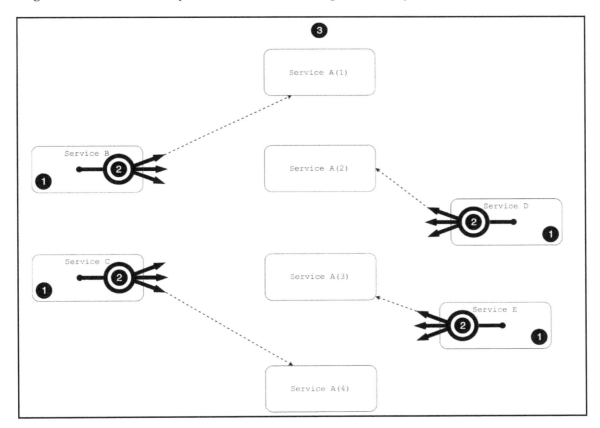

Diagram 8.2. Example of the client-side load-balancing pattern

In the preceding diagram, the numbered points mean the following:

1. This point depicts a few services that communicate with **Service A**.
2. These are the client-side load balancers. As we can see now, the load balancer is a part of each service. Consequently, all coordination should be done before the actual HTTP call occurs.
3. The actual group of **Service A** instances is depicted here.

In this example, all callers execute a call to the different replicas of **Service A**. Even though the technique provides independence from a dedicated external load balancer (thereby providing better scalability), it has its limitations. First of all, the mentioned load-balancing technique is client-side balancing. Consequently, each caller is responsible for balancing all requests locally by choosing an instance of the target service. This helps to avoid a single point of failure, thereby providing better scalability. On the other hand, information about available services should somehow be accessible to the rest of the services in the system.

To become familiar with the modern techniques used for service discovery, we are considering one of the popular libraries in the Java and Spring ecosystem—Ribbon. The Ribbon library is an implementation of the client-side load balancer pattern created by Netflix. Ribbon offers two common techniques to provide access to the list of available services. The simplest way of providing such information is through a static preconfigured list of services' addresses. This technique is depicted in the following diagram:

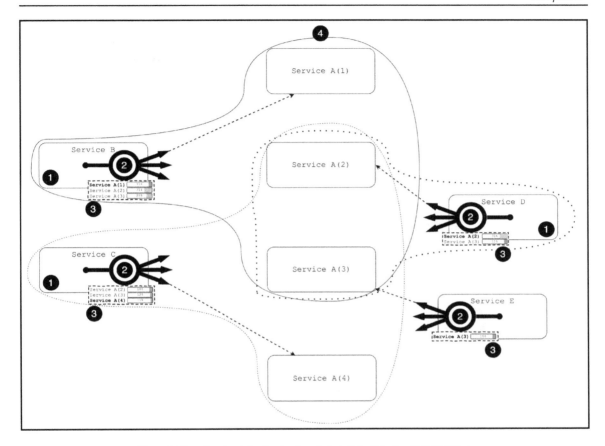

Diagram 8.3. Preconfigured static list of services for each client-side load balancing with Netflix Ribbon.

In the aforementioned diagram, the numbered points mean the following:

1. This point depicts a few services that communicate with **Service A**.
2. These are client-side load balancers. Each service has access to the particular group of service instances.
3. A representation of the internal list of pre-configured **Service A** instances. Here, each caller service independently measures the load on each target **Service A** instance and applies a balancing process concerning that. The bold service name in the list also refers to the current execution target instance of **Service A**.
4. The actual group of **Service A** instances is depicted here.

In the preceding diagram, the shapes with different borders outline areas of knowledge of different callers. Unfortunately, the client-side load balancing technique has its gaps. First of all, there is no coordination between client-side balancers, so it is possible that all callers may decide to call the same instance and overload it, as depicted in this diagram:

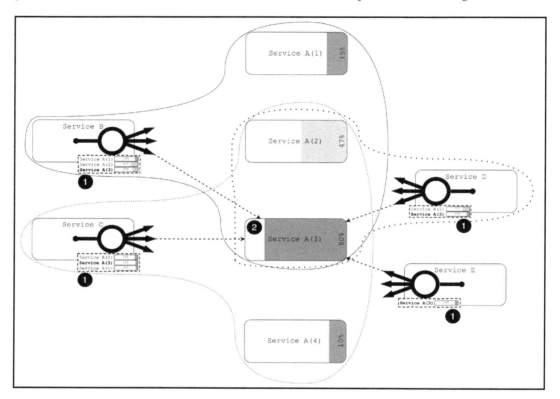

Diagram 8.4. The representation of the problematic points with unsynchronized client-side load balancing

Each section of the numbered diagram is explained as follows:

1. This refers to the caller services with their list of pre-configured **Service A** instances. Local load measurements are different across services. Consequently, in this example, the case is shown in which all services call the same target instance of **Service A**. This may cause an unexpected spike in the load.

2. This is one of the **Service A** instances. Here, the actual load on the instance is different than what each caller service assumed based on the local measurements.

Moreover, such a simple way of managing the load with a static list of service instances is far from reactive system requirements, mainly from the elastic load management standpoint.

 From the perspective of the reactive manifesto, *elasticity* refers to the ability to increase dynamically system throughput in response to the growing demand and decreased resource usage when the demand diminishes.

As a solution, Ribbon is capable of integrating with a service registry such as Eureka, so the registry service is continuously updating the list of available service replicas. Consider the following diagram:

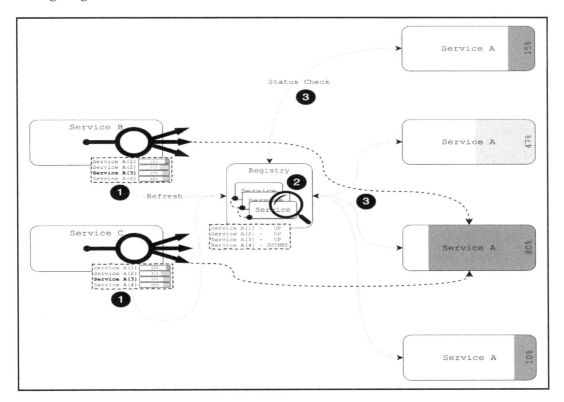

Diagram 8.5. Example of dynamic updating of the available services list

In the preceding diagram, the numbered points mean the following:

1. This refers to caller services with the list of available **Service A** instances. Here, to keep the list of alive instances in **Service A** up to date, the client-side balancer refreshes that list periodically and grabs the latest information from the registry **(2)**.
2. This is the representation of the registry service. As we can see here, the registry service keeps its own list of discovered services and their statuses.
3. The dotted lines represent the heartbeat of the services or health status check requests.

As may be noticed from the preceding diagram, the problem of coordination for client-side load balancers remains. In this case, the registry is responsible for keeping a list of healthy service instances and continuously updating them at runtime. Here, both the client-side balancer and the registry service may hold the information about a load of target service instances, and the client-side balancer may periodically synchronize internal load statistics with the load collected by a registry service. Furthermore, all interested parties can access that information and execute their load balancing based on that information. This way of managing the list of available services is much broader than the previous one, making it possible to update the list of available destinations dynamically.

First of all, that technique works well for a small cluster of services. However, the discovery of the dynamic services using a shared registry is far from ideal. As with server-side load balancing, a classic registry service such as Eureka becomes a single point of failure because there is a huge effort required to keep the information of the system's state updated and accurate. For instance, when the state of the cluster rapidly changes, the information about registered services may become outdated. To track a service's health status, service instances usually send heartbeat messages periodically. Alternatively, a registry may execute a health check request periodically. In both cases, very frequent status updates may consume an unreasonably high percentage of cluster resources. Therefore, the duration between health checks usually lasts from a couple of seconds to a few minutes (the default duration for Eureka is 30 seconds). Consequently, a registry may propose a service instance that was healthy during the last health check but has already been destroyed. Hence, the more dynamic a cluster is, the harder it is to track services' statuses accurately using a centralized registry.

In addition, all balancing is still taking place on the client side. This leads to the same problem of uncoordinated load balancing, which means that there is a chance that the actual load on the service can be unbalanced. Moreover, accurate and honest request coordination provided by the client-side load balancers based on service metrics in a distributed system is another challenge, which is probably even harder than the previous one. Hence, we have to find a better solution to build a reactive system.

In this section, we have discussed a very popular Spring Cloud ecosystem discovery/registry service: Eureka. For more information on this, see the following link: `https://cloud.spring.io/spring-cloud-netflix/`. In general, client-side load balancing is an efficient technique for distributing a load between target service instances.

Also, there are algorithms that make client-side balancing predictable, so most of the issues described here might be avoided. To learn more, please see the following: `https://www.youtube.com/watch?v=6NdxUY1La2I`.

Message brokers as an elastic, reliable layer for message transferring

Fortunately, a reactive manifesto offers a solution for problems related to server-side and client-side balancing:

> *"Employing explicit message-passing enables load management, elasticity, and flow control by shaping and monitoring the message queues in the system and applying back-pressure when necessary."*

This statement can be interpreted as the employment of an independent message brokers for the purpose of transferring messages. Consider the following diagram:

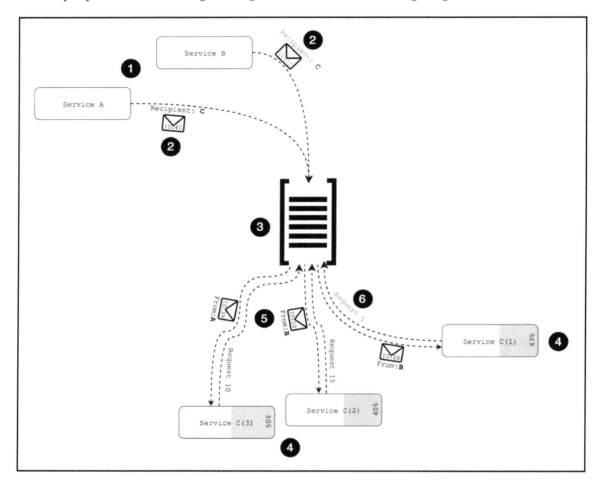

Diagram 8.6. Example of load balancing with message queue as a service

In the preceding diagram, the numbered points mean the following:

1. These are the caller services. As we can see here, caller services only know the location of the message queue and the recipient's service name, which allows the decoupling of the caller service from the actual target service instance. This communication model is similar to what we have with server-side balancing. However, one of the significant differences here is asynchronous behavior in communication between the caller and the final recipient. Here, we do not have to keep the connection open while the request is processing.

2. This is the outgoing message representation. In this example, an outgoing message may hold the information about the recipient's service name and the message correlation ID.

3. This is the representation of a message queue. Here, the message queue works as an independent service and allows users to send messages to the group of **Service C** instances so that any available instance may process messages.

4. This is the recipient's service instances. Each **Service C** instance has the same average load because each worker is capable of controlling backpressure by showing a demand **(6)** so that the message queue can send incoming messages **(5)**.

First of all, all requests are sent over the message queue, which may then send them to the available worker. Moreover, the message queue may keep the message persisted until one of the workers has asked for new messages. In this way, the message queue knows how many interested parties there are in the system and can manage the load based on that information. In turn, each worker is capable of managing backpressure internally and sending demands depending on machine possibilities. Just by monitoring the number of pending messages, we can increase the count of active workers. Furthermore, just by relying on the amount of pending workers demands, we can reduce dormant workers.

Although a message queue solves the problem of client-side load balancing, it might seem that we are getting back to a very similar solution to server-side load balancing that we had earlier, and the message queue might become a hot point in the system. However, this is not true. First of all, the communication model here is a bit different. Instead of searching for available services and making the decision of whom to send the request to, the message queue just puts the incoming message into the queue. Then, when the worker declares the intent to receive messages, the enqueued messages are transferred. Therefore, there are two separate, possibly independent stages here. These are as follows:

- Receiving the messages and putting them into the queue (which may be very fast)
- Transferring data when consumers show demand

On the other hand, we may replicate the message queue for each group of recipients. Therefore, we may enhance our system's scalability and masterfully avoid any bottlenecks. Consider the following diagram:

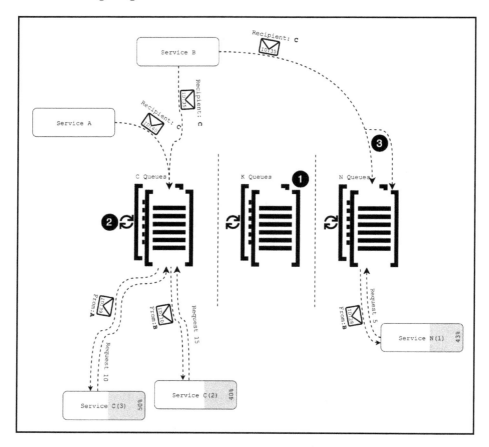

Diagram 8.7. Example of elasticity with message queues as a service

Each section of the numbered diagram is explained as follows:

1. This represents the message queue with enabled data replication. In this example, we have a few replicated message queues that are dedicated per group of the service instances.

2. This represents the state synchronization between replicas for the same group of recipients.

3. This represents possible load balancing (for example, client-side balancing) between replicas.

Here, we have a queue per recipients group and a replication set for each queue in that group. However, the load may vary from group to group, so one group may be overloaded, and another may simply lay dormant without any work, which may be wasteful. Consequently, instead of having the message queue as a separate service, we might rely on a message broker that supports virtual queues. By doing that, we can reduce the cost of the infrastructure since the load on the system may decrease so that one message broker may be shared between different recipients' groups. In turn, message broker may be a reactive system as well. Consequently, the message broker can be elastic, resilient, and can share its internal state employing asynchronous, non-blocking message passing. Consider the following diagram:

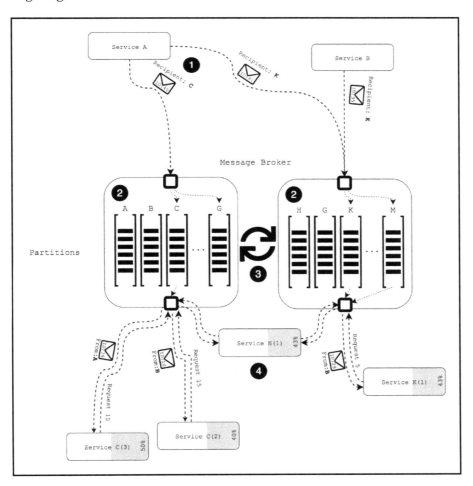

Diagram 8.8. Elasticity with distributed message broker

In the previous diagram, the numbered points mean the following:

1. This is the caller service with a partitioned client-side load balancer. In general, the message broker may use the previously mentioned techniques to organize the discovery of partitions and sharing information with its clients.
2. This refers to the representation of the message broker partition. In this example, each partition has a number of assigned recipients (topics). In turn, along with partitioning, each part may also have a replica.
3. This refers to the rebalancing of the partition. A message broker may employ an additional rebalancing mechanism, so in the case of new recipients or new nodes in the cluster, such a message broker may scale easily.
4. This is an example of the recipient, which may listen to messages from different partitions.

The preceding diagram depicts a possible design of the message broker as a system that can be a reliable backbone for the target application. As may be noticed from the preceding diagram, a message broker may hold as many virtual queues as the system requires. Modern message brokers adopt techniques for state sharing, such as eventual consistency and message multicasting, consequently achieving elasticity out of the box. Message brokers can be a reliable layer for asynchronous message transferral with backpressure support and replayability guarantees.

 For example, a message broker's reliability may be achieved by employing an effective technique for message replication and persistence on fast storages. However, experience may vary, since the performance of such message brokers may be slower than the performance of those message brokers that do not use message persistence or in cases when messages are sent peer-to-peer.

What does this mean for us? It means that in the case of the crash of the message broker, all messages are available, hence once the messaging layer becomes available, all undelivered messages can find their destinations.

In summary, we may conclude that the message broker technique improves the overall scalability of the system. In this case, we may build an elastic system easily just because the message broker can behave as a reactive system. Hence, communication is no longer a bottleneck.

The market of message brokers

In spite of the fact that the idea of employing message brokers may be a dream for most business needs, the actual implementation of our own message broker might turn out to be a nightmare. Fortunately, the market nowadays offers us a few powerful open source solutions. Some of the most popular message brokers and messaging platforms include RabbitMQ, Apache Kafka, Apache Pulsar, Apache RocketMQ, NATS, NSQ, and so on.

 We may find comparisons of the message brokers by following the following links: Apache RocketMQ versus Apache Kafka at `https://rocketmq.apache.org/docs/motivation/#rocketmq-vs-activemq-vs-kafka`; RabbitMQ versus Kafka versus NSQ at `https://stackshare.io/stackups/kafka-vs-nsq-vs-rabbitmq`; and Apache Pulsar versus Apache Kafka at `https://streaml.io/blog/pulsar-streaming-queuing`.

Spring Cloud Streams as a bridge to Spring Ecosystem

All of the previously mentioned solutions are competitive with one other and have their advantages, such as wins in low-latency or better guarantees of message delivery or persistence.

Nonetheless, this book is about the reactive possibilities in the Spring Ecosystem, so it would be valuable to get an understanding of what Spring offers for a painless integration with message brokers.

One of the powerful ways of building robust message-driven systems using Spring Cloud is through Spring Cloud Streams. Spring Cloud Streams provides a simplified programming model for async cross-service messaging. In turn, the Spring Cloud Streams module is built on top of the Spring Integration and Spring Message modules, which are the fundamental abstractions over proper integration with external services and straightforward asynchronous messaging. Moreover, Spring Cloud Streams give the ability to build an elastic application without having to deal with over-complicated configurations and without needing an in-depth knowledge of a particular message broker.

 Unfortunately, only a few message brokers have the appropriate support in Spring Framework. At the moment of writing, Spring Cloud Streams only provides integration with RabbitMQ and Apache Kafka.

To get an understanding of the fundamentals of building reactive systems with Spring Cloud Streams, we are going to upgrade the reactive chat application that we built in `Chapter 7`, *Reactive Database Access*, to a new reactive Spring Cloud Stack.

First of all, we are going to start by recapping on the design of our application, which consists of three conceptual parts. The first part is a connector service called `ChatService`. In our case, this is the implementation of communication with the Gitter service, which is a server-sent events stream. In turn, that stream of messages is shared between `ChatController`, which is responsible for transferring those messages directly to final users, and `StatisticService`, which is responsible for storing messages in the database and recalculating statistics based on changes. Previously, all three parts consisted of one monolith application. Consequently, each component in the system was connected through the use of a Spring Framework Dependency Injection. Moreover, asynchronous, non-blocking messaging was supported with Reactor 3 reactive types. The first thing that we need to understand is whether Spring Cloud Streams allows decomposing a monolith application into microservices while allowing to use reactive types for communication between components.

Fortunately, starting with Spring Cloud 2, there is direct support for communication via Reactor types. Previously, location transparency might relate to the loose-coupling of components within the monolith application. Using the **Inversion of Control (IoC)**, each component can access the component interface without any knowledge of the implementation. In the Cloud Ecosystem, along with knowing access interface, we should know the domain name (component name) or, in our case, the name of the dedicated queue. As a replacement for communication over interfaces, Spring Cloud Streams provide two conceptual annotations for wiring communication between services.

 To learn more about *Location Transparency*, please see the following link: `http://wiki.c2.com/?LocationTransparency`.

The first conceptual annotation is the `@Output` annotation. This annotation defines the queue name to which the message should be delivered. The second conceptual annotation is the `@Input` annotation which defines the queue from which messages should listen. This method of interaction between services might replace our interfaces, so instead of invocating the method, we may rely on sending messages to the particular queue. Let's consider the changes that we have to apply to our application in order to allow sending messages to the message broker:

```
@SpringBootApplication                    // (1)
@EnableBinding(Source.class)              // (1.1)
@EnableConfigurationProperties(...)       //
```

```
/* @Service */                                          // (1.2)
public class GitterService                              //
    implements ChatService<MessageResponse>  {          //

    ...                                                 // (2)

    @StreamEmitter                                      // (3)
    @Output(Source.OUTPUT)                              // (3.1)
    public Flux<MessageResponse> getMessagesStream() { ... }  //

    @StreamEmitter                                      // (4)
    @Output(Source.OUTPUT)                              //
    public Flux<MessageResponse> getLatestMessages() { ... }  //

    public static void main(String[] args) {            // (5)
        SpringApplication.run(GitterService.class, args);     //
    }                                                   //
}                                                       //
```

 Note that, along with the actual implementation, the preceding code shows the code differences. Here, `/* Commented Text */` refers to removed code-lines, and `Bold Underlined Text` means a new one. A non-styled code means that nothing has changed there.

In the preceding code, the numbered points mean the following:

1. This is the `SpringBootApplication` declaration. At point `(1.1)`, we define Spring Cloud Streams as an `@EnableBinding` annotation that enables underlying integration with the streaming infrastructure (for instance, integration with Apache Kafka). In turn, we removed the `@Service` annotation `(1.2)`, since we migrated from the monolith application to a distributed one. Now we can run that component as a small independent application and enable better scaling in that way.
2. This is the list of fields and constructors, which are left unchanged.
3. This refers to the messages' `Flux` declaration. That method returns an infinitive stream of messages from Gitter. Here, the key-role plays `@StreamEmitter` because it establishes that the given source is a reactive source. Consequently, to define a destination channel, `@Output` is used here, accepting the name of the channel. Note that the destination channel's name must be in the list of the bound channel at line `(1.1)`.

4. Here, `getLatestMessages` returns a finite stream of the latest Gitter messages and sends them to the destination channel.

5. This refers to the `main` method declaration, which is used to bootstrap a Spring Boot application.

As may be noticed from the example, there have been no significant changes made from the business logic perspective. In turn, a great deal of infrastructural logic was added here just by applying a few Spring Cloud Streams annotations. First of all, by using `@SpringBootApplication`, we defined our small service as a separate Spring Boot application. By applying `@Output(Source.OUTPUT)`, we defined the name of the destination queue in a message broker.

Finally, `@EnableBinding`, `@StreamEmitter` means that our application is bound to a message broker and the `getMessagesStream()` and `getLatestMessages()` methods are invoked at the application's start point.

 To learn more about `@StreamEmitter` and its restrictions, please see the following link: `https://docs.spring.io/spring-cloud-stream/docs/ current/reference/htmlsingle/#_reactive_sources`. Also, to get a basic understanding of Spring Cloud Stream's annotation model, please see this link: `https://docs.spring.io/spring-cloud-stream/docs/current/ reference/htmlsingle/#_programming_model`.

In addition to Java annotations, we should provide the configuration of Spring Cloud Stream's bindings. This may be done by providing Spring Application properties such as the following (`application.yaml`, in that case):

```
spring.cloud.stream:                           //
   bindings:                                    //
      output:                                   // (1)
         destination: Messages                  // (2)
         producer:                              // (3)
            requiredGroups: statistic, ui       // (4)
```

In the previous example code, at point (1), we specified the bindings' key, which is the name of the channel defined in `Source.OUTPUT`. By doing so, we may access `org.springframework.cloud.stream.config.BindingProperties` and configure the name of the destination in the message broker (2). Along with that, we may configure how our producer should behave (3). For example, we may configure a list of recipients that should receive messages with an *at least once* delivery guarantee (4).

By running the previous code as a separate application, we may see that the dedicated queue inside the message broker starts receiving messages. On the other hand, as we might remember from Chapter 7, *Reactive Database Access,* our chat application has two central message consumers: a controller layer and a statistic service. As the second step in the modification of the system, we are going to update the statistic service. In our application, the statistic service is a bit more than a plain consumer; it is responsible for updating statistics based on database changes and then sending it to the controller layer. This means that that service is a Processor, since it plays the role of Source and Sink at the same time. Hence, we have to provide an ability to consume messages from the message broker as well as sending it to the message broker. Consider the following code:

```java
@SpringBootApplication                                          // (1)
@EnableBinding(Processor.class)                                 //
/* @Service */                                                  //
public class DefaultStatisticService                            //
   implements StatisticService {                                //

   ...                                                          // (2)

   @StreamListener                                              // (3)
   @Output(Processor.OUTPUT)                                    //
   public Flux<UsersStatisticVM> updateStatistic(              //
      @Input(Processor.INPUT) Flux<MessageResponse> messagesFlux  // (3.1)
   ) { ... }                                                    //

   ...                                                          // (2)

   public static void main(String[] args) {                    // (4)
      SpringApplication.run(DefaultStatisticService.class, args);  //
   }                                                            //
}
```

Each section of the numbered code is explained as follows:

1. This is the @SpringBootApplication declaration. Here, as in the previous example, we replaced @Service with the @EnableBinding annotation. In contrast to the configuration of the GitterService component, we use the Processor interface which declares that the StatisticService component consumes data from the message broker as well as sends them to the message broker.
2. This is the part of the code that is left unchanged.

3. This is the processor's method declaration. Here, the `updateStatistic` method accepts a `Flux`, which provides access to the incoming message from the message broker's channel. We have to explicitly define that the given method listens to the message broker by providing an `@StreamListener` annotation along with the `@Input` annotation declaration.

4. This is the `main` method declaration, which is used to bootstrap the Spring Boot application.

As may be noticed, we use Spring Cloud Streams annotations just to mark that the input `Flux` and output `Flux` are streams from/to the defined queues. In that example, `@StreamListener` allows the name of the virtual queue (from/to which messages are consumed/sent) to correspond to the name defined in the `@Input`/`@Output` annotations while pre-configured interfaces are bound in the `@EnableBinding` annotation. As seen in the preceding example, along with producers configuration, we may configure the declared input and output in the same generic way using the same application's properties (YAML configuration, in this case):

```
spring.cloud.stream:                        //
   bindings:                                //
      input:                                //  (1)
         destination: Messages              //
         group: statistic                   //  (2)
      output:                               //
         producer:                          //
            requiredGroups: ui              //
         destination: Statistic             //
```

Spring Cloud Stream provides flexibility in the configuration of communication with the message broker. Here, at point (1) we define `input` which is, in fact, a consumer's configuration. Additionally (2), we have to define the name of the `group` which represents the name of the group of recipients in the message broker.

To learn more about the available configurations for Spring Cloud Stream, please visit the following link `https://docs.spring.io/spring-cloud-stream/docs/current/reference/htmlsingle/#_configuration_options`.

Finally, after the preparation of emitters we have to update our `InfoResource` component in the following way:

```
@RestController                                                    // (1)
@RequestMapping("/api/v1/info")                                    //
@EnableBinding({MessagesSource.class, StatisticSource.class})      // (1.1)
@SpringBootApplication                                             //
public class InfoResource {                                        //

    ...                                                            // (2)
/*  public InfoResource(                                           // (3)
        ChatService<MessageResponse> chatService,                  //
        StatisticService statisticService                          //
    ) { */                                                         // (3.1)
    @StreamListener                                                //
    public void listen(                                            //
        @Input(MessagesSource.INPUT) Flux<MessageResponse> messages, //
        @Input(StatisticSource.INPUT)                              //
        Flux<UsersStatisticVM> statistic                           //
    ) {                                                            //

    /*  Flux.mergeSequential(                                      // (4)
            chatService.getMessagesAfter("")                       //
                        .flatMapIterable(Function.identity()),     //
            chatService.getMessagesStream()                        //
        )                                                          //
        .publish(flux -> Flux.merge( ... */                       //

            messages.map(MessageMapper::toViewModelUnit)           // (5)
                    .subscribeWith(messagesStream);                //
            statistic.subscribeWith(statisticStream);              //

    /*  ))                                                         // (4)
        .subscribe(); */                                           //
    }                                                              //

    ...                                                            // (2)

    public static void main(String[] args) {                      // (6)
        SpringApplication.run(InfoResource.class, args);           //
    }                                                              //
}                                                                  //
```

In the preceding code, the numbered points mean the following:

1. This is the `@SpringBootAppliction` definition. As we may have noticed, `@EnableBinding` accepts two custom bindable interfaces here with the separate input channel's configurations for statistics and messages.
2. This is the part of the code that is left unchanged.
3. This is the `.listen` method declaration. As we can see, the constructor that accepted two interfaces now accepts `Fluxes` annotated by the `@Input` annotation.
4. This is the modified logic. Here, we do not need a manual stream merging and sharing anymore since we have moved that responsibility to the message broker.
5. This is the point in which we subscribe to the given streams of statistics and messages. At that point, all incoming messages are cached into `ReplayProcessor`. Note that the mentioned cache is local and to achieve better scalability, the distributed one may be employed instead.
6. This is the `main` method declaration, which is used to bootstrap the Spring Boot application.

 To learn more about possible integration with distributed caches such as **Hazelcast**, please see the available extension in the *Reactor-Addons module*: `https://github.com/reactor/reactor-addons/tree/master/reactor-extra/src/main/java/reactor/cache`.

Here, we are listening to two separate queues. Again, employing a message broker gives us transparent decoupling from both `GitterService` and `StatisticService`. In turn, when we deal with Spring Cloud Stream, we have to remember that the `@StreamListener` annotation is only applicable to methods. Consequently, we have to hack that element by applying `@StreamListener` on top of the void method, which is invoked when a connection with the message broker has been wired.

To get a better understanding of the internals of custom bindable interfaces, let's consider the following code:

```
interface MessagesSource {                    //
    String INPUT = "messages";                // (1)
                                              //
    @Input(INPUT)                             // (2)
    SubscribableChannel input();              // (3)
}                                             //

interface StatisticSource {                   //
    String INPUT = "statistic";               // (1)
                                              //
    @Input(INPUT)                             // (2)
    SubscribableChannel input();              // (3)
}                                             //
```

Each section of the numbered code is explained here:

1. This is the String constant that represents the name of the bound channel.
2. This is the @Input annotation that declares that the annotated method provides MessageChannel, through which incoming messages enter the application.
3. This is the method that indicates the type of MessageChannel. In the case of the bindable interface for the message consumer, we have to provide SubscribableChannel, which extends MessageChannel with two additional methods for asynchronous message listening.

Identically to the previous cases, we have to provide similar properties in the local application.yaml:

```
spring.cloud.stream:
    bindings:
        statistic:
            destination: Statistic
            group: ui
        messages:
            destination: Messages
            group: ui
```

By including all of the puzzles in the diagram, we get the following architecture of the system:

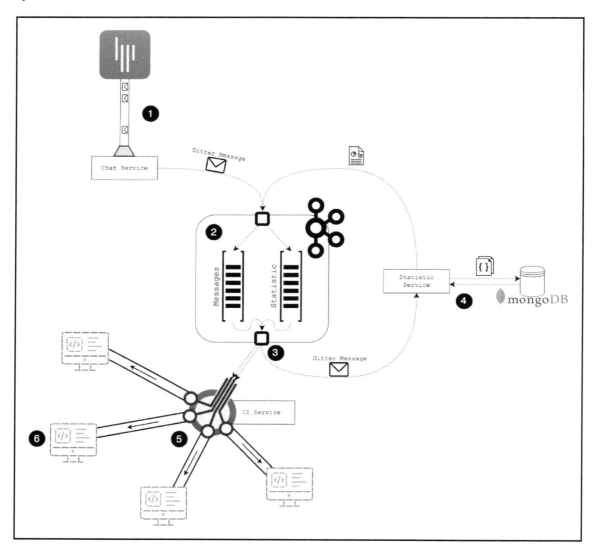

Diagram 8.9. Example of a distributed chat application

In the preceding diagram, the numbered points mean the following:

1. This is the representation of GitterService. As it may be noticed, GitterService is tightly coupled with Gitter API and Message Broker **(2)** (Apache Kafka in this case). However, there is no direct dependency on the external services.

2. This is the message broker representation. Here, we have two virtual queues inside. Note that the mentioned representation does not expose specific configurations such as replication and partitioning.

3. At this point, the message broker demultiplexes messages to the UI Service (InfoResource) and StatisticService.

4. This is the StatisticService representation. As it might be noticed, the service listens to incoming messages for the message broker, stores them in MongoDB, does some statistic aggregations, and produces an update result.

5. Finally, both queues are consumed by the UI Service, which demultiplexes all messages in turn to all subscribed clients.

6. This is the web-browser representation. Here, the clients of the UI Service are web-browsers, which receive all updates through the HTTP connection.

As we may have noticed from the preceding diagram, our application is fully decoupled at the component level. For example, GitterService, StatisticService, and the UI service run as a separate application (which may be run on separate machines) and send messages to the message broker. In addition, the Spring Cloud Streams module supports Project Reactor and its programming model which means it follows the Reactive Streams specification and enables backpressure control, hence, offers higher application's resilience. With such a setup, each service can scale independently. Therefore, we may achieve a reactive system, which is the primary goal of moving to Spring Cloud Streams.

Reactive programming in the cloud

Even though Spring Cloud Streams provide a simplified way of achieving a distributed reactive system, we still have to deal with the list of configurations (for example, the configuration of destinations) to deal with the specifics of the Spring Cloud Streams programming model, and so on. Another significant problem is reasoning about flow. As we may remember from `Chapter 2`, *Reactive Programming in Spring - Basic Concepts*, one of the main reasons for inventing reactive extensions (as a concept of asynchronous programming) was to achieve a tool that hides complex asynchronous data flow behind the functional chain of operators. Even though we can develop specific components and we can specify the interaction between components, the digging into the whole picture of the interaction between them might become a puzzle. Similarly, in reactive systems, understanding the flow interactions between microservices is a crucial part that is hard to achieve without specific tools.

Fortunately, Amazon invented its AWS Lambda in 2014. This expanded on new possibilities for reactive system development. This is mentioned on the official web page for that service:

> *"AWS Lambda is a serverless compute service (*`https://aws.amazon.com/serverless`*) that runs your code in response to events and automatically manages the underlying compute resources for you (*`https://aws.amazon.com/lambda/features`*)."*

AWS Lambda allows us to build small, independent, and scalable transformations. Moreover, we gained the ability to decouple the development life cycle of business logic from a particular data flow. Finally, a user-friendly interface allows us to use each function for building an entire business flow independently.

Amazon was a pioneer in that area, inspiring many cloud providers to adopt the same technique. Fortunately, Pivotal was one of the adopters of that technique as well.

Spring Cloud Data Flow

In early 2016, Spring Cloud introduced a new module called Spring Cloud Data Flow, with the official module description at this link: `https://cloud.spring.io/spring-cloud-dataflow`:

> *"Spring Cloud Data Flow is a toolkit for building data integration and real-time data-processing pipelines."*

To generalize, the main idea of that module is to achieve separation between the development of functional business transformations and the actual interaction between developed components. In other words, this is the separation between functions and their composition in the business flow. To solve this problem, Spring Cloud Data Flow gives us a user-friendly web interface which makes it possible to upload deployable Spring Boot applications. It then sets up data flows by using uploaded artifacts and deploying the composed pipe to the chosen platform, such as Cloud Foundry, Kubernetes, Apache YARN or Mesos. Moreover, Spring Cloud Data Flow provides an extensive list of out-of-the-box connectors to sources (DBs, message queue, and files), different built-in processors for data transformation, and sinks, which represent different ways of storing results.

> To learn more about supported sources, processors, and sinks, please visit the following links: `https://cloud.spring.io/spring-cloud-task-app-starters/` and `https://cloud.spring.io/spring-cloud-stream-app-starters/`.

As previously mentioned, Spring Cloud Data Flow employs the idea of stream processing. Hence, all deployed flows are built on top of the Spring Cloud Stream module, and all communication is done via distributed, elastic message brokers such as Kafka or distributed highly-scalable variants of RabbitMQ.

To understand the power of distributed reactive programming with Spring Cloud Data Flow, we are going to build a payments processing flow. As we might already know, payment processing is quite complicated. However, here is a simplified diagram of this process:

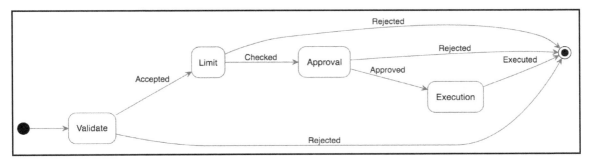

Diagram 8.10. The flow diagram of payment processing

As we may have noticed, a user's payment has to transit through a few vital steps such as validation, account limits checking, and payment approvals. In Chapter 6, *WebFlux Async Non-Blocking Communication*, we built a similar application in which one service orchestrated the entire flow. Although the whole interaction was distributed among asynchronous calls to several independent microservices, the state of the flow was held by one service within Reactor 3 internals. This means that in the case of a failure of that service, recovering the state might be challenging.

Fortunately, Spring Cloud Data Flow relies on Spring Cloud Streams, which rely on a resilient message broker. Consequently, in case of failure, the message broker will not be acknowledged about message receiving, so the message will, therefore, be redelivered to another executor without additional effort.

Since we have obtained a basic understanding of the core principles of the internals of Spring Cloud Data Flow and the business requirements for Payment Flow, we may implement that service using that technology's stack.

First of all, we have to define the entry point, which is usually accessible as an HTTP endpoint. Spring Cloud Data Flow offers an HTTP source that may be defined with the **Spring Cloud Data Flow DSL**, as in the following example:

```
SendPaymentEndpoint=Endpoint: http --path-pattern=/payment --port=8080
```

The preceding example represents a small part of Spring Cloud Data Flow pipes DSL. In the following examples, we will define more samples of how to build the complete Spring Cloud Data Flow pipes. To learn more about Stream Pipeline DSL visit the following link at https://docs.spring.io/spring-cloud-dataflow/docs/current/reference/htmlsingle/#spring-cloud-dataflow-stream-intro-dsl.

Before starting any manipulations, ensure that all supported applications and tasks have already been registered at https://docs.spring.io/spring-cloud-dataflow/docs/current/reference/htmlsingle/#supported-apps-and-tasks.

In the preceding example, we defined a new data flow function, which represents all HTTP requests as a stream of messages. Consequently, we can react to them in a defined way.

The finest-grained application with Spring Cloud Function

After defining an HTTP endpoint, we have to validate the incoming message. Unfortunately, this part of the process holds actual business logic and requires a custom implementation of a stage of the flow. Fortunately, though, Spring Cloud Data Flow allows using custom Spring Cloud Stream applications as part of the process.

We will not go into detail about the implementation of the custom Spring Cloud Data Flow stage here. However, to learn more about the creation and registration of custom Spring Boot applications, follow these links:

- `https://docs.spring.io/spring-cloud-dataflow/payment/docs/current/reference/htmlsingle/#custom-applications`
- `https://docs.spring.io/spring-cloud-dataflow-samples/docs/current/reference/htmlsingle/#_custom_spring_cloud_stream_processor`

On the one hand, we can provide our own separate Spring Cloud Stream application with a custom validation logic. But, on the other hand, we still have to deal with all configurations, uber-jars, long startup time, and the rest of the problems related to the application deployment. Fortunately, those problems can be avoided with the Spring Cloud Function project.

The main aim of Spring Cloud Function is to promote business logic via functions. This project offers the ability to decouple custom business logic from the specifics of runtime. Hence, the same function might be reused in different ways and places.

To learn more about the features of the Spring Cloud Function project, please visit the following link: `https://github.com/spring-cloud/spring-cloud-function`.

Before we start working with Spring Cloud Function, we are going to cover the principal features of the Spring Cloud Function module in this section and get a better understanding of its internals.

At its core, Spring Cloud Function is an additional level of abstraction for applications that may be running on top of Spring Cloud Streams, AWS Lambda, or any other cloud platform using any communication transport.

By default, Spring Cloud Function has adapters for the configurable deployment of functions to AWS Lambda, Azure Functions, and Apache OpenWhisk. The main benefit of using Spring Cloud Function, as opposed to direct Java function's upload, is the possibility to use most Spring features, and not to depend on a particular cloud provider SDK.

The programming model offered by Spring Cloud Function is nothing more than a definition of one of the following Java classes—`java.utils.function.Function`, `java.utils.function.Supplier`, and `java.utils.function.Consume`. Furthermore, Spring Cloud Function can be used in different framework combinations. For example, we can create a Spring Boot application, which can be a platform for an element of the functions. In turn, some of them may be represented as an ordinary Spring `@Bean`:

```
@SpringBootApplication                                            // (1)
@EnableBinding(Processor.class)                                   // (1.1)
public class Application {                                        //

    @Bean                                                        // (2)
    public Function<                                             //
        Flux<Payment>,                                          //
        Flux<Payment>                                          //
    > validate() {                                              //
        return flux -> flux.map(value -> { ... });             // (2.1)
    }                                                          //

    public static void main(String[] args) {                   // (3)
        SpringApplication.run(Application.class, args);        //
    }                                                          //
}
```

In the preceding code, the numbered points mean the following:

1. This is the `@SpringBootApplication` declaration. As it might be noticed, we still have to define a minimal declaration for a Spring Boot application. Also, we use the `@EnableBinding` annotation with the `Processor` interface as a parameter. In such a combination, Spring Cloud identifies a bean at line `(2)` to be used as a message handler. Also, the *input* and *output* of the function are bound to the external destinations exposed by the `Processor` binding.

2. This shows `Function`, which transforms `Flux` into another `Flux` as a component of the IoC container. Here, at the point `(2.1)`, we declare a lambda for elements validation, which in turn is a higher-order function that accepts a stream and returns another.

3. This is the `main` method declaration, which is used to bootstrap a Spring Boot application.

As may be noticed from the preceding example, Spring Cloud Function supports different programming models. For example, message transformation with the support of Reactor 3 reactive types and Spring Cloud Streams, which exposes those streams to external destinations.

Furthermore, Spring Cloud Function is not limited to predefined functions. For example, it has a built-in runtime compiler that makes it possible to provide a function as a string in the properties' file, as shown in the following example:

```
spring.cloud.function:                                         // (1)
   compile:                                                    // (2)
      payments:                                                // (3)
         type: supplier                                        // (4)
         lambda: ()->Flux.just(new org.TestPayment())          // (5)
```

Each section of the numbered code is explained as follows:

1. This is the Spring Cloud Function properties namespace.
2. This is the namespace related to the runtime (on-the-fly) function compilation.
3. This is the definition of the key, which is the name of the function that is visible inside Spring IoC container. This plays the role of the file name for the compiled Java bytecode.
4. This is the definition of a type of function. The available options are `supplier/function/consumer`.
5. This is the lambda definition. As we can see, the supplier is defined as a `String` that is compiled into bytecode and stored in the filesystem. The compilation is possible with the support of the `spring-cloud-function-compiler` module. This has a built-in compiler as well as making it possible to store compiled functions as bytecode and adding them to `ClassLoad`.

The preceding example shows that Spring Cloud Function offers the ability to dynamically define and run functions without also having to have them pre-compiled. Such an ability may be used to implement **Function as a Service** (**FaaS**) capabilities in our software solution.

Along with that, Spring Cloud Function provides a module called `spring-cloud-function-task`, which allows running the mentioned functions in a pipe using the same properties file:

```
spring.cloud.function:
   task:                                                       // (1)
      supplier: payments                                       // (2)
      function: validate|process                               // (3)
```

```
      consumer: print                                          // (4)
  compile:
    print:
      type: consumer
      lambda: System.out::println
      inputType: Object
    process:
      type: function
      lambda: (flux)->flux
      inputType: Flux<org.rpis5.chapters.chapter_08.scf.Payment>
      outputType: Flux<org.rpis5.chapters.chapter_08.scf.Payment>
```

The numeration in the code is explained as follows:

1. This is the namespace used for task configurations.
2. Here, we configure a `supplier` (source) function for the task. As we can see, to define a supplier we have to pass the name of the supplier's function.
3. These are the intermediate transformations of the data. Here, to pipe the execution, we may combine several functions using the (pipe) | symbol. Note that, under the hood, all functions are chained using the `Function#accept` method.
4. This is the definition of the consumer stage. Note that the task is executed only when all stages are provided.

As we can see, by using a pure Spring Boot application with Spring Cloud Function modules as dependencies, it is possible to run users' prepared functions and combine them in a complex handler.

An important role in the Spring Cloud Function ecosystem is played by the `spring-cloud-function-compiler` module. Along with on-the-fly function compilation from a property file, this module exposes web endpoints, which allow on-the-fly function deployment. For example, by calling the following `curl` command in a terminal, we can add the provided function to the running Spring Boot application:

```
curl -X POST -H "Content-Type: text/plain" \
  -d "f->f.map(s->s.toUpperCase())" \
  localhost:8080/function/uppercase\
  ?inputType=Flux%3CString%3E\
  &outputTupe=Flux%3CString%3E
```

In this example, we upload a function with `Flux<String>` as the input and output type for it.

Note, that we use the `%3C %3E` symbols here to encode `< >` in HTTP URI.

There are two options for running `spring-cloud-function-compiler` as a server:

- Download a JAR file from `maven-central` and run it independently
- Add the module as a dependency to the project and provide the following path to scan for beans: `"org.springframework.cloud.function.compiler.app"`

Following a function's deployment by running a lightweight Spring Boot application with dependencies on `spring-cloud-function-web` and `spring-cloud-function-compiler`, we obtain on-the-fly function deployment over HTTP and its dynamic deployment as a separate web application. For example, by having the same jar file and changing program arguments, we can run it with different functions as follows:

```
java -jar function-web-template.jar \
   --spring.cloud.function.imports.uppercase.type=function \
   --spring.cloud.function.imports.uppercase.location=\
file:///tmp/function-registry/functions/uppercase.fun \
\
   --spring.cloud.function.imports.worldadder.type=function \
   --spring.cloud.function.imports.worldadder.location=\
file:///tmp/function-registry/functions/worldadder.fun
```

In this example, we import two functions:

- **Uppercase**: Which transforms any given string into an uppercase equivalent
- **Worldadder**: Which adds the `world` suffix to any given string

As may be noticed from the previous example code, we use the
`spring.cloud.function.imports` namespace to define the name of the imported
functions (**in bold**) and then their types (*in italic*) and locations of the bytecode for those
functions. After the successful application's startup, we can access deployed functions by
executing the following `curl` command:

```
curl -X POST -H "Content-Type: text/plain" \
    -d "Hello" \
    localhost:8080/uppercase%7Cworldadder
```

As the result of the execution, we receive "`HELLO World`", which ensures that both
functions are present on the server and executed in the order defined in the URL.

We use the `%7C` symbol here to encode (pipe) | in HTTP URI.

In the same way, we may deploy and import other functions within the same or
independent applications.

Alternatively, Spring Cloud Function offers a deployment module that plays the role of the
container for independent functions. In the previous cases, we were able to run built-in
functions or deploy over a `spring-cloud-function-compiler` web API. We have seen
how to use deployed functions and run them as independent applications. Despite that
flexibility, the startup time of a Spring Boot application may be much longer than the
execution of that function. In some cases (along with the pure functions), we have to use
some of the Spring Framework arsenal. For example, relying on Spring Data or Spring Web
features. Hence, what could be useful in such cases is the deployment of thin jars. Spring
Cloud Function offers an additional module here called `spring-cloud-function-
deployer`.

The **Spring Cloud Function Deployer** module allows running each jar with the same Spring Deployer application but in complete isolation. At first glance, valuable benefits are not received from using that module. However, as we may remember, independent functions (which are what we want to achieve) are fast in their bootstrapping and execution. A function packed into the Spring Boot environment for its startup requires the startup of the whole Spring Boot application, which usually takes a significant amount of time in comparison to the function's startup time.

Consequently, to solve that problem, Spring Cloud Function Deployer starts itself first and pre-loads some part of the JDK classes. It then creates child `ClassLoader` for each jar with functions. The execution of each jar takes place in its own `Thread` which enables parallel execution. Since each jar is an independent micro Spring Boot application, it runs within its own Spring Context, so beans do not intersect with neighboring applications' beans. Finally, the startup of a child Spring Boot application is significantly faster because the parent `ClassLoader` has already done the difficult job of warming up the JVM.

Moreover, the killer combination of `spring-cloud-function-deployer` and `spring-boot-thin-launcher` makes it possible to solve the **fat jar** problem as well. **Spring Boot Thin Launcher** is a plugin for Maven and Gradle, which overrides the default Spring Boot fat `JarLauncher` and offers `ThinJarWrapper` and `ThinJarLauncher` instead. Those classes do all of the work required for packaging a dependency-free jar first and then—only during the bootstrap phase—they locate all required dependencies from the configured cache (for example, from the local Maven repo) or download missing dependencies from the configured Maven repositories. Behaving in that way, our application may reduce the size of the jar to a few KB and startup time to hundreds of milliseconds.

To learn more about Thin Launcher and the benefits offered by Spring Cloud Function Deployer, please visit the following links: `https://github.com/dsyer/spring-boot-thin-launcher`, `https://github.com/dsyer/spring-boot-thin-launcher/tree/master/deployer` and `https://github.com/spring-cloud/spring-cloud-function/tree/master/spring-cloud-function-deployer`.

To summarize the information gained about Spring Cloud Function, let's take a look at the following generalized diagram of the ecosystem:

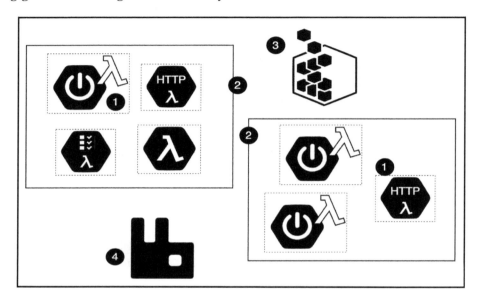

Diagram 8.11. The Spring Cloud Function's ecosystem

In the preceding diagram, the numbered points mean the following:

1. This is the representation of a function in the form of hexagons. As we can see, there are a few different types of hexagons depicted here. A few of them are a combination of functions within the Spring Boot application, or functions which are exposed over HTTP. Another can communicate with other functions with the support of a Spring Cloud Stream Adapter or can be deployed as a task for single execution.

2. This is the representation of a Spring Cloud Function Deployer. As was mentioned earlier, the Spring Cloud Function Deployer is depicted as a container. In this case, we have two independent Spring Cloud Function Deployers executed on the different nodes. Also, the dotted borders around functions inside the containers represent independent ClassLoaders.

3. This is the representation of the Spring Cloud Function Compiler module. In this case, the module plays the role of the server, which allows functions' deployment over HTTP and keeps them in storage.

4. This is the representation of a message broker, which in this case is RabbitMQ.

As we can see, using Spring Cloud Function modules along with straightforward integration with existing Cloud platforms, we can build our own **Function as a Service (FaaS)** platform that almost offers the whole arsenal of Spring Framework features, allowing the building of an application using lightweight functions. However, we have to remember that Spring Cloud Function shows the power when there is a foundation for instances' deploying, monitoring and management, so the Spring Cloud Function ecosystem can be built on top of that and exposes FaaS capabilities. Hence, in the following section, we are going to cover how Spring Cloud Function works in combination with the full-fledged Spring Cloud Data Flow ecosystem.

Spring Cloud – function as a part of a data flow

Now, having enough knowledge about the Spring Cloud Function ecosystem, we may get back on topic and see how to use this awesome module. There is an additional module called **Spring Cloud Starter Stream App Function**, which enables the use of Spring Cloud Function features in Spring Cloud Data Flow. This module allows us to use pure jars and deploy them as part of the Spring Cloud Data Flow without any redundant overhead from Spring Boot. Since we have a plain mapping here, a simplified `Validation` function can be reduced to a conventional `Function<Payment, PaymentValidation>` function and can look as follows:

```
public class PaymentValidator
        implements Function<Payment, Payment> {

   public Payment apply(Payment payment) { ... }
}
```

After the packaging and publishing of an artifact, we may be able to write the following stream pipe script to connect our HTTP source to the Spring Cloud Function Bridge:

```
SendPaymentEndpoint=Endpoint: http --path-pattern=/payment --port=8080 |
Validator: function --class-name=com.example.PaymentValidator --
location=https://github.com/PacktPublishing/Hands-On-Reactive-Programming-i
n-
Spring-5/tree/master/chapter-08/dataflow/payment/src/main/resources/payment
s-validation.jar?raw=true
```

At the time of writing, the Spring Cloud Function module for Spring Cloud Data Flow was not included in the default Applications and Tasks packages and should be registered by providing the following bulk import properties:

```
source.function=maven://org.springframework.cloud.stream.app
:function-app-rabbit:1.0.0.BUILD-SNAPSHOT

source.function.metadata=maven://org.springframework.cloud.s
tream.app:function-app-rabbit:jar:metadata:1.0.0.BUILD-
SNAPSHOT

processor.function=maven://org.springframework.cloud.stream.
app:function-app-rabbit:1.0.0.BUILD-SNAPSHOT

processor.function.metadata=maven://org.springframework.clou
d.stream.app:function-app-rabbit:jar:metadata:1.0.0.BUILD-
SNAPSHOT

sink.function=maven://org.springframework.cloud.stream.app:f
unction-app-rabbit:1.0.0.BUILD-SNAPSHOT

sink.function.metadata=maven://org.springframework.cloud.str
eam.app:function-app-rabbit:jar:metadata:1.0.0.BUILD-
SNAPSHOT
```

Finally, to complete the first part of the process, we have to deliver a validated payment to the different destinations, choosing the endpoint with regards to the result of the validation. Since the validation function is a pure function that should not have access to the infrastructure (such as RabbitMQ routings headers), we should delegate that responsibility elsewhere. Fortunately, Spring Cloud Data Flow offers **Router Sink**, which allows routing incoming messages to different queues based on an expression such as the following:

```
...  | router --expression="payload.isValid() ? 'Accepted' : 'Rejected'"
```

Alternatively, we may configure a source that listens to the particular message queue name. For example, pipe script is responsible for listening to the RabbitMQ channel called `Accepted`, which looks like the following:

```
...
Accepted=Accepted: rabbit --queues=Accepted
```

According to the payments flow diagram, the following step of a payment processing persists its status with the `Accepted` state. In that way, users can visit a particular page with their payments and check the state of the processing for each payment. Hence, we should provide integration with a database. For example, we may store states of the payment's transitions in MongoDB. Spring Cloud Data Flow offers a *MongoDB Sink*. Using that, we can easily write incoming messages to MongoDB. Relying on Spring Data Flow add-ons, we can broadcast messages to both the MongoDB sink and the next execution step. Such a technique could only be a valid solution in the case of a fully reliable message broker such as Apache Kafka. As we might know, Kafka persists messages. Hence, messages would be available in the message broker even if the execution crashes at some stage. Consequently, MongoDB holds a state intended for use in UI, while the actual processing state is held inside the message broker; therefore, it is available for replay at any point in time. On the other hand, in the case of fast, in-memory message brokers such as RabbitMQ, it would be sufficient to rely on the state stored in MongoDB as a source of truth. Consequently, we must ensure that the Payment's state has been stored before the execution of the next step. Unfortunately, to achieve such functionality, we have to write a custom Spring Cloud Stream application that wraps MongoDB as a processing stage in the process.

By repeating similar operations for the rest of the process, we can achieve the following execution flow:

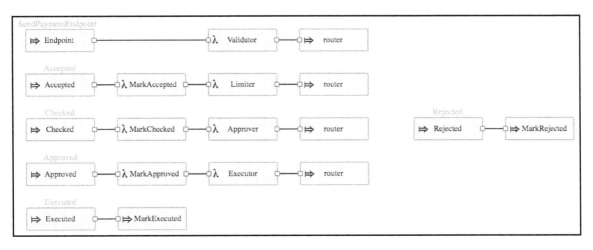

Diagram 8.12. Completed Payment's Execution Flow written with the support of the Spring Cloud Data Flow User Interface

The preceding diagram shows a built-in Spring Cloud Data Flow dashboard that allows building flows and managing applications using a browser-based GUI. We are not going into too much detail on this dashboard, but we may learn more about it by visiting the following link: `https://docs.spring.io/spring-cloud-dataflow/docs/current/ reference/htmlsingle/#dashboard`, `https://github.com/spring- projects/spring-flo/`, and `https://github.com/spring-cloud/spring- cloud-dataflow-ui`. Along with the dashboard options, there is also a data flow shell client that offers the same functionality as the dashboard. To learn more about data flow shell, please see the following link: `https:/ /docs.spring.io/spring-cloud-dataflow/docs/current/reference/ htmlsingle/#shell`.

The preceding flow visualization is represented by the following pipe script:

```
SendPaymentEndpoint=Endpoint: http --path-pattern=/payment --port=8080 |
Validator: function --class-name=com.example.PaymentValidator --
location=https://github.com/PacktPublishing/Hands-On-Reactive-Programming-i
n-
Spring-5/tree/master/chapter-08/dataflow/payment/src/main/resources/payment
s.jar?raw=true | router --expression="payload.isValid() ? 'Accepted' :
'Rejected'"

Accepted=Accepted: rabbit --queues=Accepted | MarkAccepted: mongodb-
processor --collection=payment | Limiter: function --class-
name=com.example.PaymentLimiter --
location=https://github.com/PacktPublishing/Hands-On-Reactive-Programming-i
n-
Spring-5/tree/master/chapter-08/dataflow/payment/src/main/resources/payment
s.jar?raw=true | router --expression="payload.isLimitBreached() ?
'Rejected' : 'Checked'"

Checked=Checked: rabbit --queues=Checked | MarkChecked: mongodb-processor -
-collection=payment | Approver: function --class-
name=com.example.PaymentApprover --
location=https://github.com/PacktPublishing/Hands-On-Reactive-Programming-i
n-
Spring-5/tree/master/chapter-08/dataflow/payment/src/main/resources/payment
s.jar?raw=true | router --expression="payload.isApproved() ? 'Approved' :
'Rejected'"

Approved=Approved: rabbit --queues=Approved | MarkApproved: mongodb-
processor --collection=payment | Executor: function --class-
name=com.example.PaymentExecutor --
location=https://github.com/PacktPublishing/Hands-On-Reactive-Programming-i
n-
```

```
Spring-5/tree/master/chapter-08/dataflow/payment/src/main/resources/payment
s.jar?raw=true | router --expression="payload.isExecuted() ? 'Executed' :
'Rejected'"

Executed=Executed: rabbit --queues=Executed | MarkExecuted: mongodb --
collection=payment

Rejected=Rejected: rabbit --queues=Rejected | MarkRejected: mongodb --
collection=payment
```

Finally, by deploying that stream, we can execute payment and see the execution logs in the console.

 To run the code along with the installed Spring Cloud Data Flow server, we have to have RabbitMQ and MongoDB installed.

A noticeable point here is that a deployment process is as simple as business logic development. First of all, the Spring Cloud Data Flow toolkit is built on top of Spring Cloud Deployer, which is used for deployment on to modern platforms such as Cloud Foundry, Kubernetes, Apache Mesos, or Apache YARN. The toolkit exposes Java APIs that allow the configuration of an application's source (for instance, Maven repository, **artifactId**, **groupId**, and **version**) and its subsequent deployment to the target platform. Along with that, Spring Cloud Deployer is flexible enough and provides a wider list of configurations and properties, one of which is the number of replicas for deployable instance.

 High availability, fault tolerance, or resilience of the deployed group of application instances directly depends on the platform and Spring Cloud Deployer itself, which does not provide any guarantees for that. For example, it is not recommended to use *Spring Cloud Deployer Local* for a production case. The local version of the toolkit is intended to be run within one machine using Docker. It is important to note that the Spring Cloud Deployer SPI does not provide additional monitoring or maintenance and expects an underlying platform to provide required features.

Embracing the mentioned possibilities, Spring Cloud Data Flow provides a one-button click (or one terminal command) deployment with the ability to pass the required configurations and properties.

To summarize, we have started from the foundation of Spring Cloud Streams and finished the story with a powerful abstraction over a few modules. As a result, we have seen that, with the support of those projects, we can build a reactive system by applying different abstractions of reactive programming. The mentioned technique of using a message broker for asynchronous, reliable messaging covers most business needs. Moreover, that technique may reduce the cost of the development of a reactive system in general and may be used for rapid development of a system such as big web stores, IoT, or chat applications. However, it is important to remember that, even though the described approach improves system reliability, scalability, and throughput, it may harm request processing latency due to the additional communication, especially with persistent message brokers. So, if our system tolerates a few milliseconds of additional delay between sending and receiving messages, then such an approach may apply to our case.

RSocket for low-latency, reactive message passing

In the previous section, we learned how we might achieve a reactive system easily using Spring Cloud Streams and its variant in Spring Cloud Data Flow. In turn, we learned how to build a fine-grained system using lightweight functions with the support of Spring Cloud Function and the simplicity of composing them into the flow.

However, one disadvantage of such simplicity and flexibility is losing a low-latency approach. Nowadays, there are some areas of applications where each millisecond plays a vital role. For example, with the stock exchange market, online video games, or systems of real-time manufacture control. With such systems, it is unacceptable to waste time on queuing and dequeuing messages. In turn, as may be noticed, most reliable message brokers persist a message, which increases the time it takes to deliver a message.

One of the possible solutions to achieve low-latency communication between services in a distributed system is by using a continuous direct connection between services. For example, when wiring continuous TCP connections between applications, we can achieve direct communication between services with lower latency and some delivery guarantees, depending on the given transport. Along with that, the usage of broader known protocols such as WebSocket allows the building of such communication using Spring WebFlux's `ReactorNettyWebSocketClient`, for instance.

However, as we might remember from earlier in this chapter, along with a tight coupling between services (because of the connection), the usage of WebSockets does not fit the reactive system requirements, since the protocol does not offer the possibility to control backpressure, which is a vital part of a resilient system.

Fortunately, the group behind the reactive streams specification understood the necessity of cross-network, asynchronous, low-latency communication. In mid 2015, Ben Christensen initiated a new project called RSocket with a group of experts.

The central goal of the RSocket project is to provide an application protocol with reactive streams' semantics over an asynchronous, binary boundary.

 To learn more about the motivation for creating the RSocket project, please visit the following link: `https://github.com/rsocket/rsocket/blob/master/Motivations.md`.

RSocket versus Reactor-Netty

At first glance, RSocket does not seem very innovative; nowadays, we already have web servers such as RxNetty or Reactor-Netty (the default WebFlux wrapper for Netty). These solutions offer APIs (which allow reading or writing from/to the network) built on top of reactive streams types, implying backpressure support. However, the only issue with that kind of backpressure is that it works in isolation. Subsequently, this means that proper backpressure support is wired only between the component and the network.

For example, using Reactor-Netty, we can consume incoming bytes only when we are ready to do so. Similarly, the network's readiness is exposed as the `Subscription#request` method calls. The central problem here is that the actual demand of the components does not cross the network boundaries, as depicted in the following diagram:

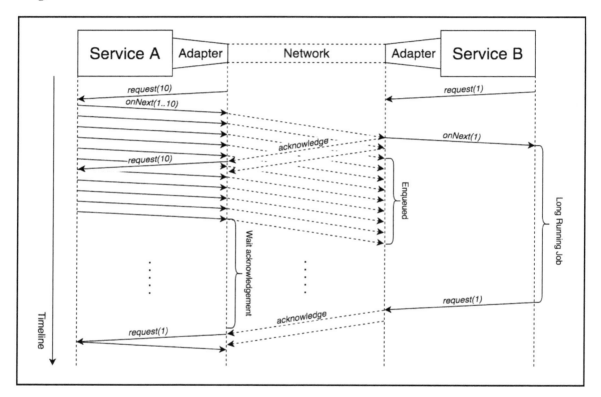

Diagram 8.13. The example of backpressure in isolation

As we can see from the preceding diagram, there are two services here (**Service A** and **Service B**). As well as that, we have an abstract **Adapter** here that allows a service (business logic) to communicate with another service over the **Network**. In this example, suppose that our adapter is Reactor-Netty, which provides reactive access. This means that backpressure control is properly implemented at the transport level. Consequently, the adapter informs the publisher of approximately how many elements it can write at that moment. In our case, **Service A** creates a continuous connection (for instance, WebSocket connection) with **Service B** and, once the connection becomes available, it starts sending elements to the adapter. Consequently, the adapter takes proper care of writing elements to the network. On the opposite side of the connection, we have **Service B**, which consumes messages from the network over the same adapter. As a `Subscriber`, **Service B** expresses the demand to the adapter and, once the proper amount of bytes have been received, the adapter converts them into the *logical* element, sending this to the business logic. In the same way, once the element has been sent to the adapter, the adapter takes care of transforming it into bytes and then following the flow control defined at the transport level to send them to the network.

As we might remember from `Chapter 3`, *Reactive Streams - the New Streams' Standard*, the worst-case scenario in communication between a producer and consumer arises when the consumer is slow enough that the producer may easily overflow the consumer. To emphasize the problem of isolated backpressure, let's suppose that we have a slow consumer and a fast producer, so some part of the events are buffered in the **Socket Buffer**. Unfortunately, the size of the buffer is limited, and at some point, the network packets may start dropping. Of course, in many aspects, a transport's behavior depends on the interaction protocol. For example, reliable network transports such as TCP have a flow control (backpressure control) that embraces the notion of the *sliding window* and *acknowledgement*. This means that, in general, backpressure is achievable on a binary level (on the level of the received bytes and the corresponding acknowledgment). In such a case, TCP takes care of redelivering the messages and cases in which the lack of acknowledgments slows down the publisher on the side of **Service A**. The drawback here is that the impact on the performance of the applications itself is high since we have to take care of the redelivery of dropped packages. Moreover, the performance of the communication may also be decreased, so the overall stability of the system may be lost. Although such a transport flow control may be acceptable, the utilization of the connection is low. This is because we can't reuse the same connection for multiplexing several logical streams. Another aspect is when the consumer can't follow the transport flow control so the consumer continues buffering bytes internally which may end up with `OutOfMemoryError`.

To learn more about TCP flow control, please see the following link:
`https://hpbn.co/building-blocks-of-tcp/#flow-control`

In contrast to the isolated reactive `Publisher-Subscriber` communication, which may be easily achieved using Reactor Netty or RxNetty, RSockets offers a binary protocol that is an application protocol for reactive streams semantics across an asynchronous, network boundary:

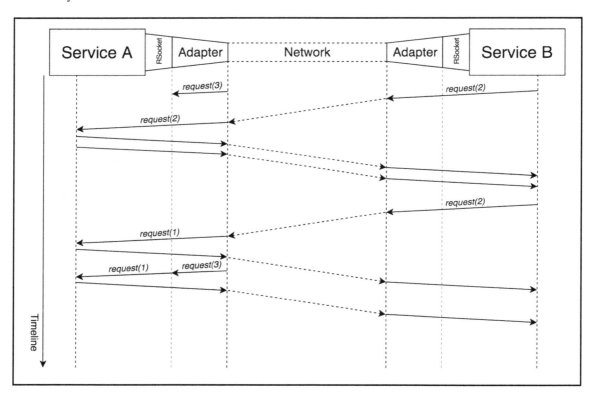

Diagram 8.14. An example of backpressure with RSocket

As we can see from the preceding diagram, with the RSocket protocol, we get support for transmitting demand over network boundaries. Hence, the producer service may react to the request and send the corresponding number of `onNext` signals that are transmitted through the network as well. Besides, RSocket works on top of the adapter that takes care of the data writing to the network so that the local demand may be coordinated in isolation with the received demand from the consumer service. In general, RSocket is a transport agnostic that, along with TCP, supports Aeron and communication over WebSocket.

At first glance, it seems that the connection's usage is inefficient since the interaction between services may be low. However, one of the powerful features of the RSocket protocol is that it allows reusing the same socket connection for many streams between the same server and client. Hence, it may optimize the use of one connection.

Along with the protocol, RSockets enables symmetric interaction models such as the following:

- **Request/response**: A stream of one element in the request and response
- **Request/stream**: A stream of one element in the request stream and a finite/infinite stream as the response
- **Fire-and-forget**: A stream of one element in the request and a `Void` (no elements) response stream
- **Channel**: Fully bi-directional finite/infinite streams for both the request and response

As we can see, RSocket provides a wide list of commonly used interaction models for async message passing, acquiring only a single connection at the very beginning.

RSocket in Java

The RSocket protocol and interaction model found a place and a high demand in Java (along with implementations in C++, JS, Python, and Go) and is implemented on top of Reactor 3. The following programming model is offered by the RSocket-Java module:

```
RSocketFactory                                                  // (1)
    .receive()                                                  // (1.1)
    .acceptor(new SocketAcceptorImpl())                         // (1.2)
    .transport(TcpServerTransport.create("localhost", 7000))    // (1.3)
    .start()                                                    // (1.4)
    .subscribe();                                               //

RSocket socket = RSocketFactory                                 // (2)
    .connect()                                                  // (2.1)
```

```
        .transport(TcpClientTransport.create("localhost", 7000))      //
        .start()                                                        //
        .block();                                                       // (2.2)

    socket                                                              // (3)
        .requestChannel(                                                // (3.1)
            Flux.interval(Duration.ofMillis(1000))                      //
                .map(i -> DefaultPayload.create("Hello [" + i + "]")))  // (3.2)
        )                                                               //
        .map(Payload::getDataUtf8)                                      // (3.3)
        .doFinally(signalType -> socket.dispose())                      //
        .then()                                                         //
        .block();                                                       //
```

Each section of the numbered code is explained here:

1. This is the Server (receiver) RSocket definition. At point (1.1), we established that we aim to create an RSocket Server, so we want to use the `.receive()` method here. At point (1.2), we provided the `SocketAcceptor` implementation, which is the definition of the handlers method called on incoming client connections. In turn, at point (1.3), we defined preferable transport, which is TCP transport in this case. Note that the TCP transport provider is Reactor-Netty. Finally, to start listening to the defined socket address, we start the server and `.subscribe()` to it.

2. This is the Client RSocket definition. Here (2.1), instead of the `.receive()` factory-method, we use `.connect()`, which provides the client's `RSocket` instance. For the sake of simplicity in that example, notice that we used the `.block()` method in order to wait for the successful connection and obtain an instance of active `RSocket`.

3. This demonstrates the execution of the request to the server. In this example, we use the channel interaction (3.1), so along with sending the stream of messages, we receive a stream as well. Notice that the default representation of a message in the stream is the `Payload` class. Hence, at point (3.2), we have to wrap a message into the Payload (in this case, into the default implementation `DefaultPayload`) or unwrap it (3.3), for example, to `String`.

In the preceding example, we wired duplex communication between the client and server. Here, all communication has been done with the support for the Reactive Streams specification and Reactor 3.

Furthermore, it is important to mention the implementation of `SocketAcceptor`:

```
class SocketAcceptorImpl implements SocketAcceptor {              // (1)

    @Override                                                     // (2)
    public Mono<RSocket> accept(                                  //
        ConnectionSetupPayload setupPayload,                      // (2.1)
        RSocket reactiveSocket                                    // (2.2)
    ) {
        return Mono.just(new AbstractRSocket() {                  // (3)
            @Override                                             //
            public Flux<Payload> requestChannel(                  // (3.1)
                Publisher<Payload> payloads                       // (3.2)
            ) {                                                   //
                return Flux.from(payloads)                        // (3.3)
                        .map(Payload::getDataUtf8)                //
                        .map(s -> "Echo: " + s)                   //
                        .map(DefaultPayload::create);             //
            }                                                     //
        });                                                       //
    }                                                             //
}
```

The numeration in the code is explained as follows:

1. This is the implementation of the `SocketAcceptor` interface. Note that `SocketAcceptor` is a representation of the server-side acceptor.

2. The `SocketAcceptor` interface has only one method called `accept`. This method takes two parameters, including the `ConnectionSetupPayload` argument (`2.1`), which represents the first **handshake** from the client's side during the connection wiring. As we may remember from this section, RSocket is a duplex connection by nature. That nature is represented by the second parameter of the `accept` method, called `sendingRSocket` (`2.2`). Using the second parameter, the server may start streaming requests to the client as if the server was the initiator of the interaction.

3. This is the handler RSocket declaration. In this case, the `AbstractRSocket` class is an abstract implementation of the `RSocket` interface that emits `UnsupportedOperationException` for any handling method. Subsequently, by overriding one of the methods (`3.1`), we can declare which interaction models our server supports. Finally, at point (`3.3`), we provide the **echo** functionality, which takes the ongoing stream (`3.2`) and modifies the incoming messages.

As we can see, the definition of `SocketAcceptor` does not mean the definition of the handler. In that case, the invocation of the `SocketAcceptor#accept` method refers to a new incoming connection. In turn, in RSocket-Java, the `RSocket` interface is a representation of the client and server's handler at the same time. Finally, the communication between parties is peer-to-peer communication, which means that both can handle requests.

Furthermore, to achieve scalability, RSocket-Java offers the RSocket `LoadBalancer` module, which can be integrated with a service registry such as Eureka. For example, the following code shows naive integration with Spring Cloud Discovery:

```
Flux
    .interval(Duration.ofMillis(100))                           // (1)
    .map(i ->
        discoveryClient
            .getInstances(serviceId)                            // (2)
            .stream()                                           //
            .map(si ->
                new RSocketSupplier(() ->
                    RSocketFactory.connect()                    // (3)
                                  .transport(                   //
                                      TcpClientTransport.create( //
                                          si.getHost(),         // (3.1)
                                          si.getPort()          // (3.2)
                                      )                         //
                                  )                             //
                                  .start()                      //
                ) {
                    public boolean equals(Object obj) { ... }   // (4)
                                                                //
                    public int hashCode() {                     //
                        return si.getUri().hashCode();          // (4.1)
                    }                                           //
                }
            )
            .collect(toCollection(ArrayList<RSocketSupplier>::new))
    )
    .as(LoadBalancedRSocketMono::create);                       // (5)
```

In the previous code, the numbered points mean the following:

1. This is the `.interval()` operator declaration. Here, the idea is to run periodic retrieving of available instances with some `serviceId`.
2. This shows the retrieval of the list of instances.

3. This is the `Supplier` from the `Mono<RSocket>` creation. We use information such as the server host (`3.1`) and port (`3.2`) from each given `ServiceInstance` to create a proper transport connection.

4. This is the anonymous `RSocketSupplier` creation. Here, we override `equals` and `hashCode` in order to distinguish which `RSocketSupplier` are the same. Note, under the hood, `LoadBalancedRSocketMono` uses `HashSet`, in which all received instances are stored. In turn, we use URI as a unique identifier of an instance in the group.

5. This is the stage of transformation of `Flux<Collection<RSocketSupplier>>` to the `LoadBalancedRSocketMono`. Note that even though the result is an instance of type `Mono` the `LoadBalancedRSocketMono` is a stateful one. Consequently, each new subscriber potentially receives different results. Under the hood, `LoadBalancedRSocketMono` makes a selection of the RSocket instances using predictive load balancing algorithm and returns selected one to a subscriber.

The previous example shows a naive method of integrating `LoadBalancedRScoketMono` with `DiscoveryClient`. Even though the mentioned example is not efficient, we still may learn how to work with `LoadBalancedRSocketMono` properly.

To generalize, RSocket is a communication protocol that follows Reactive Streams semantics and expands the new horizons for streaming communication across network boundaries with backpressure control support. In turn, there is a powerful Reactor 3 based implementation, which offers a straightforward API for wiring a connection between peers and efficiently utilizes it over the interaction's life cycle.

RSocket versus gRPC

We may still wonder why we need a separate framework if there is a well-known framework called gRPC. The gRPC is described as follows:

> *"A high performance, open source, general-purpose RPC framework* (`https://github.com/grpc`)*"*

This project was initially developed by Google and aimed to provide asynchronous messaging over HTTP/2. It uses **Protocol Buffers (Protobuf)** as the **Interface Description Language (IDL)** and as its underlying message interchange format.

 To learn more about Service Definition using IDL and Protobuf, please see the following link:
https://grpc.io/docs/guides/concepts.html#service-definition

In general, gRPC offers an almost identical messaging semantic to a Reactive Streams one and provides the following interface:

```
interface StreamObserver<V>  {

    void onNext(V value);

    void onError(Throwable t);

    void onCompleted();
}
```

As we can see, the semantic is 1:1 to `Observer` from RxJava 1. In turn, the gRPC's API offers the `Stream` interface, which expands the following methods:

```
public interface Stream {

    void request(int numMessages);

    ...

    boolean isReady();
    ...
}
```

Looking at the preceding code, we may get the feeling that gRPC, along with asynchronous message passing, gives backpressure control support as well. However, that part is a bit tricky. In general, the interaction flow is somewhat similar to what we saw in *Diagram 8.13*, with the only difference being that it supports the flow control with a higher granularity. Since gRPC is built on top of HTTP/2, the framework employees HTTP/2 flow control as the building block for providing a fine-grained backpressure control. Nevertheless, the flow control still relies on the sliding window size in bytes, so the backpressure control on the logical elements' level granularity is left uncovered.

Another significant difference between gRPC and RSocket is that gRPC is an RPC framework while RSocket is a protocol. gRPC is based on the HTTP/2 protocol and provides code-generation for service stubs and clients. By default, gRPC uses Protobuf for messaging format; however, it may also support other formats such as JSON. At the same time, RSocket gives only a reactive implementation for the server and the client. Also, there is a separate RPC framework called RSocket-RPC, which is built on top of the RSocket protocol and provides all the capabilities of gRPC. RSocket-RPC allows code generation based on Protobuf models in a fashion identical to gRPC. So, any project that uses gRPC can migrate smoothly to RSocket-RPC.

To learn more about RSocket-RPC, please see the following link: `https://github.com/netifi/rsocket-rpc`.

To learn more about backpressure control support in gRPC, please see the following link: `https://github.com/salesforce/reactive-grpc#back-pressure`.

RSocket in Spring Framework

Although the implementation gives broader possibilities in writing asynchronous, low-latency, and high-throughput communication using Reactor API, it left much work with infrastructure configurations for developers. Fortunately, Spring teams valued that project and started experimenting with adopting such a great solution to the Spring Ecosystem with a simplified programming model over annotations.

One of the experiments was called Spring Cloud Sockets and was aimed at providing a familiar (in comparison to Spring Web) programming model for declaring annotations:

```
@SpringBootApplication                                          // (1)
@EnableReactiveSockets                                          // (1.1)
public static class TestApplication {                           //

    @RequestManyMapping(                                        // (2)
        value = "/stream1",                                     // (2.1)
        mimeType = "application/json"                           // (2.2)
    )                                                           //
    public Flux<String> stream1(@Payload String a) {           // (2.3)
        return Flux.just(a)                                     //
                .mergeWith(                                     //
                    Flux.interval(Duration.ofMillis(100))       //
                        .map(i -> "1. Stream Message: [" + i + "]")//
                );                                              //
    }                                                           //
```

```
@RequestManyMapping(                                              // (2)
   value = "/stream2",                                           // (2.1)
   mimeType = "application/json"                                 // (2.2)
)                                                                //
public Flux<String> stream2(@Payload String b) {                // (2.3)
   return Flux.just(b)                                          //
             .mergeWith(                                        //
                Flux.interval(Duration.ofMillis(500))          //
                   .map(i -> "2. Stream Message: [" + i + "]")//
             );                                                 //
}                                                               //
}
```

The numeration in the code is explained here:

1. This is the @SpringBootApplication definition. Here, at point (1.1), we define the @EnableReactiveSockets annotation, which provides the required configurations and enables RSocket in the application.

2. This is the handler method declaration. Here, we use the @RequestManyMapping annotation to specify that the current method works in the **request stream** interaction model. One noticeable feature offered by the Spring Cloud Sockets module is that it provides out-of-the-box mapping (routing) and allows the definition of the handler mapping's path (2.1) and mime-type for incoming messages (2.2). Finally, there is an additional @Payload annotation (2.3), which suggests that the given parameter is the incoming request's payload.

Here, we have the familiar Spring Boot application, which, with the support of Spring Cloud Socket, enables additional features of the RSocket-Java library. In turn, Spring Cloud Sockets provide simplification for interactions with a server from the client's perspective as well:

```
public interface TestClient {                                    // (1)
   @RequestManyMapping(                                          // (2)
      value = "/stream1",                                       //
      mimeType = "application/json"                             //
   )                                                            //
   Flux<String> receiveStream1(String a);                      //

   @RequestManyMapping(                                          // (2)
      value = "/stream1",                                       //
      mimeType = "application/json"                             //
   )                                                            //
   Flux<String> receiveStream2(String b);                      //
}
```

Here, all we have to do is declare an RSocket Client using Spring Cloud Sockets when providing an interface `(1)`. In order to enable the RSocket client, we have to define identical annotations, as in the server example on top of client's methods, and define the corresponding handler path.

As a result, the interface can easily be transformed into a `Proxy` at runtime using the `ReactiveSocketClient` factory, as in the following example:

```
ReactiveSocketClient client = new ReactiveSocketClient(rSocket);
TestClient clientProxy = client.create(TestClient.class);

Flux.merge(
        clientProxy.receiveStream1("a"),
        clientProxy.receiveStream2("b")
    )
    .log()
    .subscribe();
```

Spring Cloud Socket is an experimental project. For now, it is hosted outside the official Spring Cloud organization. The source code might be found at the following GitHub repository at `https://github.com/viniciusccarvalho/spring-cloud-sockets`.

In the preceding example, we created a client (please note that, in this example, we have to provide RSocket client's instance manually). For demonstration purposes, we merged two streams and endeavored to `.log()` the results.

RSocket in other frameworks

As previously mentioned, the Spring Cloud Socket module is experimental and is no longer supported by the original author. Despite the fact that Spring teams continue internal experiments and keep an eye on the RSocket since this is the powerful solution for Reactive Streams through the network boundaries, there are a few other frameworks that have also adopted the implementation of the protocol in Java.

The ScaleCube Project

As the original authors of the framework say, the ScaleCube is defined as follows:

> *"An open source project that is focused on streamlining the reactive programming of Microservices reactive systems that scale (*`http://scalecube.io`*)."*

The central goal of the project is to build highly scalable low latency, distributed systems.

For interaction between services, the toolkit uses Project Reactor 3 and is generally transport agnostic. However, as this book is being written, the default transport is RSocket-Java.

Along with this, ScaleCube offers integration with Spring Framework and provides an annotation based API in order to build scalable, low latency, distributed systems. We will not go into the details of the frameworks' integration here. However, to learn more, please see the following link: `https://github.com/scalecube/scalecube-spring`.

The Proteus Project

Another powerful toolkit is the Netifi Proteus Project. In contrast to the ScaleCube Project, Proteus is positioned as follows:

> *"A fast and easy RSocket-based RPC layer for microservices (*`https://github.com/netifi-proteus`*)"*

In general, Proteus offers a cloud-native microservices platform that uses the RSocket protocol and the RSocket-RPC framework and provides a list of modules for message routing, monitoring, and tracing.

In addition, the Proteus Project offers integration with Spring Framework and provides a straightforward, annotation-based programming model along with a powerful code generation feature. We will not go into the details of the frameworks' integration; however, to learn more, please visit this link: `https://github.com/netifi-proteus/proteus-spring`.

Summarizing RSocket

As we may have noticed throughout this section, RSocket is a convenient way to build a high-throughput and low-latency reactive system based on asynchronous peer-to-peer communications employing a Reactive Streams specification. In general, the RSocket protocol seeks to reduce perceived latency and increase system efficiency. That may be achievable with the support of non-blocking communication via a duplex connection. Along with that, RSocket is designed with the purpose of reducing a hardware footprint. In turn, RSocket is a protocol that may be implemented in any language. Finally, the implementation of RSocket in Java is built on top of Project Reactor, which gives a powerful programming model out of the box.

In general, the RSocket community is skyrocketing and looks promising. For now, the project is actively maintained by Facebook and Netifi, and, in the near future, is going to be joined by other companies.

Summary

In this chapter, we went on a journey of evolving a monolith application into a reactive system. Here, we understood the pros and cons of using plain server-side load-balancing techniques for achieving a scalable system. However, these techniques cannot provide elasticity, since the load balancer might become a bottleneck in this case. In turn, this technique may add additional costs to operations as well as a powerful infrastructure for load balancers.

Furthermore, in this chapter, we explored the technique of client-side load balancing. However, this technique has its limitations and does not provide balancing coordination with the client-side load balancers installed on all services in the system.

Finally, we looked at how the reactive manifesto advises us to use a message queue for robust, asynchronous message passing. As a result, we have learned that employing a message broker as a separate reactive system for asynchronous communication allows us to achieve elasticity, making this an entirely reactive system.

Moreover, we covered how the Spring ecosystem helps us to build reactive systems with the support of the Reactor and Spring Cloud Stream project. We also learned new programming paradigms for backpressure supported communication with message brokers such as Apache Kafka or RabbitMQ using Reactor 3. In turn, we saw a few examples of applying that technique to a real project.

Following this, we saw how Spring Cloud Data Flow helps us to separate particular business logic from actual, specific configurations related to communication with a message broker or integration with a particular cloud platform.

Finally, we learned about an additional library for achieving low-latency, high-throughput communication with RSocket. Consequently, we saw an experimental project that might easily integrate RSocket into the Spring ecosystem.

To complete our knowledge of reactivity, Chapter 9, *Testing the Reactive Application,* explores the essential techniques of testing reactive systems built using Spring 5. To finalize our knowledge, we are going to look at how to release, support, and monitor a reactive system.

Testing the Reactive Application

9

So far, we have covered almost everything about reactive programming using Spring 5.x. We have also looked at how to build a clean, asynchronous execution using Project Reactor 3 and how to use that knowledge for building web applications using WebFlux. Moreover, we learned how Reactive Spring Data complements the whole system, and how quickly we can upgrade our application to a cloud level one using Spring Cloud and Spring Cloud Streams.

In this chapter, we will finalize our knowledge base by learning how to test each component in our system. We will cover the testing techniques and utilities that help in the verification code, which is written using Reactor or any library that is compatible with the Reactive Streams specification. We will also look at features offered by the Spring Framework to test the reactive application from end to end.

In this chapter, we will cover the following topics:

- The demand for additional testing tools
- The essentials of `Publisher` testing using `StepVerifier`
- Advanced `StepVerifier` usage scenarios
- The tool set for end-to-end WebFlux testing

Why are reactive streams hard to test?

Nowadays, enterprise applications are enormous. This is why the verification of such systems is a very important stage in any modern development life cycle. However, we should remember that in large systems there are a vast number of components and services, which in turn may include a large number of classes. For this reason, we should follow the **Test Pyramid** suggestions in order to cover everything. Here, the basic part of system testing is unit testing.

In our case, the subject of the testing is code written using the reactive programming technique. As we discovered in Chapter 3, *Reactive Streams - the New Streams' Standard* and Chapter 4, *Project Reactor - the Foundation for Reactive Apps*, reactive programming gives us a bunch of benefits. The first of these is the ability to optimize resource usage by enabling asynchronous communication. In turn, such a model fits well for building non-blocking I/O communication. Moreover, the ugly asynchronous code may be transformed into clean code using a reactive library such as Reactor. Reactor brings substantial functionality that simplifies the application's development.

However, along with the benefits, there is also a considerable drawback to testing such code. First of all, since that code is asynchronous, there is no easy way to pick the returned element and check whether it is correct. As we might remember from Chapter 3, *Reactive Streams - the New Streams' Standard*, we may collect elements from any Publisher by implementing the Subscriber interface and using it to check the accuracy of the emitted results. We may potentially end up with a complex solution from this, which is not an ideal situation for a developer when testing code.

Fortunately, Reactor's team did their best to simplify the verification of the code written using Reactive Streams.

Testing reactive streams with StepVerifier

For testing purposes, Reactor offers an additional reactor-test module that provides StepVerifier. StepVerifier provides a fluent API for building a verification flow for any Publisher. In the following subsections, we will cover everything about the **Reactor Test** module, starting with the essentials and finishing with advanced testing cases.

Essentials of StepVerifier

There are two main methods for verifying a `Publisher`. The first one
is `StepVerifier.<T>create(Publisher<T> source)`. The test that can be built with
this technique looks like the following:

```
StepVerifier
    .create(Flux.just("foo", "bar"))
    .expectSubscription()
    .expectNext("foo")
    .expectNext("bar")
    .expectComplete()
    .verify();
```

In this example, our `Publisher` should produce two particular elements, and subsequent
operations verify whether particular elements have been delivered to the final subscriber.
From the preceding example, we might understand the workings of a part of
the `StepVerifier` API. The builder technique offered by that class allows us to define the
order in which events will occur during the verification process. According to the
preceding code, the first emitted event must be the event concerning the subscription, and
the next events must be the `"foo"` and `"bar"` strings. Finally,
`StepVerifier#expectCompletion` defines the presence of a terminal signal, which in
our case must be the invocation of `Subscriber#onComplete` or simply the successful
completion of the given `Flux`. To execute the verification or in other words, subscribe to
creating a flow—we must call the `.verify()` method. This is a blocking call, so it will
block the execution until the flow has emitted all expected events.

By using this simple technique, we may verify `Publisher` with a countable amount of
elements and events. However, it will be hard to verify the flow with a huge amount of
elements. In cases in which it is more important to check whether our publisher has emitted
the particular amount of elements rather than the particular values, the
`.expectNextCount()` method might be useful. This is depicted in the following code:

```
StepVerifier
    .create(Flux.range(0, 100))
    .expectSubscription()
    .expectNext(0)
    .expectNextCount(98)
    .expectNext(99)
    .expectComplete()
    .verify();
```

As we might remember from previous chapters, `Flux.range(0, 100)` produces the range of elements from 0 to 99 inclusively. In such cases, it is more important to check whether this emitted the particular amount of elements and, for example, that the elements are emitted in the right order. The case mentioned here might be achievable by applying `.expectNext()` and `.expectNextCount()` together. According to the code, the first element will be checked by the `.expectNext(0)` statement. The test flow will then check that the given publisher produced another 98 elements, so the given producer emits 99 elements at a given point in total. Since our publisher should produce 100 elements, the last element should then be 99, which is verified using the `.expectNext(99)` statement.

Despite the fact that the `.expectNextCount()` method addresses a part of the problem, there are some cases where it is not enough to simply check the count of emitted elements. For example, when it comes to verifying the part of the code that is responsible for filtering or selecting elements by specific rules, it is important to check that all emitted items match the defined filtering rule. For that purpose, `StepVerifier` makes it possible to record emitted data and its verification at once, using tools such as Java Hamcrest (see `http://hamcrest.org/JavaHamcrest`). The following code depicts a unit test that uses this library:

```
Publisher<Wallet> usersWallets = findAllUsersWallets();
StepVerifier
   .create(usersWallets)
   .expectSubscription()
   .recordWith(ArrayList::new)
   .expectNextCount(1)
   .consumeRecordedWith(wallets -> assertThat(
      wallets,
      everyItem(hasProperty("owner", equalTo("admin"))))
   ))
   .expectComplete()
   .verify();
```

Using the preceding example, we can see how to record all elements and then match them with the given matcher. In contrast to the previous examples, where each expectation covered the verification of only one element or a specified count of elements, `.consumeRecordedWith()` makes it possible to verify all elements that are published by a given `Publisher`. It should be noted that `.consumeRecordedWith()` only works if `.recordWith()` is specified. In turn, we should carefully define the collection class in which records will be stored. In the case of a multithreaded publisher, the type of collection used for recording events should support the concurrent access, so in these cases, it is better to use `.recordWith(ConcurrentLinkedQueue::new)` instead of `.recordWith(ArrayList::new)`, because `ConcurrentLinkedQueue` is thread safe in contrast with `ArrayList`.

From the previous few paragraphs, we can familiarize ourselves with the essentials of the Reactor Test API. Along with this, there are also other functionally similar methods. For example, an expectation of the next element might be defined as depicted in the following code:

```
StepVerifier
    .create(Flux.just("alpha-foo", "betta-bar"))
    .expectSubscription()
    .expectNextMatches(e -> e.startsWith("alpha"))
    .expectNextMatches(e -> e.startsWith("betta"))
    .expectComplete()
    .verify();
```

The only difference between `.expectNextMatches()` and `.expectNext()` is that the former makes it possible to define the custom matcher `Predicate`, making it more flexible than the latter. This is because `.expectNext()` is based on the element's comparison using the `.equals()` method.

Similarly, `.assertNext()` and `.consumeNextWith()` make it possible to write custom assertions. It should be noted that `.assertNext()` is the alias for `.consumeNextWith()`. The difference between `.expectNextMatches()` and `.assertNext()` is that the former accepts a `Predicate`, which has to return `true` or `false`, while the latter accepts a `Consumer` that could throw an exception, and any `AssertionError` thrown by the consumer will be captured and thrown by the `.verify()` method, as shown in the following code:

```
StepVerifier
    .create(findUsersUSDWallet())
    .expectSubscription()
    .assertNext(wallet -> assertThat(
        wallet,
        hasProperty("currency", equalTo("USD"))
    ))
    .expectComplete()
    .verify();
```

Finally, we are left with uncovered error cases, which are also part of the normal system's life cycle. There are few API methods that make it possible to check error signals. The simplest one is `.expectError()`, with no arguments, as shown in the following code:

```
StepVerifier
    .create(Flux.error(new RuntimeException("Error")))
    .expectError()
    .verify();
```

Despite the fact that we may verify that the error was emitted, there are cases in which it is vital to test the particular error type. For example, if an incorrect credential is entered during a user's login, then the security service should emit `BadCredentialsException.class`. To verify the emitted error, we may use `.expectError(Class<? extends Throwable>)`, as demonstrated in the following code:

```
StepVerifier
    .create(securityService.login("admin", "wrong"))
    .expectSubscription()
    .expectError(BadCredentialsException.class)
    .verify();
```

In cases in which the checking of the error type is still not enough, there are additional extensions called `.expectErrorMatches()` and `.consumeErrorWith()` that allow a direct interaction with a signaled `Throwable`.

At this point, we may discover the essentials of the testing code written using Reactor 3 or any Reactive Streams specification compatible library. The `StepVerifier` API covers most of the reactive workflows. However, when it comes to the real development, there are some extra cases.

Advanced testing with StepVerifier

The first step of the publisher's testing is the verification of the infinite `Publisher`. According to the Reactive Streams specification, an infinite stream means that the stream will never call the `Subscriber#onComplete()` method. In turn, this means that the testing techniques that we may have learned before will not work anymore. The problem here is that `StepVerifier` is going to wait for the completion signal infinitely. Consequently, the test will be blocked until it is killed. To fix that problem, `StepVerifier` offers a cancellation API that unsubscribes from the source when some expectations are satisfied, as shown in the following code:

```
Flux<String> websocketPublisher = ...
StepVerifier
    .create(websocketPublisher)
    .expectSubscription()
    .expectNext("Connected")
    .expectNext("Price: $12.00")
    .thenCancel()
    .verify();
```

The preceding code tells us that we will disconnect or unsubscribe from the WebSocket after getting `Connected` and after receiving the `Price: $12.00` message.

Another crucial stage during the system's verification is checking for the backpressure behavior of the `Publisher`. For example, interaction with an external system over WebSocket results in a push-only `Publisher`. A naive way to prevent such behavior is by protecting downstream with the `.onBackpressureBuffer()` operator. To check that the system behaves as expected with the selected backpressure strategy, we have to control the subscriber demand manually. In order to do this, `StepVerifier` offers the `.thenRequest()` method, which allows us to control the subscriber demand. This is depicted in the following code:

```
Flux<String> websocketPublisher = ...
Class<Exception> expectedErrorClass =
    reactor.core.Exceptions.failWithOverflow().getClass();

StepVerifier
    .create(websocketPublisher.onBackpressureBuffer(5), 0)
    .expectSubscription()
    .thenRequest(1)
    .expectNext("Connected")
    .thenRequest(1)
    .expectNext("Price: $12.00")
    .expectError(expectedErrorClass)
    .verify();
```

From the preceding example, we might learn how to use the `.thenRequest()` method for verifying backpressure behavior. In turn, it is expected that at some point in time, the overflow will take place and we will get an overflow error. Please note that in the preceding example, we used the `StepVerifier.create()` method's overload, which accepts the initial subscriber's demand as the second argument. In one argument method's overload, the default demand is `Long.MAX_VALUE`, which refers to unlimited demand.

One of the advanced features offered by the `StepVerifiers` API is the ability to run an additional action after a particular verification. For example, in the case where elements producing the process require some additional external interaction, this might be done with the `.then()` method.

We will also use `TestPublisher` from the test package of the Reactor Core library. `TestPublisher` implements the Reactive Stream `Publisher` and makes it possible to directly trigger the `onNext()`, `onComplete()`, and `onError()` events for testing purposes. The next example demonstrates how to trigger new events during the test execution:

```
TestPublisher<String> idsPublisher = TestPublisher.create();

StepVerifier
    .create(walletsRepository.findAllById(idsPublisher))
    .expectSubscription()
    .then(() -> idsPublisher.next("1"))                           // (1)
    .assertNext(w -> assertThat(w, hasProperty("id", equalTo("1"))))  // (2)
    .then(() -> idsPublisher.next("2"))                           // (3)
    .assertNext(w -> assertThat(w, hasProperty("id", equalTo("2"))))  // (4)
    .then(idsPublisher::complete)                                 // (5)
    .expectComplete()
    .verify();
```

In this example, it is a requirement to verify that `WalletRepository` searching wallets are correctly given `ids`. In turn, one of the specific requirements of the wallet repository is searching for data as it comes, which means that the upstream should be a hot `Publisher`. In our example, we use `TestPublisher.next()` in combination with `StepVerifier.then()`. Steps `(1)` and `(3)` send new requests only after previous steps were verified. Step `(2)` verifies that requests generated with step `(1)` were processed successfully and correspondingly, while line `(4)` verifies step `(3)`. Step `(5)` commands `TestPublisher` to complete the request stream, after which `StepVerifier` verifies that the response stream is also completed.

This technique plays an important role by enabling event production after the subscription has actually happened. In this way, we may verify that emitted IDs have been found right after that action, and that the `walletsRepository` behaves as expected.

Dealing with virtual time

Despite the fact that the essence of testing is in covering business logic, there is another very important part that should be given thought as well. To understand this characteristic, we should consider the following example of the code first:

```
public Flux<String> sendWithInterval() {
    return Flux.interval(Duration.ofMinutes(1))
        .zipWith(Flux.just("a", "b", "c"))
        .map(Tuple2::getT2);
}
```

This example shows a naive way of publishing events with a specific interval. In a real-world scenario, behind the same API, there might be a more complex mechanism hidden that involves long delays, timeouts, and event intervals. To verify such code using `StepVerifier`, we might end up with the following test case:

```
StepVerifier
    .create(sendWithInterval())
    .expectSubscription()
    .expectNext("a", "b", "c")
    .expectComplete()
    .verify();
```

The proceeding test will be passed toward our previous implementation of `sendWithInterval()`, which is something that we really want to achieve. However, there is a problem with this test. If we run it a few times, we will find that the average duration of the test is a bit more than three minutes. This occurs because the `sendWithInterval()` method produces three events with a delay of one minute before each element. In cases in which the interval or schedule time will be hours or days, verification of the system may take a huge amount of time, which is unacceptable when it comes to continuous integration nowadays. To solve this problem, the Reactor Test module offers the ability to replace real time with virtual time, as shown in the following code:

```
StepVerifier.withVirtualTime(() -> sendWithInterval())
    // scenario verification ...
```

When using the `.withVirtualTime()` builder method, we explicitly replace every `Scheduler` in the Reactor with `reactor.test.scheduler.VirtualTimeScheduler`. In turn, such a replacement means that `Flux.interval` will be run on that `Scheduler` as well. Consequently, all control of the time may be done using `VirtualTimeScheduler#advanceTimeBy`, as shown in the following code:

```
StepVerifier
    .withVirtualTime(() -> sendWithInterval())
    .expectSubscription()
    .then(() -> VirtualTimeScheduler
        .get()
        .advanceTimeBy(Duration.ofMinutes(3))
    )
    .expectNext("a", "b", "c")
    .expectComplete()
    .verify();
```

As we might notice, in the preceding example we use `.then()` in combination with the `VirtualTimeScheduler` API to advance the time by a certain amount. If we run that test, it will take a few milliseconds instead of minutes! This result is much better, since now our test behaves regardless of the actual time intervals with which the data is produced. Finally, to make our test clean, we may replace the combination of `.then()` and `VirtualTimeScheduler` with `.thenAwait()`, which behaves identically.

 Be aware that in cases in which `StepVerifier` does not advance time enough, the test may hang forever.

To limit the time spent on the verification scenario, the `.verify(Duration t)` overload may be used. This will throw `AssertionError` when the test fails to verify during the allowed duration. Furthermore, the `.verify()` method returns how long the verification process actually took. The following code depicts such a use case:

```
Duration took = StepVerifier
    .withVirtualTime(() -> sendWithInterval())
    .expectSubscription()
    .thenAwait(Duration.ofMinutes(3))
    .expectNext("a", "b", "c")
    .expectComplete()
    .verify();

System.out.println("Verification took: " + took);
```

In cases in which it is important to check that there were no events during the specified waiting time, there is an additional API method called `.expectNoEvents()`. Using this method, we may check that events are produced using the specified interval, as follows:

```
StepVerifier
    .withVirtualTime(() -> sendWithInterval())
    .expectSubscription()
    .expectNoEvent(Duration.ofMinutes(1))
    .expectNext("a")
    .expectNoEvent(Duration.ofMinutes(1))
    .expectNext("b")
    .expectNoEvent(Duration.ofMinutes(1))
    .expectNext("c")
    .expectComplete()
    .verify();
```

From the preceding examples, we might learn a list of techniques that help us make our test fast.

It might be noted that there is an additional overload of the .thenAwait() method with no arguments. The main idea behind this method is the triggering of any tasks that have not yet been executed and that are scheduled to be executed at or before the current virtual time. For example, to receive the first scheduled event in the next set up, Flux.interval(Duration.ofMillis(0), Duration.ofMillis(1000)) will require an additional call of .thenAwait(), as shown in the following code:

```
StepVerifier
    .withVirtualTime(() ->
        Flux.interval(Duration.ofMillis(0), Duration.ofMillis(1000))
            .zipWith(Flux.just("a", "b", "c"))
            .map(Tuple2::getT2)
    )
    .expectSubscription()
    .thenAwait()
    .expectNext("a")
    .expectNoEvent(Duration.ofMillis(1000))
    .expectNext("b")
    .expectNoEvent(Duration.ofMillis(1000))
    .expectNext("c")
    .expectComplete()
    .verify();
```

Without .thenAwait(), the test will hang forever.

Verifying reactive context

Finally, the most uncommon verification is that of the Reactor's Context. We covered the role and mechanics of Context in Chapter 4, *Project Reactor - the Foundation for Reactive Apps*. Let's assume that we want to verify the reactive API of the authentication service. In order to authenticate a user, LoginService expects that a subscriber will provide a Context that holds the authentication information:

```
StepVerifier
    .create(securityService.login("admin", "admin"))
    .expectSubscription()
    .expectAccessibleContext()
    .hasKey("security")
    .then()
    .expectComplete()
    .verify();
```

In the preceding code, we can see how to check whether there is an accessible `Context` instance. We can see that there is only one case in which the `.expectAccessibleContext()` verification may fail. This happens only when the returned `Publisher` is not a Reactor type (`Flux` or `Mono`). Consequently, subsequent `Context` verifications will be executed only if there is an accessible context. Along with the `.hasKey()`, there are a bunch of other methods that allow a detailed verification of the current context. To exit the context verification, the builder provides the `.then()` method.

To summarize this section, we learned how the Reactor Test helps with Reactive Streams testing. This section covers almost everything required to unit test a small piece of reactive code, but there is still a lot more offered by the Spring Framework for testing reactive systems.

Testing WebFlux

In this section, we are going to cover additions that were introduced for the verification of WebFlux-based applications. Here, we will focus on checking the modules' compatibility, application integrity, exposed communication protocols, external APIs, and client libraries. So it is not about simple unit tests anymore, but more about the component and integration testing.

Testing Controllers with WebTestClient

Imagine that we test a *Payment* service. In this scenario, suppose that the *Payment* service supports the GET and POST methods for the /payments endpoint. The first HTTP call is responsible for retrieving the list of executed payments for the current user. In turn, the second makes it possible to submit a new payment. Implementation of that rest controller looks like the following:

```
@RestController
@RequestMapping("/payments")
public class PaymentController {
    private final PaymentService paymentService;

    public PaymentController(PaymentService paymentService) {
        this.paymentService = paymentService;
    }

    @GetMapping("/")
    public Flux<Payment> list() {
```

```
        return paymentService.list();
    }

    @PostMapping("/")
    public Mono<String> send(Mono<Payment> payment) {
        return paymentService.send(payment);
    }
}
```

The first step toward the verification of our service is writing all expectations from the web exchange with the service. For interaction with WebFlux endpoints, the updated spring-test module offers us the new org.springframework.test.web.reactive.server.WebTestClient class. WebTestClient is similar to org.springframework.test.web.servlet.MockMvc. The only difference between those test web clients is that WebTestClient is aimed at testing WebFlux endpoints. For example, using WebTestClient and the Mockito library, we may write the verification for retrieving the list of user payments in the following way:

```
@Test
public void verifyRespondWithExpectedPayments() {
    PaymentService paymentService = Mockito.mock(PaymentService.class);
    PaymentController controller = new PaymentController(paymentService);

    prepareMockResponse(paymentService);
    WebTestClient
        .bindToController(controller)
        .build()
        .get()
        .uri("/payments/")
        .exchange()
        .expectHeader().contentTypeCompatibleWith(APPLICATION_JSON)
        .expectStatus().is2xxSuccessful()
        .returnResult(Payment.class)
        .getResponseBody()
        .as(StepVerifier::create)
        .expectNextCount(5)
        .expectComplete()
        .verify();
}
```

In this example, we built a verification of PaymentController using WebTestClient. In turn, using the WebTestClient fluent API, we may check the correctness of the response's status code and headers. Also, we can use .getResponseBody() to get a Flux of responses, which is finally verified using StepVerifier. This example shows how easily both tools can be integrated with each other.

In the preceding example, we might see that PaymentService is mocked and we do not communicate with external services when testing PaymentController. However, to check the system integrity, we have to run complete components, not just a few layers. To run the completed integration test, we need the whole application to be started. For that purpose, we may use a common @SpringBootTest annotation in combination with @AutoConfigureWebTestClient. WebTestClient provides the ability to establish an HTTP connection with any HTTP server. Furthermore, WebTestClient can directly bind to WebFlux-based applications using mock request and response objects, eliminating the need for an HTTP server. It plays the same role in testing WebFlux applications as TestRestTemplate for WebMVC applications, as shown in the following code:

```
@RunWith(SpringRunner.class)
@SpringBootTest
@AutoConfigureWebTestClient
public class PaymentControllerTests {
    @Autowired
    WebTestClient client;
    ...
}
```

Here, we do not need to configure WebTestClient anymore. This is because all of the required defaults are configured by Spring Boot's autoconfiguration.

 Please note that if an application uses the Spring Security module, additional configuration for tests might be required. We may add a dependency on the spring-security-test module that provides the @WithMockUser annotation targeted especially at mocking user authentication. Out of the box, the @WithMockUser mechanism supports WebTestClient. However, even if @WithMockUser does its job, enabled by default CSRF may add some undesirable obstacles to the end-to-end tests. Pay attention; additional configuration regarding CSRF is required only for @SpringBootTest or any other Spring Boot test runner except @WebFluxTest, which disables CSRF by default.

To test the second part of the *Payment* service example, we need to look through the business logic of the PaymentService implementation. This is defined using the following code:

```
@Service
public class DefaultPaymentService implements PaymentService {

    private final PaymentRepository paymentRepository;
    private final WebClient          client;
```

```
public DefaultPaymentService(PaymentRepository repository,
                               WebClient.Builder builder) {
   this.paymentRepository = repository;
   this.client = builder.baseUrl("http://api.bank.com/submit").build();
}

@Override
public Mono<String> send(Mono<Payment> payment) {
  return payment
            .zipWith(
                ReactiveSecurityContextHolder.getContext(),
                (p, c) -> p.withUser(c.getAuthentication().getName())
            )
            .flatMap(p -> client
                .post()
                .syncBody(p)
                .retrieve()
                .bodyToMono(String.class)
                .then(paymentRepository.save(p)))
            .map(Payment::getId);
}

@Override
public Flux<Payment> list() {
   return ReactiveSecurityContextHolder
            .getContext()
            .map(SecurityContext::getAuthentication)
            .map(Principal::getName)
            .flatMapMany(paymentRepository::findAllByUser);
}
}
```

First of all, the thing that should be noted here is that the method that returns all the user's payments interacts only with the database. In contrast, the payment's submission logic, along with the database interaction, requires additional interaction with an external system via `WebClient`. In our example, we are using a reactive Spring Data MongoDB module, which supports an embedded mode for testing purposes. In contrast, interaction with an external bank provider, for instance, cannot be embedded. Consequently, we need to mock an external service with a tool such as WireMock (`http://wiremock.org`) or somehow mock outgoing HTTP requests. Mocking services with WireMock is a valid option for both WebMVC and WebFlux.

However, when comparing WebMVC and WebFlux functionality from a test perspective, the former has an advantage, because of the out-of-the-box ability to mock an outgoing HTTP interaction. Unfortunately, there is no support for a similar functionality with `WebClient` in Spring Boot 2.0 and Spring Framework 5.0.x. However, there is a trick here that makes it possible to mock the response of an outgoing HTTP call. In situations in which developers follow the technique of constructing a `WebClient` using `WebClient.Builder`, it is possible to mock `org.springframework.web.reactive.function.client.ExchangeFunction`, which plays an essential role in `WebClient` request processing, as shown in the following code:

```
public interface ExchangeFunction {
    Mono<ClientResponse> exchange(ClientRequest request);
    ...
}
```

Using the following test's configuration, it is possible to customize `WebClient.Builder` and provide a *mocked*, or *stubbed* implementation of `ExchangeFunction`:

```
@TestConfiguration
public class TestWebClientBuilderConfiguration {
    @Bean
    public WebClientCustomizer testWebClientCustomizer(
        ExchangeFunction exchangeFunction
    ) {
        return builder -> builder.exchangeFunction(exchangeFunction);
    }
}
```

This hack gives us the ability to verify the correctness of the formed `ClientRequest`. In turn, by properly implementing `ClientResponse`, we may simulate the network activity and interaction with the external service. The completed test may look like the following:

```
@ImportAutoConfiguration({
    TestSecurityConfiguration.class,
    TestWebClientBuilderConfiguration.class
})
@RunWith(SpringRunner.class)
@WebFluxTest
@AutoConfigureWebTestClient
public class PaymentControllerTests {
    @Autowired
    WebTestClient client;
    @MockBean
    ExchangeFunction exchangeFunction;
```

```
@Test
@WithMockUser
public void verifyPaymentsWasSentAndStored() {
    Mockito
        .when(exchangeFunction.exchange(Mockito.any()))
        .thenReturn(
            Mono.just(MockClientResponse.create(201, Mono.empty())));

    client.post()
            .uri("/payments/")
            .syncBody(new Payment())
            .exchange()
            .expectStatus().is2xxSuccessful()
            .returnResult(String.class)
            .getResponseBody()
            .as(StepVerifier::create)
            .expectNextCount(1)
            .expectComplete()
            .verify();

    Mockito.verify(exchangeFunction).exchange(Mockito.any());
    }
}
```

In this example, we used the `@WebFluxTest` annotation to disable full autoconfiguration and apply only WebFlux's relevant configuration, including `WebTestClient`. The `@MockBeen` annotation is used to inject a mocked instance of `ExchangeFunction` into the Spring IoC container. In turn, the combination of `Mockito` and `WebTestClient` allows us to build an end-to-end verification of the desired business logic.

Even though it is possible to mock outgoing HTTP communication in WebFlux applications in a similar way to WebMVC, do this with caution! This approach has its pitfalls. Now, application tests are built under the assumption that all HTTP communications are implemented with `WebClient`. This is not a service contract, but rather an implementation detail. Consequently, if any service changes its HTTP client library for any reason, the corresponding tests will break for no reason. Consequently, it is preferable to use *WireMock* to mock external services. Such an approach not only assumes an actual HTTP client library, but also tests actual request-response payloads sent over the network. As a rule of thumb, it may be acceptable to mock the HTTP client library when testing separate classes with business logic, but it is a definite no-go for black-box testing the entire service.

In general, in the following techniques, we may verify all business logic built on top of a standard Spring WebFlux API. `WebTestClient` has an expressive API that allows us to verify regular REST controllers and new Router functions using `.bindToRouterFunction()` or `.bindToWebHandler()`. Moreover, using `WebTestClient`, we may perform black-box testing by using `.bindToServer()` and providing a full server HTTP address. The following test checks some assumptions regarding the website `http://www.bbc.com` and fails (as expected) because of the difference between the expected and actual response bodies:

```
WebTestClient webTestClient = WebTestClient
    .bindToServer()
    .baseUrl("http://www.bbc.com")
    .build();

webTestClient
    .get()
    .exchange()
    .expectStatus().is2xxSuccessful()
    .expectHeader().exists("ETag")
    .expectBody().json("{}");
```

This example shows that WebFlux's `WebClient` and `WebTestClient` classes not only give us asynchronous non-blocking clients for HTTP communication, but also a fluent API for integration testing.

Testing WebSocket

Finally, one topic that should be covered here is the verification of streaming systems. In this section, we will cover the testing of the WebSocket server and client only. As we will learn in Chapter 6, *WebFlux Async Non-Blocking Communication*, along with the WebSocket API, there is a **Server-Sent Events** (**SSE**) protocol for streaming data, which gives us similar capabilities. Nevertheless, since the implementation of SSE is almost identical to the implementation of the regular controller, all verification techniques from the previous section will be valid for that case as well. Consequently, the only thing that remains unclear now is how to test WebSocket.

Unfortunately, WebFlux does not provide an out-of-the-box solution for WebSocket API testing. Nonetheless, we may use a standard tool set for building the verification classes. Namely, we may use `WebSocketClient` to connect to the target server and verify the correctness of the received data. The following code depicts such an approach:

```
new ReactorNettyWebSocketClient()
        .execute(uri, new WebSocketHandler() {...})
```

Despite the fact that we may connect to the server, it is difficult to verify incoming data using `StepVerifier`. First of all, `.execute()` returns `Mono<Void>` instead of incoming data from the WebSocket connection. In turn, we need to check the two side interactions, which means that there are cases in which it is important to check that incoming data is the result of outgoing messages. An example of such a system might be a trading platform. Suppose that we have a crypto-trading platform that offers the ability to send trades and receive the results of the deals. One of the business requirements is the ability to make Bitcoin trades. This means that the user may sell or buy bitcoins using the platform and observe the result of the deal. To verify the functionality, we need to check that incoming trade is the result of the outgoing request. From a testing perspective, it is hard to deal with `WebSocketHandler` to check all corner cases. Consequently, from a testing perspective, the WebSocket client's interface would ideally look as follows:

```
interface TestWebSocketClient {
    Flux<WebSocketMessage> sendAndReceive(Publisher<?> outgoingSource);
}
```

To adapt the standard `WebSocketClient` to the proposed `TestWebSocketClient`, we need to go through the following steps.

First, we need to handle `WebSocketSession`, given in `WebSocketHandler` via `Mono<WebSocketSession>`, as shown in the following code:

```
Mono.create(sink ->
    sink.onCancel(
        client.execute(uri, session -> {
                sink.success(session);
                return Mono.never();
            })
            .doOnError(sink::error)
            .subscribe()
    )
);
```

Using `Mono.create()` and `MonoSink`, we may adopt the old school way of handling asynchronous callbacks with a session and redirect it to another stream. In turn, we need to care about the correct return type for the `WebSocketHandler#handle` method. This is because the return type controls the time of the opened connection's life. On the other hand, the connection should be cancelled as soon as `MonoSink` notifies us about this. Consequently, `Mono.never()` is the best candidate, which, in combination with the redirection error via `.doOnError(sink::error)` and the handling cancellation via `sink.onCancel()` , makes that adoption complete.

The second step that should be performed regarding the proposed API is adapting the WebSocketSession using the following technique:

```
public Flux<WebSocketMessage> sendAndReceive(
    Publisher<?> outgoingSource
) {
    ...
    .flatMapMany(session ->
        session.receive()
            .mergeWith(
                Flux.from(outgoingSource)
                    .map(Object::toString)
                    .map(session::textMessage)
                    .as(session::send)
                    .then(Mono.empty())
            )
    );
}
```

Here, we downstream incoming WebSocketMessages and send outgoing messages to the server. As we might have noticed, in this example, we use plain object conversion, which might be replaced with sophisticated message mapping.

Finally, using that API, we may build the following verification's flow for the mentioned functionality:

```
@RunWith(SpringRunner.class)
@SpringBootTest(webEnvironment =
                SpringBootTest.WebEnvironment.DEFINED_PORT)
public class WebSocketAPITests {
    @Test
    @WithMockUser
    public void checkThatUserIsAbleToMakeATrade() {
        URI uri = URI.create("ws://localhost:8080/stream");
        TestWebSocketClient client = TestWebSocketClient.create(uri);
        TestPublisher<String> testPublisher = TestPublisher.create();
        Flux<String> inbound = testPublisher
            .flux()
            .subscribeWith(ReplayProcessor.create(1))
            .transform(client::sendAndReceive)
            .map(WebSocketMessage::getPayloadAsText);

        StepVerifier
            .create(inbound)
            .expectSubscription()
            .then(() -> testPublisher.next("TRADES|BTC"))
            .expectNext("PRICE|AMOUNT|CURRENCY")
```

```
        .then(() -> testPublisher.next("TRADE: 10123|1.54|BTC"))
        .expectNext("10123|1.54|BTC")
        .then(() -> testPublisher.next("TRADE: 10090|-0.01|BTC"))
        .expectNext("10090|-0.01|BTC")
        .thenCancel()
        .verify();
    }
}
```

The first thing we do in this example is configuring the `WebEnvironment`. By setting the `WebEnvironment.DEFINED_PORT`, we tell Spring Framework that it should be available on a configured port. This is an essential step because `WebSocketClient` can connect to the defined handler only over the real HTTP call. We then prepare the inbound stream. In our case, it is important to cache the first message, sent via `TestPublisher` in the `.then()` step. This is because `.then()` may be called before the session can be retrieved, which means that the first message may be ignored, and we may not connect to our bitcoin trades. The next step is to verify that the sent trades have been passed, and that we have received the correct response.

Lastly, it should be mentioned that, along with the WebSocket API verification, there may be cases in which we need to mock interaction over `WebSocketClient` with external services. Unfortunately, there is no easy way to mock an interaction. First of all, this is because we do not have a common `WebSocketClient.Build` that might be mocked. In turn, there is no out-of-the-box way to autowire `WebSocketClient`. Consequently, the only solution that we might have is wiring a mock server.

Summary

In this chapter, we learned how to test asynchronous code written using Reactor 3 or any Reactive Streams-based libraries. In turn, we covered the essential points of testing reactive Spring applications, based on the WebFlux module and the Spring Test module. Then, using `WebTestClient`, we learned a way to verify a single controller in isolation, or the whole application with mocked external interaction. Furthermore, we learned knowing how to test Reactor 3 helps us in testing the whole system in integration. Along with everyday business logic checking, we learned a few tips for working with mocked security, which is also a crucial part of modern web applications. Finally, this chapter ended with some tips and tricks for WebSocket testing. Here, we saw some of the limitations of the 5.0.x Spring Test module. Nevertheless, by adopting `WebSocketClient`, we learned how to build a testable data flow and check the correctness of the client-server interaction. Unfortunately, we also discovered that there is no simple way to mock `WebSocketClient` for a server-to-server interaction.

Since we have finished testing our system, it is time to learn how to deploy a web application to the cloud and learn how to monitor it in production. Consequently, in the next chapter, we will cover how to work with Pivotal Cloud, the toolset that helps us to monitor the entire reactive system. We will also cover how Spring 5 helps us to solve problems.

10
And, Finally, Release It!

Throughout this book, we have covered everything about Reactivity in Spring 5. This includes the concepts and patterns of reactive programming with Reactor 3, the new features of Spring Boot 2, Spring WebFlux, Reactive Spring Data, Spring Cloud Streams, and testing techniques for reactive programming. Now that we are familiar with these concepts, it is time to prepare our reactive application for production. The application should expose logs, metrics, traces, feature toggles, and other information that is useful for ensuring a successful operation. The application should also discover runtime dependencies such as database or message broker without violating security concerns. With all of this in mind, we can build an executable artifact ready for an on-premise or cloud deployment.

In this chapter, we will cover the following topics:

- The challenges of a software operation
- The need for operational metrics
- The aim and features of a Spring Boot Actuator
- How to extend Actuator capabilities
- Techniques and libraries for monitoring the reactive application
- Tracing services interaction inside the reactive system
- Tips and tricks for an application's deployment in the cloud

The importance of DevOps-friendly apps

We may look at almost any software from three distinct angles. Each angle represents the needs of different target audiences that work with the system, namely the following:

- Business users are interested in the business functions that the system provides
- Developers want the system to be development-friendly
- Operational teams want the system to DevOps-friendly

Now let's explore the operational aspect of a software system. From the standpoint of a DevOps team member, a software system is DevOps-friendly when it is not hard to support the system in production. This means that the system exposes proper health checks and metrics, and provides the ability to measure its performance and update different components smoothly. Furthermore, because nowadays microservices architecture is a default software development technique, it is mandatory to have the proper monitoring capabilities even to deploy to the cloud. Without a proper monitoring infrastructure, our software would not be able to survive more than a few days in production.

The appearance of cloud environments for application deployment simplified and democratized software delivery and operational processes by providing the proper infrastructure even for the most demanding software designs. IaaS, PaaS, and container management systems such as Kubernetes (https://kubernetes.io) or Apache Mesos (http://mesos.apache.org) have removed many headaches related to OS and network configurations, file backups, metrics gathering, automatic service scaling, and much, much more. However, such external services and techniques still cannot determine on their own whether our business application delivers the appropriate quality of service. Besides, the cloud provider cannot suggest whether the underlying resources are used efficiently depending on the tasks that our system is doing. Such responsibility still rests on the shoulders of software developers and DevOps.

To operate software efficiently, mainly when it consists of dozens or even sometimes thousands of services, we need some ways to do the following:

- Identify services
- Check the service's health status
- Monitor operational metrics
- Look through the logs and dynamically change log levels
- Trace requests or data flows

Let's go through each of the concerns one by one. Service identification is a must in microservice architecture. This is because in most cases some orchestration systems (such as Kubernetes) will spawn a multitude of service instances on different nodes, shuffling them, creating and destroying nodes as a client's demand grows and decreases. Even though containers or runnable JAR files usually have meaningful names, it is essential to be able to identify the service name, type, version, build time, and event commit revision of the source code at the time of running. This makes it possible to spot an incorrect or buggy service version in production, trace the changes that introduced a regression (if any) and automatically track performance characteristics of different versions of the same service.

When it comes to being able to distinguish between services at runtime, we want to know whether all services are healthy. If not, we want to know whether this is critical, depending on the role of a service. Service health check endpoints are often used by an orchestration system itself to identify and restart a failing service. It's not mandatory to have only two states here: healthy and unhealthy. Usually, a health status provides the whole set of essential checks—some of these are critical, some are not. For example, we may calculate a service health level based on processing a queue size, error rate, available disc space, and free memory. It is worth only considering essential metrics when calculating the overall health. In other cases, we may risk building a service that can hardly ever be considered healthy. In general, the ability to offer a health status request means that the service is at least capable of serving requests. This characteristic is often used by the containers' management systems to check service availability and make a decision about a service restart.

Even when the service operates correctly and has a healthy status, we often want to have a deeper insight into operational details. A successful system not only consists of healthy components but also behaves in a predicted and acceptable way for an end user. The critical metrics for the system could include average response time, error rate, and, depending on a request's complexity, the time it takes to process a request. Having an understanding of how our system behaves under the load not only allows us to scale it adequately but also allows us to plan expenses on the infrastructure. It also enables spotting hot codes, inefficient algorithms, and limiting factors for scalability. Operational metrics give a snapshot of the current state of the system and bring a lot of value, but metrics are much more informative when gathered continuously. Operational metrics provide trends and may deliver insights into some correlated characteristics like service memory usage with regards to uptime. Wisely implemented metric reporters do not consume a lot of server resources, but keeping metrics history over time requires some additional infrastructure, usually a time-series database such as Graphite (`https://graphiteapp.org`), InfluxDB (`https://www.influxdata.com`), or Prometheus (`https://prometheus.io`). To visualize a time-series on meaningful dashboards and to set up alerts in response to critical situations, we often need additional monitoring software such as Grafana (`https://grafana.com`) or Zabbix (`https://www.zabbix.com`). Cloud platforms often provide such software to their clients in the form of extra services.

When monitoring the service's operational characteristics and investigating incidents, a DevOps team often reads logs. Nowadays, all the application logs should ideally be stored or at least analyzed in one centralized place. For that purpose, in a Java ecosystem, ELK stack (`https://www.elastic.co/elk-stack`) (consisting of Elasticsearch, Logstash, and Kibana) is often used. Although such a software stack is excellent and makes it possible to treat the dozens of services as one system, it is very inefficient to transfer over the network and store logs for all logging levels. Usually, it is enough to save INFO messages and turn on DEBUG or TRACE levels only to investigate some repeatable anomalies or errors. To do dynamic log level management, we need some hassle-free interfaces.

When logs do not reveal enough to represent the whole picture, our last resort attempt before laborious debugging would be the ability to trace processes inside our software. Tracing could represent a detailed log of recent server requests, or it could describe the complete topology of subsequent requests, including queueing time, DB-requests with timing, external calls with correlation IDs, and so on. Tracing is very helpful for visualizing request processing in real-time and it is indispensable when improving software performance. Distributed tracing does the same in a distributed system, making it possible to track all requests, messages, network delays, errors, and so on. Later in this chapter, we will describe how to enable distributed tracing with Spring Cloud Sleuth and Zipkin (`https://zipkin.io`).

 Adrian Cole, the head of the Zipkin project, gave a great talk about the importance of different perspectives in application monitoring: `https://www.dotconferences.com/2017/04/adrian-cole-observability-3-ways-logging-metrics-tracing`.

Most importantly, for the successful operation of the software system, all of the techniques mentioned are required or at least desired. Fortunately, in a Spring ecosystem, we have a Spring Boot Actuator.

All previously mentioned operational techniques are well-understood and well-described for an ordinary Servlet-based application. However, since reactive programming on a Java platform is still a novelty, achieving similar objectives for a reactive application may require some code modifications or even entirely different implementation approaches.

Nevertheless, from an operational standpoint, a service implemented with reactive programming should not differ from an ordinary well-implemented synchronous service. It should follow the Twelve-Factor App guidelines (`https://12factor.net`), it should be DevOps friendly, and it should be easy to operate and evolve.

Monitoring the Reactive Spring application

In general, it is possible to implement all the monitoring infrastructure for a Spring application in a custom way, but this would apparently be a pretty wasteful venture, especially when doing so repeatedly for each service in a microservice system. Hopefully, Spring Framework provides a pretty good tool set to help build a DevOps-friendly application. This tool set is called Spring Boot Actuator. With only one additional Spring Boot dependency, this brings some important capabilities. At the same time, it also gives a skeleton for the desired monitoring infrastructure.

Spring Boot Actuator

Spring Boot Actuator is a sub-project of Spring Boot that brings a lot of production-ready features to the Spring Boot application. This includes service info, health checks, metrics gathering, tracing traffic, state of the database, and so on. The central idea behind a Spring Boot actuator is to provide the application's essential metrics and make it possible to extend them with ease.

A Spring Boot actuator exposes HTTP endpoints and JMX beans with a lot of operational information, and this allows seamless integration with a lot of monitoring software. Its numerous plugins extend those capabilities even more. As with most of Spring's modules, it is enough to add one dependency to get a consistent tool set for application monitoring.

Adding an actuator to the project

Adding a Spring Boot actuator is as simple as adding the next dependency to the project. Consider the following dependency in the Gradle-built file:

```
compile('org.springframework.boot:spring-boot-starter-actuator')
```

Here, we rely on the fact that the actual version of the library and all its dependencies are specified in the **Spring Boot Bill of Materials** (**BOM**).

A Spring Boot actuator was initially introduced with Spring Boot Version 1.x, but with Spring Boot 2.x it has been improved a lot. At the moment, an actuator is technologically agnostic and supports both Spring Web MVC and Spring WebFlux. It also shares the security model with the rest of the application, so it could easily be used in a reactive application and leverage all benefits of reactive programming.

The default configuration of an actuator exposes all endpoints under URL `/actuator`, but this could be changed with the `management.endpoints.web.base-path` property. So, after the application has started, we may immediately begin by exploring the internals of the service.

 As Spring Boot actuator heavily depends on the web infrastructure of the application, it is required to have either Spring Web MVC or Spring WebFlux as an application dependency.

Now let's go through the main concerns described earlier and look at how to implement them in a reactive application.

Service info endpoint

By default, a Spring Boot actuator provides the most valuable information for system monitoring, scaling, and evolving over time. Depending on the application configuration, it exposes information about the application executable artifact (service group, artifact ID, artifact name, artifact version, build time) and Git coordinates (branch name, commit ID, commit time). Of course, we may extend this list with additional information, if required.

 To expose the information collected during the build of the application, we may add the following configuration to the Gradle build file in the `springBoot` section: `buildInfo()`. Of course, the same functionality is available for Maven builds. The following article provides more details about this: `https://docs.spring.io/spring-boot/docs/current/reference/htmlsingle/#howto-build`.

An actuator displays application information with an `/actuator/info` endpoint. In general, this endpoint is enabled by default, but its accessibility may be configured by the `management.endpoint.info.enabled` property.

We may add some custom information exposed over that REST endpoint by configuring the `application.property` file in the following way:

```
info:
    name: "Reactive Spring App"
    mode: "testing"
    service-version: "2.0"
        features:
            feature-a: "enabled"
            feature-b: "disabled"
```

Alternatively, we may provide similar information programmatically by registering a bean that implements the `InfoContributor` interface. The following code depicts this capability:

```
@Component
public class AppModeInfoProvider implements InfoContributor {        // (1)
    private final Random rnd = new Random();

    @Override
    public void contribute(Info.Builder builder) {                   // (2)
        boolean appMode = rnd.nextBoolean();
        builder
            .withDetail("application-mode",                          // (3)
                    appMode ? "experimental" : "stable");
    }
}
```

Here, we have to implement an `InfoContributor` interface (1) with only the `contribute(...)` (2) method, which provides a builder that can be used to add the required information using the `withDetail(...)` (3) builder method:

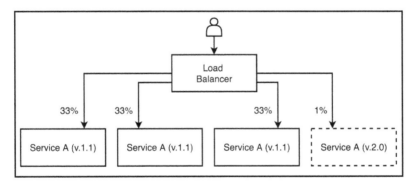

Diagram 10.1. An example of the Canary Deployment pattern. The load balancer routes traffic to service instances, according to their versions

When discussing advanced usage scenarios, an actuator service info endpoint may be leveraged when doing a canary deployment (`https://martinfowler.com/bliki/CanaryRelease.html`). Here, a load balancer may use the information about the service version to route incoming traffic.

 To learn all details related to Spring Boot Actuator `/info` endpoint, follow this link: `https://docs.spring.io/spring-boot/docs/current/reference/htmlsingle/#production-ready-application-info`.

Because a Spring Boot actuator does not provide any reactive or asynchronous APIs for information exposure, a reactive service is not any different than a blocking one.

Health information endpoint

The next essential point of the system's monitoring is the capability to check the service health status. In the most straightforward approach, service health might be interpreted as an ability for the service to respond to requests. Such a scenario is depicted in the following diagram:

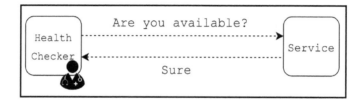

Diagram 10.2. An example of naive health checking over checking whether a service is available

The central problem here is that the service might be accessible via a network. However, some vital components such as a hard drive (if used), underlying database, or a dependent service might be inaccessible. Because of this, the service cannot be fully functional. From the operational perspective, a health check means much more than just an availability status. First of all, a healthy service is one in which sub-components are fitted and available as well. Moreover, the health information should include all details that allow an operational team to react to potential threats of failure as soon as possible. Responding to the unavailability of the database or free disc space shortage will enable DevOps to take corresponding actions. So, health information may include more details as depicted in the following diagram:

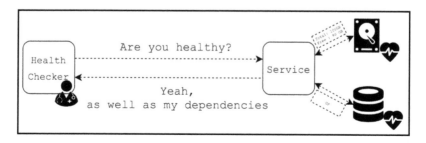

Diagram 10.3. An example of a health check with details about underlying resources

To our delight, the Spring Boot actuator offers a fully-fledged approach to health monitoring. Essential details of the service health might be accessed via the `/actuator/health` endpoint. This endpoint is enabled and exposed by default. Moreover, a Spring Boot actuator has an extensive list of built-in health indicators for the most common components such as Cassandra, MongoDB, JMS, and other popular services integrated into the Spring Ecosystem.

 To get the full list of built-in `HealthIndicators`, please visit the following link: `https://docs.spring.io/spring-boot/docs/current/reference/html/production-ready-endpoints.html#autoconfiguredhealthindicators`.

Along with a built-in indicator, we may provide a custom implementation of a `HealthIndicator`. However, the most exciting part of Spring Boot Actuator 2.0 is proper integration with Spring WebFlux and Reactor 3. That mixture provides a new reactive interface for health indicators called `ReactiveHealthIndicators`. This may be vital when the health status requires additional I/O requests that could be processed more efficiently with WebClient, as described in Chapter 6, *WebFlux Async Non-Blocking Communication*. The following code implements a custom health indicator using the new API:

```
@Component
class TemperatureSensor {                                        // (1)
  public Mono<Integer> batteryLevel() {                          // (1.1)
    // A network request here
  }
  ...
}

@Component
class BatteryHealthIndicator implements ReactiveHealthIndicator {  // (2)
    private final TemperatureSensor temperatureSensor;             // (2.1)

    @Override
    public Mono<Health> health() {                                 // (3)
        return temperatureSensor
            .batteryLevel()
            .map(level -> {
                if (level > 40) {
                    return new Health.Builder()
                        .up()                                      // (4)
                        .withDetail("level", level)
                        .build();
                } else {
                    return new Health.Builder()
```

```
                      .status(new Status("Low Battery"))              // (5)
                      .withDetail("level", level)
                      .build();
              }
          }).onErrorResume(err -> Mono.                                // (6)
              just(new Health.Builder()
                  .outOfService()                                      // (6.1)
                  .withDetail("error", err.getMessage())
                  .build())
          );
      }
  }
```

The preceding example code shows how to wire communication with an external sensor that can be installed in a house but is available via a network:

1. The `TemperatureSensor` service has a `Mono<Integer> batteryLevel()` (`1.1`) method, which makes a request to the sensor, and, if this is available, returns the current battery level from 0 to 100 percent. This method returns a `Mono` with a response and uses `WebClient` for efficient communication.

2. To use the data about the sensor's battery level when calculating the service health status, we have to define a custom `BatteryHealthIndicator` class. This implements the `ReactiveHealthIndicator` interface and has a reference to the `TemperatureSensor` service (`2.1`).

3. To implement the interface, the health indicator implements the `Mono<Health> health()` method with a reactive return type. Consequently, the health status may be reactively calculated at the point when a network response arrives from the temperature sensor.

4. Depending on the battery level, we may return a predefined UP status with some additional details.

5. An example of a completely custom `Health` status. In this example, we receive a `Low Battery` status.

6. Furthermore, using reactor capabilities, we may react to communication errors and return an OUTOFSERVICE status with some details about the actual error (`6.1`).

A Spring Boot actuator has a few modes that establish when to expand the health information and when to show only the top-level status (`UP`, `DOWN`, `OUTOFSERVICE`, `UNKNOWN`). For our testing purposes, it is enough to set the application property `management.endpoint.health.show-details` to the value `always`. The following article describes available options in greater detail: `https://docs.spring.io/spring-boot/docs/current/reference/htmlsingle/#production-ready-health`. Also, to avoid overwhelming the sensor and limiting the request's rate, we may cache the battery level for a period with Reactor capabilities or configure caching for the service health status with the `management.endpoint.health.cache.time-to-live=10s` property.

Such a monitoring approach enables users to arrange corresponding actions such as raising a ticket for battery replacement or sending notifications to the housekeeper about the low battery status.

Spring Boot Actuator 2 provides a few built-in `ReactiveHealthIndicators` that may be found at the following link: `https://docs.spring.io/spring-boot/docs/current/reference/html/production-ready-endpoints.` `html#autoconfiguredreactivehealthindicators`.

Metrics endpoint

The next vital part of successfully monitoring the application is through operational metrics gathering. Of course, a Spring Boot actuator covers this aspect too and provides monitoring for basic JVM characteristics such as the process uptime, memory usage, CPU usage, and GC pauses. Furthermore, WebFlux provides some statistics regarding the processing of incoming HTTP requests. However, to provide a meaningful insight into what is going on in the service from a business standpoint, we have to extend operational metrics on our own.

Starting with Spring Boot 2.0, an actuator changed an underlying library used for metrics gathering and now uses a micrometer library: `https://micrometer.io`.

If exposed, the /actuator/metrics REST endpoint provides a list of tracked metrics and makes it possible to navigate to a desired gauge or timer, also giving additional contextual information in the form of tags. A summary for one metric, let's say jvm.gc.pause, may look the following way:

```json
{
  "name": "jvm.gc.pause",
  "measurements": [
    {
      "statistic": "COUNT",
      "value": 5
    },
    {
      "statistic": "TOTALTIME",
      "value": 0.347
    }
  ],
  "availableTags": [
    {
      "tag": "cause",
      "values": [
        "Heap Dump Initiated GC",
        "Metadata GC Threshold",
        "Allocation Failure"
      ]
    }
  ]
}
```

One drawback of the new metrics endpoint, when compared to its Spring Boot 1.x counterpart, is the inability to retrieve all the tracked metric summaries with a single REST request. However, this is probably only a minor issue.

As usual, we are free to register new metrics using a micrometer metrics registry. Later in this chapter, we will cover the mechanics of this process and will see what operational metrics are useful for the reactive application.

The `/actuator/metrics` endpoint is not exposed by default. Instead, the default configuration exposes only `info` and `health` endpoints. Consequently, the metrics endpoint should be exposed by providing the following property in the `application.property` file—`management.endpoints.web.expos ure.include: info, health, metrics`. The same is relevant to all of the endpoints mentioned later in this chapter. In the case in which it is necessary to expose all endpoints, we may follow the next technique and provide a wildcard instead—`management.endpoints.web.exposure.include: *`. For more details, see the following link: `https://docs.spring.io/spring-boot/docs/current/reference/htmlsingle/#production-ready-endpoints-enabling-endpoints`.

Loggers management endpoint

Likewise, the Spring Boot actuator provides two valuable endpoints for log management. The first one is `/actuator/loggers`, which allows accessing and changing logging levels at runtime without the application restart. This endpoint is very helpful since switching the granularity of information without a service restart is an essential part of a successful application operation. In light of the complicated debug experience related to reactive applications, the ability to switch log levels and analyze the outcome on the fly is crucial. Of course, it is not very convenient to change log levels from a console with a `curl` command, but this feature plays well with Spring Boot admin, which provides a pretty UI for such purposes.

This feature makes it possible to enable or disable dynamically generated logs by a Reactor `log()` operator that was described in `Chapter 4`, *Project Reactor - the Foundation for Reactive Apps*. The following code depicts a reactive service that pushes events to the SSE stream:

```
@GetMapping(path = "/temperature-stream",
            produces = MediaType.TEXTEVENTSTREAMVALUE)
public Flux<TemperatureDto> temperatureEvents() {
    return temperatureSensor.temperatureStream()
                            .log("sse.temperature", Level.FINE)      // (1)
                            .map(this::toDto);
}
```

Here, the `log()` operator registers a logger `sse.temperature` with a `Level.FINE` (1). Consequently, we may dynamically enable or disable the output for this logger using the `/actuator/loggers` endpoint.

On the other hand, an ability to access application logs without a need to copy files from a remote server might be advantageous. To simplify that, Spring Boot actuator provides an `/actuator/logfile` endpoint that exposes a file with logs over the web. Spring Boot admin also has a neat web page that streams application logs to a UI in a pretty convenient way.

 Note that in the case of unavailability of the `/actuator/logfile` endpoint, it might be that the log file is not configured in the application. Consequently, we have to configure it explicitly, as in the following example—`logging.file: my.log`.

Other valuable endpoints

Along with the endpoints mentioned previously, a Spring Boot actuator provides an extensive list of handy web-endpoints. The proper documentation is available from the following link: `https://docs.spring.io/spring-boot/docs/current/actuator-api/html`.

Nevertheless, the most important are listed here with brief descriptions (all endpoints are located under the base Actuator URL `/actuator`):

- `/configprops`: This provides access to all possible configuration properties in the application.
- `/env`: This provides access to environment variables.
- `/mappings`: This provides access to all exposed web endpoints in the application.
- `/httptrace`: This provides access to recorded HTTP interaction for server-side and client-side.
- `/auditevents`: This gives access to all audited events in the application.
- `/beans`: This provides the list of available beans in the Spring context.
- `/caches`: This provides access to the cache management of the application.
- `/sessions`: This provides a list of active HTTP sessions.
- `/threaddump`: This makes it possible to get a thread dump for the application's JVM.
- `/heapdump`: This makes it possible to generate and download a heap dump. Note that in that case, the resulting file will be in HPROF format: `https://docs.oracle.com/javase/8/docs/technotes/samples/hprof.html`.

Writing custom actuator endpoints

A Spring Boot actuator allows registering custom endpoints that will not only display data but also may update the application's behavior. For that purpose, a Spring bean should be decorated with an @Endpoint annotation. To register read/write operations as an actuator endpoint, the library provides @ReadOperation, @WriteOperation, and @DeleteOperation annotations that are in turn mapped to HTTP GET, POST, and DELETE respectively. Note though, generated REST endpoints consume and produce the following content type:
application/vnd.spring-boot.actuator.v2+json, application/json.

To demonstrate how this feature can be used within the reactive application, let's create a custom endpoint that reports the current server time and the time difference with the **Network Time Protocol** (**NTP**) server. Sometimes, such capability helps in resolving issues related to incorrect time due to a server or network misconfiguration. This is especially handy for distributed systems. To do so, we need to register a bean decorated with an @Endpoint annotation and configured ID property (in our case server-time). We will also return the data of interest through a method annotated with @ReadOperation as follows:

```
@Component
@Endpoint(id = "server-time")                                   // (1)
public class ServerTimeEndpoint {
    private Mono<Long> getNtpTimeOffset() {                     // (2)
        // Actual network call to get the current time offset
    }
    @ReadOperation                                             // (3)
    public Mono<Map<String, Object>> reportServerTime() {      // (4)
        return getNtpTimeOffset()                              // (5)
            .map(timeOffset -> {                              // (6)
                Map<String, Object> rsp = new LinkedHashMap<>();    //
                rsp.put("serverTime", Instant.now().toString());    //
                rsp.put("ntpOffsetMillis", timeOffset);            //
                return rsp;
            });
    }
```

The preceding code example shows how to create a custom actuator `@Endpoint` using reactive types from Project Reactor. The aforementioned code sample may be explained as follows:

1. This is an endpoint class with the `@Endpoint` annotation. Here, the `@Endpoint` annotation exposes the `ServerTimeEndpoint` class as the REST endpoint. In addition, the `id` parameter of the `@Endpoint` annotation identifies the URL of the endpoint. In such a combination, the URL is `/actuator/server-time`.

2. This is a method definition that asynchronously reports an offset with the current time on the NTP server. The `getNtpTimeOffset()` method returns `Mono<Long>`, so it could be composed in a reactive fashion.

3. Here is a `@ReadOperation` annotation that marks the `reportServerTime()` method as a method that should be exposed via Actuator mechanisms as a REST `GET` operation.

4. This is the `reportServerTime()` method that returns a reactive type `Mono<Map<String, Object>>`, so it may be efficiently used within a Spring WebFlux application.

5. Here we have a declaration of the asynchronous call to NTP server, the result of which defines the start of a reactive stream.

6. This is a result transformation operation. When a response arrives, it is transformed with a `map()` operator, where we fill in the map with a result (current server time and NTP offset) that should be returned to a user. Note that all the fancy techniques for error handling covered in Chapter 4, *Project Reactor - the Foundation for Reactive Apps* can also be used here.

 The NTP (`http://www.ntp.org`) is a very popular protocol for synchronizing computer clocks over a network. NTP servers are publicly available, but be careful not to abuse the system with too many requests because NTP servers may block our application IP address.

With custom endpoints, we may quickly implement dynamic feature toggles, custom request tracking, modes of operation (master/slave), old sessions invalidation, or a lot of other functionalities that are relevant to successful application operations. It is now also possible to do this in a reactive fashion.

Securing actuator endpoints

In the previous sections, we covered the essentials of a Spring Boot actuator and implemented our custom reactive actuator endpoint. Notice that, when exposing useful information, a Spring Boot actuator may also disclose sensitive information. Access to environment variables, a structure of the application, configuration properties, ability to do heap and thread dumps, and other factors might simplify the lives of bad guys who are trying to hack our application. In these cases, a Spring Boot actuator may also expose private users' data. Therefore, we have to care about secured access for all actuator endpoints as well as the usual REST endpoints.

Due to the fact that a Spring Boot actuator shares a security model with the rest of the application, it is easy to configure access permissions in the place where the main security configuration is defined. For example, the following code only permits access to the /actuator/ endpoint for users who have the ACTUATOR authority:

```
@Bean
public SecurityWebFilterChain securityWebFilterChain(
    ServerHttpSecurity http
) {
    return http.authorizeExchange()
        .pathMatchers("/actuator/").hasRole("ACTUATOR")
        .anyExchange().authenticated()
        .and().build();
}
```

Of course, we may configure access policies differently. Usually, it is appropriate to give unauthenticated access to /actuator/info and /actuator/health endpoints, which are often used for application identification and health-check procedures, and to secure other endpoints that could potentially hold some sensitive information or information that may help during an attack on the system.

On the other hand, we may expose all management endpoints on a separate port and configure network access rules. Consequently, all management will only happen through the internal virtual network. To provide such a configuration, all we have to do is provide the management.server.port property with the desired HTTP port.

To generalize, a Spring Boot actuator brings a lot of features that simplify application identification, monitoring, and management. With tight Spring WebFlux integration, Actuator 2.x uses resources efficiently thanks to the fact that most of its endpoints support reactive types. Actuator 2.x simplifies the overall development process without causing a lot of hassle, expanding application capabilities, consolidating better default application behavior, and making the life of the DevOps team easier.

Although a Spring Boot Actuator is quite useful on its own, it shines even more in conjunction with tools that automatically gather monitoring information and represent such information in a visual form through charts, trends, and alerts. Therefore, later in the chapter, we cover a handy module called Spring Boot Admin that allows accessing all vital management information for multiple services with a single pretty UI.

Micrometer

Starting with Spring Boot 2.0, Spring Framework changed the default library used for metrics gathering. This was previously Dropwizard Metrics (`https://metrics.dropwizard.io`), but now it is a brand new library called Micrometer (`https://micrometer.io`). Micrometer is a standalone library with a minimal list of dependencies. This is developed as a separate project, but it targets Spring Framework as its primary consumer. The library provides a facade over clients for the most popular monitoring systems. Micrometer gives a vendor-neutral monitoring API in the same way that SLF4J gives such an API for logging. At the moment, Micrometer integrates well with Prometheus, Influx, Netflix Atlas, and a dozen other monitoring systems. It also has an embedded in-memory metrics store that allows using the library even without an external monitoring system.

Micrometer is designed to support dimensional metrics where each metric besides a name may contain tags in key/value. Such an approach makes it possible to overview aggregated values and also to drill-down with tags when required. When the target monitoring system does not support dimensional metrics, the library flattens associated tags and adds them to the name.

 To learn more about Micrometer design, its API, and supported monitoring systems, please refer to the project site at `https://micrometer.io`.

A Spring Boot actuator uses Micrometer to report application metrics via the `/actuator/metrics` endpoint. With an actuator module, we get a bean of the `MeterRegistry` type auto-configured by default. This is a Micrometer interface that guards the client code against the details of how and where all metrics are stored. Each supported monitoring backend has a dedicated implementation of the `MeterRegistry` interface, so for Prometheus support, an application has to instantiate the `PrometheusMeterRegistry` class. Of course, Micrometer provides a `CompositeMeterRegistry` to report metrics to more than one registry at once. Furthermore, a `MeterRegistry` interface is an entry point that allows adding custom application metrics from the user code.

There are different types of metrics (such as `Timer`, `Counter`, `Gauge`, `DistributionSummary`, `LongTaskTimer`, `TimeGauge`, `FunctionCounter`, `FunctionTimer`) and all of these extend the `Meter` interface. Every metric type has a versatile API and makes it possible to configure monitoring behavior in the desired way.

Default Spring Boot metrics

By default, the Spring Boot actuator configures Micrometer to gather the most commonly used metrics such as the process uptime, CPU usage, memory usage by regions, GC pauses, treads count, loaded classes, and the number of open file descriptors. It also tracks Logback logger events as counters. All of this behavior is defined by an actuator's `MetricsAutoConfiguration` and gives a pretty evident picture regarding the service metrics.

For reactive applications, an actuator provides `WebFluxMetricsAutoConfiguration`, which adds a specialized `WebFilter`. This filter adds callbacks to the `ServerWebExchange` to intersect the moment when the request processing is finished. It is possible to report the request time. In addition, in the metric's report that filter includes information such as the request URI, HTTP method, response status, and exception type (if any) in the form of tags. In this way, reactive processing of an HTTP request can be easily metered with the Micrometer library. Metrics results are reported with a metric called `http.server.requests`.

Similarly, a Spring Boot actuator instruments `RestTemplate` and registers the `http.client.requests` metric to report on outgoing requests. Starting with Spring Boot 2.1, an actuator does the same with the `WebClient.Builder` bean. Nevertheless, even for Spring Boot 2.0, it is still easy to add the desired metrics for `WebClient` related workflows. Such an approach is explained in the following section.

Along with other useful things, a Spring Boot actuator makes it possible to add common tags to all `Meter`s of the application. This is especially handy in multi-node service deployment, as it allows us to clearly distinguish service nodes by tags. For this purpose, an application should register a bean that implements the `MeterRegistryCustomizer` interface.

 To read more about customizations that the Spring Boot actuator enables over the Micrometer library, please read the following article: https://docs.spring.io/spring-boot/docs/current/reference/htmlsingle/#production-ready-metrics-getting-started.

Monitoring Reactive Streams

Starting with Version 3.2, Project Reactor itself added an essential integration with the Micrometer library. Project Reactor works fine without the Micrometer library, but in case it detects a Micrometer presence in the application's classpath, it may report some elemental metrics that may reveal valuable insights about application operational conditions. Now it is time to describe how to monitor reactive streams using built-in functions and how to add custom meters for the desired operational aspects.

 Project Reactor 3.2 is bundled with Spring Framework 5.1 and Spring Boot 2.1. However, in general, it is possible to bump the reactor version even for applications with Spring Framework 5.0 and Spring Boot 2.0. Furthermore, all the code related to custom metric registration should work fine with previous versions of Project Reactor.

Monitoring reactor flows

In Project Reactor 3.2, reactive types `Flux` and `Mono` obtained a `metrics()` operator. This reports operational metrics regarding the stream when called. The `metrics()` operator behaves similarly to the `log()` operator. It cooperates with the `name()` operator to build a target metric name and add a tag. For example, the following code demonstrates how to add metrics to an outgoing SSE stream:

```
@GetMapping(
        path = "/temperature-stream",
        produces = MediaType.TEXTEVENTSTREAMVALUE)
public Flux<Temperature> events() {
   return temperatureSensor.temperatureStream()                      // (1)
       .name("temperature.stream")                                   // (2)
       .metrics();                                                   // (3)
}
```

Here, the `temperatureSensor.temperatureStream()` returns `Flux<Temperature>` (1), while the `name("temperature.stream")` method adds a name for a monitoring point (2). The `metrics()` method (3) registers a new metric into the `MeterRegistry` instance.

As a result, the Reactor library registers the following counters—reactor.subscribed, reactor.requested and the following timers—reactor.flow.duration, reactor.onNext.delay, each of which has a tag (dimension) called flow with a temperature.stream value. These metrics alone allow us to track the number of stream instantiations, the number of requested elements, the maximum and total time for stream existence as well as onNext delay.

> Please note that Reactor uses the name of the stream as the flow tag in terms of Micrometer metric. As a Micrometer library has a limit for the amount of tracked tags, it is important to configure that limit to collect information about all metered streams.

Monitoring reactor schedulers

Because reactive streams usually operate on different reactor schedulers, it may be beneficial to track fine-grained metrics regarding their operation. In some cases, it is plausible to use a custom ScheduledThreadPoolExecutor with a manual metric instrumentation. For example, let's assume we have the following class:

```
public class MeteredScheduledThreadPoolExecutor
        extends ScheduledThreadPoolExecutor {                          // (1)

    public MeteredScheduledThreadPoolExecutorShort(
        int corePoolSize,
        MeterRegistry registry                                         // (2)
    ) {
        super(corePoolSize);
        registry.gauge("pool.core.size", this.getCorePoolSize());      // (3)
        registry.gauge("pool.active.tasks", this.getActiveCount());    //
        registry.gauge("pool.queue.size", this.getQueue().size());     //
    }
}
```

Here, the MeteredScheduledThreadPoolExecutor class extends an ordinary ScheduledThreadPoolExecutor (1) and additionally receives a MeterRegistry instance (2). In the constructor, we register a few gauges (3) to track the core size of the thread pool, the number of active tasks, and the queue size.

With a small modification, such executors can also track the number of successful and failed tasks as well as time spent executing these tasks. For such purposes, an executor's implementation should also override `beforeExecute()` and `afterExecute()` methods.

Now we may use such an instrumented executor in the following reactive stream:

```
MeterRegistry meterRegistry = this.getRegistry();

ScheduledExecutorService executor =
    new MeteredScheduledThreadPoolExecutor(3, meterRegistry);

Scheduler eventsScheduler = Schedulers.fromExecutor(executor);

Mono.fromCallable(this::businessOperation)
    .subscribeOn(eventsScheduler)
    ....
```

Even though such an approach is pretty powerful, it does not cover built-in `Schedulers` like `parallel()` or `elastic()`. To instrument all reactor schedulers, we may use a custom `Schedulers.Factory`. For example, let's look at the following implementation of such a factory:

```
class MetersSchedulersFactory implements Schedulers.Factory {        // (1)
    private final MeterRegistry registry;

    public ScheduledExecutorService decorateExecutorService(         // (2)
        String type,                                                 // (2.1)
        Supplier<? extends ScheduledExecutorService> actual          // (2.2)
    ) {
        ScheduledExecutorService actualScheduler = actual.get();     // (3)
        String metric = "scheduler." + type + ".execution";          // (4)

        ScheduledExecutorService scheduledExecutorService =
                          new ScheduledExecutorService() {           // (5)
            public void execute(Runnable command) {                  // (6)
                registry.counter(metric, "tag", "execute")           // (6.1)
                        .increment();
                actualScheduler.execute(command);                    // (6.2)
            }

            public <T> Future<T> submit(Callable<T> task) {          // (7)
                registry.counter(metric, "tag", "submit")            // (7.1)
                        .increment();
                return actualScheduler.submit(task);                 // (7.2)
            }

            // other method overrides ...
```

```
    };

    registry.counter("scheduler." + type + ".instances")        // (8)
            .increment();
    return scheduledExecutorService;                              // (9)
    }
}
```

The preceding code is explained as the following:

1. This is a custom implementation of the reactor's `Schedulers.Factory` class.

2. Here, we have a declaration of the method that allows decorating a scheduled executor service where `type` (`2.1`) represents a type of a scheduler (`parallel`, `elastic`) and `actual` (`2.2`) holds a reference to the actual service to be decorated.

3. At this point, there is an extraction of the actual executor service instance, as it is used in a decorator.

4. This is the definition of the counter name that includes the type of `Scheduler` to increase metrics' readability.

5. This is the declaration, the anonymous `ScheduledExecutorService` instance, that decorates the actual `ScheduledExecutorService` and provides additional behavior.

6. This is the overridden `execute(Runnable command)` method, which executes `MeterRegistry#counter` with additional `execute` tag (`6.1`) and increments the number of collected metrics by one. Then, the delegate calls the actual method's implementation (`6.2`).

7. Similar to the `execute` method, we override the `Future<T> submit(Callable<T> task)` method here. With each method's execution, call the `MeterRegistry#counter` method with an additional `submit` tag and finally increment the number of calls in the registry (`7.1`). After all actions, we delegate the method execution to the actual service (`7.2`).

8. This is a declaration of the registering the count of created instances of the executor service.

9. At this point, we finally return the decorated `ScheduledExecutorService` instance with an additional Micrometer metrics processing.

To use the `MetersSchedulersFactory`, we have to register the factory as follows:

```
Schedulers.setFactory(new MeteredSchedulersFactory(meterRegistry));
```

Now all Reactor schedulers (including custom schedulers defined on `MeteredScheduledThreadPoolExecutor`) are metered with Micrometer metrics. Such an approach gives plenty of flexibility but requires some discipline to prevent metrics gathering from becoming the most resource-demanding part of an application. For example, even though a meter (counter/timer/gauge) lookup in a meter registry should be fast, it is better to save a retrieved reference to a local variable or an instance field to reduce redundant lookups. Also, not all aspects of the application execution deserve a dedicated set of metrics. Usually, an application domain and using our common sense helps to select the essential application characteristics to monitor.

Adding custom Micrometer meters

In reactive streams, we may easily add a custom monitoring logic even without built-in support. For example, the following code explains how to add an invocation counter for a `WebClient` that does not have any default instrumentation:

```
WebClient.create(serviceUri)                                   // (1)
        .get()
        .exchange()
        .flatMap(cr -> cr.toEntity(User.class))               // (2)
        .doOnTerminate(() -> registry
                .counter("user.request", "uri", serviceUri)   // (3)
                .increment())
```

Here, we create a new `WebClient` for a target `serviceUri` (1), make a request and deserialize the response to a `User` entity (2). When the operation is terminated, we manually increase the counter with a custom tag `uri` where the value represents `serviceUri` (3).

Similarly, we may combine stream hooks (such as `.doOnNext()`, `.doOnComplete()`, `.doOnSubscribe()`, or `.doOnTerminate()`) with different types of Micrometer meters (such as `.counter()`, `.timer()`, or `.gauge()`) to measure the desired operational characteristics of reactive streams with a sufficient level of detail provided by tags that represent different dimensions.

Distributed tracing with Spring Boot Sleuth

Another crucial ingredient for a successful reactive system operation is to have an understanding of how events flow across the services, how requests stack-up, and how long this takes. As stated in Chapter 8, *Scaling Up with Cloud Streams*, communication between services is an essential part of a distributed system operation and some problems can not be resolved without the full picture of the data flow. However, taking all the complexity of communications in a distributed system into account, such capturing is a very complicated task. Fortunately, Spring Cloud provides an excellent module called spring-cloud-sleuth. Spring Cloud Sleuth is a project well-integrated with Spring Boot 2.x infrastructure, enabling distributed tracing with just a few bits of auto-configuration.

 To read more about Spring Cloud Sleuth, please refer to the following page:
https://cloud.spring.io/spring-cloud-sleuth/single/spring-cloud-sleuth.html.

Even though most modern tracing tools such as Zipkin or Brave do not fully support new Spring reactive web services, Spring Cloud Sleuth naturally fills that gap.

First of all, there is an identical replacement of WebMVC filters for WebFlux called org.springframework.cloud.sleuth.instrument.web.TraceWebFilter. That filter guarantees that all incoming HTTP requests are carefully analyzed and any tracing headers that are found are reported to Zipkin. In turn, with the support of org.springframework.cloud.sleuth.instrument.web.client.TracingHttpClientInstrumentation, all outgoing requests are adjusted with additional tracing headers as well. To track outgoing requests, we have to register WebClient as a context bean instead of creating it each time; otherwise, the proper instrumentation does not happen.

We also have to clarify how all the tracing spans are stored and passed in the reactive programming paradigm. As we might learn from the previous chapters, reactive programming does not guarantee that all of the transformations are executed on the same thread. This means that metadata transferring through ThreadLocal, the primary tracing pattern for **WebMVC**, does not work here in the same way as in the imperative programming paradigm. However, thanks to the composition of the reactor's Context mechanism (described in Chapter 4, *Project Reactor - the Foundation for Reactive Apps*), Reactor's global Hooks, and org.springframework.cloud.sleuth.instrument.web.client.TraceExchangeFilterFunction, it became possible to transfer additional contextual metadata through the reactive flow without ThreadLocal.

Finally, Spring Cloud Sleuth provides a few ways to report collected tracing information to the Zipkin server. The most common method of delivery is through HTTP. Unfortunately, at the moment this method is implemented in a blocking manner. Nevertheless, the default `zipkin2.reporter.AsyncReporter` sends spans (pieces of tracing information) to the Zipkin server on a separate `Thread`. So despite the blocking nature, such a technique might be pretty efficient even in a reactive application since callers on the reactive side are protected from blocking request latency or potential exceptions.

Along with the traditional data delivery protocol over HTTP, there is a message queue-based option. Spring Cloud Sleuth provides excellent support for Apache Kafka and RabbitMQ. Even though the client for Apache Kafka supports asynchronous, non-blocking message passing, the underlying mechanism still uses the same `AsyncReporter` that downgrades non-blocking communication to a blocking one.

Spring Cloud Sleuth brings distributed tracing support for Reactive Spring WebFlux and Spring Cloud Streams. Moreover, to start using this great tool in the project, all that is needed is to require the following dependencies in the project (Gradle config):

```
compile('org.springframework.cloud:spring-cloud-starter-sleuth')
compile('org.springframework.cloud:spring-cloud-starter-zipkin')
```

Furthermore, relying on project dependencies and available environment, Spring Boot Autoconfiguration prepares all beans needed for distributed tracing at runtime.

 When it comes to available Message Broker dependencies such as `org.springframework.amqp:spring-rabbit`, communication over message broker is preferred automatically over HTTP-based communication. In the case in which the HTTP is the preferred option for sending the tracing data, there is a property called `spring.zipkin.sender.type`, which accepts one of the following preferences for communication with Zipkin—`RABBIT`, `KAFKA`, `WEB`.

Pretty UI with Spring Boot Admin 2.x

From the very beginning, the central idea behind the **Spring Boot Admin** project (**SBA**) was to provide a handy admin interface for the managing and monitoring of Spring Boot applications. Spring Boot Admin stands out in its beautiful and user-friendly UI, which is built on top of Spring Actuator endpoints. This gives access to all required operational information such as application health status, CPU and memory metrics, JVM startup flags, an application classpath, application metrics, HTTP traces, and audit events. It also makes it possible to inspect and delete active sessions (using spring-session), manage log levels, make thread and heap dumps, and so on:

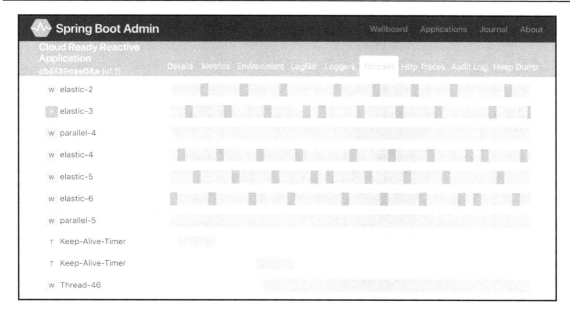

Diagram 10.4. Spring Boot Admin UI showing apps thread statuses in real time

In general, Spring Boot Admin is designed to help operate on microservice applications. Also, Spring Boot Admin consists of two parts:

- The server part. The server acts as a central point of gathering information from all available microservices. Also, the server part exposes the UI through which the gathered information is displayed.
- The client part. This part is included and runs within each service in the system and registers the host service to the Spring Boot Admin server.

Even though the server part of Spring Boot Admin was designed to be a standalone application (recommended configuration), it is possible to assign this role to one of the existing services. To give a service Spring Boot Admin server a role, it is enough to provide the application with the `de.codecentric:spring-boot-admin-starter-server` dependency and add the `@EnableAdminServer` annotation to enable the required auto-configuration. In turn, to integrate all neighboring services with the Spring Boot Admin Server, they may include the `de.codecentric:spring-boot-admin-starter-client` dependency and point to an SBA server, or SBA may leverage a pre-existing Spring Cloud Discovery infrastructure based on Eureka or Consul. Alternatively, it is possible to create a static configuration on the SBA server side.

SBA Server also supports cluster replications, so an SBA Server should not be a single point of failure in the highly-available Microservice application:

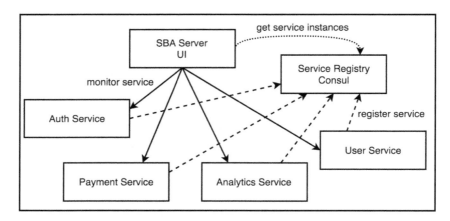

Diagram 10.5. Spring Boot Admin discovering and monitoring services

In the case, when the Spring Boot Admin's dashboard is correctly configured, it contains a mesh of services with the number of registered instances. In turn, each service in the mesh shows its health status, so we may easily understand the whole state of the system. Moreover, it supports push notifications for browsers such as Slack, Hipchat, Telegram, and others, so it may proactively inform the DevOps team about a substantial change within the application infrastructure or it may even be a part of the Pager Duty infrastructure.

Before Version 2.0, as any Spring-oriented add-on, Spring Boot Admin was based on the Servlet API. This meant that both client and server applications were based on blocking I/O that might be inefficient for a high-load reactive system. With 2.0, an SBA server was rewritten from scratch to benefit from Spring WebFlux and do all communications over async non-blocking I/O.

Of course, Spring Boot Admin gives options for adequately securing the SBA server UI as it may expose some sensitive information. Spring Boot Admin also provides integration with a Pivotal Cloud Foundry. In a case in which a Spring Boot Admin Server or client detects the presence of the Cloud Platform, all necessary configurations are applied. Consequently, the clients and the server discovery are simplified. Likewise, an SBA has an extension point, so it is entirely possible to add the desired behavior to an SBA infrastructure. For example, this may include a management page that features toggles or custom auditing.

To learn more about Spring Boot Admin, please follow the following link at `http://codecentric.github.io/spring-boot-admin/current`.

To summarize, Spring Boot Admin gives an excellent opportunity for a DevOps team to easily monitor, operate, and evolve a reactive system using a handy and customizable UI, and we're going to do this with all the benefits of async non-blocking I/O.

Deploying to the cloud

While software development is fun, the essential part of a software life cycle is **production.** This refers to serving actual client requests, doing business processes, and improving the industry in general by offering an amazing business service. For our application, this vital step is called **release**. Now, after being mainly under the guardianship of developers and testers, our software system is ready to meet the real world and the real production environment with its many hidden difficulties.

Taking into account how different target environments and extraordinary customer needs may be, or whatever operational qualities are required, we may notice that the release process itself could be complicated and deserves at least a few books on its own. Here, we do not cover topics related to delivering software but only take a quick look at different software deployment options and how these affect a reactive application.

With the IoT boom, although our reactive applications may soon be running on wearable devices such as smartwatches or heart-rate sensors, here we consider the most common target environments, which are on-premise and in the cloud. The introduction of the cloud changed the way we deploy and operate applications. In a sense, the cloud made us more *reactive* with regard to user demand, as we may now acquire new computation resources in minutes or sometimes even seconds instead of weeks or months in the era of on-premise data centers. However, from the developer standpoint, both these approaches are pretty similar. The main difference is that in the former case, actual servers are located in the building, and in the latter case, they are hosted by the cloud provider.

More critical differences arise in the way we use computation resources to deploy applications, and this distinction relates to both on-premise and cloud deployments:

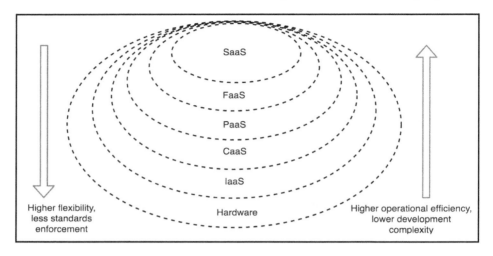

Diagram 10.6. Platform hierarchy and deployment options for software

The following is a brief description of the previous diagram:

- **Hardware**: These are bare-metal servers that do not run a hypervisor and consequently are not virtualized but still may be provided as a cloud service. Examples of these are Scaleway (https://www.scaleway.com) and Packet (https://www.packet.net). A user has to manage everything. Even though the setup does not provide a hypervisor, usually some OS is still installed on the server. From a developer's viewpoint, this option is not very different from IaaS.

- **Infrastructure as a Service (IaaS)**: This cloud provider gives a virtual machine with a Software Define Network and attached storage. Here, a user has to manage an environment and deploy applications. Deployment options choose the user. An example of these are AWS (https://aws.amazon.com) and Microsoft Azure (https://azure.microsoft.com).

- **Containers as a Service (CaaS)**: This is a form of virtualization where a cloud provider allows clients to deploy containers (for example, Docker or CoreOS Rocket containers). Container technology defines deployment mode, but inside a container, the client may use any technology stack. Examples of these are AWS Elastic Container Service (https://aws.amazon.com/ecs) and the Pivotal Container Service (https://pivotal.io/platform/pivotal-container-service).

- **Platform as a Service (PaaS)**: This cloud provider gives everything for an application up to runtime and build pipelines, but it also limits the set of technologies and libraries. Examples of these are Heroku (`https://www.heroku.com`) and the Pivotal Cloud Foundry (`https://pivotal.io/platform`).

- **Function as a Service (FaaS, Serverless)**: This is an extremely recent development. Here, a cloud provider manages all the infrastructure, and users deploy and use simple data transformation functions that are expected to start within milliseconds to handle individual requests. Examples of these are AWS Lambda (`https://aws.amazon.com/lambda`) and Google Cloud Function (`https://cloud.google.com/functions`).

- **Software as a Service (SaaS)**: With this on-demand software, everything is managed by a vendor. End users have to use this and cannot deploy their own applications there. Examples of these are Dropbox (`https://www.dropbox.com`) and Slack (`https://slack.com`).

> To read more about the difference between *IaaS*, *PaaS*, and *SaaS* please refer to this article: `http://www.bmc.com/blogs/saas-vs-paas-vs-iaas-whats-the-difference-and-how-to-choose`. A short description of *CaaS* can be found here: `https://blog.docker.com/2016/02/containers-as-a-service-caas`, while an introduction article to *FaaS* may be found here: `https://stackify.com/function-as-a-service-serverless-architecture`.

Reactive applications built with a Spring stack may deploy to any environment type except for SaaS as it does not offer a deployment option. `Chapter 8`, *Scaling Up with Cloud Streams*, describes potential options for running reactive applications in the form of FaaS. This chapter also describes the available options for deploying Spring applications to PaaS, CaaS and IaaS environments. The main difference between such target environments lies in the format of deployable artifacts and through the way in which such artifacts are built.

It is still possible to build sophisticated installers for JVM applications targeted at manual installations. Although it is possible to install such software rapidly using automation tools such as Chef (`https://www.chef.io/chef`) or Terraform (`https://www.terraform.io`), such deployment options are not very attractive for a fast application spin-up in the cloud, as this brings additional unnecessary operational costs.

At the moment, probably the most universal deployment unit for a Java application is uber-jar, also known as fat jar. In one file, this not only contains a Java program but also all the dependencies. Even though uber-jar usually increases the application distribution footprint, especially in a case with lots of services, it is still convenient, easy to use, and has a universal approach. Most other distribution options are built on top of an uber-jar approach. There is a `spring-boot-maven-plugin` Maven plugin that builds an uber-jar with a Spring Boot application, and `spring-boot-gradle-plugin` gives the same functionality for Gradle setups.

 To read more about executable jars with Spring Boot, please read the following article: `https://docs.spring.io/spring-boot/docs/current/reference/htmlsingle/#getting-started-first-application-executable-jar`. Also, Chapter 8, *Scaling Up with Cloud Streams* describes a `spring-boot-thin-launcher` plugin (`https://github.com/dsyer/spring-boot-thin-launcher`) for Maven and Gradle that helps to reduce an artifact's size, which is crucial for FaaS use cases.

Deploying to Amazon Web Services

Amazon Web Services (**AWS**) provides a few different software deployment options, but at the heart of the service lives the IaaS model. This model imposes a minimal amount of restrictions so we may deploy an application to AWS in a dozen ways, but for the sake of brevity, here we will only consider the option of building fully-provisioned images that may be directly executed on AWS or VirtualBox.

The Boxfuse (`https://boxfuse.com`) project is doing exactly what we need: it is generating minimal images for Spring Boot applications that boot and run directly on virtual hardware. Boxfuse takes uber-jar and wraps it into a minimal VM image. It has excellent integration with Spring Boot and may leverage information from Spring Boot configuration files to configure ports and health checks. Furthermore, it has built-in integration with AWS and enables a straightforward deployment procedure for Spring Boot applications.

 The following articles describe the steps for building a Spring Boot application as an image for AWS:
`https://boxfuse.com/blog/spring-boot-ec2.html`.

Deploying to the Google Kubernetes Engine

The **Google Kubernetes Engine** (**GKE**) is a cluster manager and orchestration system built by Google on top of Kubernetes (`https://kubernetes.io`), their open source system for automated deployment, scaling, and management of containerized applications. GKE is an example of a CaaS platform and is consequently a deployment unit for an application. In this case, this should be a Docker image.

With this approach, we initially build a fat jar with an application and then wrap it into a Docker image. For that purpose, we may add `Dockerfile` and run the `docker build` command manually or by using Maven or Gradle plugins to do it as part of a standard build pipeline. After testing, we may deploy an image to the Google Cloud Container Registry (`https://cloud.google.com/container-registry`) or even use the Google Cloud Container Build service (`https://cloud.google.com/cloud-build`) to perform actual build and container deployment procedures.

The following article outlines steps describing how to deploy a Spring Boot application to GKE:
`https://cloud.google.com/community/tutorials/kotlin-springboot-c ontainer-engine`.

Along with containers that hold our production service, we may deploy all the monitoring infrastructure just by referencing public Docker images. For example, we may reference Prometheus, Grafana, and Zipkin in the same cluster configuration file. With Kubernetes based platforms, it is easy to reach system elasticity with embedded auto-scaling mechanisms.

Similarly, we may deploy applications to any CaaS platform including, but not limited to, Amazon Elastic Container Service, Azure Container Service, Pivotal Container Service, or even on-premise solutions such as OpenShift (`https://www.openshift.com`) or Rancher (`https://rancher.com`).

Deploying to Pivotal Cloud Foundry

When talking about PaaS options of an application deployment, Spring Boot brings excellent support for the **Google Cloud Platform (GCP)**, **Heroku**, and **Pivotal Cloud Foundry (PCF)**. Here, we cover integration with PCF, but other options are treated similarly and with almost the same level of detail.

As the first step in setting up the releasing process with PCF, it is essential to understand how the Spring ecosystem helps in deploying an application onto the PaaS platform.

Suppose that we have a microservice streaming application that has three major parts:

- A **UI Service** that provides a UI to users and additionally plays the role of a service gateway
- A **Storage Service** that persists streaming data and transforms them into a user's view model so that a UI Service may handle it and multicast to each subscriber
- A **Connectors Service** that is responsible for setting proper configurations between particular data sources and then transferring events from them to the storage service

All of these services interact with one another over a message queue that, in our example, is a RabbitMQ broker. Moreover, to persist received data, the application uses MongoDB as a flexible, partition tolerant and a fast data-storage provider.

To generalize, we have three deployable services that message each other over RabbitMQ, and one of them communicates with MongoDB. For a successful operation, all those services should be running. With IaaS and CaaS it would be our responsibility to deploy and support RabbitMQ and MongoDB. With PaaS, the cloud provider serves those services if required and reduces operational responsibilities even more.

To deploy service to the PCF, we have to install a Cloud Foundry CLI, package our service with `mvn package`, log in to PCF and run the following command:

```
cf push <reactive-app-name> -p target/app-0.0.1.jar
```

After a few seconds of the deployment process, the application should be available at `http://<reactive-app-name>.cfapps.io`. CPF recognizes Spring Boot applications and makes an educated guess about the most optimal configuration for the service, but of course, developers may define his/her preferences with the `manifest.yml` file.

 To read more about deploying Java application to CPF, please read the following article:
`https://docs.cloudfoundry.org/buildpacks/java/java-tips.html`

It is neat that the platform takes care of the application startup and basic configuration. On the other hand, PaaS is highly opinionated about service discovery and network topology, so we can't deploy all services on the same server or configure the overall virtual network. Consequently, all external services could be located via a `localhost` URI. Such limitation leads to the fact that we lose configuration flexibility. Fortunately, modern PaaS providers expose platform information and the knowledge about add-ons or connected services to the deployed application. Therefore, all crucial data can be retrieved, and all necessary configurations can be done right after that. However, we still have to write clients or particular infrastructure code to integrate with a concrete PaaS provider's API. At that moment, Spring Cloud Connectors (`https://cloud.spring.io/spring-cloud-connectors`) came to the rescue:

> *Spring Cloud Connectors simplify the process of connecting to services and gaining operating environment awareness in cloud platforms such as Cloud Foundry and Heroku, especially for Spring applications.*

Spring Cloud Connectors reduce dedicated boilerplate codes for interaction with Cloud platforms. Here, we do not outline details of service configuration since that information will be described on the official page of the project. Instead, we are going to achieve out of the box support for Reactive features within a Reactive Application deployed to PCF. We will also describe what is needed to run Reactive Spring Application inside a PaaS.

Discovering RabbitMQ in PCF

Let's return to our application. The whole system is based on asynchronous communication over RabbitMQ. As we might have learned from Chapter 8, *Scaling Up with Cloud Streams*, all we have to do to set up a connection with a local RabbitMQ instance is to provide two additional Spring Boot dependencies. Additionally, for the Cloud infrastructure, we have to add `spring-cloud-spring-service-connector` and `spring-cloud-cloudfoundry-connector` dependencies. Finally, we have to provide a configuration depicted in the following code snippet and additional `@ScanCloud` annotation:

```
@Configuration
@Profile("cloud")
public class CloudConfig extends AbstractCloudConfig {
  @Bean
  public ConnectionFactory rabbitMQConnectionFactory() {
    return connectionFactory().rabbitConnectionFactory();
  }
}
```

For better flexibility, we use the @Profile("cloud") annotation, which enables the RabbitMQ configuration only when running on the cloud, and not locally during development.

 For RabbitMQ on a PCF case, it is not necessary to provide additional configurations since Cloud Foundry is highly tuned for a Spring ecosystem, so all required injections take place at runtime without extra hassle. However, it is essential to follow that practice (at least providing a @ScanCloud annotation) to be compatible with all cloud providers. In case of the deployed Application crashing, please check whether the RabbitMQ service provided by the PCF is bound to the application.

Discovering MongoDB in PCF

Along with a simple RabbitMQ configuration, there is a slightly more complicated configuration for Reactive Data Storages. One of the conceptual differences between non-Reactive and Reactive Data Storages is a client or a driver. Non-Reactive clients and drivers are well integrated into the Spring ecosystem and battle-tested by many solutions. In contrast, Reactive Clients are still a novelty.

At the time of writing, PCF Version 2.2 does not provide out-of-the-box configuration for Reactive MongoDB (as well as for any other DB with reactive clients). Fortunately, using the Spring Cloud Connectors module, we may access the required information and configure Reactive MongoDB Client, as shown in the following example code:

```
@Configuration
@Profile("cloud")
public class CloudConfig extends AbstractCloudConfig {          // (1)
  ...
  @Configuration                                                 // (2)
  @ConditionalOnClass(MongoClient.class)                         //
  @EnableConfigurationProperties(MongoProperties.class)          //
  public class MongoCloudConfig
              extends MongoReactiveAutoConfiguration {
    ...
    @Bean
    @Override
    public MongoClient reactiveStreamsMongoClient(               // (3)
      MongoProperties properties,
      Environment environment,
      ObjectProvider<List<MongoClientSettingsBuilderCustomizer>>
        builderCustomizers
    ) {
```

```
    List<ServiceInfo> infos = cloud()                       // (3.1)
      .getServiceInfos(MongoDbFactory.class);

    if (infos.size() == 1) {
      MongoServiceInfo mongoInfo =
        (MongoServiceInfo) infos.get(0);
      properties.setUri(mongoInfo.getUri());                // (3.2)
    }
    return super.reactiveStreamsMongoClient(               // (3.3)
      properties,
      environment,
      builderCustomizers
    );
  }
 }
}
```

The following is a description of the code sample:

1. This extension of the `AbstractCloudConfig` class gives access to the MongoDB location.
2. This is a common approach to checking that the `MongoClient` is present in the classpath.
3. This is the configuration of a reactive `MongoClient` bean, where at point `(3.1)` we get information about MongoDB from the cloud connector including connection URI `(3.2)`. At `(3.3)` we create a new reactive stream MongoDB client by reusing the original logic.

Here, we extended a configuration class from `org.springframework.boot.autoconfigure.mongo.MongoReactiveAutoConfiguration` and dynamically customized `MongoProperties` with regards to available `cloud()` configurations.

After following Cloud Foundry instructions available at `https://docs.run.pivotal.io/devguide/deploy-apps/deploy-app.html` and appropriately configuring the MongoDB service, Storage Service should become available and streamed data should be stored in MongoDB.

Configurationless deployment with Spring Cloud Data Flow for PCF

Even though Pivotal Cloud Foundry simplifies the overall deployment process and Spring Cloud ecosystem provides the comprehensive assistance to minimize the amount of configuration inside the application, we still have to deal with some of them. However, as we might remember from Chapter 8, *Scaling Up with Cloud Streams*, there is a fantastic solution that simplifies application development for a cloud. That solution is called Spring Cloud Data Flow. The central idea behind the project is the simplification of a reactive system development over a user-friendly interface. Along with that central feature, Spring Cloud Data Flow provides an extensive list of implementations for different Cloud providers which may be found at the following link: https://cloud.spring.io/spring-cloud-dataflow/#platform-implementations. The most significant for our use cases are the implementations for PCF. Spring Cloud Data Flow may be installed on PCF and provides a serverless solution out of the box for deploying pipelines directly on to the PCF.

 All required documentation regarding Spring Cloud Data Flow installation onto PCF may be found here: http://docs.spring.io/spring-cloud-dataflow-server-cloudfoundry/docs/current/reference/htmlsingle.

To summarize, a Pivotal Cloud Foundry as a PaaS provides extensive support for simplifying the application deployment process with the minimum required effort from the developers. It handles a lot of infrastructural responsibilities for our applications like provisioning message brokers or database instances. Also, PCF integrates well with Spring Cloud Data Flow. Hence, the development of Reactive Cloud Native Applications becomes a developer's dream.

Knative for FaaS over Kubernetes and Istio

In the middle of 2018, Google and Pivotal announced the Knative project (https://pivotal.io/knative). This aims to make Kubernetes able to deploy and run serverless workloads. For communication routing between services, Knative uses the Istio project (https://istio.io), which may also provide a dynamic route configuration, release canaries, gradually upgrade versions, and conduct A/B testing. One of the goals of Knative is to unroll a private FaaS platform on any cloud provider that may run Kubernetes (or on-premise).

Another Pivotal project called Project Riff (`https://projectriff.io`) is built on top of Knative. The main idea behind Project Riff is to package functions as containers, deploy to Kubernetes, connect those functions with event brokers, and scale containers with functions depending on the rate of incoming events. Also, Project Riff support functions that may process streams in the reactive fashion with the support of Project Reactor and Spring Cloud Function.

> Knative and Project Riff are still in the early stages of development, but the following articles describe the motivation, use-cases, and ideas behind these projects: `https://projectriff.io/blog/first-post-announcing-riff-0-0-2-release`, `https://content.pivotal.io/blog/knative-powerful-building-blocks-for-a-portable-function-platform`, `https://medium.com/google-cloud/knative-2-2-e542d71d531d`.
>
> Also, the following article explains how to use Riff step by step: `https://www.sudoinit5.com/post/riff-intro`.

In some aspects, Knative and Project Riff may extend the capabilities of a Spring Cloud Data Flow and Spring Cloud Function modules, but in other aspects, they are competitors. In any case, the most likely initiative around Knative will bring us one more platform for deploying Reactive Applications implemented in the FaaS paradigm.

Bits of advice for successful application deployment

In short, a successful process of software delivery includes a lot of steps and actions, which happens in stages of planning and development. It is apparent that without a proper automated testing infrastructure, we would not be able to release any non-trivial applications, and it is evident that such tests should evolve with the production code itself, from the first prototypes to the end of the application's life. Given the complexity of real applications, test scenarios nowadays should also contain suites for performance testing to identify the software limits and adequately calculate expenses on infrastructure such as servers, network, storage, and so on.

To simplify the product shipment, enable a fast feedback loop, and at the same time have the ability to fix problems before an end user notices, techniques such as **Continuous Delivery** and **Continuous Deployment** are crucial. It is also essential to monitor all vital metrics of the system, gather logs, trace errors, and react to the system behavior whether it is desired or not. A wide range of application metrics and real-time reports allow us not only to be informed about the current status but also to craft an automated infrastructure capable of auto-scaling, self-healing, and self-improvement.

Moreover, as was shown in this book, a reactive stack of Spring Framework gives a basis for very efficient applications that, in contrast to their imperative counterparts, are not limited by blocking I/O. Spring Boot auto-configurations bring the necessary well-tested combinations of functionality, so developers rarely have to make bean configurations manually. A Spring Boot Actuator gives all the necessary tooling for a successful application operation with regards to best practices and standards. Spring Cloud modules easily integrate Spring applications with Message Brokers (RabbitMQ, Apache Kafka), Distributed Tracing (Spring Cloud Sleuth and Zipkin), and much more. Moreover, community projects such as Spring Boot Admin fulfil the additional needs for out-of-the-box solutions regarding a software operation. A Spring ecosystem also provides excellent support for all popular software deployment options, including IaaS, CaaS, PaaS, and FaaS. This clever combination of a few of the previously described patterns and techniques in the right proportion should allow designing, building, operating, and evolving a successful reactive system. We hope that this book simplifies such a challenge.

Summary

In this chapter, we covered the challenges of software delivery and operation. We also named a few techniques and Spring modules that help to simplify the software product release and operation hassle. A Spring Boot Actuator provides service identification, health status, metrics, configuration information, elemental request tracing, the ability to dynamically change log levels, and much more. Spring Cloud Sleuth and Zipkin also bring distributed tracing to our microservice system, even to reactive components. Spring Boot Admin 2.x gives a unique UI experience, exposing all metrics in the form of charts and expressive reports. All of this significantly simplifies the life of DevOps or operational teams, enabling us to focus mainly on business tasks since Spring Boot modules and plugins cover most of the boilerplate.

In addition to this, we have covered how easy it is to configure a reactive Spring application to run in the cloud, including IaaS, CaaS, and PaaS modes of operation. We have described how to deploy applications to AWS with Boxfuse, to GKE with Docker, and to PCF, which was designed to run Spring applications properly from the beginning.

With all that said, a reactive system built with a Spring stack already has all the crucial elements not only for efficient resource utilization but also for a successful operation in the cloud.

Other Books You May Enjoy

If you enjoyed this book, you may be interested in these other books by Packt:

C++ Reactive Programming
Praseed Pai, Peter Abraham

ISBN: 9781788629775

- Understand language-level concurrency in C++
- Explore advanced C++ programming for the FRP
- Uncover the RxCpp library and its programming model
- Mix the FP and OOP constructs in C++ 17 to write well-structured programs
- Master reactive microservices in C++
- Create custom operators for RxCpp
- Learn advanced stream processing and error handling

Hands-On Spring Security 5 for Reactive Applications
Tomcy John

ISBN: 9781788995979

- Understand how Spring Framework and Reactive application programming are connected
- Implement easy security confgurations with Spring Security expressions
- Discover the relationship between OAuth2 and OpenID Connect
- Secure microservices and serverless applications with Spring
- Integrate add-ons, such as HDIV, Crypto Module, and CORS support
- Apply Spring Security 5 features to enhance your Java reactive applications

Leave a review - let other readers know what you think

Please share your thoughts on this book with others by leaving a review on the site that you bought it from. If you purchased the book from Amazon, please leave us an honest review on this book's Amazon page. This is vital so that other potential readers can see and use your unbiased opinion to make purchasing decisions, we can understand what our customers think about our products, and our authors can see your feedback on the title that they have worked with Packt to create. It will only take a few minutes of your time, but is valuable to other potential customers, our authors, and Packt. Thank you!

Index

wire protocol, for database access 332, 333, 334
synchronous repository
transforming, into reactive 389, 390

T

tailable cursor 380
TCK, Reactive Streams spec
Publisher verification 107
reference 114
Subscriber verification 109, 114
TCK
reference 106
thread scheduling model, Reactor
about 201
publishOn operator 201
time
dealing with 189

U

Universal Scalability Law 281, 282, 284

V

verifying payment info state 328
Vert.x
reference 72

W

Web module
reactive programming 230
Web MVC
processing models 284, 286
WebClient

non-blocking cross-service communication 256, 258, 259
WebFlux processing model
challenges 296, 297, 299
WebFlux WebSocket
versus Spring WebSocket module 263
WebFlux
applications 307
as central reactive server foundation 240, 242, 243
MVC frameworks 247
processing models 284, 286
purely functional web 251, 253, 254, 256
reactive web core 243, 244, 245, 246
reactive web framework 247
testing 474
versus Web MVC 275
working 310, 312, 313, 314
WebMVC 509
WebSocket
about 260
testing 480, 483
WebTestClient
used, for testing controllers 474, 480
wrk
reference 288

Z

Zabbix
URL 487
Zipkin
URL 488
Zuul
reference 69

Printed in the USA
CPSIA information can be obtained
at www.ICGtesting.com
CBHW080904050524
7765CB00014B/170

9 781787 284951